THE HBJ READER

RICHARD HASWELL
JOHN EHRSTINE
ROBERT WILKINSON

Washington State University

HARCOURT BRACE JOVANOVICH, PUBLISHERS

San Diego   New York   Chicago   Austin   Washington, D.C.
London   Sydney   Tokyo   Toronto

COVER: Laszlo Moholy-Nagy, "AL3." The Blue Four, Galka Scheyer Collection, Norton Simon Museum.

Illustrations by Mark Donnelly.

Copyright © 1987 by Harcourt Brace Jovanovich, Inc.

All rights reserved. No part of this publication may be reproduced or transmitted in any form or by any means, electronic or mechanical, including photocopy, recording, or any information storage and retrieval system, without permission in writing from the publisher.

Requests for permission to make copies of any part of the work should be mailed to: Permissions, Harcourt Brace Jovanovich, Publishers, Orlando, Florida 32887.

ISBN: 0-15-535323-3

Library of Congress Catalog Card Number: 86-81626

Printed in the United States of America

Copyrights and Acknowledgments appear on pages 461–63, which constitute a continuation of the copyright page.

PREFACE

> *Books are to be call'd for, and supplied, on the assumption that the process of reading is not a half-sleep, but, in the highest sense, an exercise, a gymnast's struggle; that the reader is to do something for himself, must be on the alert, must himself or herself construct indeed the poem, argument, history, metaphysical essay—the text furnishing the hints, the clue, the start or frame-work. Not the book needs so much to be the complete thing, but the reader of the book does.*
> —Walt Whitman, Democratic Vistas, 1871

Whitman's metaphor, "a gymnast's struggle," describes what good reading ought to be. To that end, we have selected for *The HBJ Reader* 54 fine essays by 18 writers from a variety of crafts and disciplines. Each writer is represented by three quite different essays, and some of our choices radically stretch the boundaries of the genre. The collection easily exhausts Whitman's list, "the poem, argument, history, metaphysical essay," and adds others: the book review, sermon, reminiscence, lecture, magazine column, and public or "open" letter. We have generally arranged the writers and essays by their difficulty to advance the exercise required for the gymnast's struggle. And we have always reprinted pieces whole. What all the essays have in common is excellence; they demand that readers be alert, as Whitman urged.

Each selection is followed by three kinds of commentary: suggestions for rhetorical analysis, for intellectual analysis, and for writing. Rhetorical analysis focuses on the forms and devices of each essay. Our goal is first to recognize and then *play* with the details of expression—an important step toward improved writing.

Yet writing consists not only of expressions but of ideas. The intellectual analysis of an essay begins not with our agreement or disagreement with a writer, but with our coming to grips with a writer's meaning. The goal of intellectual analysis is comprehension first, evaluation second. Again, a kind of play is involved.

Because reading well requires that each of us must actively "construct" a text (as Whitman says), ultimately we must learn to depend on ourselves, to compose our own ideas, and to map our own strategies in our own arena. The important thing is for readers to develop the necessary blend of intellect and rhetoric to make them independent, resourceful writers. The suggestions for writing are the final bridge to independence, and are the last element to follow each selection.

"Excellence" literally means a rising beyond, "exercise" a release from confinement, "essay" a trial or testing or trying out. We hope that these essays will encourage and free writers, through the creative act of reading, to excel and thereby surpass themselves.

We have a good many debts of gratitude connected with this book. Above all, our thanks go to Paul Nockleby of Harcourt Brace Jovanovich for his abiding and steady interest and enthusiasm, and for his painstaking editorial support. Second on our list ought certainly to be Leota Day of the Department of English, Washington State University: she did much more than act as principal typist. Three other pleasant people also helped us with the typing: Nellie Zamora, Sherri Lippiat, and Anne Ehrstine. We are grateful, too, for the use of facilities in the Humanities Research Center of Washington State University.

While all this work was going on, we received both encouragement and patience from John Elwood, Chairman of the Department of English, and friend to the three of us. Finally, who can say what all we owe our families for putting up with us while we were absorbed in this enterprise?

RICHARD HASWELL
JOHN EHRSTINE
ROBERT WILKINSON

Contents

Preface	iii
Eudora Welty	**1**
A Sweet Devouring	2
My Grandmother's House	8
The Little Store	14
Langston Hughes	**24**
Salvation	26
Theme for English B	30
Brown America in Jail: Kilby	32
Barry Lopez	**36**
The Log Jam	38
Wolfing for Sport	47
Buffalo	60
E. B. White	**66**
The Gastropods	68
Calculating Machine	72
Death of a Pig	76
Isak Dinesen	**86**
The Iguana	88
Pooran Singh	90
On Mottoes of My Life	94
Lewis Thomas	**106**
How to Fix the Premedical Curriculum	108
Late Night Thoughts on Listening to Mahler's Ninth Symphony	112
Seven Wonders	117

George Orwell — 124
- A Hanging — 126
- As I Please — 132
- Politics and the English Language — 136

Alice Walker — 150
- Nuclear Madness: What You Can Do — 152
- Beauty: When the Other Dancer Is the Self — 156
- In Search of Our Mothers' Gardens — 165

William Styron — 176
- The Habit — 178
- The Oldest America — 183
- This Quiet Dust — 188

E. M. Forster — 212
- My Wood — 214
- Tolerance — 218
- Anonymity: An Enquiry — 224

Virginia Woolf — 236
- Old Mrs. Grey — 238
- Professions for Women — 241
- Gas — 248

Stephen Jay Gould — 252
- A Biological Homage to Mickey Mouse — 254
- The Nonscience of Human Nature — 265
- Crazy Old Randolph Kirkpatrick — 272

James Baldwin — 282
- Notes of a Native Son — 284
- An Open Letter to My Sister, Miss Angela Davis — 305
- If Black English Isn't a Language, Then Tell Me, What Is? — 312

Joan Didion — 318
- On Keeping a Notebook — 320
- Bureaucrats — 329
- On Morality — 334

Bertrand Russell — 342
- Nightmares — 344
- How I Write — 352
- "Useless" Knowledge — 357

Barbara Tuchman — 368
- On Our Birthday—America as Idea — 370
- The Historian as Artist — 374
- "Perdicaris Alive or Raisuli Dead" — 381

Loren Eiseley — 398
- How Flowers Changed the World — 400
- The Judgment of the Birds — 411
- One Night's Dying — 421

Paul Tillich — 430
- Faith and Uncertainty — 432
- The Decline and the Validity of the Idea of Progress — 436
- The Riddle of Inequality — 451

Glossary of Useful Terms — 464
Index of Rhetorical Modes — 476
Index of Subject Matter — 480

Eudora Welty

Born in Jackson, Mississippi, in 1909, the only daughter of an insurance executive and a schoolteacher, Eudora Welty was brought up in a protective, bookish household. In 1925 she enrolled at Mississippi State College for women, where as a freshman reporter for the school newspaper she wrote an April-fool editorial lamenting five members of her class drowned in recent floods, but suggesting on the bright side that it had relieved somewhat the overcrowding in the dorms. The Baltimore writer H. L. Mencken picked up the squib for his magazine, American Mercury, printing it seriously "as sample thinking from the Bible Belt."

Welty returned to Jackson after graduation from the University of Wisconsin in 1929 and from the Columbia University business school in 1931. There she remained, for more than 50 years, living in her parents' house. But it would be a mistake to think that her life was simply sheltered. "A sheltered life can be a daring life," she wrote; "all serious daring starts from within."

In 1936 her first story, "Death of a Traveling Salesman," was published, to be followed by many other short stories and novels that have placed her in the very front rank of modern American writers. But again, although the landscape of her writing is confined mostly to the environs of Jackson, its ultimate meaning has nothing confined about it. The three essays reprinted here exhibit the qualities inherent in all her work: a quest into the local to find the universal, and a delicate sense of language that still has the depth and toughness to search out connections between the self and other human beings, and between human beings and the nonhuman landscape. As she has said in her autobiographical One Writer's Beginnings, "beginning to write stories about people, I drew near slowly; noting and guessing, apprehending, hoping, drawing my eventual conclusions out of my own heart, I did venture closer to where I wanted to go." The pun in the title of her collected essays, The Eye of the Story, is a serious one.

A Sweet Devouring

When I used to ask my mother which we were, rich or poor, she refused to tell me. I was then nine years old and of course what I was dying to hear was that we were poor. I was reading a book called *Five Little Peppers* and my heart was set on baking a cake for my mother in a stove with a hole in it. Some version of rich, crusty old Mr. King—up till that time not living on our street—was sure to come down the hill in his wheelchair and rescue me if anything went wrong. But before I could start a cake at all I had to find out if we were poor, and poor *enough*; and my mother wouldn't tell me, she said she was too busy. I couldn't wait too long; I had to go on reading and soon Polly Pepper got into more trouble, some that was a little harder on her and easier on me.

Trouble, the backbone of literature, was still to me the original property of the fairy tale, and as long as there was plenty of trouble for everybody and the rewards for it were falling in the right spots, reading was all smooth sailing. At that age a child reads with higher appetite and gratification, and with those two stars sailing closer together, than ever again in his growing up. The home shelves had been providing me all along with the usual books, and I read them with love—but snap, I finished them. I read everything just alike—snap. I even came to the *Tales from Maria Edgeworth* and went right ahead, without feeling the bump—then. It *was* noticeable that when her characters suffered she punished them for it, instead of rewarding them as a reader had rather been led to hope. In her stories, the children had to make their choice between being unhappy and good about it and being unhappy and bad about it, and then she helped them to choose wrong. In *The Purple Jar*, it will be remembered, there was the little girl being taken through the shops by her mother and her downfall coming when she chooses to buy something beautiful instead of something necessary. The purple jar, when the shop sends it out, proves to have been purple only so long as it was filled with purple water, and her mother knew it all the time. They don't deliver the water. That's only the cue for stones to start coming through the hole in the victim's worn-out shoe. She bravely agrees she must keep walking on stones until such time as she is offered another choice between the beautiful and the useful. Her father tells her as far as he is concerned she can stay in the house. If I had been at all easy to disappoint, that story would have disappointed me. Of course, I did feel, what is the good of walking on rocks if they are going to let the water out of the jar too? And it seemed to me that even the illustrator fell down on the characters in that book, not alone Maria Edgeworth, for when a rich, crusty old gentleman gave Simple Susan a guinea for some kind deed she'd done him, there was a picture of the transaction and where was the guinea? I couldn't make out a feather. But I liked *reading* the book all right—except that I finished it.

My mother took me to the Public Library and introduced me: "Let her have any book she wants, except *Elsie Dinsmore*." I looked for the book I couldn't have and it was a row. That was how I learned about the Series Books. The *Five Little Peppers* belonged, so did *The Wizard of Oz*, so did *The Little Colonel*, so did *The Green Fairy Book*. There were many of everything, generations of everybody, instead of one. I wasn't coming to the end of reading, after all—I was saved.

Our library in those days was a big rotunda lined with shelves. A copy of *V. V.'s Eyes* seemed to follow you wherever you went, even after you'd read it. I didn't know what I liked, I just knew what there was a lot of. After *Randy's Spring* there came *Randy's Summer*, *Randy's Fall* and *Randy's Winter*. True, I didn't care very much myself for her spring, but it didn't occur to me that I might not care for her summer, and then her summer didn't prejudice me against her fall, and I still had hopes as I moved on to her winter. I was disappointed in her whole year, as it turned out, but a thing like that didn't keep me from wanting to read every word of it. The pleasures of reading itself—who doesn't remember?—were like those of a Christmas cake, a sweet devouring. The "Randy Books" failed chiefly in being so soon over. Four seasons doesn't make a series.

All that summer I used to put on a second petticoat (our librarian wouldn't let you past the front door if she could see through you), ride my bicycle up the hill and "through the Capitol" (shortcut) to the library with my two read books in the basket (two was the limit you could take out at one time when you were a child and also as long as you lived), and tiptoe in ("Silence") and exchange them for two more in two minutes. Selection was no object. I coasted the two new books home, jumped out of my petticoat, read (I suppose I ate and bathed and answered questions put to me), then in all hope put my petticoat back on and rode those two books back to the library to get my next two.

The librarian was the lady in town who wanted to be it. She called me by my full name and said, "Does your mother know where you are? You know good and well the fixed rule of this library: *Nobody is going to come running back here with any book on the same day they took it out.* Get both those things out of here and don't come back till tomorrow. And I can practically see through you."

My great-aunt in Virginia, who understood better about needing more to read than you *could* read, sent me a book so big it had to be read on the floor—a bound volume of six or eight issues of *St. Nicholas* from a previous year. In the very first pages a serial began: *The Lucky Stone* by Abbie Farwell Brown. The illustrations were right down my alley: a heroine so poor she was ragged, a witch with an extremely pointed hat, a rich, crusty old gentleman in—better than a wheelchair—a runaway carriage; and I set to. I gobbled up installment after installment through the whole luxurious book, through the last one, and then came the words, turning me to *un*lucky stone: "To be concluded." The book had come to an end and *The Lucky Stone* wasn't finished! The witch had it! I couldn't believe this infidelity from my aunt. I still had my secret childhood feeling that if you hunted long enough in a book's pages, you could find what you were looking for, and long after I knew books better than that, I used to hunt again for the end of *The Lucky Stone*. It never occurred to me that the story had an existence anywhere else outside the pages of that single green-bound book. The last chapter was just something I would have to do without. Polly Pepper could do it. And then suddenly I tried something—I read it again, as much as I had of it. I was in love with books at least partly for what they looked like; I loved the printed page.

In my little circle books were almost never given for Christmas, they cost too much. But the year before, I'd been given a book and got a shock. It was from the same classmate who had told me there was no Santa Claus. She gave me a book, all right—*Poems by Another Little Girl*. It looked like a real book, was printed like a real book—but it was *by her*. *Homemade* poems? Illusion-dispelling was her favorite game. She was in such a hurry, she had such a pile to get rid of—her mother's electric runabout was stacked to the bud vases with copies—that she hadn't even time to say, "Merry Christmas!" With only the same raucous laugh with which she had told me, "Been filling my own stocking for years!" she shot me her book, received my Japanese pencil box with a moonlight scene on the lid and a sharpened pencil inside, jumped back into the car and was sped away by her mother. I stood right where they had left me, on the curb in my Little Nurse's uniform, and read that book, and I had no better way to prove when I got through than I had when I started that this was not a real book. But of course it wasn't. The printed page is not absolutely everything.

Then this Christmas was coming, and my grandfather in Ohio sent along in his box of presents an envelope with money in it for me to buy myself the book I wanted.

I went to Kress's. Not everybody knew Kress's sold books, but children just before Christmas know everything Kress's ever sold or will sell. My father had showed us the mirror he was giving my mother to hang above her desk, and Kress's is where my brother and I went to reproduce that by buying a mirror together to give her ourselves, and where our little brother then made us take him and he bought her one his size for fifteen cents. Kress's had also its version of the Series Books, called, exactly like another series, "The Camp Fire Girls," beginning with *The Camp Fire Girls in the Woods*.

I believe they were ten cents each and I had a dollar. But they weren't all that easy to buy, because the series stuck, and to buy some of it was like breaking into a loaf of French bread. Then after you got home, each single book was as hard to open as a box stuck in its varnish, and when it gave way it popped like a firecracker. The covers once prized apart would never close; those books once open stayed open and lay on their backs helplessly fluttering their leaves like a turned-over June bug. They were as light as a matchbox. They were printed on yellowed paper with corners that crumbled, if you pinched on them too hard, like old graham crackers, and they smelled like attic trunks, caramelized glue, their own confinement with one another and, over all, the Kress's smell—bandannas, peanuts and sandalwood from the incense counter. Even without reading them I loved them. It was hard, that year, that Christmas is a day you can't read.

What could have happened to those books?—but I can tell you about the leading character. His name was Mr. Holmes. He was not a Camp Fire Girl: he wanted to catch one. Through every book of the series he gave chase. He pursued Bessie and Zara—those were the Camp Fire Girls—and kept scooping them up in his touring car, while they just as regularly got away from him. Once Bessie escaped from the second floor of a strange inn by climbing down a gutter pipe. Once she escaped by driving away from Mr. Holmes in his own automobile, which she had learned to drive by watching him. What Mr. Holmes wanted with them—either Bessie or Zara would do—didn't give me pause; I was too young to be a Camp Fire Girl; I was just keeping up. I wasn't alarmed by Mr. Holmes—when I cared for a chill, I knew to go to Dr. Fu Manchu, who had his own series in the library. I wasn't fascinated either. There was one thing I wanted from those books, and that was for me to have ten to read at one blow.

Who in the world wrote those books? I knew all the time they were the false "Camp Fire Girls" and the ones in the library were the authorized. But book reviewers sometimes say of a book that if anyone else had written it, it might not have been this good, and I found it out as a child—their warning is justified. This was a proven case, although a case of the true not being as good as the false. In the true series the characters were either totally different or missing (Mr. Holmes was missing), and there was too much time given to teamwork. The Kress's Campers, besides getting into a more reliable kind of trouble than the Carnegie Campers, had adventures that even they themselves weren't aware of: the pages were in wrong. There were transposed pages, repeated pages, and whole sections in upside down. There was no way of telling if there was anything missing. But if you knew your way in the woods at all, you could enjoy yourself tracking it down. I read the library "Camp Fire Girls," since that's what they were there for, but though they could be read by poorer light they were not as good.

And yet, in a way, the false Campers were no better either. I wonder whether I felt some flaw at the heart of things or whether I was just tired of not having any taste; but it seemed to me when I had finished that the last nine of those books weren't as good as the first one. And the same went for all Series Books. As long as they are keeping a series going, I was afraid, nothing can really happen. The whole thing is one grand prevention. For my greed, I might have unwittingly dealt with myself in the same way Maria Edgeworth dealt with the one who put her all into the purple jar—I had received word it was just colored water.

And then I went again to the home shelves and my lucky hand reached and found Mark Twain—twenty-four volumes, not a series, and good all the way through.

Rhetorical Analysis

1. It may seem that Welty expects the reader of "A Sweet Devouring" to have read all the books she mentions. If we have read Margaret Sidney's *Five Little Peppers and How They Grew*, for instance, we would know that Polly Pepper is the central character, that her parents are very poor, that the stove had a crack in it, and so forth. But notice that the important facts can be inferred from Welty's first paragraph even if we have not read Sidney's book. Welty's stance toward the reader is a good one to be aware of: she treats readers as though they are knowledgeable, but helps them along just the same. Look for other places where she does this (¶ 2 has an especially instructive instance).
2. This essay is mostly descriptive. The danger in lengthy verbal description is that the reader will be lost to boredom.
    a. Welty counters the danger partly by peppering her essay with lively items of human interest. Find a paragraph or two and underline those details which you find entertaining, whether or not they have any bearing on the main subject of Welty's childhood reading.
    b. She avoids boredom also by the ideas she has about this reading. She does not make the same point over and over, but a new one with almost every paragraph. Record her major points. Do they progress toward a main conclusion? If so, what is it?
3. When writers force us to pause and reflect, they are frequently making their most interesting and far-reaching points. Consider the following striking statements, each of which could serve as the thesis of an essay:
    a. "Trouble [is] the backbone of literature. . . ." (¶ 2)
    b. "It *was* noticeable that when her characters suffered she punished them for it, instead of rewarding them as a reader had rather been led to hope." (¶ 2)
    c. "Of course I did feel, what is the good of walking on rocks if they are going to let the water out of the jar too?" (¶ 2)
    d. "My great aunt in Virginia . . . understood better about needing more to read than you *could* read." (¶ 7)

Find other such statements and explore their implications.

Intellectual Analysis

1. What do you make of the title, and of other references to eating throughout the essay (as in ¶s 4, 7, and 11)?
    a. All along, Welty emphasizes quantity. Why?
    b. Her emphasis leads in turn to the point of the whole essay, which is that pulp reading is somehow like the "purple jar." How so?
    c. The only way for Welty to learn of this connection, however, is through indiscriminate feeding of an appetite. In that case, the meaning of this piece becomes rather fierce, and at odds with the witty, graceful presentation and tone. That persistent conflict, or paradox, is laid before us from the title on. Trace that contrast through the essay.
    d. What does Welty's discovery of Twain have to do with the point she is making about reading?
2. How is this piece humorous and witty? Where, and on what, does the wit turn? On the speaker herself (as a child), on literature itself, on education?

Suggestions for Writing

1. Write an essay in which you discuss pulp reading today, among adults or among children.
2. Write an essay in which you describe some similar childhood appetite and its effects.
3. The end of the essay makes it clear that Welty is describing a life-long interest that kept changing, kept growing—in a word, that developed. Select an interest of your own, and show and explain the stages of its development.

MY GRANDMOTHER'S HOUSE

*T*his was not the first time I'd been brought here to visit Grandma in West Virginia, but the first visit I barely remembered. Where I stood now was inside the house where my mother had been born and where she grew up. It was a low, gray-weathered wooden house with a broad hall through the middle of it with the light of day at each end, the house that Ned Andrews, her father, had built to stand on the very top of the highest mountain he could find.

"And here's where I first began to read my Dickens," Mother said, pointing. "Under that very bed. Hiding my candle. To keep them from knowing what I was up to all night."

"But where did it all *come* from?" I asked her at last. "All that Dickens?"

"Why, Papa gave me that set of Dickens for agreeing to let them cut off my hair," she said, as if surprised that a reason like that wouldn't have occurred to me. "In those days, they thought very long thick hair like mine would sap a child's strength. I said *No!* I wanted my hair left the very way it was. They offered me gold earrings first—in those days little girls often developed a wish to have their ears pierced and fitted with little gold rings. I said *No!* I'd rather keep my hair. Then Papa said, 'What about books? I'll have them send a whole set of Charles Dickens to you, right up the river from Baltimore, in a barrel.' I agreed."

Ned Andrews had been the county's youngest member of the bar. He quickly made a name for himself on the side as an orator. When he gave the dedicatory address for the opening of a new courthouse in Nicholas County, West Virginia, my mother put away a copy. He is praising the architecture of the building: "The student turns with a sigh of relief from the crumbling pillars and columns of Athens and Alexandria to the symmetrical and colossal temples of the New World. As time eats from the tombstones of the past the epitaphs of primeval greatness, and covers the pyramids with the moss of forgetfulness, she directs the eye to the new temples of art and progress that make America the monumental beacon-light of the world."

People may have expected the highfalutin in oratory in those days, but they might not have expected Ned's courtroom flair. There was a murder trial of a woman given to fortunetelling. She had been overheard reading in an old man's cards that his days were numbered. When, the very next day, this old man had been found in his bed dead from a gunshot wound, it appeared to the public that that fortuneteller might have known too much about it. She was put on trial for murder. Ned Andrews' defense centered on the well-known fact that the old man kept his loaded gun mounted at all times over the head of his bed. This was the gun that had shot him. The old man could have discharged it perfectly easily himself, Ned argued, by carelessly bouncing on the bed a little bit. He proposed to prove it, and invited the jury of dubious mountaineers to watch him do it. Leading them all the way up the mountain to the old man's cabin, he mounted the gun in place on its rests, having first loaded it with blank shells, and while they watched he mimicked the old man and made a running jump onto the bed. The gun jarred loose, tumbled down, and fired at him. He rested his case. The fortuneteller was without any more ado declared not guilty.

He was brim full of talents. He'd attended Trinity College (later, Duke University) where he organized a literary society; he'd been a journalist and a photographer in Norfolk, Virginia, and in West Virginia where he'd run away to, to seek adventure, he'd turned into a lawyer. He seems to have been a legendary fisherman in those mountain streams, is still now and then referred to in local sportsmen's tales. Ned was impervious to the sting of bees and could always be summoned to capture a wild swarm. Ned was the one they sent for when someone fell down an empty well, because he was not afraid to harness himself and be lowered into the deathly gasses at the bottom and bring the unconscious victim up again.

Yet the human failings Mother could least forgive in other people, she regarded with only tenderness in him. I gathered—slowly and over the years I gathered—that sometimes he drank. He told tall tales to his wife, Eudora Carden. He told one to begin with, in order to marry her, saying he was of age to do so, when he was nineteen and four years younger than she. She was superstitious; he loved to tease her with tricks, to stage elaborate charades with the connivance of one of his little boys, that preyed on her fear of ghosts. He shocked her with a tale—Mother said there was nothing to prove it wasn't a fact—that one of the Andrews ancestors had been hanged in Ireland. Eudora Carden came from the home of a strongly dedicated Baptist preacher, and about all preachers he was irreverent and irrepressible. I have seen photographs he took of her—tintypes; it's clear that he took them with great care to show how beautiful he found her. In one she is standing up behind a chair, with her long hands crossed at the wrist over the back of it; she is dressed in her best, with her dark hair drawn high above her oval face and tucked with a flower that looks like a wild rose. She is very young. She has long gray eyes over high cheekbones; she is gazing to the front, looking straight at him. Her mouth is sensitive, her lips youthfully full. She told her daughter Chessie years later that she was objecting to his taking this picture because she was pregnant at the time, and the pose—the crossed hands on the back of a chair—had been to hide that. (With my mother herself, I wondered, her first child?) When she came back from the well on cold mornings, her hands would be bleeding from breaking the ice on it: this is what my mother would remember when she looked at those soft hands in the tintypes.

I don't know from whom it came or to whom it was passed, but at one time an old, home-made drawing of the Andrews family tree came into my mother's hands. It was rolled up; if unrolled it was capable of rattling shut the next instant. The tree was drawn as a living tree, spreading from a rooted trunk, every branch, twig, and leaf in clear outline, all with names and dates on them in a copperplate handwriting. The most riveting feature was the thick branch stemming from near the base of the main trunk: it was broken off short to a jagged end, branchless and leafless, and labeled "Joseph, Killed by lightning."

It had been executed with the finest possible pen in ink grown very pale, as if it had been drawn in watered maple syrup. The leaves weren't stiffly drawn or conventional ellipses, all alike, but each one daintily fashioned with a pointed tip and turned on its stem this way or that, as if this family tree were tossed by a slight breeze. The massed whole had the look, at that time to me, of a children's puzzle in which you were supposed to find your mother. I found mine—only a tiny leaf on a twig of a branch near the top, hardly big enough to hold her tiny name.

The Andrews branch my mother came from represents the mix most usual in the Southeast—English, Scottish, Irish, with a dash of French Huguenot. The first American one, Isham, who fought in the Revolutionary War, was born in Virginia and moved to Georgia, where succeeding generations lived. The Andrewses were not a rural clan, like the Weltys; they lived in towns, were educators and preachers, with some Methodist circuit riders; one cousin of Ned's (Walter Hines Page) was an ambassador to England. Trinity College educated some of them, including, for an impatient time, young Ned. By the time my mother's father, Edward Raboteau Andrews (Ned) was born in 1862, the family had returned to Virginia. He broke from the mold and at eighteen ran away from a home of parents, grandparents, sisters, brothers, and aunts in Norfolk to become the first West Virginian.

Here in the center of the Andrews kitchen, at the same long table where the family always ate, not too far from where Grandma seemed to be always busy at the warm stove, Ned had sat and worked up his cases for the defense in Clay Courthouse, far below and out of sight straight down the mountain. Mother remembered him transposing band music there, too; he had sent off for the instruments, got together a band, and proceeded to teach them to play in concert, lined up on the courthouse lawn: he had a strong need of music. His children had an instrument to learn to play too: he assigned my mother the cornet. (When I think back to how she sang "Blessed Assurance" while washing the dishes, I realize she flatted her high notes just where a child's cornet might.)

It was in the quilted bed in the front room of this house where he lay in so much pain (probably from the affliction that brought on his death, an infected appendix) that he once told Mother, a little girl, to bring the kitchen knife and plunge it into his side; she, hypnotized, almost believed she must obey. It was from that door that later she went with him on the frozen winter night when it was clear he had to get, somehow, to a hospital. The mountain roads were impassable, there was ice in the Elk River: but a neighbor vowed he could make way by raft. She was fifteen. Leaving her mother and the five little brothers at home, Chessie went with him. Her father lay on the raft, on which a fire had been lit to warm him, Chessie beside him. The neighbor managed to pole the raft through the icy river and eventually across it to a railroad. They flagged the train. (It seems likely that the place they flagged it was the same as where my mother and I were let off that train when I was three, arriving on that nearly forgotten visit. It was an early summer dawn; everything was a cloud of mist—we were standing on the bank of a river and I didn't know it. When my mother pulled the rope of an iron bell, we watched a boat come out of the mist to meet us, with her five brothers all inside.)

Mother had to return by herself from Baltimore, her father's body in a coffin on the same train. He had died on the operating table in Johns Hopkins, of a ruptured appendix, at thirty-seven years of age. The last lucid remark he'd made to my mother was "If you let them tie me down, I'll die." (The surgeon had come out where she stood waiting in the hall. "Little girl," he'd said, "you'd better get in touch now with somebody in Baltimore." "Sir, I don't know anybody in Baltimore," she said, and what she never forgot was his astounded reply: "You don't know anybody in *Baltimore*?")

It was from this house that my mother very soon after that piled up her hair and went out to teach in a one-room school, mountain children little and big alike. The first day, some fathers came along to see if she could whip their children, some who were older than she. She told the children that she did intend to whip them if they became unruly and refused to learn, and invited the fathers to stay if they liked and she'd be able to whip them too. Having been thus tried out, she was a great success with them after that. She left home every day on her horse; since she had the river to cross, a little brother rode on her horse behind her, to ride him home, while she rowed across the river in a boat. And he would be there to meet her with her horse again at evening. All this way, to pass the time, she told me, she recited the poems in McGuffey's Readers out loud.

She could still recite them in full when she was lying helpless and nearly blind, in her bed, an old lady. Reciting, her voice took on resonance and firmness, it rang with the old fervor, with ferocity even. She was teaching me one more, almost her last, lesson: emotions do not grow old. I knew that I would feel as she did, and I do.

16

Rhetorical Analysis

1. This part of *One Writer's Beginnings* is a unified piece, but Welty left it untitled. "My Grandmother's House" is the title we have given it. What title would you have given it? What makes a good title?
2. At first glance, this essay reads like a family chronicle. But it is more than that. It is an account of Eudora Welty's coming to know that history, and by its telling we learn the value of that history for Welty.
    a. Thus the organization is not merely a patching together of family stories. The essay includes references to items when her mother's past impinged on Welty's life. Four of those times receive special treatment, in ¶s 1, 9, 13, and 16. Look to see whether these four passages give the whole essay a larger organization. Is their sequence meaningful, for example?
    b. The final paragraph serves as a conclusion in that it binds together the rest of the essay. How does that paragraph work? Is it sufficient in giving the reader a satisfying sense of closure?
3. It is easy to bore strangers with family history. What strategy does Welty use to keep from boring us here?

Intellectual Analysis

1. Since this essay appears, perhaps deceptively, to have been developed spontaneously, it is important to ask if its central subject matter is
    a. The speaker's memory and its actions?
    b. The speaker's mother? or grandfather? or family?
    c. The fact that "emotions do not grow old" (last ¶)?
2. There are two particularly prominent images in the essay—the house and the family tree. How do these images contribute to the ideas?
    a. The image of the old house in one sense holds this whole set of recollections together; you will need to track that image through the essay. We are told of a

"gray-weathered wooden house," "with the light of day at each end." What do those words imply, especially with the image of light?
    b. Several details about the picture of the family tree stand out: the broken trunk, the danger of it rolling up, its pale ink, its appearance of being "tossed by a slight breeze," and her mother as only a tiny leaf in it. What do you make of these details?
3. Once again, note how the final paragraph, with its statement about the timelessness of emotions, binds the whole essay together.
    a. Why does Welty delay this key statement until the very end?
    b. How does it operate in connection with the fact that the bulk of the essay is about her grandfather? Is there a conflict between Welty's conclusion and her memory of her grandfather's flamboyant character?

Suggestions for Writing

1. Tell how your family has gone about passing its history down to you. This will not be an account of your family's past, but a study of the special ways one family keeps its memories and traditions alive.
2. In this anthology are a number of other essays that explore the author's past in a search for self-understanding: Welty's "The Little Store"; "On Mottoes of my Life" by Isak Dinesen; and "Beauty: When the Other Dancer Is the Self" by Alice Walker. Choose one of these and compare it with "My Grandmother's House."
3. In the last paragraph, Welty tells us that her mother could recite poems from the famous 19th-century schoolbook series, McGuffey's Readers, poems first read by her mother half a century earlier. Welty herself recalls events that happened to her more than fifty years earlier. Select a memory of your own that you know you will still remember no matter how long you live. Explore it and its implications in an essay similar to Welty's.

The Little Store

*T*wo blocks away from the Mississippi State Capitol, and on the same street with it, where our house was when I was a child growing up in Jackson, it was possible to have a little pasture behind your backyard where you could keep a Jersey cow, which we did. My mother herself milked her. A thrifty homemaker, wife, mother of three, she also did all her own cooking. And as far as I can recall, she never set foot inside a grocery store. It wasn't necessary.

For her regular needs, she stood at the telephone in our front hall and consulted with Mr. Lemly, of Lemly's Market and Grocery downtown, who took her order and sent it out on his next delivery. And since Jackson at the heart of it was still within very near reach of the open country, the blackberry lady clanged on her bucket with a quart measure at your front door in June without fail, the watermelon man rolled up to your house exactly on time for the Fourth of July, and down through the summer, the quiet of the early-morning streets was pierced by the calls of farmers driving in with their plenty. One brought his with a song, so plaintive we would sing it with him:

> "Milk, milk,
> Buttermilk,
> Snap beans—butterbeans—
> Tender okra—fresh greens . . .
> And buttermilk."

My mother considered herself pretty well prepared in her kitchen and pantry for any emergency that, in her words, might choose to present itself. But if she should, all of a sudden, need another lemon or find she was out of bread, all she had to do was call out, "Quick! Who'd like to run to the Little Store for me?"

I would.

She'd count out the change into my hand, and I was away. I'll bet the nickel that would be left over that all over the country, for those of my day, the neighborhood grocery played a similar part in our growing up.

Our store had its name—it was that of the grocer who owned it, whom I'll call Mr. Sessions—but "the Little Store" is what we called it at home. It was a block down our street toward the capitol and half a block further, around the corner, toward the cemetery. I knew even the sidewalk to it as well as I knew my own skin. I'd skipped my jumping-rope up and down it, hopped its length through mazes of hopscotch, played jacks in its islands of shade, serpentined along it on my Princess bicycle, skated it backward and forward. In the twilight I had dragged my steamboat by its string (this was homemade out of every new shoebox, with candle in the bottom lighted and shining through colored tissue paper pasted over windows scissored out in the shapes of the sun, moon and stars) across every crack of the walk without letting it bump or catch fire. I'd "played out" on that street after supper with my brothers and friends as long as "first-dark" lasted; I'd caught its lightning bugs. On the first Armistice Day (and this will set the time I'm speaking of) we made our own parade down that walk on a single velocipede—my brother pedaling, our little brother riding the handlebars, and myself standing on the back, all with arms wide, flying flags in each hand. (My father snapped that picture as we raced by. It came out blurred.)

As I set forth for the Little Store, a tune would float toward me from the house where there lived three sisters, girls in their teens, who ratted their hair over their ears, wore headbands like gladiators, and were considered to be very popular. They practiced for this in the daytime; they'd wind up the Victrola, leave the same record on they'd played before, and you'd see them bobbing past their dining-room windows while they danced with each other. Being three, they could go all day, cutting in:

> "Everybody ought to know-oh
> How to do the Tickle-Toe (how to do the Tickle-Toe)"—

they sang it and danced to it, and as I went by to the same song, I believed it.

A little further on, across the street, was the house where the principal of our grade school lived—lived on, even while we were having vacation. What if she would come out? She would halt me in my tracks—she had a very carrying and well-known voice in Jackson, where she'd taught almost everybody—saying, "Eudora Alice Welty, spell OBLIGE." OBLIGE was the word that she of course knew had kept me from making 100 on my spelling exam. She'd make me miss it again now, by boring her eyes through me from across the street. This was my vacation fantasy, one good way to scare myself on the way to the store.

Down near the corner waited the house of a little boy named Lindsey. The sidewalk here was old brick, which the roots of a giant chinaberry tree had humped up and tilted this way and that. On skates, you took it fast, in a series of skittering hops, trying not to touch ground anywhere. If the chinaberries had fallen and rolled in the cracks, it was like skating through a whole shooting match of marbles. I crossed my fingers that Lindsey wouldn't be looking.

During the big flu epidemic he and I, as it happened, were being nursed through our sieges at the same time. I'd hear my father and mother murmuring to each other, at the end of a long day, "And I wonder how poor little *Lindsey* got along today?" Just as, down the street, he no doubt would have to hear his family saying, "And I wonder how is poor *Eudora* by now?" I got the idea that a choice was going to be made soon between poor little Lindsey and poor Eudora, and I came up with a funny poem. I wasn't prepared for it when my father told me it wasn't funny and my mother cried that if I couldn't be ashamed for myself, she'd have to be ashamed for me:

> There was a little boy and his name was Lindsey.
> He went to heaven with the influinzy.

He didn't, he survived it, poem and all, the same as I did. But his chinaberries could have brought me down in my skates in a flying act of contrition before his eyes, looking pretty funny myself, right in front of his house.

Setting out in this world, a child feels so indelible. He only comes to find out later that it's all the others along his way who are making themselves indelible to him.

Our Little Store rose right up from the sidewalk; standing in a street of family houses, it alone hadn't any yard in front, any tree or flowerbed. It was a plain frame building covered over with brick. Above the door, a little railed porch ran across on an upstairs level and four windows with shades were looking out. But I didn't catch on to those.

Running in out of the sun, you met what seemed total obscurity inside. There were almost tangible smells—licorice recently sucked in a child's cheek, dill-pickle brine that had leaked through a paper sack in a fresh trail across the wooden floor, ammonia-loaded ice that had been hoisted from wet croker sacks and slammed into the icebox with its sweet butter at the door, and perhaps the smell of still-untrapped mice.

Then through the motes of cracker dust, cornmeal dust, the Gold Dust of the Gold Dust Twins that the floor had been swept out with, the realities emerged. Shelves climbed to high reach all the way around, set out with not too much of any one thing but a lot of things—lard, molasses, vinegar, starch, matches, kerosene, Octagon soap (about a year's worth of octagon-shaped coupons cut out and saved brought a signet ring addressed to you in the mail. Furthermore, when the postman arrived at your door, he blew a whistle). It was up to you to remember what you came for, while your eye traveled from cans of sardines to ice cream salt to harmonicas to flypaper (over your head, batting around on a thread beneath the blades of the ceiling fan, stuck with its testimonial catch).

Its confusion may have been in the eye of its beholder. Enchantment is cast upon you by all those things you weren't supposed to have need for, it lures you close to wooden tops you'd outgrown, boy's marbles and agates in little net pouches, small rubber balls that wouldn't bounce straight, frazzly kite-string, clay bubble-pipes that would snap off in your teeth, the stiffest scissors. You could contemplate those long narrow boxes of sparklers gathering dust while you waited for it to be the Fourth of July or Christmas, and noisemakers in the shape of tin frogs for somebody's birthday party you hadn't been invited to yet, and see that they were all marvelous.

You might not have even looked for Mr. Sessions when he came around his store cheese (as big as a doll's house) and in front of the counter looking for you. When you'd finally asked him for, and received from him in its paper bag, whatever single thing it was that you had been sent for, the nickel that was left over was yours to spend.

Down at a child's eye level, inside those glass jars with mouths in their sides through which the grocer could run his scoop or a child's hand might be invited to reach for a choice, were wineballs, all-day suckers, gumdrops, peppermints. Making a row under the glass of a counter were the Tootsie Rolls, Hershey Bars, Goo-Goo Clusters, Baby Ruths. And whatever was the name of those pastilles that came stacked in a cardboard cylinder with a cardboard lid? They were thin and dry, about the size of tiddlywinks, and in the shape of twisted rosettes. A kind of chocolate dust came out with them when you shook them out in your hand. Were they chocolate? I'd say rather they were brown. They didn't taste of anything at all, unless it was wood. Their attraction was the number you got for a nickel.

Making up your mind, you circled the store around and around, around the pickle barrel, around the tower of Cracker Jack boxes; Mr. Sessions had built it for us himself on top of a packing case, like a house of cards.

If it seemed too hot for Cracker Jacks, I might get a cold drink. Mr. Sessions might have already stationed himself by the cold-drinks barrel, like a mind reader. Deep in ice water that looked black as ink, murky shapes that would come up as Coca-Colas, Orange Crushes, and various flavors of pop, were all swimming around together. When you gave the word, Mr. Sessions plunged his bare arm in to the elbow and fished out your choice, first try. I favored a locally bottled concoction called Lake's Celery. (What else could it be called? It was made by a Mr. Lake out of celery. It was a popular drink here for years but was not known universally, as I found out when I arrived in New York and ordered one in the Astor bar.) You drank on the premises, with feet set wide apart to miss the drip, and gave him back his bottle.

But he didn't hurry you off. A standing scales was by the door, with a stack of iron weights and a brass slide on the balance arm, that would weigh you up to three hundred pounds. Mr. Sessions, whose hands were gentle and smelled of carbolic, would lift you up and set your feet on the platform, hold your loaf of bread for you, and taking his time while you stood still for him, he would make certain of what you weighed today. He could even remember what you weighed the last time, so you could subtract and announce how much you'd gained. That was goodbye.

Is there always a hard way to go home? From the Little Store, you could go partway through the sewer. If your brothers had called you a scarecat, then across the next street beyond the Little Store, it was possible to enter this sewer by passing through a privet hedge, climbing down into the bed of a creek, and going into its mouth on your knees. The sewer—it might have been no more than a "storm sewer"—came out and emptied here, where Town Creek, a sandy, most often shallow little stream that ambled through Jackson on its way to the Pearl River, ran along the edge of the cemetery. You could go in darkness through this tunnel to where you next saw light (if you ever did) and climb out through the culvert at your own street corner.

I was a scarecat, all right, but I was a reader with my own refuge in storybooks. Making my way under the sidewalk, under the street and the streetcar track, under the Little Store, down there in the wet dark by myself, I could be Persephone entering into my sixth-month sojourn underground—though I didn't suppose Persephone had to crawl, hanging onto a loaf of bread, and come out through the teeth of an iron grating. Mother Ceres would indeed be wondering where she could find me, and mad when she knew. "Now am I going to have to start marching to the Little Store for *myself*?"

I couldn't picture it. Indeed, I'm unable today to picture the Little Store with a grown person in it, except for Mr. Sessions and the lady who helped him, who belonged there. We children thought it was ours. The happiness of errands was in part that of running for the moment away from home, a free spirit. I believed the Little Store to be a center of the outside world, and hence of happiness—as I believed what I found in the Cracker Jack box to be a genuine prize, which was as simply as I believed in the Golden Fleece.

But a day came when I ran to the store to discover, sitting on the front step, a grown person, after all—more than a grown person. It was the Monkey Man, together with his monkey. His grinding-organ was lowered to the step beside him. In my whole life so far, I must have laid eyes on the Monkey Man no more than five or six times. An itinerant of rare and wayward appearances, he was not punctual like the Gipsies, who every year with the first cool days of fall showed up in the aisles of Woolworth's. You never knew when the Monkey Man might decide to favor Jackson, or which way he'd go. Sometimes you heard him as close as the next street, and then he didn't come up yours.

But now I saw the Monkey Man at the Little Store, where I'd never seen him before. I'd never seen him sitting down. Low on that familiar doorstep, he was not the same any longer, and neither was his monkey. They looked just like an old man and an old friend of his that wore a fez, meeting quietly together, tired, and resting with their eyes fixed on some place far away, and not the same place. Yet their romance for me didn't have it in its power to waver. I wavered. I simply didn't know how to step around them, to proceed on into the Little Store for my mother's emergency as if nothing had happened. If I could have gone in there after it, whatever it was, I would have given it to them—putting it into the monkey's cool little fingers. I would have given them the Little Store itself.

In my memory they are still attached to the store—so are all the others. Everyone I saw on my way seemed to me then part of my errand, and in a way they were. As I myself, the free spirit, was part of it too.

All the years we lived in that house where we children were born, the same people lived in the other houses on our street too. People changed through the arithmetic of birth, marriage and death, but not by going away. So families just accrued stories, which through the fullness of time, in those times, their own lives made. And I grew up in those.

But I didn't know there'd ever been a story at the Little Store, one that was going on while I was there. Of course, all the time the Sessions family had been living right overhead there, in the upstairs rooms behind the little railed porch and the shaded windows; but I think we children never thought of that. Did I fail to see them as a family because they weren't living in an ordinary house? Because I so seldom saw them close together, or having anything to say to each other? She sat in the back of the store, her pencil over a ledger, while he stood and waited on children to make up their minds. They worked in twin black eyeshades, held on their gray heads by elastic bands. It may be harder to recognize kindness—or unkindness, either—in a face whose eyes are in shadow. His face underneath his shade was as round as the little wooden wheels in the Tinker Toy box. So was her face. I didn't know, perhaps didn't even wonder: were they husband and wife or brother and sister? Were they father and mother? There were a few other persons, of various ages, wandering singly in by the back door and out. But none of their relationships could I imagine, when I'd never seen them sitting down together around their own table.

29 The possibility that they had any other life at all, anything beyond what we could see within the four walls of the Little Store, occurred to me only when tragedy struck their family. There was some act of violence. The shock to the neighborhood traveled to the children, of course; but I couldn't find out from my parents what had happened. They held it back from me, as they'd already held back many things, "until the time comes for you to know."

30 You could find out some of these things by looking in the unabridged dictionary and the encyclopedia—kept to hand in our dining room—but you couldn't find out there what had happened to the family who for all the years of your life had lived upstairs over the Little Store, who had never been anything but patient and kind to you, who never once had sent you away. All I ever knew was its aftermath: they were the only people ever known to me who simply vanished. At the point where their life overlapped into ours, the story broke off.

31 We weren't being sent to the neighborhood grocery for facts of life, or death. But of course those are what we were on the track of, anyway. With the loaf of bread and the Cracker Jack prize, I was bringing home the intimations of pride and disgrace, and rumors and early news of people coming to hurt one another, while others practiced for joy—storing up a portion for myself of the human mystery.

Rhetorical Analysis

1. The ideal paragraph, according to some style books, should consist of at least three but never more than ten sentences (ideally, 100 to 200 words). The style books may also say that one sentence does not make a paragraph (except occasionally, for emphasis), and that two-sentence paragraphs are considered awkward or inadequately developed. In "The Little Store" ¶s 4 and 18 are both one

sentence long, and ¶s 5 and 11 are two sentences long. Study these four short paragraphs in the context of the whole essay, and be ready to argue the issue. Do the "rules" expressed in style books make sense?

2. Reread ¶ 11. One point that Welty wishes to make in this essay is that certain events in one's life are "indelible," or unforgettable. As a writer, then, she would like to describe events in this essay so vividly that they remain indelibly imprinted in the reader's memory. How does Welty achieve this goal? Study ¶s 13, 15, 17, or any other that contains an image or event you find especially memorable. List the particular writing strategies Welty uses to make her material unforgettable.

3. Welty uses an event—a trip to the store and back—to give her essay an overall shape, or "frame." But that event accounts only for ¶s 3-22. How does she organize the two preceding paragraphs (¶s 1–2) and the following nine (¶s 23–31)? What is the rhetorical purpose of those eleven paragraphs?

Intellectual Analysis

1. Based on the opening paragraphs, one cannot foresee that Welty's essay will eventually lead to a stern lesson about the "human mystery." How does Welty make the transition from the rather ordinary tone and setting of the first paragraph to the almost cosmic sense of mystery at the end of the essay?
    a. All along there are clues that a trip to the "little store" is fraught with a multitude of dreads and tests and pitfalls. Examine the details carefully, noting the setting of the capitol, the house, the store, maybe even the windows of ¶ 12.
    b. What is the point of building the essay this way?
    c. How does the rhetorical strategy of ¶ 12 contribute to the meaning of the essay?
2. By the end, the little store has been left behind. What is the essay's ultimate subject?
    a. In many different ways Welty tells us that the trip to the store is an adventure, an intellectual and spiritual odyssey. What are those ways, and what do they tell us about what is finally discovered? What does she in fact discover?
    b. Is the reference to "death," "disgrace," and "hurt" in the last paragraph expected? Has Welty prepared the reader for that downward turn?
    c. Note has been made already of Welty's use of the word "indelible" in ¶ 12 of the essay. How does that word help identify her subject?

Suggestions for Writing

1. Describe your first encounter with violence, or with violent change. What strategies might you use to make experience objective in order to communicate it accurately to the reader? Is it possible you may have to "tell some stories" in order to get at the truth of the experience?

2. During the Great Depression in the 1930s, Welty worked for the WPA as a photographer. In *One Writer's Beginnings* she uses photography as a metaphor for her writing.

> *I learned in the doing how ready I had to be. Life doesn't hold still. A good snapshot stopped a moment from running away. Photography taught me that to be able to capture transience, by being ready to click the shutter at the crucial moment, was the greatest need I had. Making pictures of people in all sorts of situations, I learned that every feeling waits upon its gesture; and I had to be prepared to recognize this moment when I saw it.*

Choose some moment in your own life that seems about to run away, some feeling awaiting its gesture, and, using Welty as a model (any of these three essays will do), "click the shutter at a crucial moment." Later, in reviewing what you have written, ask yourself whether the photography metaphor helped you record a complete picture.

Langston Hughes

Langston Hughes first acted on his decision to write out of first-hand experience, and not out of books, while on a ship bound for the Azores and Africa. The year was 1922 and he was working as a mess boy. He had dropped out of Columbia University the previous year. "I leaned over the rail of the S.S. Malone," he wrote in his autobiography, The Big Sea, "and threw the books as far as I could out into the sea—all the books I had had at Columbia, and all the books I had lately bought to read." The lost volumes were to be replaced by many volumes of his own.

More than twenty books—poetry, fiction, nonfiction, and plays—followed. There were also translations of other writers from the French and Spanish, many anthologies, and the almost uncountable articles, essays and journalistic pieces. That first voyage to Africa also confirmed a pattern of restless wandering begun in childhood. Hughes, born in Joplin, Missouri, in 1902, lived—at times with his grandmother, at times with one or the other of his divorced parents—in Cleveland, Ohio, in Lawrence and Topeka, Kansas, in Mexico City, and elsewhere. He once remarked that "if strange beds had been given to upsetting me, I would have lost many a good night's sleep in my life." A peripatetic childhood led to an adult life that largely consisted of moving from place to place.

After graduating from Central High

in Cleveland, and before entering Columbia, Hughes published his first poem, "The Negro Speaks of Rivers," still a popular anthology piece. As seaman, following his first voyage on the Malone, he sailed to the West Indies and to Europe. In 1924, he disembarked in Rotterdam, went to Paris, and worked for a time as a doorman in Montmartre. At the end of that year he returned to New York City, working his way back as a deck hand. He arrived with twenty-five cents in his pocket, and landed a job as a bus boy at the Wardman Park Hotel. By the next year he had become a member of the coterie of writers and artists who made up what was later named the Harlem Renaissance, and in 1926 published his first book of poems, The Weary Blues. In the 1930s Hughes traveled to Russia, and also to Spain where, as a correspondent, he wrote about the Civil War. In 1961 he was elected a member of the National Academy of Arts and Letters, and in 1962 his song play, Black Nativity, was performed at the music festival in Spoleto, Italy.

Since Langston Hughes's death in 1967—and despite a brief period in the 1960s when he was criticized by a younger generation of writers for being out of touch with contemporary black issues—his reputation as one of the masters of twentieth-century American writing has become firmly established. Because of his many accomplishments, there is something of the Renaissance Man in Langston Hughes—perhaps as much as in any other national figure in modern letters.

SALVATION

I was saved from sin when I was going on thirteen. But not really saved. It happened like this. There was a big revival at my Auntie Reed's church. Every night for weeks there had been much preaching, singing, praying, and shouting, and some very hardened sinners had been brought to Christ, and the membership of the church had grown by leaps and bounds. Then just before the revival ended, they held a special meeting for children, "to bring the young lambs to the fold." My aunt spoke of it for days ahead. That night I was escorted to the front row and placed on the mourners' bench with all the other young sinners, who had not yet been brought to Jesus. 1

My aunt told me that when you were saved you saw a light, and something happened to you inside! And Jesus came into your life! And 2

God was with you from then on! She said you could see and hear and feel Jesus in your soul. I believed her. I had heard a great many old people say the same thing and it seemed to me they ought to know. So I sat there calmly in the hot, crowded church, waiting for Jesus to come to me.

The preacher preached a wonderful rhythmical sermon, all moans and shouts and lonely cries and dire pictures of hell, and then he sang a song about the ninety and nine safe in the fold, but one little lamb was left out in the cold. Then he said: "Won't you come? Won't you come to Jesus? Young lambs, won't you come?" And he held out his arms to all us young sinners there on the mourners' bench. And the little girls cried. And some of them jumped up and went to Jesus right away. But most of us just sat there.

A great many old people came and knelt around us and prayed, old women with jet-black faces and braided hair, old men with work-gnarled hands. And the church sang a song about the lower lights are burning, some poor sinners to be saved. And the whole building rocked with prayer and song.

Still I kept waiting to *see* Jesus.

Finally all the young people had gone to the altar and were saved, but one boy and me. He was a rounder's son named Westley. Westley and I were surrounded by sisters and deacons praying. It was very hot in the church, and getting late now. Finally Westley said to me in a whisper: "God damn! I'm tired o' sitting here. Let's get up and be saved." So he got up and was saved.

Then I was left all alone on the mourners' bench. My aunt came and knelt at my knees and cried, while prayers and songs swirled all around me in the little church. The whole congregation prayed for me alone, in a mighty wail of moans and voices. And I kept waiting serenely for Jesus, waiting, waiting—but he didn't come. I wanted to see him, but nothing happened to me. Nothing! I wanted something to happen to me, but nothing happened.

I heard the songs and the minister saying: "Why don't you come? My dear child, why don't you come to Jesus? Jesus is waiting for you. He wants you. Why don't you come? Sister Reed, what is this child's name?"

"Langston," my aunt sobbed.

"Langston, why don't you come? Why don't you come and be saved? Oh, Lamb of God! Why don't you come?"

Now it was really getting late. I began to be ashamed of myself, holding everything up so long. I began to wonder what God thought about Westley, who certainly hadn't seen Jesus either, but who was now sitting proudly on the platform, swinging his knickerbockered legs and grinning down at me, surrounded by deacons and old women on their knees praying. God had not struck Westley dead for taking his name in vain or for lying in the temple. So I decided that maybe to save further trouble, I'd better lie, too, and say that Jesus had come, and get up and be saved.

So I got up. 12

Suddenly the whole room broke into a sea of shouting, as they saw me rise. Waves of rejoicing swept the place. Women leaped in the air. My aunt threw her arms around me. The minister took me by the hand and led me to the platform. 13

When things quieted down, in a hushed silence, punctuated by a few ecstatic "Amens," all the new young lambs were blessed in the name of God. Then joyous singing filled the room. 14

That night, for the last time in my life but one—for I was a big boy twelve years old—I cried. I cried, in bed alone, and couldn't stop. I buried my head under the quilts, but my aunt heard me. She woke up and told my uncle I was crying because the Holy Ghost had come into my life, and because I had seen Jesus. But I was really crying because I couldn't bear to tell her that I had lied, that I had deceived everybody in the church, that I hadn't seen Jesus, and that now I didn't believe there was a Jesus any more, since he didn't come to help me. 15

Rhetorical Analysis

1. As a rhetorical device, what is the effect of continually making the reader aware of the room—"the hot, crowded church"—in which this episode takes place? What are the various ways in which Hughes emphasizes the setting? Here are three observations with which to begin:
    a. He mentions the "mourners' bench" (¶s 1, 3, and 7), coupled with the adults gathered around it (¶ 4).
    b. Hughes speaks repeatedly of sounds in the room: ¶s 3, 4, and 13, for example. Then he mentions the sudden "hushed silence" of ¶ 14, followed by singing.
    c. Hughes tells us the room is hot and crowded in ¶ 2, and the "whole building rocked" in ¶ 4.
    How do these details intensify the climax of the essay in the last three paragraphs?
2. Hughes uses three one-sentence paragraphs in this piece, and one other paragraph is constructed of four short, rapid-fire questions. What is the function of

such a technique? Note that handbooks on writing often advise against such paragraphing; here, however, this percussive approach may aid Hughes in pacing and emphasis. Evaluate the technique further.
3. Hughes's diction all through this essay is noteworthy for its balance between poetry and plainness. Compare expressions like "songs swirled all around me," with the flatness of "I wanted something to happen to me, but nothing happened" (both in ¶ 7). What is the effect of matching charged expressions with plain statement? What reason might Hughes have for doing this?

Intellectual Analysis

1. A fundamental irony, at several levels, operates in this essay from the title onward. The first two sentences establish clearly that what apparently happened did not happen at all. Everything else follows from that self-conscious irony.
   a. It conditions the diction. For example, ¶ 3 opens with, "The preacher preached a wonderful rhythmical sermon, all moans and shouts and lonely cries. . . ." Evaluate the verbal irony of that statement. Search for others that continue the irony.
   b. It conditions larger elements, too. For example, Hughes's ironic build-up to the opening of ¶ 7: "Then I was left all alone on the mourners' bench." What does he achieve with that build-up (which begins at the end of ¶ 1)?
   c. It conditions a still larger pattern: the immense pressure on the children to be saved. Look at ¶ 6.
   d. It conditions, finally, the structure of the whole essay in Hughes's juxtaposition of the "little church" with his own room at the end.
2. The simple point of this essay is that though Hughes appears to have been saved, he has not been; the last paragraph makes clear that the opposite has occurred. Yet the point may be more complex than that. Consider these two possibilities.
   a. He weeps at the end, he says, because "I had deceived everybody in the church. . . ." To learn that deception is wrong is a great virtue. Was that the only reason he "cried . . . and couldn't stop?"
   b. Suppose Hughes was, at least in one sense, "saved." What if, in the last analysis, the title is not ironic? And if that is the case, then what has he been "saved" from?

Suggestions for Writing

1. As pointed out above, Hughes demonstrates the pressure placed on the children of the church to be saved. Write an essay on other "pressured" situations where conformity to some practice, situation, or code is the object.
2. What does Hughes himself learn from this experience? Write a speculative essay on that question. You should begin with details in his essay, though you should go beyond them.

THEME FOR ENGLISH B

The instructor said,

>   Go home and write
>   a page tonight.
>   And let that page come out of you—
>   Then, it will be true.

I wonder if it's that simple?
I am twenty-two, colored, born in Winston-Salem.
I went to school there, then Durham, then here
to this college on the hill above Harlem.
I am the only colored student in my class.
The steps from the hill lead down into Harlem,
through a park, then I cross St. Nicholas,
Eighth Avenue, Seventh, and I come to the Y,
the Harlem Branch Y, where I take the elevator
up to my room, sit down, and write this page:

It's not easy to know what is true for you or me
at twenty-two, my age. But I guess I'm what
I feel and see and hear, Harlem, I hear you:
hear you, hear me—we two—you, me, talk on this page.
(I hear New York, too.) Me—who?
Well, I like to eat, sleep, drink, and be in love.
I like to work, read, learn, and understand life.
I like a pipe for a Christmas present,
or records—Bessie, bop, or Bach.
I guess being colored doesn't make me *not* like
the same things other folks like who are other races.
So will my page be colored that I write?
Being me, it will not be white.
But it will be
a part of you, instructor.
You are white—
yet a part of me, as I am a part of you.
That's American.
Sometimes perhaps you don't want to be a part of me.
Nor do I often want to be a part of you.

But we are, that's true!
As I learn from you,
I guess you learn from me—
although you're older—and white—
and somewhat more free.   40

This is my page for English B.

Rhetorical Analysis

1. Since this is the only piece in the form of a poem in this anthology, it raises some unique questions.
    a. Rhetorically, what does Hughes gain by metering his statements here, and lining them out poetically? If you were to write out this poem in prose paragraphs, what would be changed?
        (1) One advantage might be that Hughes can pace the statements more forcefully this way (for example, the short lines, 13 from the end).
        (2) Another possibility is that he can make more use of sound effects by such things as occasional rhymes and near-rhymes.
        (3) If the object of the professor's assignment is to fill the page, then Hughes fulfills the requirement. The word, "page," is repeated, and to what rhetorical effect?
    b. But, finally, Hughes makes the rhetorical choice to write his "Theme for English B" in verse for reasons that have less to do with matters of technique, and more with what sort of statement he wanted to make by disrupting the instructor's expectations implicit in the assignment: "Go home and write/a page tonight." What effect do you think Hughes hoped to achieve by controverting those expectations? (See question 1 under "Intellectual Analysis.")
2. What persuasive function does the early line—"I wonder if it's that simple?"—serve? Do you think this poem is "that simple"? Is the surface of the poem deceptive in any way? Or, is it utterly straightforward?

Intellectual Analysis

1. In his assignment the instructor enjoins his students, "And let that page come out of you—/Then, it will be true." What sort of assumptions is he making about writing and about this assignment?
2. How much do we learn about Hughes, or at least the speaker of this poem? Since he has been told to let it "come out" of "himself," how much does he reveal? What sort of person does he reveal himself to be?

3. In the second verse paragraph, Hughes makes two identifications, one between himself and Harlem (ll. 18–19), and one between himself and his instructor (l. 32). What point do these identifications, or alliances, make? Do both identifications have the same weight? The same intent? They are worth exploring: they have to do with himself and what is outside of him. They consequently have to do with the most fundamental question we can ask.

Suggestions for Writing

1. Here is an even briefer poem by Langston Hughes. Write a critical essay on it and its implications.

>WHAT HAPPENS TO A DREAM DEFERRED?
>
>Does it dry up
>like a raisin in the sun?
>
>Or fester like a sore—
>And then run?
>Does it stink like rotten meat?
>Or crust and sugar over—
>like syrupy sweet?
>
>Maybe it just sags
>like a heavy load.
>
>*Or does it explode?*

   Trace out the differences in tone, imagery, and theme, between this poem and "Theme for English B."

2. Answering question 3 of "Intellectual Analysis" brings us squarely up against the long and tangled history of race relations in America. Quoting lines 18–19 and 32 as a starting point, discuss the complex relationships, and the ambiguities of Hughes's own position (as he presents it in this poem) in those relationships, of white and black, teacher and student, youth and (relative) age. You might read (or reread) such essays as Baldwin's "Notes of a Native Son" and Walker's "In Search of Our Mothers' Gardens" to deepen your discussion.

BROWN AMERICA IN JAIL: KILBY

The steel doors closed. Locked. Here, too, was Brown America. Like monkeys in tiered cages, hundreds of Negroes barred away from life.   1

Animals of crime. Human zoo for the cast-offs of society. Hunger, ignorance, poverty: civilization's major defects woven into a noose for the unwary. Men in jail, months and months, years and years after the steel doors have closed. Vast monotony of guards and cages. The State Penitentiary at Kilby, Alabama, in the year of our Lord, 1932.

Our Lord . . . Pilate . . . and the thieves on the cross.

For a moment the fear came: even for me, a Sunday morning visitor, the doors might never open again. WHITE guards held the keys. (The judge's chair protected like Pilate's.) And I'm only a nigger. Nigger. Niggers. Hundreds of niggers in Kilby Prison. Black, brown, yellow, near-white niggers. The guards. WHITE. Me—a visiting nigger.

Sunday morning: In the Negro wing. Tier on tier of steel cells. Cell doors are open. Within the wing, men wander about in white trousers and shirts. Sunday clothes. Day of rest. Cards, checkers, dice, story telling from cell to cell. Chapel if they will. One day of rest, in jail. Within the great closed cell of the wing, visiting, laughing, talking, *on Sunday.*

But in the death house, cells are not open. You enter by a solid steel door through which you cannot see. White guard opens the door. White guard closes the door, shuts out the world, remains inside with you.

THE DEATH HOUSE. Dark faces peering from behind bars, like animals when the keeper comes. All Negro faces, men and young men in this death house at Kilby. Among them the eight Scottsboro boys. Sh-s-s-s! Scottsboro boys? SCOTTSBORO boys. SCOTTSBORO BOYS! (Keep silent, world. The State of Alabama washes its hands.) Eight brown boys condemned to death. No proven crime! Farce of a trial. Lies. Laughter. Mob. Music. Eight poor niggers make a country holiday. (Keep silent, Germany, Russia, France, young China, Gorki, Thomas Mann, Romain Rolland, Theodore Dreiser. Pilate washes his hands. Listen Communists, don't send any more cablegrams to the Governor of Alabama. Don't send any more telegrams to the Supreme Court. What's the matter? What's all this excitement about, over eight young niggers? Let the law wash its hands in peace.)

There are only two doors in the death house. One from the world, in. The other from the world, out—to the electric chair. To DEATH. Against this door the guard leans. White guard, watching Brown America in the death house.

Silence. The dark world is silent. Speak! Dark world:

>Listen, guard: Let the boys out.
>Guard with the keys, let 'em out.

>   Guard with the law books, let them out.
>   Guards in the Supreme Court! Guards in the White
>   House!
>   Guards of the money bags made from black hands sold
>   in the cotton fields, sold in mines, sold on Wall
>   Street:
>   Let them out!

Daily, I watch the guards washing their hands.

The world remembers for a long time a certain washing of hands. The world remembers for a long time a certain humble One born in a manger—straw, manure, and the feet of animals—standing before Power washing its hands. No proven crime. Farce of a trial. Lies. Laughter. Mob. Hundreds of years later Brown America sang: *My Lord! What a morning when the stars began to fall!*

For eight brown boys in Alabama the stars have fallen. In the death house I heard no song at all. Only a silence more ominous than song. All of Brown America locked up there. And no song.

>   *Even as ye do unto the least of these, ye do it unto Me.*
>   White guard.
>   The door that leads to DEATH.
>   Electric chair.
>   No song.

Rhetorical Analysis

1. Hughes's first paragraph is a perfect example of inductive logic: a sequence of staccato details, ending with a general statement which locates us. Stylistically, the paragraph also demonstrates paratactic structure: that is, a string of details, not necessarily subordinated rationally, is suddenly drawn into focus by a final statement. Evaluate the effectiveness of such style and structure here.

2. Why does Hughes use so many fragmentary sentences in this essay? What sense do they make? How does he get away with such an excess? Are they effective?
    a. One effect of the style in this essay is to make the description of this visit to the jail more dramatic and immediate. The fragments imitate the speed with which the speaker is taking in impressions, and the horror of them as well.
    b. Another effect is that these slivers of sentences make the whole essay seem something like an incantation. Select some spots where Hughes is nearly chanting. What is their effect?

3. Why is this essay so short? What reasons can Hughes have for making brevity a rhetorical device? Is the essay finished? Does its ending work?

4. Paragraphs 5–8 form a unit in this piece: how does this unit fit into the progression of the whole? The governing image here is the "Death House."
   a. How is this subsection built within itself? For instance, from the inner Death House we move within to the faces, then to the inner door; then the speaker, by going further in his mind, goes past that door. Chart this rhetorical strategy in more detail.
   b. In ¶ 6, there is a great deal of rhetorical maneuvering: the focus on the Scottsboro case, the mention of specific names, and quick changes of point of view. Analyze Hughes's persuasive powers in this one paragraph.

Intellectual Analysis

1. The content of this essay is partly carried by the effect of the scene on the controlling voice, presumably Hughes himself (there is no reason to assume a persona here). What are the details that impress him most? In this context, consider the key images and key, or striking, statements.
   a. The imagery first: doors, zoo, guards, keys, the washing of hands. What are we to make of these counters? In what ways are they powerful?
   b. Now for two of the more striking statements: "civilization's major defects woven into a noose for the unwary" (¶ 1); and "Dark faces peering from behind bars, like animals when the keeper comes" (¶ 6). In both examples, Hughes takes particular pains to weight his diction carefully: for instance, what thematic weight does the "noose" carry here? Evaluate the diction carefully in these two expressions; then select other sentences which seem crucial to you.
2. Why does Hughes, with all his focus on the prison itself, keep reaching outward from it, thematically and verbally?
   a. Why mention the governor of Alabama, the Supreme Court, Wall Street? (In this regard, several other allusions, especially those of ¶ 6, need to be identified; keep in mind this essay was written in 1932.)
   b. What does Hughes gain by emphasizing repeatedly that it is Sunday? And, how does he extend the possibilities, by allusion, of the connection of "Sunday" and the prison? Recollect the "washing of hands."
3. Why mention the falling of the stars (¶s 10–11)?

Suggestions for Writing

1. After rereading this essay, read Baldwin's "An Open Letter to My Sister, Miss Angela Davis." Though the two essays are separated by more than 40 years, what have they in common?
2. Try your hand at writing a descriptive piece, making use of vivid details and lots of fragmentary or half sentences to build a brief scene.

Barry Lopez

Barry Holstun Lopez began his pursuit of nature and the primitive early. He was born in New York state in 1945, but was raised in southern California (he now lives in the Cascade mountains in Oregon). After receiving degrees in English at Notre Dame and enrolling briefly in the writing program at the University of Oregon, Lopez began to study North American folklore as well as anthropology and natural history. Dropping out of the university, he pursued these interests as a free-lance writer. His first book, Giving Birth to Thunder, Sleeping with His Daughter (1977), is a collection of native American folktales; and his second, Of Wolves and Men, is an integrated study of wolves in nature, in human history, and in the human psyche. The second book was awarded the John Burroughs Medal for distinguished natural history writing in 1978.

Between 1978 and 1982 Lopez traveled all across the Arctic, in the company of wildlife biologists, petroleum geologists, and Eskimo hunters. Those experiences, including a harrowing account of being trapped in a small boat by Arctic ice, are told in his most recent book, Arctic Dreams (1986). Both River Notes (1979) and Winter Count (1980), represented in this anthology by "Log Jam" and "Buffalo," respectively, contain pieces which may properly be read either as essays or as fiction; they amount, in fact, to something of a new genre (or an old one revived—

Lamb, Hunt and DeQuincey having produced similar work), or of a hybrid of several genres, that has emerged in the past thirty or so years. Lopez has himself spoken to this issue, most eloquently in an essay called "Story at Anaktuvuk Pass." "Distinctions between fiction and nonfiction are sometimes obscured by arguments over what constitutes 'the truth.' In the aboriginal literature I am familiar with, the first distinction made among narratives is to separate the authentic from the inauthentic."

One of the challenges in reading the selections below is to understand Lopez's distinction between the authentic and inauthentic, and to see why it is of much more importance to Lopez than that between fiction and nonfiction. Somehow in the natural and in the primitive world Lopez finds a way of living, a way of seeing, and a way of believing more satisfying and, above all, more genuine than that way fostered by the highly civilized world that most of us know, with its insistence on technological progress, on abstract knowledge, and on objective "truth."

The Log Jam

1946

*I*n September, when bearberry leaves were ready to pick, after the first storm had come upvalley like a drunken miner headed home, snapping limbs as thick as your arms off the maples, Olin Sanders caught a big tree barberchairing and was dead before they could get him out of the woods. They laid him across the laps of two men in the back of the truck and sent word ahead. When they got down to the road his wife was there crying, with pink curlers like pine cones in her hair and in black knit slacks too small for her stout legs and a loose hanging white blouse. And two county sheriffs, drawn by the word of death, wearing clean, pressed clothing, like clerks. When she looked in through the window of the truck and saw him broken in half like a buckled tin can she raised her fists to beat at the thing responsible and began beating the truck. When the sheriff held her back and said in a polite voice, "Now, control yourself," she began beating her thighs. One of the men stepped up and punched the sheriff.

1

All this time the son, in whose lap the father's broken head was cradled, sat silent. He was aware of the beginning of something else, more than his father's end. His pants were wet with his father's blood.

That night the boy left the house, walked past his father's shirts hanging to dry on the line, and drove up the Warner Creek Road to the place where they had been cutting. He sidestepped downslope with the chainsaw in his hands to reach the stump of the tree (the blood congealed like dark sap on the wood) and cut it off, cut off the top of the stump with the stain of his father's death on it, the saw screaming in the dim night. With a choker and a length of cable he hauled the butt round uphill and cursed and jacked it into the back of his pickup.

He came off Warner Mountain to the Granite Creek Road and went down Granite Creek until he came to the equipment shed, where a logging bridge crossed the river to the highway side. With a front loader and a length of chain he yanked the slab of wood out of the pickup, drove out onto the bridge and with jerking motions and the hiss of hydraulics he twisted the machine crosswise, tipped the bucket and dumped the slab of fir into the river.

He put the front loader away and drove home.

No one had ever done anything like this before. The lack of any tradition in it bothered the boy. As he walked past the trees near the house he was suddenly afraid. His mother was awake, sitting in the darkened living room when he walked in, wearing the tattered quilt robe that embarrassed him when his friends were around. Behind the glow of her cigarette she asked where he had been.

The butt round came back to the surface of the river, the thunderous sound of its plunge evaporating in the night, and it moved off like a dark iceberg riding low in the water. A few miles and it beached quietly on the cobbles of an island.

1951

Cawley Besson and his family—a wife called June, two boys, and a mixed-breed dog—came to work for the Forest Service. There was timber then, timber uncruised in backcountry valleys. Douglas firs ten feet through at the base and straight-grained for two hundred and fifty feet. Dense, slow-grown wood. It was show-off timber and no need to spare it.

Cawley opened roads to it. He was tight-bellied, dedicated, and clipped in his manners. He left early for work and came home late, with a reputation, he said, to think about. He had places to go after this job he told his wife (lying next to him, listening to him, wondering when they would make love again), places to go.

On a hot Sunday in June, Cawley sat at the river's edge in a pair of shorts, eating a picnic lunch, thinking about Monday, drinking cold beer and watching his sons. The boys were throwing rocks into the river, which the dog chased until he felt the current at his legs and stepped back. Cawley liked the feel of this: he looked toward his wife, feeling the warmth of his own body. The boy swept past him, gesticulating silently, before the scream arrived in his ears, as the dog ran over him barking, and he looked to see the other son standing motionless at the river's edge with his hands over his mouth.

Cawley leaped to his feet, spilling food away, calling out, running to catch up, cursing jibberish. He could not swim, the boy either. He saw the small white face in the dark water, the sunlight bright in his short wet hair, and what lay ahead began to close in on him. The boy, wide-eyed and quiet, went with the river.

Cawley continued to run. The panic got into him like leeches. The beer was coming up acid in his mouth. The river bore the boy on and he calculated how fast, running harder to get ahead, yelling to the boy Hold on! Hold on! Jesus hold on. A little ahead now. He saw the vine maple coming at him, grabbed it, bent it, broke it so fast he felt hope, ran hard into the shallows ahead of the boy to throw the end of the long branch to him—who spun off its tip with his hands splayed, rigid. Cawley dropped the limb and churning high-legged and mad, chest deep and with a sudden plunge had the boy, had his shirt, and was flailing for shore, grabbing for rocks in the river bed that swept by under him. His feet touched ground and held. His fist was white with his grip twisted in the boy's tee-shirt—the boy could hardly breathe against his clutch.

The maple limb drifted downriver and came to rest among willows, near a log round on which dark stains were still visible.

1954

A storm came this year, against which all other storms were to be measured, on a Saturday in October, a balmy afternoon. Men in the woods cutting firewood for winter, and children outside with melancholy thoughts lodged somewhere in the memory of summer. It built as it came up the valley as did every fall storm, but the steel-gray thunderheads, the first sign of it anyone saw, were higher, much higher, too high. In the stillness before it hit, men looked at each other as though a fast and wiry man had pulled a knife in a bar. They felt the trees falling before they heard the wind, and they dropped tools and scrambled to get out. The wind came up suddenly and like a scythe, like piranha after them, like seawater through a breach in a dike. The first blow bent trees half to the ground, the second caught them and snapped them like kindling, sending limbs raining down and twenty-foot splinters hurtling through the air like mortar shells to stick quivering in the ground. Bawling cattle running the fences, a loose lawnmower bumping across a lawn, a stray dog lunging for a child racing by. The big trees went down screaming, ripping open holes in the wind that were filled with the broken-china explosion of a house and the yawing screech of a pickup rubbed across asphalt, the rivet popping and twang of phone and electric wires.

It was over in three or four minutes. The eerie, sucking silence it left behind seemed palpably evil, something that would get into the standing timber, like insects, a memory.

No one was killed. Roads were cut off, a bridge buckled. No power. A few had to walk in from places far off in the steep wooded country, arriving home later than they'd ever been up. Some said it pulled the community together, others how they hated living in the trees with no light. No warning. The next day it rained and the woods smelled like ashes. It was four or five days before they got the roads opened and the phones working, electricity back. Three sent down to the hospital in Holterville. Among the dead, Cawley Besson's dog. And two deer, butchered and passed quietly in parts among neighbors.

Of the trees that fell into the river, a number came up like beached whales among willows at the tip of an island.

1957

Rebecca Grayson drove forty-one miles each morning to work in a men's clothing store in town and came back each evening in time to fix her husband's dinner. It was a job that had paid for births and funerals, for weddings and a second automobile but it left her depressed and stranded now, at fifty-six, as if it were a clear defeat, invisible but keenly known to her.

Her husband operated a gas station and logging supply shop in Beaver Creek, a small town on the river. They had had four daughters, which had caused Clarence Grayson a kind of dismay from which he never recovered. It wasn't a country for raising daughters, he thought. He lived as though he were waiting for wounds to heal before moving on.

He hardly noticed, when she helped him in the shop on Saturdays, that someone often came by with wildflowers for her, or to tell a story, to ask had she seen the skunk cabbage in Danmeier's field or the pussy willows blooming, sure signs of spring. Clarence appreciated these acts of kindness, while he finished a job for whoever it was, as a duty done that he had no way with.

Men were attracted to Rebecca in an innocent but almost hungry way, as though needing the pleasure she took in them. Because there was never a hint of anything but friendship, their attentions both pleased her and left her with a deep longing, out of which, unashamed, she lay awake at night in a self-embrace of fantasy.

Late at night, when he couldn't sleep, Clarence would roll over to her and try to speak. Sometimes he would begin to cry and sob in anger at a loss he couldn't find the words for. He cried against her negligee and drove his fist weakly into his pillow. On those nights she held him until the pain ran its course, and said nothing of her own yearning.

After the last daughter had married she thought they could go away. In a deeply private place she wished to go to Europe, alone; but she could not bear the thought of his loneliness and did not believe that in a journey together there could be any joy.

One summer evening while Clarence was in the living room reading, she sat on their bed with her face lowered to a glass bowl of dried blossoms in her lap, a pool of musky odor that triggered memory and passion in her and to which she would touch her face in moments when she needed friendship. Twenty years of anniversary roses, flowers from her first gardens, wildflowers from men who were charmed by her, a daughter's wedding bouquet. She felt the tears run the length of her nose and the tightness of her small fists pressing against her knees. She wished to be rid of it, and she rose with the bowl and left.

In the dark yard by the side of the house she took off her dress and her soft underclothes. With the bowl firmly in her grip she walked down to the river and stepped in. The cold water rose against her as she moved away from the shore, lapped at her pale belly, and she felt a resolve as strong as any love she could ever remember. Her breasts hardened in the cold air. Waist deep in the water, her feet bent painfully around the stones (on the far bank she could see into the living rooms of people she knew), she scattered the first handful on the water. The pieces landed soundlessly and teetered quickly away. She flung the dry petals, the shrunken blossoms and the discolored flakes until the bowl was empty, and then dipped its lip to the current to swirl it clean.

She stood there, numb to the cold, until the wind had dissipated the perfume, listening to the wash around her hips, feeling the excitement of something she could not grasp. She thought of herself going on, like the river, without a break, with two herons flying overhead, untouchable and graceful, toward an undetermined destination. She had no wish to explain the feeling to anyone.

Of the flowers she threw on the water, some floated down as far as the log jam and hung up in its crevices.

1964

By this time beaver had come back to the valley, once having been trapped out. They were few and save for the sight of alders cut along the creeks their lives went unnoticed. One of the dams blocked a feeder stream above Bear Creek and was found one morning in the fall by a boy hunting deer. He walked across, testing it idly as he went, then throwing his weight to it, trying to make it spring. He came to a halt and surveyed the dam with surprise, for it did not give. On the far side he set his gun against a tree and cut an alder pole, stripping the leaves and sharpening the point with swift, deft strokes of his knife. Walking back across the span he began to probe the structure, looking for an opening with depth. He found such a place and twisting the pole into it began to pry and root with the tip, seeking better leverage. Bracing his legs and putting all the strength of his back and upper arms into it, he broke out a wedge of mud and twigs. Against this breach he began to use the pole like a post-hole digger, raising it above his head and ramming deeper and deeper, prying against any purchase. The green twigs were supple and difficult to break so he turned to the knife. Cut through, then pry. He was beginning to sweat. As he took off his jacket he saw the beaver surface in the middle of the pond. He hunkered quietly off the dam and hid in the brush. The beaver, motionless in the center of departing concentric rings of water, followed each movement.

The boy stared at the beaver, angry for having allowed himself to be seen. He could feel his heart pounding, the sudden compression of his muscles, smell his own warm odors. His hand located a rock. In one fluid motion he rose to fire it with tremendous strength, so hard the hair jumped on his head with the snap of his body. He missed. The beaver slipped under. He picked up another rock. *Twoosh.* The sound of the stone cutting into the pond steadied him. *Twoosh. Twoosh.*

He returned to the dam, to the place where he had gouged an opening. Prying, batting, cutting, and kicking; finally, against a fulcrum of boulders carried from the shore, he broke through the mesh of limbs. He stepped aside, disheveled. As the water flowed cleanly through the cut he came to realize the break was too shallow, only several inches below the surface of the pond; and that it was too late in the day to go hunting. And that the beaver had not shown himself again. He cursed the beaver, threw the pry pole into the pond and, taking his gun, walked off sullenly.

The pond drained to the level of the cut. After dark the beaver came to the breach and began to weave a closure.

The boy threatened to return to the valley and trap beaver that winter but did not.

Alder branches from the dam were swept down Bear Creek and into the river, where they wedged in the log jam.

1973

The fir that grew next to the Thompson's house was, by a count of its rings, 447 years old when it fell at dusk on a March day during dinner. Before it fell the sounds outside were only those of the river coming up softly through the trees and the calls of grosbeaks. Gene Thompson was able to hear other things as he sat at the table. He could hear trees growing and dying. (When he walked in the woods he could distinguish between the creaking of cedar and the creaking of hemlock, between the teeter of rocks in a stream and the heartbeat of a spotted owl. He lay in the woods with his ear pressed to the damp earth listening to the slow burrowing of tree roots, which he distinguished from the digging of moles or worms, or the sound of rivers moving deep in the earth.) When he listened with his forehead against a tree he heard the thinking of woodpeckers asleep inside. He heard the flow of sap which sounded like stratospheric winds to him.

Gene sat quietly at dinner listening to the fir by the house. He heard the sudden spread of a filigree of cracks in the termite-ridden roots, the groaning of fibers stretched as the tree shifted its weight, seventy tons, toward the river and a muffled popping in the earth as it gave way. He heard (the fork poised before his mouth) the sweeping brush of trailing limbs high overhead as it began its descent. With the first loud crack, the terrible whining screech of separation, the gasping, sucking noise in its wake as the tree sailed down, everyone looked up. The tree struck the earth like a sheet of iron and dinner leaped from the table. A soft after-rain of twigs.

Gene went out the door with his father.

"Holy cow!" he said, striding toward it.

It had taken other trees with it, broken the highway and lay with its top in the river. It had to be removed, said his father, right away, to let traffic through. "Six or seven feet," he said to an approaching neighbor, "through the butt and clean for two hundred feet." Lucky no one had been killed, he said. He knew its value. Prime old growth. Overmature. Cut right it could be worth $3,000. He figured it roughly, climbed up on it and paced off a measurement in the falling light while another son jerked a chain saw to life to begin to clear the road.

The boy squatted at the stump with his hands spread wide in the tawny sap. He had heard the slow movement of air through the lengthening termite tunnels and had known. He raised his hands from the stump and the sap hung stiffly from his fingers like spirals of honey.

The crown of the tree eventually washed downriver and became entangled at the tip of the island. In the years that followed a pair of osprey came and built a nest, and lived as well as could be expected in that country.

Rhetorical Analysis

1. This essay establishes the authority of the writer in the very first sentence with words such as "bearberry," "upvalley," and "barberchairing." Part of the persuasion of the piece is accomplished by the use of this vocabulary; and it could be used

correctly only by someone with a thorough knowledge of the countryside. Find other examples. Is the vocabulary too technical, in your opinion?

2. Rhetorically, this is as unconventional an essay as you are likely to find. Discuss the following characteristics. What effects is Lopez trying to achieve with them?
   a. The separateness of six narratives, the only connection among them being the chronology of the dates and the final references to the log jam.
   b. The absence of any explicit statement of thesis or even subject.
   c. The absence of any explicit statement indicating the attitudes of the writer.
   d. The use of techniques commonly found in fiction writing, such as metaphoric language and direct narration.

Intellectual Analysis

1. Above we note that rhetorically this essay is unconventional. This eccentricity of form means we as readers may have to look for meaning in ways we are not used to.
   a. It borders on being a set of notebook entries. Thematically, what links these episodes together? Are they stories, or are they prose accounts of information and fact?
   b. Taken as a whole, this piece forms the most extreme kind of inductive argument: we move through details and particulars toward some conclusion. Yet the generalization that ought to result from induction is absent. Or is it? Is there an implicit generalization? Check the phrasing in ¶s 8 and 28, for example; are natural resources somehow the point of the whole?

2. How do the island and the log jam function in this essay? What can be observed about them?
   a. In the first section, Lopez refers to "an island"; by the last, it has become "the island." Why the change?
   b. The log jam seems to be at the island, too. Does it also become an image of something? What would be its meaning?
   c. Consider that in one way or another, the remnants of all these episodes are collected at the island or in the jam. What does that imply?
   d. How does the presence of the woman in episode 4 figure in these two images, within this whole structure?

Suggestions for Writing

1. Write an essay, on a subject of your choice, with three or more sections unified by theme but with no explicit connections between them.

2. Write an essay in which you analyze the relationship between the land and the people in "Log Jam." Is there conflict? Does Lopez see people exploiting the land or living in harmony with it? Or does he see a relationship that is more complex?

Wolfing for Sport

Man has always sought to legitimize his hunting of wolves, even when it was at the ragged edges of decency. One of the defenses he offered was that it was simply "good sport" to hunt wolves—the wolf was taken for the admired enemy. Even though many of these men bore the wolf no overt hatred, their methods could not always be called sporting, however.

Theodore Roosevelt hunted wolves in Russia and North America with dogs, sometimes on a grand scale, and he made no apology for it. (He once set off with seventy fox hounds, sixty-seven greyhounds, sixty saddle and packhorses, and forty-four hunters, beaters, wranglers, and journalists, all in a private train of twenty-two cars.) In Russia there was a veneer of upper-class respectability to such hunts; in America there was rarely legitimate claim to sport in coursing, though that was often its guise. Roosevelt was quite clear on this point. Writing of an acquaintance who hunted wolves with dogs in North Dakota, he said: "The only two requisites were that the dogs be fast and fight gamely; and in consequence they formed as wicked a hard-biting crew as ever throttled a wolf. They were usually taken out ten at a time, and by their aid Massinggale killed over two hundred wolves, including pups. Of course there was no pretense of giving them fair play. The wolves were killed for vermin, not sport. . . ."

Wolf hunting in Europe and Russia with hounds was an aristocratic amusement, popular around the turn of the century. While nobility and its guests dined and relaxed in the hunting lodge, the head huntsman and his helpers scoured the countryside for wolf sign or learned from local peasants where the wolves were. On the day of the hunt the gentlemen arrayed themselves in a line at the edge of a promising wood and the head huntsman tried to howl up a wolf. If an answering howl was heard—"commingling the lament of a dying dog with the wailing of an Irish Banshee"—the dogs began driving the woods from the far side. A beater might have as many as six dogs on leashes as he moved through the woods. Deerhounds, staghounds, and Siberian wolfhounds, the slender white borzoi, as well as smaller greyhounds and foxhounds. When he saw a wolf, he would shout: "Loup! Loup! Loup!" and slip the dogs. The idea was to trap the wolf between pursuing dogs and the hunters sitting astride their horses at the edge of the wood. Bursting from cover, the wolf would either be shot or pinned by the dogs and then speared or clubbed. Sometimes the dogs, especially the larger mastiff crossbreeds and hounds, would kill the wolf.

Wolves were also coursed, or chased, by dogs and horsemen through open prairie country where they were worried by the hounds until lassoed or shot. George Armstrong Custer was a devotee of coursing and usually traveled with a retinue of dogs. He was partial to larger greyhounds and staghounds and took two of the latter, large, white, shaggy dogs, with him into the Sioux's sacred Black Hills where he turned them loose on deer and wolves. The southern Cheyenne, who hated Custer, killed one of his favorite staghounds, Blucher, at the Battle of the Washita in Oklahoma in 1868.

A popular kind of wolf hunting in the winter in Russia was done from a flat sled drawn by horses. A butchered calf or pig or a bale of bloody straw was trailed behind, or a live pig's leg was twisted to make it squeal, until wolves fell in behind the sled. The wolves were then shot. Stories of sled hunting abound in Russia and the failure of this scheme—the horses tire or there are too many wolves or the wolves are too fast or the sled flips over in an icy turn—is a staple incident in Russian fiction. Commonly the hunters lose their driver and horses to the wolves and spend a harrowing night under the upturned sled, holding the wolves off in a manner of a wagon train surrounded by Indians until morning. The wolves drift off at first light, having killed their own wounded and eaten their own dead, and human help usually arrives in the person of distraught friends who feared the worst when the adventurers didn't return.

The most exotic sort of wolf hunting involves the use of eagles. It has been seen only occasionally in Europe; its real home is Kirgizia, in south-central Russia. The specially bred birds—a subspecies of golden eagle called a berkut—are flown by nomadic tribesmen. The birds weigh only ten or twelve pounds but can slam into a wolf's back and bind its spine with such force that the wolf is almost paralyzed. Often the bird binds the spine with one foot and, as the wolf turns its head to bite, binds its nose with the other foot, suffocating the animal or holding it down until the hunter kills it. The birds are deceptively strong; there is almost a ton of binding force in each foot and the blow of a thirty-six-inch wing can break a man's arm.

Eagles probably never attack adult wolves in the wild; wolf hunting is something they have to be trained to. A former German military officer, F. W. Remmler, hunted wolves with eagles in Finland in the 1930s and later in Europe before moving to Canada. He trained his birds by first turning them loose on children. The children were dressed in leather armor and covered with a wolf skin, and raw meat was strapped to their backs. When the eagles were used to knocking the children down for the meat, Remmler put them in an enclosure into which he loosed wolves purchased from European zoos. It might take days for the birds to learn how to kill the wolves. (Remmler doesn't say, but they were presumably muzzled.) The final step was to hunt wolves that had been turned loose on an island. Remmler and his friends would put themselves in position and the wolves would be driven toward them by dogs. When the wolves came in sight, the birds were cast off.

Writing thirty years later about one such hunt, Remmler recalled an afternoon when one of his eagles, Louhi, had killed two wolves in ten minutes. That night as Remmler and his friends sipped cognac around the fire they heard the howling of the other five wolves on the island. "First the female and then the pack stretched their noses toward the starlit heavens," he wrote, "and both gave a howl so dreadful that my blood almost hardened in my veins. It may be that I had drunk too much that night, but the horror that filled me was very real. If I could have given the two dead wolves their lives back I would have done it immediately."

Kirgizian tribesmen still hunt wolves in Russia with eagles, on horseback, with the aid of dogs.

Because he roamed so widely and more often than not avoided man, the wolf had to be routed out with dogs or eagles or drawn to a bait. Still hunting, where a sheep or goat was staked out, was never very successful, though a horse or cow might be slaughtered and its carcass dragged through the woods to leave a trail ending at a spot where the meat was hung in a tree and the hunter concealed himself. (Residents of rural northern Minnesota laughed up their sleeves when hunters from urban Minneapolis, threatening to wipe out wolves preying on deer herds in the early 1970s, bought steaks and lunch meat at local supermarkets, set it out on frozen lakes, and waited in blinds for the wolves to show up.)

The reasoning behind hunting wolves for sport as opposed to hunting them because they were hated or considered a menace to livestock was often confused. Consider the following hunt that took place near Tamworth, New Hampshire, in 1830, described by Charles Beals in *Passaconaway in the White Mountains*.

On the evening of Nov. 14 couriers rode furiously through Tamworth and the surrounding towns, proclaiming that 'countless numbers' of wolves had come down from the Sandwich Range mountains and had established themselves in the woods on Marston Hill. All able-bodied males, from ten years old to eighty, were therefore summoned to report at Marston Hill by daylight on the following morning.

Marston Hill was crowned by about twenty acres of woods, entirely surrounded by cleared land. Sentinels were posted around the hill and numerous fires were lighted to prevent the wolves from effecting a return to the mountains. All through the night a continuous and hideous howling was kept up by the besieged wolves and answering howls came from the slopes of the great mountains. The shivering besiegers were regaled with food and hot coffee furnished by the women of the country-side throughout their long lonely watch.

All night long reinforcements kept arriving. By daylight there were six hundred men and boys on the scene, armed with rifles, shotguns, pitchforks and clubs. A council of war was held and a plan of campaign agreed upon. General Quimby, of Sandwich, a war-seasoned veteran, was made commander-in-chief. The general immediately detailed a thin line of sharpshooters to surround the hill, while the main body formed a strong line ten paces in the rear of the skirmishers. The sharpshooters then were commanded to advance towards the center, that is, towards the top of the hill. The firing began. The reports of the rifles and the unearthly howling of wolves made the welkin ring. The beleaguered animals, frenzied by the ring of flame and noise, and perhaps by wounds, made repeated attempts to break through "the thin red line," but all in vain. They were driven back into the woods, where they unceasingly continued running, making it difficult for the marksmen to hit them. In about an hour the order was given for the main line to advance, which was done.

Closing in on the center, the circular battle-line at last massed itself in a solid body on the hilltop, where, for the first time in sixteen hours, the troops raised their voices above a whisper, bursting out into wild hurrahs of victory. Joseph Gilman records that few of the besieged wolves escaped. But the historian of Carroll County maintains that the greater part of the frantic animals broke through the line of battle and escaped to the mountains whence they had come. Returning to the great rock on which the commander-in-chief had established headquarters, the victorious warriors laid their trophies at the feet of their leader—four immense wolves—and once more gave thrice three thundering cheers.

The little army then formed column, with the general, in a barouche, at its head. In the barouche also reposed the bodies of the slain wolves. After a rapid march of thirty-five minutes, the triumphant volunteers entered the village and formed a hollow square in front of the hotel, the general, mounted on the top of his barouche, being in the center of the square. What a cheering and waving of handkerchiefs by the ladies, in windows and on balconies, there was! General Quimby then made a speech befitting the occasion, after which the thirsty soldiers stampeded to the bar to assuage the awful thirst engendered by twenty mortal hours of abstinence and warfare.

The paramilitary aspect, the mock nobility, and the odd air of gaiety were frequently the major themes of such hunts.

Saturday afternoon wolf killings were a popular social pastime in the Midwest at the turn of the century. Bounties collected on the dead wolves were pooled to pay for end-of-the-season parties. "In three ways," wrote one participant, "does the most popular spring enjoyment of the prairie states—the wolf hunt—originate. The farmers may desire earnestly to rid the township of 'varmints'; the men of the community may want a day of entertainment; an enterprising hardware dealer may wish to enliven the market for gunpowder and shotguns. With them all wolf hunts become increasingly numerous, not because wolves are more common, but because it is an occasion of healthful outdoor exercise and fun." These farmers more often killed a coyote than a wolf during these outings. Their casual attitude toward the hundreds of rabbits, prairie dogs, burrowing owls, gophers, and other small game killed in the process, and their habit of hanging the wolf's carcass from a pole and parading it through the streets on a Saturday night, was part of the barbarism of the times. There were few, if any, misgivings. A contemporary writer, O. W. Williams, comments: "If the lobo has any useful qualities or habits I have not yet learned of them. If it destroys any noxious animal, reptile or insect in appreciative quantity, I have no account of it. It seems to be a specialist in carnage and to have brought professional skill to the slaughter of cattle. Possibly it has its uses—but it will require a skillful man with a very high powered magnifying glass to ascertain them."

Aerial hunting for wolves in the modern age is a difficult practice to understand. It seems unfair and cruel. Wolves caught out in the open on the arctic tundra or on a frozen lake are approached with highly maneuverable aircraft and blasted with automatic shotguns. The plane lands and the trophy hunter picks up his prize. In Alaska, where the practice was widespread before it was outlawed in 1972, it was not uncommon for two men in a plane to catch ten or fifteen animals—the whole pack—in the open with no cover and methodically kill every one of them. In their defense pilots claim it was difficult to shoot a moving target from a moving plane, that in such low-level, low-speed flying it is easy to stall the aircraft, that a bad shot could blow away a wing strut, and that winter flying—in intense cold with a possibility of whiteouts and crashing in unpopulated regions—was dangerous.

The pilots were right. Planes were shot up, apparently chances to kill were missed, and people were killed when wolves turned to snap at the plane's skis and caused it to crash. But, overwhelmingly, it was a case of dead wolves, healthy hunters, and pilots exaggerating the dangers to lure still more clients—and coming to believe their own exaggerations when an outraged public tried to stop the practice. Adding to the shabbiness of the episode was the fact that the hunter-clients were usually rich, urban men who knew nothing about wolves and nothing about the Arctic. They commonly believed all wolves weighed two hundred pounds and that any movement a wounded wolf might make once they were on the ground was an attempt to attack them. The illusions were encouraged by the pilots, who took the pelt and left the carcass behind on the snow. Back in Kotzebue or Bettles or Fairbanks the story was embellished and hunter and pilot congratulated for their bravery and daring. It is both ludicrous and tragic that the death of a wolf so cheaply killed confers such enormous prestige.

There is something deep-seated in men that makes them want to "take on" the outdoors, as though it were something to be whipped, and to kill wolves because killing a wolf stands for real triumph. In view of the way most wolves are killed it is hard to see how the image is sustained, but it is. Hunting is an ingrained male activity, especially in rural America, where few male children grow up not wanting to hunt. I hunted as a boy and I remember very clearly the first time I thought there was something wrong with the men I admired, something fundamentally backward about the kind of hunting that was held out to me as what men were supposed to do in the course of things. I was reading a book about big game animals in which Jack O'Connor, then the gun editor of *Outdoor Life*, described suddenly coming on seven wolves on a river bar in the Yukon. O'Connor dismounted and opened fire. "With considerable expenditure of ammunition," he wrote, he killed four of them, and then said he was sorry he'd done it for two reasons. "For one it was August and the hides were worthless. For another, my shooting spooked an enormous grizzly bear."

I couldn't get over that.

O'Connor writes elsewhere that the greatest satisfaction he had in killing a wolf came in British Columbia while he was sheep hunting. A wolf was doggedly pursuing a sheep up a steep slope. When the wolf stopped for a breath, O'Connor leveled his gun. "It was a lovely sight to see the crosshairs in the 4X settle right behind the wolf's shoulder. Neither ram nor wolf had seen me. The wolf's mouth was open, his tongue was hanging out, and he was panting heavily. The ram, on the other hand, seemed hardly bothered by the run. When my rifle went off, the 130 grain .270 bullet cracked that wolf right through the ribs and the animal was flattened as if by a giant hammer."

O'Connor spoke for a generation of men who matured in the twenties, thirties, and forties in America. He shot at every wolf he ever saw, including the only one he ever saw in the lower forty-eight states. For all he knew about guns and camping he seemed to know next to nothing about wolves, which was also typical of his generation of hunters. He never questioned his own role as a predator, nor his right to kill another predator, like the wolf, in pursuit of its game. It was largely these sorts of hunters, smug and ignorant, weaned on stories of vicious wolves, innocent deer, and poor, starving Eskimos, who became the most righteously vocal defenders of aerial hunting. As a result, at the height of the craze its appeal was to a sense of duty (protect the defenseless herds and help the starving Eskimo), to violence (permissible in defense of the defenseless), and to a distorted sense of manhood. Argument over whether it was a sport disappeared.

One hunter, promoting the activity to a sympathetic audience, wrote ecstatically of "not being more than thirty feet above the animals, so close I saw the hair fly from one of the black wolves as the hail of buckshot hit it. The wolf went down, rolling and kicking, biting at its side. Confused, the other wolves crouched, looking up at us. Tom, an enthusiastic wolf-hunter, who had once shot a cylinder off his plane trying to kill a wolf from the air, pulled the plane up into a jubilant chandelle, then let it drop off in a screaming, side-slipping dive that brought us in behind the wolves again."

This anecdote ends with embarrassing self-parody. " 'If I could afford it,' said Tex with satisfaction as we landed to pick up the pelts, 'I wouldn't do nothin' but fly around an' hunt them varmints. Every time I kill one it makes me feel good.' "

When such "hunters" stood before national television cameras in sunglasses and flightsuits and pretended to eat raw the flesh of wolves they'd just killed, they only exposed their own foolishness and the mockery they had made of traditional hunting ethics.

The sport hunter and the roustabout do-gooder came together in an interesting character in Alaska in the 1930s. During the Depression, a number of men drifted north in hopes of making a living as trappers. Most didn't. Some who did wrote about their experiences with wolves in magazines like *The Alaska Sportsman*. These men were mostly ignorant of the woods when they arrived; their stories are full of errors and cruelty to wolves and are punctuated by a righteous hatred for the animal. They believed wolves attacked and killed men in the north country, and they seemed barely able to control themselves when they told you what the wolves did to deer. "I knew what I'd find," wrote one, "deer hair and crushed bones, rent tissues and blood," as though wolves might have left something else. Stories with titles like "Wolves Killed Crist Colby," "I Match Wits with Wolves," and "I'll Get Old Club Foot Yet!" were unconscious parodies of frontier yarns in which the trappers played the role of the sheriff going for his six-shooter or shootin' iron whenever he saw a wolf.

The men who wrote these stories passionately believed they were serving humanity in the lower forty-eight states from this distant outpost. One of them, as if writing home to his family, said, "While I do my best to destroy all the wolves in the Ward Cove Game Refuge, the other animals go unmolested. On the roof of my cabin at Third Lake, the martin jump at night and the deer, unmolested, have become very tame, seeming to sense that there are few wolves and that man bears no ill will."

An Alaskan trapper named Lawrence Carson tracked a wolf that had dragged one of his traps more than twenty miles and found him hung upside down by the dragline on a steep hillside. He disentangled the wolf for the purpose of taking pictures, then shot him in the head. "Lobo died as he had lived, in defiance of all things that would dare to conquer him. His bloody career was ended, but even in death his fiery eyes and truculent jaws opened in a look of unremitting hate. Lobo, king of his domain—and rightly a king he was called—was dead."

But Carson's thoughts reveal the ambivalence in some of these men, for he continues:

"As I looked at his lifeless form, a feeling of condonation came over me. Even though he had been a wanton destroyer of wild life and ill-deserving of mercy, somehow I felt sorry that he was gone. I wondered if the great mountains and deep silent valleys that had been his range would miss him. I wondered if at night, when the moon hung low like a great ball of fire, the dark shaggy spruce trees would miss his wild, deep-throated call. Something has been taken away that would never be put back in the scheme of things. Somehow I felt as if there was an irreparable loss. The well-known axiom had again asserted itself; the sport and fun were not in the kill, but in the chase."

Those who stayed on in Alaska eventually wrote for the very same audiences of their fondness for the wolf, debunking the old stories of wolves killing people, and saying not much at all about how cute the deer were. One ended his story by saying he would like to spend his last years with wolves. He wrote, "I think I could enjoy the companionship of that magnificent creature more fully than any other creature on earth."

The O'Connor-type hunters whose hatred of wolves was gospel gave way in the 1960s to a more "enlightened" hunter, who spoke of the beneficial value of the wolf in balancing wild ecosystems, but who still wanted to kill him. The president of the Boone and Crockett Club, a national hunters' organization, said: "If more factual information can be widely disseminated to the general public as well as to sportsmen and conservationists perhaps this magnificent animal can yet attain his well-deserved status as a useful and highly important big game trophy animal." He was no longer a varmint; he was big game. The justifications are endless.

Without airplanes no one deliberately hunts wolves anymore—they are too hard to find from the ground. (Whatever sport there may be in wolf hunting, in the sense of earning a right to kill, is probably down there on the ground with the trapper who does it for a living. He works alone over long distances during a harsh season. He has to know something about wolf habits and a lot about the territory.) The wolf becomes a big game trophy animal today only when someone is lucky enough to see one while he is hunting something else. This kind of wolf hunting brings us to the present day.

Big game hunting in North America became popular after World War II. Books and articles about the romance of the sport in Alaska and Canada were suddenly everywhere. The formula for these stories was always the same: the author flew to the north country, explored widely with a guide, shot record numbers of animals, and sat around a campfire lamenting the loss of North America's best trophy animals to wolves, Indians, and Eskimos. It was agreed that if something wasn't done to thin the wolf population the herds would soon be gone.

One such book, *From Out of the Yukon* by James Bond, contains the requisite scenes and sentiments. It is worth reviewing not so much for its appeal to armchair adventurers as for the portrait it paints of the wolf and the hunting philosophy it endorses.

Around the campfire one evening Mr. Bond suggests it's not the wolves but excessive human hunting that is to blame for the depletion of the game herds. Everyone agrees. The solution they arrive at is twofold: first, increase the wolf bounty and get furriers to raise the price of wolf pelts to encourage more wolf trapping; second, "encourage all hunters to be good sportsmen and not shoot more than they need."

In his north country adventures Mr. Bond encounters wolves twice. The first time he can't get a clear shot but the guide does. "Well, I do not have to tell you," he writes, "that I badly wanted that big black devil for my trophy room, but I am glad Norman killed it, for it means one less wolf in the country."

The second wolf he meets, one howled up by the guide, he cripples and as he approaches, he thinks: "What excitement! These wolves had no conception of man." After he has killed the wolf, Mr. Bond inspects the head. "I was really amazed to find the numerous and tremendous muscles in the head and neck of this great wolf. They could only have developed through usage—ripping and tearing at our game animals.... It pleased me greatly to see this leader of destruction lying dead on the ground before me." The dimensions Mr. Bond reports for the wolf, typically, exceed those of any wolf on record.

I do not think men thoughtlessly kill wolves; they have reasons for doing so. Prime among them is the belief that they are doing something deeply and profoundly right. Whatever arguments are put forth—predation on big game, wolves are cowards and deserve to die—all seem rooted in the belief that the wolf is "wrong" in the scheme of things, like cancer, and has to be rooted out.

It is a convention of popular sociology that modern man leads a frustratingly inadequate life in which hunting becomes both overcompensation for a sense of impotence and an attempt to reroot oneself in the natural world. As man has matured, the traditional reason for hunting—to obtain food—has disappeared, along with the sacred relationship with the hunted. The modern hunter pays lip service to the ethics of the warrior hunter—respect for the animal, a taboo against waste, pride taken in highly developed skills like tracking—but his actions betray him. What has most emphatically not disappeared, oddly, is the almost spiritual sense of identification that comes over the hunter in the presence of a wolf.

Here is an animal capable of killing a man, an animal of legendary endurance and spirit, an animal that embodies marvelous integration with its environment. This is exactly what the frustrated modern hunter would like: the noble qualities imagined; a sense of fitting into the world. The hunter wants to be the wolf.

The first time I understood this I was talking with a man who had killed some thirty-odd wolves himself from a plane, alone, and flown hunters who had killed almost four hundred more. As he described with his hands the movement of the plane, the tack of its approach, his body began to lean into the movement and he shook his head as if to say no words could tell it. For him the thing was not the killing; it was that moment when the blast of the shotgun hit the wolf and flattened him—because the wolf's legs never stopped driving. In that same instant the animal was fighting to go on, to stay on its feet, to shake off the impact of the buckshot. The man spoke with awed respect of the animal's will to live, its bone and muscle shattered, blood streaking the snow, but refusing to fall. "When the legs stop, you know he's dead. He doesn't quit until there's nothing left." He spoke as though he himself would never be a quitter in life because he had seen this thing. Four hundred times.

It does not demean men to want to be what they imagine the wolf to be, but it demeans them to kill the animal for it. 44

Rhetorical Analysis

1. "Wolfing for Sport" has the same basic constraints as a college research paper in that it must respect its secondary sources and help readers find their way back to those sources should they wish to do so. Lopez appends the following bibliographical note to this piece:

   > Information on wolf hunting with dogs in Russia and America comes largely from popular magazines of the period, including various issues of *Scribner's Magazine*, *Outdoor Life*, and *English Illustrated Magazine*. In general, outdoor magazines of the period covered (roughly 1850 to the present) are an excellent guide to attitudinal changes concerning the wolf. Especially useful, and mentioned in the text, are copies of *The Alaska Sportsman* from the 1930s, and *Outdoor Life*, which began publication in 1897. Roosevelt's quote on hunting wolves with dogs, at the beginning of chapter 8, is from "A Wolf Hunt in Oklahoma" (*Scribner's Magazine* 38 (5): 513–32, 1905).
   >
   > Material on hunting wolves with eagles is from Remmler's own account, "Reminiscences of My Life with Eagles" (*Journal of the American Falconer's Association* 9, 1970), but I am indebted to Stephen Bodio, Harry Reynolds, and Alberto Palleroni for clarifications. The Tamworth incident is from Charles Edward Beals, *Passaconoway in the White Mountains* (Boston: R. G. Badger, 1916). The Saturday-afternoon wolf killing is distilled from Charles Harger, "Hunting Wolves by Automobile" (*World Today* 16: 429–32, April 1909). The O'Connor book is *The Big Game Animals of North America* (N.Y.: Outdoor Life/ E. P. Dutton, 1961). See also his "Wolf" (*Outdoor Life* 127 (4): 72–75, 144–45, 148–49, April 1961). The aerial hunting incident quoted is from Russell Annabel, *Hunting and Fishing in Alaska* (N.Y.: Knopf, 1948). The James H. Bond book, *From Out of the Yukon*, was published by Binfords and Mort, Portland, Ore., in 1948.

Along with citations in the text itself, is this note adequate for readers to find their way through the author's sources?
2. Reread the material Lopez quotes. Deduce his principles for selecting what to cite verbatim and what to express in his own words. This is not an idle exercise. You will learn more about the tactics of direct quotation than you would from most writing textbooks. Compare especially the different strategies of ¶s 12–16, 18, and 21.
3. This is a long essay, and the reader must stay on course.
   a. Generally, the longer the stretch of discourse, the simpler the organization of it. How is this essay arranged on its most basic level?
   b. Breaks divide the essay into eight parts. Write headings for these eight major sections. What now is the organization?
   c. What other sequences do you find giving shape to this piece?

Intellectual Analysis

1. Lopez begins this essay in a quite matter-of-fact way, letting the material speak for itself. Yet by the end, we know of his strong feelings.
   a. Where does Lopez first make clear his own attitude? And how?
   b. What does he gain by withholding his own emotional bias at first?
   c. Summarize his feelings about the hunting of wolves. Do you think these feelings have undermined the objectivity of his account of the history of such hunting?
2. Lopez claims (¶ 24) that Jack O'Connor, "For all he knew about guns and camping," knew "next to nothing about wolves."
   a. Ignorance is an important theme throughout. Trace it.
   b. An important question is, "How has such ignorance persisted?" And with that, "How has such a body of false knowledge built up around wolves?" Consider, too, the possibility of wolves being considered as scapegoats (as in ¶ 26).
3. The theme of ignorance and superstition is countered, especially toward the end of the essay, by that of what men *do* know about wolves.
   a. What do hunters admire about them?
   b. In ¶ 42, Lopez boldly claims, "The hunter wants to be the wolf." What does he mean by such a statement? What is the irony of it?

Suggestions for Writing

1. Elsewhere Lopez says, "I write now in a country and at a time when man's own brutal nature is cause for concern and when the wolf, whom man has historically accused of craven savagery, has begun to emerge as a benign creature." The

words were written in the United States and published in 1978. Write an essay in response, using the material in "Wolfing for Sport" as needed.
2. Read Barbara Tuchman's "The Historian as Artist" in this anthology. Evaluate "Wolfing for Sport" in light of Tuchman's ideas about the writing of history.
3. Write an essay, for a lay audience, on a subject in which you are technically expert—sailing, sewing, skiing, horse-raising, whatever. Imitate Lopez's use of technical terms ("coursing," "slip," "welkin," "lobo"), without pretension, without having to reach for them.

Buffalo

In January 1845, after a week of cold but brilliantly clear weather, it began to snow in southern Wyoming. Snow accumulated on the flat in a dead calm to a depth of four feet in only a few days. The day following the storm was breezy and warm—chinook weather. A party of Cheyenne camped in a river bottom spent the day tramping the snow down, felling cottonwood trees for their horses, and securing game, in response to a dream by one of them, a thirty-year-old man called Blue Feather on the Side of His Head, that they would be trapped by a sudden freeze. 1

That evening the temperature fell fifty degrees and an ice crust as rigid, as easily broken, as sharp as window glass formed over the snow. The crust held for weeks. 2

Access across the pane of ice to game and pasturage on the clear, wind-blown slopes of the adjacent Medicine Bow Mountains was impossible for both Indian hunters and a buffalo herd trapped nearby. The buffalo, exhausted from digging in the deep snow, went to their knees by the thousands, their legs slashed by the razor ice, glistening red in the bright sunlight. Their woolly carcasses lay scattered like black boulders over the blinding white of the prairie, connected by a thin crosshatching of bloody red trails. 3

Winds moaned for days in the thick fur of the dead and dying buffalo, broken by the agonized bellows of the animals themselves. Coyotes would not draw near. The Cheyenne camped in the river 4 bottom were terrified. As soon as they were able to move they departed. No Cheyenne ever camped there again.

The following summer the storm and the death of the herd were depicted on a buffalo robe by one of the Cheyenne, a man called Raven on His Back. Above the scene, in the sky, he drew a white buffalo. The day they had left camp a man was supposed to have seen a small herd of buffalo, fewer than twenty, leaving the plains and lumbering up the Medicine Bow River into the mountains. He said they were all white, and each seemed to him larger than any bull he had ever seen. There is no record of this man's name, but another Cheyenne in the party, a medicine man called Walks Toward the Two Rivers, carried the story of the surviving white buffalo to Crow and Teton Sioux in an effort to learn its meaning. In spite of the enmity among these tribes their leaders agreed that the incident was a common and disturbing augury. They gathered on the Box Elder River in southeastern Montana in the spring of 1846 to decipher its meaning. No one was able to plumb it, though many had fasted and bathed in preparation.

Buffalo were never seen again on the Laramie Plains after 1845, in spite of the richness of the grasses there and the size of the buffalo herds nearby in those days. The belief that there were still buffalo in the Medicine Bow Mountains, however, survivors of the storm, persisted for years, long after the disappearance of buffalo (some 60 million animals) from Wyoming and neighboring territories by the 1880s.

In the closing years of the nineteenth century, Arapaho and Shoshoni warriors who went into the Medicine Bow to dream say they did, indeed, see buffalo up there then. The animals lived among the barren rocks above timberline, far from any vegetation. They stood more than eight feet at the shoulder; their coats were white as winter ermine and their huge eyes were light blue. At the approach of men they would perch motionless on the granite boulders, like mountain goats. Since fogs are common in these high valleys in spring and summer it was impossible, they say, to tell how many buffalo there were.

In May 1887 a Shoshoni called Long Otter came on two of these buffalo in the Snowy Range. As he watched they watched him. They began raising and lowering their hooves, started drumming softly on the rocks. They began singing a death song, way back in the throat like the sound of wind moaning in a canyon. The man, Long Otter, later lost his mind and was killed in a buckboard accident the following year. As far as I know this is the last report of living buffalo in the Medicine Bow.

It is curious to me that in view of the value of the hides no white man ever tried to find and kill one of these buffalo. But that is the case. No detail of the terrible storm of that winter, or of the presence of a herd of enormous white buffalo in the Medicine Bow, has ever been found among the papers of whites who lived in the area or who might have passed through in the years following.

It should be noted, however, by way of verification, that a geology student from Illinois called Fritiof Fryxell came upon two buffalo skeletons in the Snowy Range in the summer of 1925. Thinking these barren heights an extraordinary elevation at which to find buffalo, he carefully marked the location on a topographic map. He measured the largest of the skeletons, found the size staggering, and later wrote up the incident in the May 1926 issue of the *Journal of Mammalogy*.

In 1955, a related incident came to light. In the fall of 1911, at the request of the Colorado Mountain Club, a party of Arapaho Indians were brought into the Rocky Mountains in the northern part of the state to relate to white residents the history of the area prior to 1859. The settlers were concerned that during the years when the white man was moving into the area, and the Indian was being extirpated, a conflict in historical records arose such that the white record was incomplete and possibly in error.

The Arapaho were at first reluctant to speak; they made up stories of the sort they believed the whites would like to hear. But the interest and persistence of the white listeners made an impression upon them and they began to tell what had really happened.

Among the incidents the Arapaho revealed was that in the winter of 1845 (when news of white settlers coming in covered wagons first reached them) there was a terrible storm. A herd of buffalo wintering in Brainard Valley (called then Bear in the Hole Valley) began singing a death song. At first it was barely audible, and it was believed the wind was making the sound until it got louder and more distinct. As the snow got deeper the buffalo left the valley and began to climb into the mountains. For four days they climbed, still singing the moaning death song, followed by Arapaho warriors, until they reached the top of the mountain. This was the highest place but it had no name. Now it is called Thatchtop Mountain.

During the time the buffalo climbed they did not stop singing. They turned red all over; their eyes became smooth white. The singing became louder. It sounded like thunder that would not stop. Everyone who heard it, even people four or five days' journey away, was terrified.

At the top of the mountain the buffalo stopped singing. They stood motionless in the snow, the wind blowing clouds around them. The Arapaho men who had followed had not eaten for four days. One, wandering into the clouds with his hands outstretched and a rawhide string connecting him to the others, grabbed hold of one of the buffalo and killed it. The remaining buffalo disappeared into the clouds; the death song began again, very softly, and remained behind them. The wind was like the singing of the buffalo. When the clouds cleared the men went down the mountain.

The white people at the 1911 meeting said they did not understand the purpose of telling such a story. The Arapaho said this was the first time the buffalo tried to show them how to climb out through the sky.

The notes of this meeting in 1911 have been lost, but what happened there remained clear in the mind of the son of one of the Indians who was present. It was brought to my attention by accident one evening in the library of the university where I teach. I was reading an article on the introduction of fallow deer in Nebraska in the August 1955 issue of the *Journal of Mammalogy* when this man, who was apparently just walking by, stopped and, pointing at the opposite page, said, "This is not what this is about." The article he indicated was called "An Altitudinal Record for Bison in Northern Colorado." He spoke briefly of it, as if to himself, and then departed.

Excited by this encounter I began to research the incident. I have been able to verify what I have written here. In view of the similarity between the events in the Medicine Bow and those in Colorado, I suspect that there were others in the winter of 1845 who began, as the Arapaho believe, trying to get away from what was coming, and that subsequent attention to this phenomenon is of some importance.

I recently slept among weathered cottonwoods on the Laramie Plains in the vicinity of the Medicine Bow Mountains. I awoke in the morning to find my legs broken.

Rhetorical Analysis

1. Lopez develops "Buffalo" in two ways, both at the same time. It is instructive to read the essay a second time, tracing the two methods of development through the essay. Lopez writes
   a. as historian, setting down incidents in chronological order, and
   b. as detective, laying out pieces of a puzzle in a way that will lead to a solution.
   How is each method apt for this essay?
2. Whether this piece is fiction or nonfiction, Lopez wants to persuade the reader of the truth of these events. What rhetorical strategies does he use to win the readers' trust? Look especially at ¶s 3, 5, 8, and 10.
3. The last sentence of "Buffalo" is arresting. Study how Lopez has set it up so that it achieves a particular effect on the reader. There may not be a specific "answer" to the question posed at the ending, but you should be able to discuss the effect it has on you.

Intellectual Analysis

1. This piece combines essay and story, research and invention, fact and fiction, even dream and observation.
   a. How do we know this? Where in the essay do these (apparently) mutually exclusive, polar possibilities meet and blend?
   b. What is the effect of such a melding of intentions? It may even be that the subject matter here expresses both myth and reality. How can this be?
2. This essay draws on the tradition common to nearly all Native American cultures of the vision-quest. There is much that is visionary in the piece, and there are several hints throughout that the narrator is not comfortable with that tradition.
   a. What are those hints and how do they advance the argument of the essay?
   b. Specifically, what is Lopez referring to in ¶ 18 when he describes the buffalo "trying to get away from what was coming"? What else may Lopez be thinking of? Do his words here have any connection with the broken legs in the next paragraph?
   c. Suppose that the author's purpose in "Buffalo" is to criticize our concept of history, or our need to understand the past. Or suppose it is to understand the relationship between history and myth, or our need as "rational" beings to make clear-cut distinctions between history and myth. If one of these is indeed the author's purpose, what then would the implications be?

Suggestions for Writing

1. Recall a particularly vivid dream, recent or not, and write an essay in which you discuss it as you would any waking experience. You may need to mingle dream experience with waking experience to achieve a credible effect.

2. Lopez challenges our culture's blind adherence to the scientific world view. Write an essay in which you define what you think that world view is; and attack or defend the author's belief that the mythic dimension is as "authentic" as the scientific.
3. Think about the old relationship between Plains Indians and the buffalo. Do present-day Americans have a relationship to animals in any way similar? What *are* animals to us today? Take one of these questions as a topic, and write an essay developing it as you wish, even on the level of personal, first-hand experience.

E. B. White

Though Elwyn Brooks White (nicknamed "Andy") left no mark on the history of poetry, his first published book was The Lady is Cold (1929), a volume of light verse. And although it is his essays and his children's books—Stuart Little and Charlotte's Web—on which his reputation stands, White always remained something of a poet. His friend, James Thurber, wrote of him, "Andy White understands begonias and children, canaries and goldfish, dachshunds and Scottish terriers, men and motives. His ear not only notes the louder cosmic rhythms but catches the faintest ticking sounds." The poet's ability to point to where the cosmic is rooted in the minute and to match the rhythms of language to the contours of the concrete things of the world are the virtues of White's best prose. Indeed, the reader is able, sometimes, to catch the loud, cosmic crashing and a barely audible ticking within a single sentence.

Born in Mount Vernon, New York, in 1889, to a well-to-do manufacturer of piano cases, White's childhood was happy, but not, as he says, untroubled: "I was uneasy about practically everything: the uncertainty of the future, the dark of the attic, the panoply and discipline of school, the transitoriness of life, the mystery of the church and of God, the frailty of the body, the sadness of afternoon, the shadow of sex, the distant challenge of love and marriage, the far-off problem of a livelihood. I brooded them all, lived with them day by day. Being the youngest in a large family, I was usually in a crowd but often felt lonely and removed. I took to writing early, to assuage my uneasiness and collect my thoughts, and I was a busy writer long before I went into long pants." White's shyness, which his friends knew was also a jealous guarding of his privacy, lasted into adulthood. Thurber notes that when White was writing and editing for the New Yorker magazine, it was White's practice to slip out of his office by the fire escape to avoid visitors he did not know.

But shyness was not timidity. In 1922, recently graduated from Cornell University, White set out with a friend in a Ford Model T, on a trip to the Far West (in those years no mean undertaking), during which they often had to mark their route by following stripes painted on telephone poles. And he overcame his passion for avoiding personal entanglements enough to marry Katherine Angell, an editor at the New Yorker, in 1929. In 1934 the Whites bought a farmhouse in Maine where they moved and where they stayed (with the exception of a return to New York to write the editorial page for the New Yorker during World War II). In 1942 White's first collection of essays appeared as One Man's Meat (the name of a column he had written for Harper's Magazine), and in 1954 a second collection, The Second Tree from the Corner, was published. His Essays appeared in 1977. His legacy includes The Elements of Style, by William Strunk, Jr., which White revised and expanded for publication in 1959. In 1986 E. B. White died, at his farm, in Maine.

THE GASTROPODS
(An answer to a hard question)

Q: I have an aquarium, and I got a snail for it because they told me it would keep the water clean, and the snail unexpectedly bore young, although it was in there all alone. I mean there weren't any other snails in there, only fish. How could it have young, very well?

A: The snail in your aquarium is a mollusk. It is quite likely an hermaphrodite, even though it came from a reputable department store. For being hermaphroditic, nobody can blame a snail. We cannot tell you everything we know about the gastropods because we know, possibly, more than is good for us. In the absence of specific information to the contrary, we would say that the snail in your aquarium had been going around a good deal with other snails before you got him (her). Some mollusks (not many) can have children merely by sitting around and thinking about it. Others can have children by living in a state of reciprocity with other hermaphrodites. Still others are like us, dioecious, possessed of only one sexual nature but thankful for small favors.

The shellfish and the snails are a great group, though it is a pose with many people to consider them dull. Usually the people who find mollusks dull are dull themselves. We have met mollusks in many parts of the world: in gardens in France, on the rocks at low tide on Long Island Sound, in household aquaria, on the sidewalks of suburban towns in the early mornings, in restaurants, and in forests. Everywhere we found them to be sensitive creatures, imaginative and possessed of a lively sense of earth's pleasant rhythm. Snails have a kind of nobility. Zoologists will tell you that they occupy, in the animal kingdom, a position of enviable isolation. They go their own way.

We can understand your curiousity about sex in snails. Mollusks are infinitely varied in their loves, their hates, and their predilections. They have a way of carrying out ideas they get in their head. They are far from cold, as many people suppose them; indeed, one of the most fascinating love stories we ever read was in the *Cambridge Natural History*, in which was described the tryst kept by a pair of snails on a garden wall. We have never forgotten the first sentence of that romantic and idyllic tale, nor have we forgotten the name of the snail, L. Maximus. The story started: "L. Maximus has been observed at midnight to ascend a wall or some perpendicular surface." It then went on to relate how, after some moments spent greeting each other, crawling round and round, the snails let themselves down on a little ladder of their own devising, and there, suspended in the air ten inches or so from the top of the wall, they found love.

Often very fecund, mollusks are rarely too busy to give attention to their children after birth, or to prepare for their coming. There is, in Algeria, a kind of mollusk whose young return for shelter to the body of their mother, somewhat in the manner of little kangaroos. There is, in the Philippines, a snail who is so solicitous for her expected babies that she goes to the trouble of climbing, with infinite pains and no little discomfort, to the top of a tall tree, and there deposits her eggs in a leaf, folding the leaf adroitly for protection. Another kind of mollusk, having laid her eggs upon a stone, amuses herself by arranging them like the petals of a rose, and hatches them by holding her foot on them. Mollusks tend to business.

Sometimes different species intermarry, but this is rare. The interesting point about it is that such unions generally take place when the air is heavily charged with electricity, as before a storm, or when great rains have made the earth wet. The Luxembourg Garden in Paris is a place snails go to for clandestine matches of this sort. H. Variabilis goes there, and Pisana. The moisture, the electricity, the fragrant loveliness of a Paris night, stir them strangely.   6

Probably, if you know so little of the eroticism of snails, you have not heard of the darts some of them carry—tiny daggers, hard and sharp, with which they prick each other for the excitement it affords. These darts are made of carbonate of lime. The Germans call them *Liebespfeil*, "love shaft." Many British mollusks are without them, but that's the way it goes.   7

We could tell much more. We could tell about mollusks that possess the curious property of laying their eggs on the outside of their own shell, and of the strange phenomenon of the Cephalopod, who, when he takes leave of his lady, leaves one of his arms with her, so that she may never lack for an embrace. But we feel we have answered your question.   8

Rhetorical Analysis

1. This essay has an unusual appearance: a brief question, followed by a much longer answer. Any essay, of course, is an attempt at an answer to an implicit question (if not an actual one), and the best essays usually raise more questions than they answer.
    a. Look at the question that prompts this essay. It is chatty, but puzzled: the kind of question one reads in "Information Please" columns of some daily newspapers. The answer, however, is quite different in tone.
    b. White takes the opportunity of the question (whether real or invented by himself—his friend, Thurber, was given to inventing his own questions to answer, usually humorously) to satirize human attitudes toward sex, as well as our tendency to assume exclusive rights on any form of expression beyond basic biological urges. For example, White assures his interlocutor that the snail might be hermaphroditic, "even though it came from a reputable department store." Even at that, one can't *blame* the snail for being hermaphroditic (containing within itself both male and female reproductive organs). Others are, White explains, like ourselves, dioecious, and must rely on the opposite sex "for small favors" (with a pun on the phrase, "sexual favors").

c. Though the beginning of the essay is dominated by White's (gently) satiric intent, and though he carries this through the first sentence of the fourth paragraph with the sentence, "Mollusks are infinitely varied in their loves, their hates, and their predilections," the tone (and certainly the intent) of the essay shifts from the satiric to the poignant. The satire remains as an echo. White uses the technique of the pun insistently to develop the theme of this piece by which the delicate sensitivity of snails in sexual matters is implicitly contrasted with what is too often the boorish clumsiness of human sexual activity. The obvious biological sensitivity of snails (to excess light or heat, for instance) becomes, in ¶ 3, imaginative sensitivity to "earth's pleasant rhythm." Their coldness (as in cold-bloodedness) White puns into emotional coldness, which he then refutes by telling the "story" of a snail "tryst." Locate other puns (they are especially rich in ¶s 5—7), and note how White subtilizes his argument even further.

2. One constant device for verbal wit is surprise: our expectations are upset in some way, and the ending of a sentence cannot be anticipated from its beginning.
    a. Check the sentences in the answer-paragraph; many end in a way we could not have expected when they began. For example, in ¶ 2, "We cannot tell you everything we know about the gastropods because we know, possibly, more than is good for us."
    b. The same sort of surprise can function in a whole paragraph. Again in ¶ 2, no one could have anticipated the end of the last sentence: "Still others are like us, dioecious, possessed of only one sexual nature but thankful for small favors."
    c. In still larger terms, the great differences in size of the question and the answer may be understood: the questioner gets much more than was bargained for.

3. What audience is White aiming at? Or, what is White's intention? Are we given any clues? (Note the use of the editorial "we.")
    a. Short pieces, such as this, White referred to as "sketches." (White himself quotes Webster in defining "sketch" as "a brief, light, or informal short story, essay, or other literary composition.") Does such a word indicate anything about audience or intention?
    b. It is also possible that the whole essay is a kind of exercise, meant to entertain or please the author. Why then publish such a piece? (Might it tell us something rather admirable about White?)

Intellectual Analysis

1. The structure of this essay is so simple and entertaining that one could well ask, after reading it, "What point does it make?"
    a. It tells us that other species are different from us, and quite fascinating, too.

From there, the essay tells us something of the assumptions we tend to make, even about something so important as reproduction.
  b. The essay also serves as a tiny window opened onto the immense world of nature and its eccentricities. White uses details garnered from scientific sources, but he uses them in ways that few scientists, who are not also philosophers, would use them.
2. Because of its wit and tone, especially in the "answer" portion, this essay is partly a satire, too, as noted above. Here are a couple of possible lines of discussion:
  a. *Curiosity:* White is satirizing the questioner's curiosity, which is clumsy, and limited to the practical matter of too many snails in his aquarium.
  b. *Mock pedantry:* Is it possible to see the answerer as an object of satire as well? Who would go on at such length about mollusks? About the eroticism of snails? The same man who would go on about the death of a pig? What kind of man is that?

Suggestions for Writing

1. Compare this piece with another essay in this anthology—Isak Dinesen's "The Iguana." Dinesen focuses, with a very delicate handling of detail, on a kind of creature with which humans do not readily identify (as they often do with dogs, chimpanzees, or horses). Dinesen, like White, closely describes such a creature to comment on human failures. What are the similarities and differences between Dinesen's and White's treatments of unfamiliar (even exotic) creatures, in their respective essays?
2. Attempt a satiric essay built on the model of this one by White. That is, pose an innocent question about something eccentric or unusual, then write an answer in the style of a know-it-all.

CALCULATING MACHINE

A publisher in Chicago has sent me a pocket calculating machine by which I may test my writing to see whether it is intelligible. The calculator was developed by General Motors, who, not satisfied with giving the world a Cadillac, now dream of bringing perfect understanding to men. The machine (it is simply a celluloid card with a dial) is called the Reading-Ease Calculator and shows four grades of "reading ease"—Very Easy, Easy, Hard, and Very Hard. You count your

1

words and syllables, set the dial, and an indicator lets you know whether anybody is going to understand what you have written. An instruction book came with it, and after mastering the simple rules I lost no time in running a test on the instruction book itself, to see how *that* writer was doing. The poor fellow! His leading essay, the one on the front cover, tested Very Hard.

My next step was to study the first phrase on the face of the calculator: "How to test Reading-Ease of written matter." There is, of course, no such thing as reading ease of written matter. There is the ease with which matter can be read, but that is a condition of the reader, not of the matter. Thus the inventors and distributors of this calculator get off to a poor start, with a Very Hard instruction book and a slovenly phrase. Already they have one foot caught in the brier patch of English usage.

Not only did the author of the instruction book score badly on the front cover, but inside the book he used the word "personalize" in an essay on how to improve one's writing. A man who likes the word "personalize" is entitled to his choice, but I wonder whether he should be in the business of giving advice to writers. "Whenever possible," he wrote, "personalize your writing by directing it to the reader." As for me, I would as lief simonize my grandmother as personalize my writing.

In the same envelope with the calculator, I received another training aid for writers—a booklet called "How to Write Better," by Rudolf Flesch. This, too, I studied, and it quickly demonstrated the broncolike ability of the English language to throw whoever leaps cocksurely into the saddle. The language not only can toss a rider but knows a thousand tricks for tossing him, each more gay than the last. Dr. Flesch stayed in the saddle only a moment or two. Under the heading "Think Before You Write," he wrote, "The main thing to consider is your *purpose* in writing. Why are you sitting down to write?" And Echo answered: Because, sir, it is more comfortable than standing up.

Communication by the written word is a subtler (and more beautiful) thing than Dr. Flesch and General Motors imagine. They contend that the "average reader" is capable of reading only what tests Easy, and that the writer should write at or below this level. This is a presumptuous and degrading idea. There is no average reader, and to reach down toward this mythical character is to deny that each of us is on the way up, is ascending. ("Ascending," by the way, is a word Dr. Flesch advises writers to stay away from. Too unusual.)

It is my belief that no writer can improve his work until he discards the dulcet notion that the reader is feebleminded, for writing is an act of faith, not a trick of grammar. Ascent is at the heart of the matter. A country whose writers are following a calculating machine downstairs is not ascending—if you will pardon the expression—and a writer who questions the capacity of the person at the other end of the line is not a writer at all, merely a schemer. The movies long ago decided that a wider communication could be achieved by a deliberate descent to a lower level, and they walked proudly down until they reached the cellar. Now they are groping for the light switch, hoping to find the way out.

I have studied Dr. Flesch's instructions diligently, but I return for guidance in these matters to an earlier American, who wrote with more patience, more confidence. "I fear chiefly," he wrote, "lest my expression may not be *extra-vagant* enough, may not wander far enough beyond the narrow limits of my daily experience, so as to be adequate to the truth of which I have been convinced. . . . Why level downward to our dullest perception always, and praise that as common sense? The commonest sense is the sense of men asleep, which they express by snoring."

Run that through your calculator! It may come out Hard, it may come out Easy. But it will come out whole, and it will last forever.

Rhetorical Analysis

1. White's humor in this essay is based on two kinds of irony: that of his statements (verbal irony), and the irony inherent in the very idea of applying an essentially mathematical tool to language. One notes, for example, that the first thing White does after he reads the instructions is to apply the machine to the instructions themselves—and finds them wanting.
    a. By ¶ 5 White has shifted from irony (which here includes mockery) to a more serious affirmation of the subtleties, and difficulties, inherent in language. From this point "Calculating Machine" rests with White's heavier statements about "Communication by the written word." Rhetorically, this little piece moves from ironic bemusement to serious statement, with only the slightest return to verbal irony in the last two sentences. Why does White

take so much time to play with the subject before he gets down to business? Why does he return to mockery at the end?
b. In the first four paragraphs, what are the elements of verbal irony, from which mild wit flashes? For example, examine how each of those paragraphs ends with a witty but strong, rather pointed statement.
2. White admires Thoreau's statement on writing, quoted in ¶ 7. Take the terms of the quotation and apply them to White's own rhetorical finesse. For example, are his expressions *"extra-vagant"* enough?

Intellectual Analysis

1. From White's point of view, what is wrong with the advice given by the Calculating Machine and Dr. Flesch? (Focus on ¶s 5–7.)
   a. The key words or phrases in White's comments are "average reader," "ascending," and "ascent," which he plays off against "reach down," "below this level," and "degrading." The word "whole" and the way it reinforces Thoreau's idea that writing must go beyond one's "narrow limits of ... daily experience" in the last sentence could be added also.
   b. White's strongest statements have to do with levels—both of expression and comprehension. Which statements can you pick out (for example, in ¶ 5, "This is a presumptuous and degrading idea")?
2. From a wider perspective, what do the Calculating Machine and Dr. Flesch leave out of their advice? What do they ignore? For one thing, they could be said to leave out the writer-as-human: even the advice to "personalize" is ironic (¶ 3). They do not take into account the value of the subject matter, or its nature, nor do they recognize the wholeness or integrity of any given discourse. For example, what would be the effect of quantifying (as one might count so many marbles) by use of a calculating machine, so subtle a human experience as love, or grief over the death of a parent? Is it possible to characterize as "Very Easy" or "Hard" whatever language one might find to express the nearly inexpressible?
3. Does White overstate his case?
   a. Look carefully at ¶ 2: is he correct to say, "There is, of course, no such thing as reading ease of written matter?"
   b. Is White advising us to eschew simplicity, to be *extra-vagant* in expression?

Suggestions for Writing

1. Write an essay in which you analyze why such a device as this Calculating Machine would not work. Make use of White's terms, but carry them further.
2. Select some other phony device—say, "painting by number"—and discuss why it is phony. Identify what the device leaves out of the whole endeavor. You could invent the device and the names of authorities who advocate its use.

Death of a Pig

Autumn 1947

I spent several days and nights in mid-September with an ailing pig and I feel driven to account for this stretch of time, more particularly since the pig died at last, and I lived, and things might easily have gone the other way round and none left to do the accounting. Even now, so close to the event, I cannot recall the hours sharply and am not ready to say whether death came on the third night or the fourth night. This uncertainty afflicts me with a sense of personal deterioration; if I were in decent health I would know how many nights I had sat up with a pig.

The scheme of buying a spring pig in blossomtime, feeding it through summer and fall, and butchering it when the solid cold weather arrives, is a familiar scheme to me and follows an antique pattern. It is a tragedy enacted on most farms with perfect fidelity to the original script. The murder, being premeditated, is in the first degree but is quick and skillful, and the smoked bacon and ham provide a ceremonial ending whose fitness is seldom questioned.

Once in a while something slips—one of the actors goes up in his lines and the whole performance stumbles and halts. My pig simply failed to show up for a meal. The alarm spread rapidly. The classic outline of the tragedy was lost. I found myself cast suddenly in the role of pig's friend and physician—a farcical character with an enema bag for a prop. I had a presentiment, the very first afternoon, that the play would never regain its balance and that my sympathies were now wholly with the pig. This was slapstick—the sort of dramatic treatment that instantly appealed to my old dachshund, Fred, who joined the vigil, held the bag, and, when all was over, presided at the interment. When we slid the body into the grave, we both were shaken to the core. The loss we felt was not the loss of ham but the loss of pig. He had evidently become precious to me, not that he represented a distant nourishment in a hungry time, but that he had suffered in a suffering world. But I'm running ahead of my story and shall have to go back.

My pigpen is at the bottom of an old orchard below the house. The pigs I have raised have lived in a faded building that once was an icehouse. There is a pleasant yard to move about in, shaded by an apple tree that overhangs the low rail fence. A pig couldn't ask for anything better—or none has, at any rate. The sawdust in the icehouse makes a comfortable bottom in which to root, and a warm bed. This sawdust, however, came under suspicion when the pig took sick. One of my neighbors said he thought the pig would have done better on new ground—the same principle that applies in planting potatoes. He said there might be something unhealthy about that sawdust, that he never thought well of sawdust.

It was about four o'clock in the afternoon when I first noticed that there was something wrong with the pig. He failed to appear at the trough for his supper, and when a pig (or a child) refuses supper a chill wave of fear runs through any household, or ice-household. After examining my pig, who was stretched out in the sawdust inside the building, I went to the phone and cranked it four times. Mr. Dameron answered. "What's good for a sick pig?" I asked. (There is never any identification needed on a country phone; the person on the other end knows who is talking by the sound of the voice and by the character of the question.)

"I don't know, I never had a sick pig," said Mr. Dameron, "but I can find out quick enough. You hang up and I'll call Henry."

Mr. Dameron was back on the line again in five minutes. "Henry says roll him over on his back and give him two ounces of castor oil or sweet oil, and if that doesn't do the trick give him an injection of soapy water. He says he's almost sure the pig's plugged up, and even if he's wrong, it can't do any harm."

I thanked Mr. Dameron. I didn't go right down to the pig, though. I sank into a chair and sat still for a few minutes to think about my troubles, and then I got up and went to the barn, catching up on some odds and ends that needed tending to. Unconsciously I held off, for an hour, the deed by which I would officially recognize the collapse of the performance of raising a pig; I wanted no interruption in the regularity of feeding, the steadiness of growth, the even succession of days. I wanted no interruption, wanted no oil, no deviation. I just wanted to keep on raising a pig, full meal after full meal, spring into summer into fall. I didn't even know whether there were two ounces of castor oil on the place.

Shortly after five o'clock I remembered that we had been invited out to dinner that night and realized that if I were to dose a pig there was no time to lose. The dinner date seemed a familiar conflict: I move in a desultory society and often a week or two will roll by without my going to anybody's house to dinner or anyone's coming to mine, but when an occasion does arise, and I am summoned, something usually turns up (an hour or two in advance) to make all human intercourse seem vastly inappropriate. I have come to believe that there is in hostesses a special power of divination, and that they deliberately arrange dinners to coincide with pig failure or some other sort of failure. At any rate, it was after five o'clock and I knew I could put off no longer the evil hour.

When my son and I arrived at the pigyard, armed with a small bottle of castor oil and a length of clothesline, the pig had emerged from his house and was standing in the middle of his yard, listlessly. He gave us a slim greeting. I could see that he felt uncomfortable and uncertain. I had brought the clothesline thinking I'd have to tie him (the pig weighed more than a hundred pounds) but we never used it. My son reached down, grabbed both front legs, upset him quickly, and when he opened his mouth to scream I turned the oil into his throat—a pink, corrugated area I had never seen before. I had just time to read the label while the neck of the bottle was in his mouth. It said Puretest. The screams, slightly muffled by oil, were pitched in the hysterically high range of pig-sound, as though torture were being carried out, but they didn't last long: it was all over rather suddenly, and, his legs released, the pig righted himself.

In the upset position the corners of his mouth had been turned down, giving him a frowning expression. Back on his feet again, he regained the set smile that a pig wears even in sickness. He stood his ground, sucking slightly at the residue of oil; a few drops leaked out of his lips while his wicked eyes, shaded by their coy little lashes, turned on me in disgust and hatred. I scratched him gently with oily fingers and he remained quiet, as though trying to recall the satisfaction of being scratched when in health, and seeming to rehearse in his mind the indignity to which he had just been subjected. I noticed, as I stood there, four or five small dark spots on his back near the tail end, reddish brown in color, each about the size of a housefly. I could not make out what they were. They did not look troublesome but at the same time they did not look like mere surface bruises or chafe marks. Rather they seemed blemishes of internal origin. His stiff white bristles almost completely hid them and I had to part the bristles with my fingers to get a good look.

Several hours later, a few minutes before midnight, having dined well and at someone else's expense, I returned to the pighouse with a flashlight. The patient was asleep. Kneeling, I felt his ears (as you might put your hand on the forehead of a child) and they seemed cool, and then with the light made a careful examination of the yard and the house for sign that the oil had worked. I found none and went to bed.

We had been having an unseasonable spell of weather—hot, close days, with the fog shutting in every night, scaling for a few hours in midday, then creeping back again at dark, drifting in first over the trees on the point, then suddenly blowing across the fields, blotting out the world and taking possession of houses, men, and animals. Everyone kept hoping for a break, but the break failed to come. Next day was another hot one. I visited the pig before breakfast and tried to tempt him with a little milk in his trough. He just stared at it, while I made a sucking sound through my teeth to remind him of past pleasures of the feast. With very small, timid pigs, weanlings, this ruse is often quite successful and will encourage them to eat; but with a large, sick pig the ruse is senseless and the sound I made must have made him feel, if anything, more miserable. He not only did not crave food, he felt a positive revulsion to it. I found a place under the apple tree where he had vomited in the night.

At this point, although a depression had settled over me, I didn't suppose that I was going to lose my pig. From the lustiness of a healthy pig a man derives a feeling of personal lustiness; the stuff that goes into the trough and is received with such enthusiasm is an earnest of some later feast of his own, and when this suddenly comes to an end and the food lies stale and untouched, souring in the sun, the pig's imbalance becomes the man's, vicariously, and life seems insecure, displaced, transitory.

As my own spirits declined, along with the pig's, the spirits of my vile old dachshund rose. The frequency of our trips down the footpath through the orchard to the pigyard delighted him, although he suffers greatly from arthritis, moves with difficulty, and would be bedridden if he could find anyone willing to serve him meals on a tray.

He never missed a chance to visit the pig with me, and he made many professional calls on his own. You could see him down there at all hours, his white face parting the grass along the fence as he wobbled and stumbled about, his stethoscope dangling—a happy quack, writing his villainous prescriptions and grinning his corrosive grin. When the enema bag appeared, and the bucket of warm suds, his happiness was complete, and he managed to squeeze his enormous body between the two lowest rails of the yard and then assumed full charge of the irrigation. Once, when I lowered the bag to check the flow, he reached in and hurriedly drank a few mouthfuls of the suds to test their potency. I have noticed that Fred will feverishly consume any substance that is associated with trouble—the bitter flavor is to his liking. When the bag was above reach, he concentrated on the pig and was everywhere at once, a tower of strength and inconvenience. The pig, curiously enough, stood rather quietly through this colonic carnival, and the enema, though ineffective, was not as difficult as I had anticipated.

I discovered, though, that once having given a pig an enema there is no turning back, no chance of resuming one of life's more stereotyped roles. The pig's lot and mine were inextricably bound now, as though the rubber tube were the silver cord. From then until the time of his death I held the pig steadily in the bowl of my mind; the task of trying to deliver him from his misery became a strong obsession. His suffering soon became the embodiment of all earthly wretchedness. Along toward the end of the afternoon, defeated in physicking, I phoned the veterinary twenty miles away and placed the case formally in his hands. He was full of questions, and when I casually mentioned the dark spots on the pig's back, his voice changed its tone.

"I don't want to scare you," he said, "but when there are spots, erysipelas has to be considered."

Together we considered erysipelas, with frequent interruptions from the telephone operator, who wasn't sure the connection had been established.

"If a pig has erysipelas can he give it to a person?" I asked.

"Yes, he can," replied the vet.

"Have they answered?" asked the operator.

"Yes, they have," I said. Then I addressed the vet again. "You better come over here and examine this pig right away."

"I can't come myself," said the vet, "but McFarland can come this evening if that's all right. Mac knows more about pigs than I do anyway. You needn't worry too much about the spots. To indicate erysipelas they would have to be deep hemorrhagic infarcts."

"Deep hemmorrhagic what?" I asked.

"Infarcts," said the vet.

"Have they answered?" asked the operator.

"Well," I said, "I don't know what you'd call these spots, except they're about the size of a housefly. If the pig has erysipelas I guess I have it, too, by this time, because we've been very close lately."

"McFarland will be over," said the vet.

I hung up. My throat felt dry and I went to the cupboard and got a bottle of whiskey. Deep hemorrhagic infarcts—the phrase began fastening its hooks in my head. I had assumed that there could be nothing much wrong with a pig during the months it was being groomed for murder; my confidence in the essential health and endurance of pigs had been strong and deep, particularly in the health of pigs that belonged to me and that were part of my proud scheme. The awakening had been violent and I minded it all the more because I knew that what could be true of my pig could be true also of the rest of my tidy world. I tried to put this distasteful idea from me, but it kept recurring. I took a short drink of the whiskey and then, although I wanted to go down to the yard and look for fresh signs, I was scared to. I was certain I had erysipelas.

It was long after dark and the supper dishes had been put away when a car drove in and McFarland got out. He had a girl with him. I could just make her out in the darkness—she seemed young and pretty. "This is Miss Owen," he said. "We've been having a picnic supper on the shore, that's why I'm late."

McFarland stood in the driveway and stripped off his jacket, then his shirt. His stocky arms and capable hands showed up in my flashlight's gleam as I helped him find his coverall and get zipped up. The rear seat of his car contained an astonishing amount of paraphernalia, which he soon overhauled, selecting a chain, a syringe, a bottle of oil, a rubber tube, and some other things I couldn't identify. Miss Owen said she'd go along with us and see the pig. I led the way down the warm slope of the orchard, my light picking out the path for them, and we all three climbed the fence, entered the pighouse, and squatted by the pig while McFarland took a rectal reading. My flashlight picked up the glitter of an engagement ring on the girl's hand.

"No elevation," said McFarland, twisting the thermometer in the light. "You needn't worry about erysipelas." He ran his hand slowly over the pig's stomach and at one point the pig cried out in pain.

"Poor piggledy-wiggledy!" said Miss Owen.

The treatment I had been giving the pig for two days was then repeated, somewhat more expertly, by the doctor, Miss Owen and I handing him things as he needed them—holding the chain that he had looped around the pig's upper jaw, holding the syringe, holding the bottle stopper, the end of the tube, all of us working in darkness and in comfort, working with the instinctive teamwork induced by emergency conditions, the pig unprotesting, the house shadowy, protecting, intimate. I went to bed tired but with a feeling of relief that I had turned over part of the responsibility of the case to a licensed doctor. I was beginning to think, though, that the pig was not going to live.

He died twenty-four hours later, or it might have been forty-eight—there is a blur in time here, and I may have lost or picked up a day in the telling and the pig one in the dying. At intervals during the last day I took cool fresh water down to him and at such times as he found the strength to get to his feet he would stand with head in the pail and snuffle his snout around. He drank a few sips but no more; yet it seemed to comfort him to dip his nose in water and bobble it about, sucking in and blowing out through his teeth. Much of the time, now, he lay indoors half buried in sawdust. Once, near the last, while I was attending him I saw him try to make a bed for himself but he lacked the strength, and when he set his snout into the dust he was unable to plow even the little furrow he needed to lie down in.

He came out of the house to die. When I went down, before going to bed, he lay stretched in the yard a few feet from the door. I knelt, saw that he was dead, and left him there: his face had a mild look, expressive neither of deep peace nor of deep suffering, although I think he had suffered a good deal. I went back up to the house and to bed, and cried internally—deep hemorrhagic intears. I didn't wake till nearly eight the next morning, and when I looked out the open window the grave was already being dug, down beyond the dump under a wild apple. I could hear the spade strike against the small rocks that blocked the way. Never send to know for whom the grave is dug, I said to myself, it's dug for thee. Fred, I well knew, was supervising the work of digging, so I ate breakfast slowly.

It was a Saturday morning. The thicket in which I found the gravediggers at work was dark and warm, the sky overcast. Here, among alders and young hackmatacks, at the foot of the apple tree, Lennie had dug a beautiful hole, five feet long, three feet wide, three feet deep. He was standing in it, removing the last spadefuls of earth while Fred patrolled the brink in simple but impressive circles, disturbing the loose earth of the mound so that it trickled back in. There had been no rain in weeks and the soil, even three feet down, was dry and powdery. As I stood and stared, an enormous earthworm which had been partially exposed by the spade at the bottom dug itself deeper and made a slow withdrawal, seeking even remoter moistures at even lonelier depths. And just as Lennie stepped out and rested his spade against the tree and lit a cigarette, a small green apple separated itself from a branch overhead and fell into the hole. Everything about this last scene seemed overwritten—the dismal sky, the shabby woods, the imminence of rain, the worm (legendary bedfellow of the dead), the apple (conventional garnish of a pig).

But even so, there was a directness and dispatch about animal burial, I thought, that made it a more decent affair than human burial: there was no stopover in the undertaker's foul parlor, no wreath nor spray; and when we hitched a line to the pig's hind legs and dragged him swiftly from his yard, throwing our weight into the harness and leaving a wake of crushed grass and smoothed rubble over the dump, ours was a businesslike procession, with Fred, the dishonorable pallbearer, staggering along in the rear, his perverse bereavement showing in every seam in his face; and the post-mortem performed handily and swiftly right at the edge of the grave, so that the inwards that had caused the pig's death preceded him into the ground and he lay at last resting squarely on the cause of his own undoing.

I threw in the first shovelful, and then we worked rapidly and without talk, until the job was complete. I picked up the rope, made it fast to Fred's collar (he is a notorious ghoul), and we all three filed back up the path to the house, Fred bringing up the rear and holding back every inch of the way, feigning unusual stiffness. I noticed that although he weighed far less than the pig, he was harder to drag, being possessed of the vital spark.

The news of the death of my pig traveled fast and far, and I received many expressions of sympathy from friends and neighbors, for no one took the event lightly and the premature expiration of a pig is, I soon discovered, a departure which the community marks solemnly on its calendar, a sorrow in which it feels fully involved. I have written this account in penitence and in grief, as a man who failed to raise his pig, and to explain my deviation from the classic course of so many raised pigs. The grave in the woods is unmarked, but Fred can direct the mourner to it unerringly and with immense good will, and I know he and I shall often revisit it, singly and together, in seasons of reflection and despair, on flagless memorial days of our own choosing.

Rhetorical Analysis

1. White's mode of argumentation in this essay is narration, and he keeps to that mode throughout. Note how the structure of narrative conditions the essay as a whole, and how it influences the particular rhetorical devices White chooses.
    a. Examine ¶ 3, for example. White, at this point, checks himself to stay with strict narrative: "But I'm running ahead of my story. . . ." Continually, there are time references used as transitions. What other techniques does White use to advance his argument?
    b. Throughout the essay is a pattern of allusion to tragedy (one of the basic patterns of story-telling). Look carefully at ¶s 2, 3, and 30. There are a host of elements that connect this essay with the traditions of tragedy: its ceremonial grounding; the strict sense of chronology that tragedy demands; White himself as a kind of chorus; even the gravedigging scene (¶s 37–38) alludes to the famous gravedigging scene in *Hamlet*, act 4. In Greek tragedy the members of the chorus, while not direct participants, have ultimately as much to gain or lose by the protagonists' actions as the tragic figures themselves; the function of the chorus is to represent the community and to comment on the action. How closely does White conform to this function?
    c. "Death of a Pig" plays with the tension between literature and life. Not only is there the controlling reference to tragedy, but a quotation from John Donne's famous essay in his *Devotions*, "Never send to know for whom the bell tolls. . . ," which White uses to connect the death of a pig with his or any individual's death. An overreliance on the device of literary allusion obviously would make the essay silly. Read through the essay noting where (and how often) White uses these specific allusions. Do you find him successful in avoiding silliness?
    d. Beginning at ¶ 17 and running through ¶ 29 there occurs the telephone conversation between White and the veterinarian about the sick pig. Twice the operator interjects, wanting to know if the connection had been properly established. Both times the operator asks, "Have they answered?" referring, of course, to the veterinarian. Both interruptions occur at dramatic points in the conversation, the first time when White finds out that the pig can communicate erysipelas to a human. What is the function of this conversation in the broader context of the essay? What is the function of the operator's presence in the context of the conversation? Given the tragic frame of reference in "Death of a Pig," how might we read the operator's question, "Does he answer?"
2. Given the large questions of life and death which White treats in "Death of a Pig," one of its most striking stylistic aspects is his use of clearly denoted particulars. What place, for example, does his noticing of the engagement ring (¶ 32) on Miss Owen's hand have in an essay devoted to such big questions? Or including the fact that McFarland and Miss Owen had just come from a picnic?
3. One of the striking aspects of style in this essay is White's plain description of

barnyard details: enemas and enema-bags, vomit, pig-slop, and so on. How does he avoid vulgarity?

Intellectual Analysis

1. In ¶ 1, White says he feels "driven to account" for the several days he spent with his sick pig, and in the last paragraph that he has "written this account in penitence and grief." What is the effect of framing the essay with these two statements? As a start, these admissions give an unusually strong sense of the presence of the author himself. But there is more to it.
   a. From what does his compulsion spring? Check ¶ 17 again, for example.
   b. How does White keep this account from becoming sentimental? After all, a pig is simply a pig! Or is it?
   c. How did the event become so important to White?
2. The subject of this essay is obviously much more than merely the death of a pig. Time, for example, is not simply a matter of rhetoric, of narrative structure (see question 1a above), but an integral part of the subject of this essay.
   a. How, where, and why does White align himself with the pig? Reread ¶ 14, for example. Note how, gradually, the pig ceases to become bacon, or ham hock, and is finally established as simply a creature among creatures.
   b. Death itself, together with suffering, sickness, and burial are all under discussion in this piece. Find and discuss the spots where the subject matter broadens to include such other aspects of the event.
   c. White is distressed that this event threatens his "tidy world" (¶ 30). The same threat is present in ¶ 8, and elsewhere. How is that possible?
3. What role does the dog, Fred, play in this drama, as White describes it? He is persistently, ironically, *there* in the scene. Is it possible to compare his function with that of the fool in *King Lear*?
4. In the final paragraph, White broadens the essay's framework to include not only the central characters, the pig, McFarland, Fred, but the community of which they are a part. What are his reasons for doing so? Do we believe him? Would such an inclusion work as well had this death taken place, say, in New York City? Why, or why not?

Suggestions for Writing

1. In an essay, analyze the ways in which White keeps this essay from being foolish, saccharine, or embarrassing.
2. If you have experienced the death of a pet, attempt a description of it. Note, however, you will face all the dangers and risks White faces. You will have to strike the right tone and voice, and fill the essay with interesting detail.

Isak Dinesen

Isak Dinesen (1883–1962) is the pen name of Baroness Karen Blixen of Denmark. Of the many remarkable facts of her life and career, one is that she wrote masterly prose in both English and Danish. Her book of descriptive pieces, Out of Africa, appeared in both languages in 1937. It is based on her experiences while running a coffee plantation in British East Africa (now Kenya) from 1914 to 1931. The book became famous for its clarity of style as well as the rich variety of the scenes described. Dinesen was also well-known as a writer of fiction. One of her books of stories, Winter's Tales, had to be smuggled out of Nazi-occupied Denmark in 1942 to be published in England and America.

Though Dinesen wrote and published short fiction in her early twenties, it was not until the coffee plantation had failed, her lover had been killed in a plane crash, and she had returned broke from Africa to Denmark that she set to work seriously as a writer. Dinesen never actually wanted to be a writer, but, as she put it, she had to make a living, and the only other thing she knew how to do was cook. It would appear that she chose her pen name, which means laughter, or one who laughs, with some care, for it suggests the curious ambiguity that laughter expresses toward life—at once distancing and embracing.

Dinesen's prose, like her personality, is characterized by a detachment—

distinctive without being too remote or obscure, ironic without being bitter—suggestive, finally, of a fastidious passion for life. In "On Mottoes of My Life," Dinesen writes that the first motto she chose to live by was **Navigare necesse est, vivere non necesse** ("To navigate is necessary, to live is not"). Essentially, that remained her motto. Though her choice to write came from economic necessity, its main motive seems to have been to express that same restlessness and impulse to navigate that led her to Africa in the first place.

Speaking of herself at age fifty she said (in motto fashion) "I will not be one person again.... Never again will I have my heart and my whole life bound up with one woman." Her writings read as navigations across the profound distances that wash between parts of oneself, one human and another, between human and nonhuman beings, as reading "The Iguana" and "Pooran Singh" will make clear. It was by that means, that essaying, that navigation, that she told her own story, and made clear to herself "the inherent richness and strangeness" of her own life.

THE IGUANA

In the Reserve I have sometimes come upon the Iguana, the big lizards, as they were sunning themselves upon a flat stone in a riverbed. They are not pretty in shape, but nothing can be imagined more beautiful than their colouring. They shine like a heap of precious stones or like a pane cut out of an old church window. When, as you approach, they swish away, there is a flash of azure, green and purple over the stones, the colour seems to be standing behind them in the air, like a comet's luminous tail.   1

Once I shot an Iguana. I thought that I should be able to make some pretty things from his skin. A strange thing happened then, that I have never afterwards forgotten. As I went up to him, where he was lying dead upon his stone, and actually while I was walking the few steps, he faded and grew pale, all colour died out of him as in one long sigh, and by the time that I touched him he was grey and dull like a lump of concrete. It was the live impetuous blood pulsating within the animal, which had radiated out all that glow and splendour. Now that the flame was put out, and the soul had flown, the Iguana was as dead as a sandbag.   2

Often since I have, in some sort, shot an Iguana, and I have remembered the one of the Reserve. Up at Meru I saw a young Native girl with a bracelet on, a leather strap two inches wide, and embroidered all over with very small turquoise-coloured beads which varied a little in colour and played in green, light blue and ultramarine. It was an extraordinarily live thing; it seemed to draw breath on her arm, so that I wanted it for myself, and made Farah buy it from her. No sooner had it come upon my own arm than it gave up the ghost. It was nothing now, a small, cheap, purchased article of finery. It had been the play of colours, the duet between the turquoise and the "nègre",—that quick, sweet, brownish black, like peat and black pottery, of the Native's skin,—that had created the life of the bracelet.

In the Zoological Museum of Pietermaritzburg, I have seen, in a stuffed deep-water fish in a showcase, the same combination of colouring, which there had survived death; it made me wonder what life can well be like, on the bottom of the sea, to send up something so live and airy. I stood in Meru and looked at my pale hand and at the dead bracelet, it was as if an injustice had been done to a noble thing, as if truth had been suppressed. So sad did it seem that I remembered the saying of the hero in a book that I had read as a child: "I have conquered them all, but I am standing amongst graves."

In a foreign country and with foreign species of life one should take measures to find out whether things will be keeping their value when dead. To the settlers of East Africa I give the advice: "For the sake of your own eyes and heart, shoot not the Iguana."

Rhetorical Analysis

1. This brief essay leads to a piece of advice, contained in the final paragraph. As with any advice, its value partly depends on the authority of the person giving it. Thus, one of Dinesen's rhetorical tasks is to persuade the reader that she *has* the authority—the experience and the intelligence—to speak credibly. What are the main ways she does this?

2. Dinesen's prose is famous for its precise description. In noting the quickness with which the colors fade in the just-shot iguana, she is not content with "As I went up to him," but describes the time even more exactly: "actually while I was walking the few steps." "Actually" is a key word here, for it creates the feeling that the event actually happened, which in turn lends authority to the rest of the piece. Study her description of the iguana's coloring (¶ 1), the bracelet (¶ 3), the shade of the girl's skin (¶ 3), the fish (¶ 4).

3. How does Dinesen compress so much into so short a space? Notice the unadorned beginning, the rapid transitions, the condensed metaphors. Find and analyze other means of rhetorical economy.

Intellectual Analysis

1. One crucial element here is the play between inanimate and animate.
    a. How is that play achieved, and what does it mean? For example, in ¶s 1–3, the author moves from the image of "stone" to "stones" to "lump of concrete" to "sandbag," and then to turquoise stones. What are the implications of such a pattern of diction?
    b. Suppose part of Dinesen's wonder is at the fact of life even emerging from matter *at all*; then what would be the significance of these images? (You could compare Dinesen's attitude to a similar one in Eiseley's "Judgment of the Birds.")
2. The iguana are "not pretty in shape," Dinesen says, and yet she finds them exceedingly beautiful—so, also, with the beads, in a slightly different way.
    a. Such a complex perception, then, must itself be a theme. How?
    b. Does this theme become an implicit statement about aesthetics? If so, how? Is beauty in the eye of the beholder?
3. This essay is pointedly didactic, as noted above. What are we to make of the moral she ends with? It does not involve killing only (with the bracelet or the fish); thus, what is the real moral? You might compare Forster's "My Wood," in which he quotes a line from Dante: "Possession is one with loss."

Suggestions for Writing

1. How do we kill the Iguana? Write an essay in which you pursue that question.
2. Write an essay evaluating the cliche, "Beauty is in the eye of the beholder."

POORAN SINGH

Pooran Singh's little blacksmith's shop down by the mill was a miniature Hell on the farm, with all the orthodox attributes of that place. It was built of corrugated iron, and when the sun shone down upon the roof of it, and the flames of the furnace rose inside it, the air itself, in and around the hut, was white-hot. All day long, the place resounded with the deafening noise of the forge,—iron on iron, on iron once more,—and the hut was filled with axes, and broken wheels, that made it look like some ancient gruesome picture of a place of execution.

All the same the blacksmith's shop had a great power of attraction, and when I went down to watch Pooran Singh at work I always found people in it and round it. Pooran Singh worked at a superhuman pace, as if his life depended upon getting the particular job of work finished within the next five minutes, he jumped straight up in the air over the forge, he shrieked out his orders to his two young Kikuyu assistants in a high bird's voice and behaved altogether like a man who is himself being burnt at the stake, or like some chafed over-devil at work. But Pooran Singh was no devil, but a person of the meekest disposition; out of working hours he had a little maidenly affectation of manner. He was our Fundee of the farm, which means an artisan of all work, carpenter, saddler and cabinet-maker, as well as blacksmith; he constructed and built more than one waggon for the farm, all on his own. But he liked the work of the forge best, and it was a very fine, proud sight, to watch him tiring a wheel.

Pooran Singh, in his appearance, was something of a fraud. When fully dressed, in his coat and large folded white turban, he managed, with his big black beard, to look a portly, ponderous man. But by the forge, bared to the waist, he was incredibly slight and nimble, with the Indian hour-glass torso.

I liked Pooran Singh's forge, and it was popular with the Kikuyus, for two reasons.

First, because of the iron itself, which is the most fascinating of all raw materials, and sets people's imagination travelling on long tracks. The plough, the sword and cannon and the wheel,—the civilization of man—man's conquest of Nature in a nut, plain enough to be understood or guessed by the primitive people,—and Pooran Singh hammered the iron.

Secondly, the Native world was drawn to the forge by its song. The treble, sprightly, monotonous, and surprising rhythm of the blacksmith's work has a mythical force. It is so virile that it appals and melts the women's hearts, it is straight and unaffected and tells the truth and nothing but the truth. Sometimes it is very outspoken. It has an excess of strength and is gay as well as strong, it is obliging to you and does great things for you, willingly, as in play. The Natives, who love rhythm, collected by Pooran Singh's hut and felt at their ease. According to an ancient Nordic law a man was not held responsible for what he had said in a forge. The tongues were loosened in Africa as well, in the blacksmith's shop, and the talk flowed freely; audacious fancies were set forth to the inspiring hammer-song.

Pooran Singh was with me for many years and was a well-paid functionary of the farm. There was no proportion between his wages and his needs, for he was an ascetic of the first water. He did not eat meat, he did not drink, or smoke, or gamble, his old clothes were worn to the thread. He sent his money over to India for the education of his children. A small silent son of his, Delip Singh, once came over from Bombay on a visit to his father. He had lost touch with the iron, the only metal that I saw about him was a fountain pen in his pocket. The mythical qualities were not carried on in the second generation.

But Pooran Singh himself, raging above the forge, kept his halo as long as he was on the farm, and I hope as long as he lived. He was the servant of the gods, heated through, white-hot, an elemental spirit. In Pooran Singh's blacksmith's shop the hammer sang to you what you wanted to hear, as if it was giving voice to your own heart. To me myself the hammer was singing an ancient Greek verse, which a friend had translated:

> "Eros struck out, like a smith with his hammer,
> So that the sparks flew from my defiance.
> He cooled my heart in tears and lamentations,
> Like red-hot iron in a stream."

Rhetorical Analysis

1. The adjective "white-hot" is used in both the first and last paragraphs. It is a forceful expression, combining at least two sensations, sight and touch. Observe how Dinesen endows this essay throughout with words and details with a strong sensory force—not just images of sight, but of sound, weight, touch, taste, temperature, even proprioceptive or visceral sensations. What is her purpose?
2. The classic advice for drawing a convincing character sketch is to make the character "well-rounded," that is, to bring in enough facts and traits about the subject to create a picture with depth, with solidity. Above all, over-simplification

or stereotypes are to be avoided; people have many facets and some of these are self-contradictory.
    a. How does Dinesen go beyond a one-dimensional portrait of Pooran Singh?
    b. It is possible that we may learn as much about the writer-observer of the piece as we do about its subject. Analyze this possibility.

3. To tire a wooden wheel (¶ 2) is to forge and attach its outer metal hoop. How does Dinesen tire her essay? How does she forge the beginning and end into one complete circle?

Intellectual Analysis

1. The structure of this essay is intuitive and inductive, moving from a man's name to a mythological statement on Eros.
    a. Chart the very particular details Dinesen mentions, paying attention to the increasing inclusiveness of them. As she moves along, Dinesen imputes more meaning and significance to the details.
    b. What does sexuality—in the poem at the end—have to do with the forge and forger?
2. Analyze the mythological element in this short piece. What meaning does it add?
    a. The mythological element is both stated and, even more richly, implied. Develop the connection between myth and Pooran Singh.
    b. The imagination of man is involved here, building things. *Homo faber*, man the toolmaker, is an ancient formulation of human nature. How does this figure in the meaning of this essay?
    c. There seems to be some opposition of, yet connection between, Heaven and Hell here: in the descriptive language, in Singh himself, and in the Natives. Some other rugged opposites match this one, and how they all fit together is important to a full appreciation of the essay.

Suggestions for Writing

1. Attempt a character sketch of the most genuinely eccentric person you can think of.
2. Item 2 above, on the mythological element in this essay, would be an excellent subject for a short research paper, involving not only Eros, but Hephaistos, Vulcan, and even Prometheus.
3. Several pieces in this anthology—"Pooran Singh," Orwell's "The Hanging," and Barry Lopez's "Buffalo"—might be read either as essays or as stories. Certainly one of the legitimate objectives of an essayist is to recreate in the imagination what has happened in reality. Write an essay including such an imaginative retelling.

On Mottoes of My Life

A short while ago an interviewer asked me whether—after having lived for many years, having felt at home in more than one country and amongst different races, and known both good and bad luck—I could sum up the events and experience of my life in what is called a motto.

He was wise, I think, to address his question to a person of my generation. The idea of what is called "a motto" is probably far from the minds of young people of today. As I look from the one age to the other, I find this particular idea—the word, *le mot*, and the motto—to be one of the phenomena of life which in the course of time have most decidedly come down in value. To my contemporaries the name *was* the thing or the man; it was even the finest part of a man, and you praised him when you said that he was as good as his word.

Very likely it will be difficult for the younger generation to realize to what extent we lived in a world of symbols. We might, at this moment, lay before us a plain matter-of-fact object, a piece of cloth, and endeavor to agree in defining and placing it. A young man or woman would say to me: "You may give this thing a name of your own choice, but actually, in reality and for all working purposes, it is a length of bunting, of such and such measurements and such and such colors, and worth so and so much a yard." The person brought up with symbols, genuinely surprised and shocked, would protest: "What do you mean? You are all wrong. The thing before us, in reality and for all working purposes, is a thing of tremendous power. Put it to a test in real, actual life—it can at any moment call up a hundred million people and set them marching. It is the Stars and Stripes, it is Old Glory, it is the United States of America."

Children of my day, even in great houses, had very little in the way of toys. Toy shops were almost unknown; modern mechanical playthings, which furnish their own activity, had hardly come into existence. One might, of course, buy oneself a hobbyhorse, but generally speaking an individually selected knotty stick from the woods, upon which imagination might work freely, was dearer to the heart. We were not observers, as children today seem to be from birth, of their own accord; and not utilizers, as they are brought up to be; we were creators. Our knotty stick, for all working purposes, in appearance and as far as actual horsepower went, came nearer to Bucephalus and eight-hoofed Sleipner, or to Pegasus himself, than any magnificently decorated horse from a smart store.

In a similar way we liked to christen an enterprise, an epoch or a task, by hoisting our colors above it in the form of a motto, proclaiming to the whole world what this undertaking was meant to be. *In hoc signo vinces.* The word, the motto, here was both the starting-shot or program, and the summing-up. It existed before the activity or deed itself, and remained when these had been brought to their conclusion; it was the opening verse, "in the beginning was the Word," and the final statement, the sacred Amen—"so be it."

And the word, taken in such earnest, is a mighty thing. You choose your motto and have it set in your seal, but before you are aware of it the motto has sealed and stamped you. There are in my own country families who for centuries have lived under the influence of a motto; I have known members of several generations of them and have found them to vary in many ways, but the stamp has been recognizable in each of them, and the people who have lived under the sign of *Nobilis est ira leonis* will differ in countenance and even in instincts from those under *Amore non vi.* I am related to and have been friends with old and young members of a family born and brought up with the motto "And yet." They were all staunch people, difficult to argue with.

Now in going through those mottoes of my own life, which at different times I have selected for myself, which I have looked upon as belonging to me, and which have most likely finished up by making me belong to them, I feel myself walking in the steps of Jacques:

> All the world's a stage,
> and all the men and women merely players.
> They have their exits and their entrances;
> and one man in his time plays many parts,
> his acts being seven ages.

Or, as in my own case, only five such ages.

Denys Finch-Hatton, my English friend in Africa, used to laugh at me. He called me "the Great Emperor Otto." For

> The great Emperor Otto
> could never decide on a motto.
> He hovered between
> "l'Etat c'est moi" and "Ich dien."

In my particular case Denys took it that the first statement expressed my attitude towards people of my own race, and the second my state of mind in my dealings with natives, and he was probably right.

To the little girl in my mother's house the great Emperor Otto's dilemma was felt as wealth, a multitude of possibilities. On the covers of old exercise-books, now found in attics, mottoes in red and blue pencil come and go. The one that recurs most often is a highly laudable maxim: *Essayez!* Others, in a Latin which unfortunately I have now forgotten: "Still I am unconquered," or "Often in difficulties, never afraid," I take to have been written down in some kind of bitterness or rebellion against higher powers sitting on the child—our governesses, most likely, for I have never gone to school, but was taught by governesses at home, to which circumstance I owe, I think, the fact that I am totally ignorant of many things that are common knowledge to other people. Still these young or elderly women were ambitious persons; at the age of twelve we were called upon to write an essay on Racine, a task that I should fear to undertake today, and to translate Walter Scott's "The Lady of the Lake" into Danish verse, passages of which were frequently on the lips of my sisters and myself years later. Other mottoes, in themselves more appropriate to my present age than to that of eleven or twelve at which they were written down, I take to have been picked for the sake of the beauty of the words themselves: *Sicut aquila juvenescam.*

I think it must have been at the age of seventeen, when I had got my own way and was studying painting at the Royal Academy of Copenhagen, that the rich possibilities consolidated into one, and that I chose the first real motto of my youth.

Navigare necesse est, vivere non necesse! This audacious order was flung from the lips of Pompey to his timid Sicilian crew when they refused to set out against the gale and the high seas to bring provisions of grain to Rome.

It is not an original motto to choose; many young people will have made it their own. In their hearts the longing and the will to dare are waiting for the magic of *the word* to send them off. It came naturally to me to view my enterprise in life in terms of seafaring, for my home stands but a hundred yards from the sea, and through all the summers of our youth my brothers had boats in the fairways between Copenhagen and Elsinore.

To young people, who think in paradoxes, the paradox of Pompey—for a paradox it is, since that all-important voyage to Rome had for its purpose the maintenance of life, and since, in any case, if you are no longer alive you can no longer sail—appears as the true, clear logic of life. No compass-needle in the world was as infallible to me as the outstretched arm of Pompey; I steered my course by it with unswerving confidence, and had any wiser person insisted that there was no earthly sense in my motto, I might have answered: "Nay, but a heavenly sense!" and have added perhaps: "And a maritime!"

Before this gale I was swept, on the eve of the First World War, under all plain canvas to Africa. I was at that time engaged to my cousin, Bror Blixen; a mutual uncle had come back from a big-game safari to what was then the Protectorate of British East Africa, and had displayed to us a Fata Morgana of tremendous farming possibilities there. In the true spirit of Pompey: "It is necessary to farm, it is not necessary to live," we set out.

Genuine simplicity of heart at times will call forth unexpected indulgence in the governing powers of the universe. The goddess Nemesis herself is swayed by it into a gentler course. The goddess might have answered me: "All right, have it your own way. Sail on, and give up the idea of living!" This, I take it, was her answer to the Flying Dutchman. To me her answer came differently: "Bless you, you fool! *I* shall set your sails, and *I* shall turn your wheel, and I shall have you sailing straight into life!" Under the flag of my first motto I sailed into the heart of Africa and into a Vita Nuova, into what became to me my real life. Africa received me and made me her own, so thoroughly that, unconsciously faithless to the motto which had united us, I exchanged it for another.

The family of Finch-Hatton, of England, have on their crest the device *Je responderay*, "I will answer." They have had it there for a long time, I believe, since it is spelled in such antiquated French; it is a long time too since Hatton Garden in London was a garden, and a long time since it was known about one of the members of the family, a favorite of Queen Elizabeth I, that

> Sir Christopher Hatton he danced with much grace,
> He had a fine form and a very sweet face,

but that all the same he came to a sad end, for the Devil took him.

I liked this old motto so much that I asked Denys, an earlier pioneer in Africa than myself—although all we settlers who had come out before the war looked upon ourselves as one family, a kind of Mayflower people—if I might have it for my own. He generously made me a present of it and even had a seal cut for me, with the words carved in it. The device was meaningful and dear to me for many reasons, two in particular.

19 The first of these was its high valuation of the idea of the answer in itself. For an answer is a rarer thing than is generally imagined. There are many highly intelligent people who have no answer at all in them. A conversation or a correspondence with such persons is nothing but a double monologue—you may stroke them or you may strike them, you will get no more echo from them than from a block of wood. And how, then, can you yourself go on speaking?

20 In the long valleys of the African plains I have been surrounded and followed by sweet echoes, as from a sounding board. My daily life out there was filled with answering voices; I never spoke without getting a response; I spoke, freely and without restraint, even when I was silent. One explanation of this was, I believe, that I lived so high up, more than 6,000 feet above sea-level, so to say on the roof of the globe, where the air is felt to be the dominant element and is apt to turn all hearts into aeolian harps. Another was that I was here in contact with the African natives and with African big game. I have always loved animals very much, and to meet them now on their own ground, not imported into human existence—to ride straight into a herd of zebra or eland and to hear from my bed the distant, mighty roar of the hunting lion, I felt as a return to those happy days when Adam gave names to the beasts of Eden. The natives of Africa I had not met before; all the same they came into my life as a kind of answer to some call in my own nature, to dreams of childhood perhaps, or to poetry read and cherished long ago, or to emotions and instincts deep down in the mind, for I have always felt that I resembled the natives more than did other white people in the Protectorate. From the very first day an understanding sprang up between them and me, so that I may say that my love of them, of both sexes and all ages, as of all tribes—above all with the Masai, the warrior-tribe, who were my neighbors when I rode across the river—was as strong a passion as I have ever known. The dark figures around me answered me, even without speaking, in their noiseless, gentle movements and quiet, keen glances. When we were alone together the echo grew stronger. I have been out on safari, a hundred miles from another white person, with native companions only, and have become one with my surroundings, with the landscape, animals, and human beings and with the hours of day and night. This feeling was enhanced by the natives giving us white people native

names, characterizing us in words of their own language. Most of these were animals' names, although there were exceptions to this rule, and one very unsociable neighbor of mine was known as *sahani modya*, one plate or cover, and my Swedish friend Eric von Otter was given the fine name of *resarsi modya*, one cartridge, since he never needed more than one for any head of game. My husband and I were *wauhauga*, the wild geese. Later, when I was alone on the farm, my old Somali gunbearer, after returning to his own country, wrote me a letter addressed to "Lioness Blixen" and beginning "Honourable Lioness," which resulted in all my friends in the colony calling me the Lioness. I feel very sure that, to a woman at least, the presence of echoes in her life is a condition for happiness, or is in itself a consciousness of rich resources. I advise every husband: answer your wife, make her answer you.

Secondly I liked the Finch-Hatton device for its ethical content. I will answer *for* what I say or do; I will answer *to* the impression I make. I will be responsible.

I cannot quite account for the overlapping of the words and the ideas of answer and responsibility. My audience, so many of whom certainly will be better versed in etymology than I, may be able to furnish the reason. The connection exists in the languages that I know—the Danish word for responsibility is plain "Ansvar." In a colony it is a sad thing to see to what extent people who in their own country have stuck to an orthodox code of behavior, in surroundings where they cannot possibly be called to account will feel themselves free of any code. It is a very good thing there, it is probably a very good thing anywhere, to have *Je responderay* harmoniously in your blood.

Were I now, after my return from those happy hunting grounds, to advise a person looking for a motto, I should tell him that *Je responderay* is a happy sign under which to live. In looking back on my nearly twenty years in Africa, I feel that the fact that all things worked together for the good of a human being goes to prove that this human being did indeed love God.

Readers of my book *Out of Africa* will know, however, that this state of things did not last for me. When in the early thirties coffee prices fell, I had to give up my farm. I went back to my own country, at sea-level, out of earshot of the echoes of the plain—the big, wild, debonnaire inhabitants of those plains and the dark, friendly figures of the manyattas sinking below the horizon all around me. During this time my existence was without an answer from anywhere. It had often happened to me during my life to imagine things, and to find it somehow difficult to bring them into reality. Here it was the other way round: things were realizing themselves on all sides, and very insistently at that, without its being in the least possible for me to imagine them.

Under the circumstances I myself grew silent. I had, in every sense of the word, nothing to say.

And yet I had to speak. For I had my books to write.

During my last months in Africa, as it became clear to me that I could not keep the farm, I had started writing at night, to get my mind off the things which in the daytime it had gone over a hundred times, and on to a new track. My squatters on the farm, by then, had got into the habit of coming up to my house and sitting around it for hours in silence, as if just waiting to see how things would develop. I felt their presence there more like a friendly gesture than a reproach, but all the same of sufficient weight to make it difficult for me to start any undertaking of my own. But they would go away, back to their own huts, at nightfall. And as I sat there, in the house, alone, or perhaps with Farah, the infallibly loyal, standing motionless in his long white Arab robe with his back to the wall, figures, voices and colors from far away or from nowhere began to swarm around my paraffin lamp. I wrote two of my *Seven Gothic Tales* there.

Now I was back again in my old home, with my mother, who received the prodigal daughter with all the warmth of her heart, but who never quite realized that I was more than fifteen years old and accustomed, for the past eighteen years, to a life of exceptional freedom. My home is a lovely place; I might have lived on there from day to day in a kind of sweet idyl; but I could not see any kind of future before me. And I had no money; my dowry, so to say, had gone with the farm. I owed it to the people on whom I was dependent to try to make some kind of existence for myself. Those Gothic Tales began to demand to be written, and first of all they demanded a motto for the book they were to make. "Give us," they cried out, "a sign in which"—not to conquer, for I could not then conceive the idea of conquest, but—"to run, to move!"

Unexpectedly, as if on its own, the third motto of my life swooped down upon me. Even at the time I did not understand the meaning of it, it just took possession of me.

In the gypsy-moth plane in which I flew with Denys over Africa there was room for two only, the passenger sitting in front of the pilot with nothing but air in front of him. You could not, there, help feeling that you were, like one of the characters of the Arabian Nights, carried through the heavens upon the palms of a djinn. In the morning or afternoon, when I had no need to fear the sun, I used to take off my flying-helmet, and the current of African air would seize me by the hair and drag back my head, so that I felt it difficult to keep it in place. In the same way I was now, in Denmark, grasped by a current of life that seemed to know what it was about, although I myself did not know.

For it so happened that I had read in the papers about the boat of a French scientific expedition which had gone down below Iceland with her flag flying. And the boat had been named *Pourquoi pas?*—"Why not?"

Now again this motto had all the nature of a paradox, and I cannot, in so many words, account for the meaning of it. But it worked. It was encouraging and inspiring. "Why?" by itself is a wail or lament, a cry from the heart; it seems to ring in the desert and to be in itself negative, the voice of a lost cause. But when another negative, the *pas*, the "not," is added, the pathetic question is turned into an answer, a directive, a call of wild hope.

Under this sign—at times very doubtful about the whole thing, but still, as it were, in the hands of an exacting and joyful spirit—I finished my first book. And this third motto of mine may be said to stand over all my books. It will stand, I think, over whatever books I may still come to write.

My friend in Africa, Hugh Martin, when I sent him my first Tale for his personal comment, answered me in a verse by Kipling:

> Old Horn to all Atlantic said:
> Now where did Frankie learn his trade?
> For he ran me down with a three-reef mainsail,
> All round the Horn.

> Atlantic answered: Not from me.
> You'd better ask the cold North Sea.
> For he ran me down under all plain canvas,
> All round the Horn.

I might make this answer my own. I had, at the time, no teacher or adviser; I could not, at the time, have been taught or advised. I was taken and forced on by the French boat gone down in the cold sea below Iceland: *Pourquoi pas?*

"They have their exits and their entrances. . . ." So have programs and mottoes. But in a good play an exit is not a disappearance—even after his final exit a character still forms part of the play. The next motto of my life came into it very quietly, without chasing out the *Pourquoi pas?*, as if by a law of nature, like the change of the seasons, which no one really wants to alter.

An old English town had three walls around it. In each wall was a gate, and above each gate an inscription. Above the first gate was written: "Be bold," above the second: "Be bold," above the third: "Be not too bold."

Will this sound like a come-down to the ears of my audience? To me it is not so. A person who all through his life, like Mussolini, has declared: *"Non amo i sedentari"*—"I do not like sedentary people"—will recognize the moment for choosing a chair and settling down in it, trusting that "trees where you sit will crowd into a shade." The craving to impress your will and your being upon the world and to make the world your own is turned into a longing to be able to accept, to give yourself over to the universe—Thy will be done. Which of the two is the most truly bold? I have been very strong, unusually so for a woman, able to walk or ride longer than most men; I have bent a Masai bow and have felt in a moment of rapture a kinship with Odysseus. The pleasure of having been strong is still with me; the weakness of today is the natural continuation of the vigor of former days. Nietzsche has written: "I am a yea-sayer, and I have been a fighter, so that one fine day I shall have my arms free to bless"—the latter attitude being not in opposition to the former but a consequence of it.

Can a human being, fully aware of the eternity behind and before him or her, fully value and appreciate the passing hour? An hour of watching the woods or the sea or of listening to music, an hour given to friendly talk with friends? One might say in the manner of the bird in the poem which perches on a frail branch, knowing that the branch will not support it, but knowing at the same time that it has wings which, when the moment comes, will do so. Indeed, *Pourquoi pas?* The older motto after its exit upholds the new.

I have come over here to America under the sign of "Be bold. Be 40
bold. Be not too bold." I may wish that I had been able to come earlier,
in the years when the necessity of sailing was plainer to me than the
necessity of living. And yet I feel that the arrangement is no come-
down—it may even be, in its own way, a joke. It is probably a good
thing for me, at this moment and while speaking to you, to be warned
against being too long-winded, if not too bold.

I shall finish up my talk on the mottoes of my life with a short tale, 41
which a friend of mine told me.

An old Chinese mandarin, during the minority of the young 42
Emperor, had been governing the country for him. When the Emperor
came of age the old man gave him back the ring which had served as
emblem of his vicariate, and said to his young sovereign:

"In this ring I have had set an inscription which your dear 43
Majesty may find useful. It is to be read in times of danger, doubt
and defeat. It is to be read, as well, in times of conquest, triumph
and glory."

The inscription in the ring read: "This, too, will pass." 44

The sentence is not to be taken to mean that, in their passing, 45
tears and laughter, hopes and disappointments disappear into a void.
But it tells you that all will be absorbed into a unity. Soon we shall see
them as integral parts of the full picture of the man or woman.

Upon the lips of the great poet the passing takes the form of 46
mighty, harmonious beauty:

> Nothing of him that doth fade,
> but doth suffer a sea-change
> into something rich and strange.

We may make use of the words—even when we are speaking 47
about ourselves—without vainglory. Each one amongst us will feel
in his heart the inherent richness and strangeness of this one thing:
his life.

Rhetorical Analysis

1. Even though later published as an essay, "On Mottoes of My Life" was originally presented as a talk to an audience welcoming Dinesen's visit to the United States in 1960. She was then 77 years old, with an established fame as a writer. How has

Dinesen designed this piece for that rhetorical situation? How does she keep her audience in mind? (See especially ¶s 24, 33, and 40−41.)
2. Beginnings and endings are often difficult to write.
   a. The first sentences of an essay are sometimes the hardest because they must accomplish a lot within a short space. To be successful, the least they must do is to establish a tone for the rest of the essay, attract the reader's attention and interest, and chart a course that the essay will then follow. Dinesen's first paragraph does all this masterfully and is well worth study. In what other ways does the opening paragraph serve as an efficient and graceful introduction?
   b. The seventh paragraph serves a special purpose, also introductory. What is it?
   c. It is harder to say what a successful ending should do. Some conclusions merely sum up, but others create a sense of closure (or rounding off) through some innovative, speculative means. Look at Dinesen's conclusion (¶ 41−47). What do these final seven paragraphs accomplish? How do they balance or complete the first six paragraphs?

Intellectual Analysis

1. Consider the first six introductory paragraphs (see item 2 above) from the standpoint of their subject matter.
   a. The first motto taken up is from Pompey: "To navigate is necessary, to live is not." Dinesen speaks of the paradox in it; how does that paradox work, and what is its significance? She says, "many young people will have made it [the motto] their own." How so?
   b. The second motto is "I will answer." What is the ethical content she is so keen about here? She says there are "many highly intelligent people who have no answer at all in them." How can this be? And how does that remark connect with Africa and husbands (¶ 20)? The third motto quickly blends into a fourth, and perhaps into a fifth: "Why not?" becomes "Be not too bold"; does it also become "This, too, will pass"? How do these mottoes differ, especially from her first motto? How does Dinesen fit them together, in a summary way?
   c. Look at the final sentence of the essay. Do the mottoes show a development, a "life"?

Suggestions for Writing

1. Here are the mottoes which Dinesen does not translate for the reader:

> *In hoc signo vinces* (¶ 5): Under this sign you will conquer.

> *Nobilis est ira leonis* (¶ 6): Noble is the wrath of the lion.
> *Amore non vi* (¶ 6): Love, not force.
> *L'Etat c'est moi* (¶ 8): I am the State.
> *Ich dien* (¶ 8): I serve.
> *Essayez* (¶ 10): Try!
> *Sicut aquila juvenescam* (¶ 10): Just as the eagle, I will rejuvenate.

Select one and write an essay discussing and elaborating its meaning. It will be complex, or else these mottoes would not exist as such. For a model, look again at ¶s 17–23, where Dinesen expounds on the implications of *Je responderai*.

2. Have mottoes gone as much out of style as Dinesen suggests? Make a search for mottoes in *your* life. You may find them anywhere, in the stories of your parents or grandparents, in the words of your favorite songs, in the pledge of allegiance, on the coins in your pocket, or on the banner flying from your college flagpole. Write an essay making sense of what you have found.

3. Apply Dinesen's analysis of the effect of mottoes to another form of discourse (greetings, advertisements, poems) or to the language of slang expression.

Lewis Thomas

Lewis Thomas was born in 1913 in Flushing, New York, which then was still a "small country town with good trees and gardens." Thomas's father was a medical doctor, and young Lewis used to accompany him on house calls, watching him practice the physician's "gift of affection." Thomas attended Princeton University where, he says, his record was "middling fair"; after which he got into Harvard medical school by "luck" and "pull." Thomas's brilliant career, however, vindicates whatever there may have been of "pull": appointments at New York University's Bellevue Medical Center, the deanship of Yale University medical school, and the presidency of Memorial Sloan-Kettering Cancer Center. Moreover, he has written "about 200" articles for medical and scientific journals.

In 1970, a former schoolmate, Franz Inglefinger, editor of The New England Journal of Medicine, asked Thomas to contribute one essay per month on any subject he wished. This invitation eventually led to the essays collected as Lives of a Cell, which won the National Book Award in nonfiction for 1974, the same year in which he received the Distinguished Achievement in Modern Medicine award. In 1979, a second collection appeared, The Medusa and the Snail, and in 1983, Late Night Thoughts on Listening to Mahler's Ninth Symphony.

Thomas's essays, ostensibly about such things as mitochondria, the scrapie

107

virus, Tau Ceti, and other microscopic and macroscopic exotica, are actually meditations on the human future, on paying attention, on the youth of the species (and therefore the need for humility), and on the unity of all life forms. He apparently learned his father's "gift of affection" for life itself.

Thomas gives us clues about reading his essays. "Uncertainty, disillusion, and despair are prices to be paid for living in an age of science. Illumination is the product sought, but it comes in small bits, only from time to time, not ever in broad, bright flashes of public comprehension, and there can be no promise that we will ever emerge from the great depths of the mystery of being." A profound sense of that mystery, and the elegant use of language to probe its depths for "small bits," are the hallmarks of Thomas's popular essays. The ultimate object of Thomas's thinking is, in the words of his favorite author, Montaigne, "wonder, the chase, ambiguity."

How to Fix the Premedical Curriculum

T he influence of the modern medical school on liberal-arts education in this country over the last decade has been baleful and malign, nothing less. The admission policies of the medical schools are at the root of the trouble. If something is not done quickly to change these, all the joy of going to college will have been destroyed, not just for that growing majority of undergraduate students who draw breath only to become doctors, but for everyone else, all the students, and all the faculty as well.

1

The medical schools used to say they wanted applicants as broadly educated as possible, and they used to mean it. The first two years of medical school were given over entirely to the basic biomedical sciences, and almost all entering students got their first close glimpse of science in those years. Three chemistry courses, physics, and some sort of biology were all that were required from the colleges. Students were encouraged by the rhetoric of medical-school catalogues to major in such nonscience disciplines as history, English, philosophy. Not many did so; almost all premedical students in recent

2

generations have had their majors in chemistry or biology. But anyway, they were authorized to spread around in other fields if they wished.

There is still some talk in medical deans' offices about the need for general culture, but nobody really means it, and certainly the premedical students don't believe it. They concentrate on science.

They concentrate on science with a fury, and they live for grades. If there are courses in the humanities that can be taken without risk to class standing they will line up for these, but they will not get into anything tough except science. The so-called social sciences have become extremely popular as stand-ins for traditional learning.

The atmosphere of the liberal-arts college is being poisoned by premedical students. It is not the fault of the students, who do not start out as a necessarily bad lot. They behave as they do in the firm belief that if they behave any otherwise they won't get into medical school.

I have a suggestion, requiring for its implementation the following announcement from the deans of all the medical schools: henceforth, any applicant who is self-labeled as a "premed," distinguishable by his course selection from his classmates, will have his dossier placed in the third stack of three. Membership in a "premedical society" will, by itself, be grounds for rejection. Any college possessing something called a "premedical curriculum," or maintaining offices for people called "premedical advisers," will be excluded from recognition by the medical schools.

Now as to grades and class standing. There is obviously no way of ignoring these as criteria for acceptance, but it is the grades *in general* that should be weighed. And, since so much of the medical-school curriculum is, or ought to be, narrowly concerned with biomedical science, more attention should be paid to the success of students in other, nonscience disciplines before they are admitted, in order to assure the scope of intellect needed for a physician's work.

Hence, if there are to be MCAT tests, the science part ought to be made the briefest, and weigh the least. A knowledge of literature and languages ought to be the major test, and the scariest. History should be tested, with rigor.

The best thing would be to get rid of the MCATs, once and for all, and rely instead, wholly, on the judgment of the college faculties.

You could do this if there were some central, core discipline, universal within the curricula of all the colleges, which could be used for evaluating the free range of a student's mind, his tenacity and resolve, his innate capacity for the understanding of human beings, and his affection for the human condition. For this purpose, I propose that classical Greek be restored as the centerpiece of undergraduate education. The loss of Homeric and Attic Greek from American college life was one of this century's disasters. Putting it back where it once was would quickly make up for the dispiriting impact which generations of spotty Greek in translation have inflicted on modern thought. The capacity to read Homer's language closely enough to sense the terrifying poetry in some of the lines could serve as a shrewd test for the qualities of mind and character needed in a physician.

If everyone had to master Greek, the college students aspiring to medical school would be placed on the same footing as everyone else, and their identifiability as a separate group would be blurred, to everyone's advantage. Moreover, the currently depressing drift on some campuses toward special courses for prelaw students, and even prebusiness students, might be inhibited before more damage is done.

Latin should be put back as well, but not if it is handled, as it ought to be, by the secondary schools. If Horace has been absorbed prior to college, so much for Latin. But Greek is a proper discipline for the college mind.

English, history, the literature of at least two foreign languages, and philosophy should come near the top of the list, just below Classics, as basic requirements, and applicants for medical school should be told that their grades in these courses will count more than anything else.

Students should know that if they take summer work as volunteers in the local community hospital, as ward aides or laboratory assistants, this will not necessarily be held against them, but neither will it help.

Finally, the colleges should have much more of a say about who goes on to medical school. If they know, as they should, the students who are typically bright and also respected, this judgment should carry the heaviest weight for admission. If they elect to use criteria other than numerical class standing for recommending applicants, this evaluation should hold.

The first and most obvious beneficiaries of this new policy would be the college students themselves. There would no longer be, anywhere where they could be recognized as a coherent group, the "premeds," that most detestable of all cliques eating away at the heart of the college. Next to benefit would be the college faculties, once again in possession of the destiny of their own curriculum, for better or worse. And next in line, but perhaps benefiting the most of all, are the basic-science faculties of the medical schools, who would once again be facing classrooms of students who are ready to be startled and excited by a totally new and unfamiliar body of knowledge, eager to learn, unpreoccupied by the notions of relevance that are paralyzing the minds of today's first-year medical students already so surfeited by science that they want to start practicing psychiatry in the first trimester of the first year.

Society would be the ultimate beneficiary. We could look forward to a generation of doctors who have learned as much as anyone can learn, in our colleges and universities, about how human beings have always lived out their lives. Over the bedrock of knowledge about our civilization, the medical schools could then construct as solid a structure of medical science as can be built, but the bedrock would always be there, holding everything else upright.

17

Rhetorical Analysis

1. "How to Fix the Premedical Curriculum" is not a typical "how-to-fix" essay, but its organization is straightforward. Aside from the first paragraph, with its introductory statement of the problem in need of fixing, there are three basic parts to Thomas's essay. Find these, mark their boundaries, define their purpose, and study their organization. This exercise will show you how a sophisticated argument can be carried on with patterns that are simple, basic, and direct.

2. Read the first sentence of each paragraph, underlining words that refer back to the preceding paragraph. For instance, in the first sentence of ¶ 2, "medical schools" repeats the subject of the first paragraph (its first two sentences), and "used to say" indicates a connection in time with two previous phrases (locate those phrases). Most of Thomas's connective devices are more obvious than these. Note the variety of transitional devices, their frequency and aptness.

Intellectual Analysis

1. Thomas's underlying concern is the need for a "bedrock of knowledge about our civilization," which ought to be supplied by a "liberal arts education." Those two concepts frame his basic argument.
    a. Why is such a "bedrock" so important? What does it do ("holding everything else upright," as he says)? Notice that "bedrock" and "holding" are metaphors; analyze them carefully.

b. Would this need for a liberal arts education hold for those in other disciplines and professions? If so, then name the disciplines and professions and tell how they would be improved. Would you exempt any? Is he against specialization?
2. Play out the implications of Thomas's claim that his scheme for undergraduate education would benefit the colleges as well. Would it also benefit society?
3. Do you think Thomas in any way overstates his case? Is he over-fearful of the problem, over-confident of his remedy? Is it possible that he deliberately overstates?

Suggestions for Writing

1. Write an essay arguing against Thomas's proposal. To make it convincing, remember that you will have to rebut each of his arguments one by one.
2. Write a "how-to-fix" essay similar to Thomas's, with description of problem, proposed solution, and prediction of results. The subject should be one in which you are unusually knowledgeable and have a strong opinion which is contrary to the status quo (or public opinion).
3. Summarize Thomas's criticism of undergraduate education, and then apply it to your own academic plans in college. Would the required coursework of your school and of your intended major satisfy Thomas? Are there ways you could come closer to his ideals, and are those ways feasible for you? There are many issues here. Write an essay centering on one.

LATE NIGHT THOUGHTS ON LISTENING TO MAHLER'S NINTH SYMPHONY

I cannot listen to Mahler's Ninth Symphony with anything like the old melancholy mixed with the high pleasure I used to take from this music. There was a time, not long ago, when what I heard, especially in the final movement, was an open acknowledgment of death and at the same time a quiet celebration of the tranquillity connected to the process. I took this music as a metaphor for reassurance, confirming my own strong hunch that the dying of every living creature, the most natural of all experiences, has to be a peaceful experience. I rely on nature. The long passages on all the strings at the end, as close as music can come to expressing silence itself, I used to hear as Mahler's idea of leave-taking at its best. But always, I have heard this music as a solitary, private listener, thinking about death.

Now I hear it differently. I cannot listen to the last movement of the Mahler Ninth without the door-smashing intrusion of a huge new thought: death everywhere, the dying of everything, the end of humanity. The easy sadness expressed with such gentleness and delicacy by that repeated phrase on faded strings, over and over again, no longer comes to me as old, familiar news of the cycle of living and dying. All through the last notes my mind swarms with images of a world in which the thermonuclear bombs have begun to explode, in New York and San Francisco, in Moscow and Leningrad, in Paris, in Paris, in Paris. In Oxford and Cambridge, in Edinburgh. I cannot push away the thought of a cloud of radioactivity drifting along the Engadin, from the Moloja Pass to Ftan, killing off the part of the earth I love more than any other part.

I am old enough by this time to be used to the notion of dying, saddened by the glimpse when it has occurred but only transiently knocked down, able to regain my feet quickly at the thought of continuity, any day. I have acquired and held in affection until very recently another sideline of an idea which serves me well at dark times: the life of the earth is the same as the life of an organism: the great round being possesses a mind: the mind contains an infinite number of thoughts and memories: when I reach my time I may find myself still hanging around in some sort of midair, one of those small thoughts, drawn back into the memory of the earth: in that peculiar sense I will be alive.

Now all that has changed. I cannot think that way anymore. Not while those things are still in place, aimed everywhere, ready for launching.

This is a bad enough thing for the people in my generation. We can put up with it, I suppose, since we must. We are moving along anyway, like it or not. I can even set aside my private fancy about hanging around, in midair.

What I cannot imagine, what I cannot put up with, the thought that keeps grinding its way into my mind, making the Mahler into a hideous noise close to killing me, is what it would be like to be young. How do the young stand it? How can they keep their sanity? If I were very young, sixteen or seventeen years old, I think I would begin, perhaps very slowly and imperceptibly, to go crazy.

There is a short passage near the very end of the Mahler in which the almost vanishing violins, all engaged in a sustained backward glance, are edged aside for a few bars by the cellos. Those lower notes pick up fragments from the first movement, as though prepared to begin everything all over again, and then the cellos subside and disappear, like an exhalation. I used to hear this as a wonderful few seconds of encouragement: we'll be back, we're still here, keep going, keep going.

Now, with a pamphlet in front of me on a corner of my desk, published by the Congressional Office of Technology Assessment, entitled *MX Basing*, an analysis of all the alternative strategies for placement and protection of hundreds of these missiles, each capable of creating artificial suns to vaporize a hundred Hiroshimas, collectively capable of destroying the life of any continent, I cannot hear the same Mahler. Now, those cellos sound in my mind like the opening of all the hatches and the instant before ignition.

If I were sixteen or seventeen years old, I would not feel the cracking of my own brain, but I would know for sure that the whole world was coming unhinged. I can remember with some clarity what it was like to be sixteen. I had discovered the Brahms symphonies. I knew that there was something going on in the late Beethoven quartets that I would have to figure out, and I knew that there was plenty of time ahead for all the figuring I would ever have to do. I had never heard of Mahler. I was in no hurry. I was a college sophomore and had decided that Wallace Stevens and I possessed a comprehensive understanding of everything needed for a life. The years stretched away forever ahead, forever. My great-great grandfather had come from Wales, leaving his signature in the family Bible on the same page that carried, a century later, my father's signature. It never crossed my mind to wonder about the twenty-first century; it was just there, given, somewhere in the sure distance.

The man on television, Sunday midday, middle-aged and solid, nice-looking chap, all the facts at his fingertips, more dependable looking than most high-school principals, is talking about civilian defense, his responsibility in Washington. It can make an enormous difference, he is saying. Instead of the outright death of eighty million American citizens in twenty minutes, he says, we can, by careful planning and practice, get that number down to only forty million, maybe even twenty. The thing to do, he says, is to evacuate the cities quickly and have everyone get under shelter in the countryside. That way we can recover, and meanwhile we will have retaliated, incinerating all of Soviet society, he says. What about radioactive fallout? he is asked. Well, he says. Anyway, he says, if the Russians know they can only destroy forty million of us instead of eighty million, this will deter them. Of course, he adds, they have the capacity to kill all two hundred and twenty million of us if they were to try real hard, but they know we can do the same to them. If the figure is only forty million this will deter them, not worth the trouble, not worth the risk. Eighty million would be another matter, we should guard ourselves against losing that many all at once, he says.

If I were sixteen or seventeen years old and had to listen to that, or read things like that, I would want to give up listening and reading. I would begin thinking up new kinds of sounds, different from any music heard before, and I would be twisting and turning to rid myself of human language. 11

Rhetorical Analysis

1. Look at Thomas's sentences. They help us relish again the flexibility and malleability of the English sentence, and its marvelous potential for creativity and play.
   a. Notice how often Thomas adds material parenthetically in mid-sentence. Instances in ¶ 1 are "not long ago," "especially in the final movement," "the most natural of all experiences," and "as close as music can come to expressing silence itself." Find other instances in a paragraph or two. What are the advantages of this syntactic maneuver? What are the pitfalls?
   b. Thomas also likes to add material onto the end of sentences; for example, in ¶ 1, see the "thinking about death" that ends the last sentence, and the phrase beginning with "confirming" that finishes the third sentence. Look for other examples. How does this structure work in the essay? Does it have a different function than the mid-sentence addition?

   Generally, mid- and final-sentence additions (technically called free modification) occur more frequently in professional than in student writing. Why do you think that is so?

2. Thomas's style is famous for the crisp clarity of his sentences. But some of the sentences in this passage might be called hesitant, even faltering. Examine ¶s 6 and 10 in particular. Does this rhetorical effect accord with the ideas of the essay? Does it add its own kind of persuasion to Thomas's message?

3. For the reader, it is essential to catch the tone of this piece—sad, even elegiac, with one edge of anger and another of despair. Thomas projects that tone through every

aspect of his writing—his ideas, his construction of sentences, and his words, even his paragraphs and the shape of the entire piece. Find instances of this and analyze them.

Intellectual Analysis

1. Death is a fact of life in the face of which most of us grow pale and avert our gaze. Thomas, however, looks at death steadily.
   a. How has he managed to comfort himself previously on the matter of death? Analyze all the details he mentions, but especially the notion of death as "peaceful experience," and the idea of continuity. How might one describe his philosophical position here?
   b. How does the prospect of nuclear holocaust change his attitude?
   c. Why does Thomas focus on the young?
2. The central motivation for this essay is stated in ¶ 6, where he expresses what he "cannot put up with." From that point on, he is trying to describe what he "cannot imagine."
   a. From that point, too, insanity becomes a persistent motif and theme. Trace this theme through the essay. Analyze the connections between insanity—what Thomas "cannot imagine"—and his style (see the second question under Rhetorical Analysis above).
   b. Thomas clearly believes that the insanity he speaks of is already here. How is it reasonable to consider the pamphlet and the television speech insane?
3. Analyze Thomas's references to music and to language throughout the essay. How are the two connected? How do the references add to his meaning? In the last paragraph, is Lewis saying that the music and language of young people today have already been affected by the nuclear madness?

Suggestions for Writing

1. Read ¶ 9 once again, and appraise Thomas's frame of mind when he was sixteen and seventeen years old. How does his memory compare with yours, or with your friends'? Has the nuclear threat had the kind of effect on your generation Thomas guesses it would have had on him, had he been young today?
2. The Engadin (or Engadine) Valley (end of ¶ 2) is in the Swiss Alps. Think of that part of the earth which *you* "love more than any other part." Write an essay connecting, as Thomas does here, two very real things: nuclear arms and your personal attachments.
3. By his mention of Wallace Stevens (¶ 9) just before his description of the Sunday television show, Thomas may have been thinking of that American poet's famous poem "Sunday Morning." In it, Stevens asks of the main character, "Why should

she give her bounty to the dead?" That is a good question for an essay: with nuclear arms, have living Americans in effect given their bounty to the dead?

Seven Wonders

A while ago I received a letter from a magazine editor inviting me to join six other people at dinner to make a list of the Seven Wonders of the Modern World, to replace the seven old, out-of-date Wonders. I replied that I couldn't manage it, not on short order anyway, but still the question keeps hanging around in the lobby of my mind. I had to look up the old biodegradable Wonders, the Hanging Gardens of Babylon and all the rest, and then I had to look up that word "wonder" to make sure I understood what it meant. It occurred to me that if the magazine could get any seven people to agree on a list of any such seven things you'd have the modern Seven Wonders right there at the dinner table.

Wonder is a word to wonder about. It contains a mixture of messages: something marvelous and miraculous, surprising, raising unanswerable questions about itself, making the observer wonder, even raising skeptical questions like, "I *wonder* about that." Miraculous and marvelous are clues; both words come from an ancient Indo-European root meaning simply to smile or to laugh. Anything wonderful is something to smile in the presence of, in admiration (which, by the way, comes from the same root, along with, of all telling words, "mirror").

I decided to try making a list, not for the magazine's dinner party but for this occasion: seven things I wonder about the most.

I shall hold the first for the last, and move along.

My Number Two Wonder is a bacterial species never seen on the face of the earth until 1982, creatures never dreamed of before, living violation of what we used to regard as the laws of nature, things literally straight out of Hell. Or anyway what we used to think of as Hell, the hot unlivable interior of the earth. Such regions have recently come into scientific view from the research submarines designed to descend twenty-five hundred meters or more to the edge of deep holes in the sea bottom, where open vents spew superheated seawater in plumes from chimneys in the earth's crust, known to oceanographic scientists as "black smokers." This is not just hot water, or steam, or even steam under pressure as exists in a laboratory autoclave (which we have relied upon for decades as the surest way to destroy all microbial life). This is extremely hot water under extremely high pressure, with temperatures in excess of 300 degrees centigrade. At such heat, the existence of life as we know it would be simply inconceivable. Proteins and DNA would fall apart, enzymes would melt away, anything alive would die instantaneously. We have long since ruled out the possibility of life on Venus because of that planet's comparable temperature; we have ruled out the possibility of life in the earliest years of this planet, four billion or so years ago, on the same ground.

  B. J. A. Baross and J. W. Deming have recently discovered the presence of thriving colonies of bacteria in water fished directly from these deep-sea vents. Moreover, when brought to the surface, encased in titanium syringes and sealed in pressurized chambers heated to 250 degrees centigrade, the bacteria not only survive but reproduce themselves enthusiastically. They can be killed only by chilling them down in boiling water. 6

  And yet they look just like ordinary bacteria. Under the electron microscope they have the same essential structure—cell walls, ribosomes, and all. If they were, as is now being suggested, the original archebacteria, ancestors of us all, how did they or their progeny ever learn to cool down? I cannot think of a more wonderful trick. 7

  My Number Three Wonder is *oncideres*, a species of beetle encountered by a pathologist friend of mine who lives in Houston and has a lot of mimosa trees in his backyard. This beetle is not new, but it qualifies as a Modern Wonder because of the exceedingly modern questions raised for evolutionary biologists about the three consecutive things on the mind of the female of the species. Her first thought is for a mimosa tree, which she finds and climbs, ignoring all other kinds of trees in the vicinity. Her second thought is for the laying of eggs, which she does by crawling out on a limb, cutting a longitudinal slit with her mandible and depositing her eggs beneath the slit. Her third and last thought concerns the welfare of her offspring; beetle larvae cannot survive in live wood, so she backs up a foot or so and cuts a neat circular girdle all around the limb, through the bark and down into the cambium. It takes her eight hours to finish this cabinetwork. Then she leaves and where she goes I do not know. The limb dies from the 8 girdling, falls to the ground in the next breeze, the larvae feed and grow into the next generation, and the questions lie there unanswered. How on earth did these three linked thoughts in her mind evolve together in evolution? How could any one of the three become fixed as beetle behavior by itself, without the other two? What are the odds favoring three totally separate bits of behavior—liking a particular tree, cutting a slit for eggs, and then girdling the limb—happening together by random chance among a beetle's genes? Does this smart beetle know what she is doing? And how did the mimosa tree enter the picture in its evolution? Left to themselves, unpruned, mimosa trees have a life expectancy of twenty-five to thirty years. Pruned each year, which is what the beetle's girdling labor accomplishes, the tree can flourish for a century. The mimosa-beetle relationship is an elegant example of symbiotic partnership, a phenomenon now recognized as pervasive in nature. It is good for us to have around on our intellectual mantelpiece such creatures as this insect and its friend the tree, for they keep reminding us how little we know about nature.

The Fourth Wonder on my list is an infectious agent known as the scrapie virus, which causes a fatal disease of the brain in sheep, goats, and several laboratory animals. A close cousin of scrapie is the C-J virus, the cause of some cases of senile dementia in human beings. These are called "slow viruses," for the excellent reason that an animal exposed to infection today will not become ill until a year and a half or two years from today. The agent, whatever it is, can propagate itself in abundance from a few infectious units today to more than a billion next year. I use the phrase "whatever it is" advisedly. Nobody has yet been able to find any DNA or RNA in the scrapie or C-J viruses. It may be there, but if so it exists in amounts too small to detect. Meanwhile, there is plenty of protein, leading to a serious proposal that the virus may indeed be *all* protein. But protein, so far as we know, does not replicate itself all by itself, not on this planet anyway. Looked at this way, the scrapie agent seems the strangest thing in all biology and, until someone in some laboratory figures out what it is, a candidate for Modern Wonder.

My Fifth Wonder is the olfactory receptor cell, located in the epithelial tissue high in the nose, sniffing the air for clues to the environment, the fragrance of friends, the smell of leaf smoke, breakfast, nighttime and bedtime, and a rose, even, it is said, the odor of sanctity. The cell that does all these things, firing off urgent messages into the deepest parts of the brain, switching on one strange unaccountable memory after another, is itself a proper brain cell, a certified neuron belonging to the brain but miles away out in the open air, nosing around the world. How it manages to make sense of what it senses, discriminating between jasmine and anything else non-jasmine with infallibility, is one of the deep secrets of neurobiology. This would be wonder enough, but there is more. This population of brain cells, unlike any other neurons of the vertebrate central nervous system, turns itself over every few weeks; cells wear out, die, and are replaced by brand-new cells rewired to the same deep centers miles back in the brain, sensing and remembering the same wonderful smells. If and when we reach an understanding of these cells and their functions, including the moods and whims under their governance, we will know a lot more about the mind than we do now, a world away.

Sixth on my list is, I hesitate to say, another insect, the termite. This time, though, it is not the single insect that is the Wonder, it is the collectivity. There is nothing at all wonderful about a single, solitary termite, indeed there is really no such creature, functionally speaking, as a lone termite, any more than we can imagine a genuinely solitary human being; no such thing. Two or three termites gathered together on a dish are not much better; they may move about and touch each other nervously, but nothing happens. But keep adding more termites until they reach a critical mass, and then the miracle begins. As though they had suddenly received a piece of extraordinary news, they organize in platoons and begin stacking up pellets to precisely the right height, then turning the arches to connect the columns, constructing the cathedral and its chambers in which the colony will live out its life for the decades ahead, air-conditioned and humidity-controlled, following the chemical blueprint coded in their genes, flawlessly, stone-blind. They are not the dense mass of individual insects they appear to be; they are an organism, a thoughtful, meditative brain on a million legs. All we really know about this new thing is that it does its architecture and engineering by a complex system of chemical signals.

The Seventh Wonder of the modern world is a human child, any child. I used to wonder about childhood and the evolution of our species. It seemed to me unparsimonious to keep expending all that energy on such a long period of vulnerability and defenselessness, with nothing to show for it, in biological terms, beyond the feckless, irresponsible pleasure of childhood. After all, I used to think, it is one sixth of a whole human life span! Why didn't our evolution take care of that, allowing us to jump catlike from our juvenile to our adult (and, as I thought) productive stage of life? I had forgotten about language, the single human trait that marks us out as specifically human, the property that enables our survival as the most compulsively, biologically, obsessively social of all creatures on earth, more interdependent and interconnected even than the famous social insects. I had forgotten that, and forgotten that children *do* that in childhood. Language is what childhood is for.

There is another related but different creature, nothing like so wonderful as a human child, nothing like so hopeful, something to worry about all day and all night. It is *us*, aggregated together in our collective, critical masses. So far, we have learned how to be useful to each other only when we collect in small groups—families, circles of friends, once in a while (although still rarely) committees. The drive to be useful is encoded in our genes. But when we gather in very large numbers, as in the modern nation-state, we seem capable of levels of folly and self-destruction to be found nowhere else in all of Nature.

As a species, taking all in all, we are still too young, too juvenile, to be trusted. We have spread across the face of the earth in just a few thousand years, no time at all as evolution clocks time, covering all livable parts of the planet, endangering other forms of life, and now threatening ourselves. As a species, we have everything in the world to learn about living, but we may be running out of time. Provisionally, but only provisionally, we are a Wonder.

And now the first on my list, the one I put off at the beginning of making a list, the first of all Wonders of the modern world. To name this one, you have to redefine the world as it has indeed been redefined in this most scientific of all centuries. We named the place we live in the *world* long ago, from the Indo-European root *wiros*, which meant man. We now live in the whole universe, that stupefying piece of expanding geometry. Our suburbs are the local solar system, into which, sooner or later, we will spread life, and then, likely, beyond into the galaxy. Of all celestial bodies within reach or view, as far as we can see, out to the edge, the most wonderful and marvelous and mysterious is turning out to be our own planet earth. There is nothing to match it anywhere, not yet anyway.

It is a living system, an immense organism, still developing, regulating itself, making its own oxygen, maintaining its own temperature, keeping all its infinite living parts connected and interdependent, including us. It is the strangest of all places, and there is everything in the world to learn about it. It can keep us awake and jubilant with questions for millennia ahead, if we can learn not to meddle and not to destroy. Our great hope is in being such a young species, thinking in language only a short while, still learning, still growing up.

We are not like the social insects. They have only the one way of doing things and they will do it forever, coded for that way. We are coded differently, not just for binary choices, *go* or *no-go*. We can go four ways at once, depending on how the air feels: *go*, *no-go*, but also *maybe*, plus *what the hell let's give it a try*. We are in for one surprise after another if we keep at it and keep alive. We can build structures for human society never seen before, thoughts never thought before, music never heard before. 17

Provided we do not kill ourselves off, and provided we can connect ourselves by the affection and respect for which I believe our genes are also coded, there is no end to what we might do on or off this planet. 18

At this early stage in our evolution, now through our infancy and into our childhood and then, with luck, our growing up, what our species needs most of all, right now, is simply a future. 19

Rhetorical Analysis

1. Consider Thomas's task, as a writer, with each of the proposed seven new wonders. He must describe each one, since he is writing to a lay audience; and since he is arguing a point, he must show why each phenomenon is so remarkable. Pick one of the wonders between two and seven, and study how Thomas approaches these two rhetorical tasks, and especially how he moves from the one task to the other.
2. The final aim of this essay is neither expository nor argumentative, but hortatory, encouraging readers to commit themselves to a position. In switching to that final purpose, the fourth paragraph and the concluding five paragraphs are crucial. Study them carefully to see how a writer can shift from one rhetorical aim to another within an essay.
3. Thomas enjoys using a metaphor now and then: "Lobby" of a mind and "biodegradable" wonders in ¶ 1, underwater "chimneys" in ¶ 5, beetle "cabinetwork" in ¶ 8 Locate other metaphors. What is their rhetorical effect?
4. Thomas is also fond of etymology, and sometimes exploits root meanings of words without telling the reader. For instance, in ¶ 15, after noting the root of the word "world," he uses the word "geometry" (check its etymology). Can you find other instances? Why does he do this if most readers probably will not notice?

Intellectual Analysis

1. This essay could hardly be more obviously deductive in its construction and logic: Thomas begins with a definition of wonder, and moves on from there. It is also openly argued by example. How, then, does Thomas avoid dullness and at the same time keep the reader intellectually stimulated? Consider these possibilities:
    a. That what he defines ("wonder") cannot actually be defined.
    b. That each example engages us in the unknown, the unexplainable, the mystifying.
    c. That he deliberately confuses his logic by saving his first wonder till last.
    d. That he sprinkles apt metaphors throughout (consider, for example, the extended metaphors in ¶ 16 and in the final paragraph).
2. Why is "wonder" so difficult, though still important, in the modern world?
    a. Consider Thomas's definition of the word. What is there to notice about it?
    b. In discussing *Oncideres*, Thomas claims that the beetle keeps "reminding us how little we know about nature." That would be true for each of his examples, and therefore the statement seems a crucial one. Develop the implications of Thomas's claims. For example, is nature the only thing we know little about?
3. Consider the ordering of the seven wonders. Why, intellectually, would Thomas arrange them that way? Why hold the first for last? What meaning is there to the grouping or progression of them? (For example, you might wish to analyze, and demonstrate, how the last examples include, even subsume, considerations brought up in the earlier ones.)

Suggestions for Writing

1. What are the seven wonders of *your* own world?
2. Analyze, in some manner, the way Thomas's mind works, how it gets caught up in these "wonders." You should keep in mind that Thomas is a scientist and an empiricist, a thinker who bases his view of life primarily on observation and experience.
3. Read the preceding two essays, and write an essay of your own in which you compare the tone and technique of these quite different pieces. Or, read another of his many essays, and analyze it in light of what you have learned about him *as a writer* from these three.

George Orwell

When Eric Blair was eight, he was sent like many middle-class English boys to boarding school, "taken out of the warm nest and flung into a world of force and fraud and secrecy, like a gold-fish into a tank full of pike." His response was to sneak up to the worst of the bullies at St. Cyprian's and bloody his mouth. The act was characteristic. Throughout his short life (1903–1950), Orwell's response to the world at large—which he came to see as not much different from St. Cyprian's, "a civilization founded on greed and fear"—was not only direct but essentially fearless.

In Burma, where after schooling he worked for five years in the Indian Civil Service, he once sallied out to hunt tigers at night in an oxcart and armed only with a Luger pistol and a borrowed shotgun. Later, alone and out of money in Paris, he kept at his writing apprenticeship by living in the poorest slums and working as a hotel dishwasher. Back in England, determined to write truthfully about the poor, he set out for weeks at a time to live as a tramp or a migrant worker, in rags and with only a few shillings. In 1937 he pawned his share of the family silver to go fight against the Fascists in Spain (eventually he was shot through the throat because he would not trouble to bend over when walking the trenches).

Bluff courage is not only a hallmark of his actions but of his writing as well. It shows up in his opinions, where he is unafraid to take the most unpopular positions if he feels they are right, for instance arguing in print during World War II that the patriotism of himself and other Britishers was probably based in part on "childish" attachments, or that the bombing of civilians is no more unjust than the bombing of soldiers. It also shows up in his famous style, forthright and clean, shorn of what he loved to call "humbug." As he said, "To write in plain, vigorous language, one has to think fearlessly." All his autobiographical works, which are perhaps the best place to begin reading him—Such, Such Were the Joys, Down and Out in Paris and London, Homage to Catalonia—were edited by his publishers for fear of libel, and he took on his pen name, George Orwell, to protect his family.

But perhaps it is well to remember that the George Orwell famed for exposure of "force and fraud and secrecy" in the world of adult politics (Animal Farm, Nineteen Eighty-Four) also loved simple things, and wrote with affection about the appearance of spring frogs and the making of a good cup of tea. That too takes a kind of courage. "I have a sort of belly-to-earth attitude," he wrote in a letter, "and always feel uneasy when I get away from the ordinary world where grass is green, stones hard." The Orwell is a country stream he was fond of.

A Hanging

*I*t was in Burma, a sodden morning of the rains. A sickly light, like yellow tinfoil, was slanting over the high walls into the jail yard. We were waiting outside the condemned cells, a row of sheds fronted with double bars, like small animal cages. Each cell measured about ten feet by ten and was quite bare within except for a plank bed and a pot of drinking water. In some of them brown silent men were squatting at the inner bars, with their blankets draped round them. These were the condemned men, due to be hanged within the next week or two.

1

One prisoner had been brought out of his cell. He was a Hindu, a puny wisp of a man, with a shaven head and vague liquid eyes. He had a thick, sprouting moustache, absurdly too big for his body, rather like the moustache of a comic man on the films. Six tall Indian warders

2

were guarding him and getting him ready for the gallows. Two of them stood by with rifles and fixed bayonets, while the others handcuffed him, passed a chain through his handcuffs and fixed it to their belts, and lashed his arms tight to his sides. They crowded very close about him, with their hands always on him in a careful, caressing grip, as though all the while feeling him to make sure he was there. It was like men handling a fish which is still alive and may jump back into the water. But he stood quite unresisting, yielding his arms limply to the ropes, as though he hardly noticed what was happening.

Eight o'clock struck and a bugle call, desolately thin in the wet air, floated from the distant barracks. The superintendent of the jail, who was standing apart from the rest of us, moodily prodding the gravel with his stick, raised his head at the sound. He was an army doctor, with a grey toothbrush moustache and a gruff voice. "For God's sake hurry up, Francis," he said irritably. "The man ought to have been dead by this time. Aren't you ready yet?"

Francis, the head jailer, a fat Dravidian in a white drill suit and gold spectacles, waved his black hand. "Yes sir, yes sir," he bubbled. "All iss satisfactorily prepared. The hangman iss waiting. We shall proceed."

"Well, quick march, then. The prisoners can't get their breakfast till this job's over."

We set out for the gallows. Two warders marched on either side of the prisoner, with their rifles at the slope; two others marched close against him, gripping him by arm and shoulder, as though at once pushing and supporting him. The rest of us, magistrates and the like, followed behind. Suddenly, when we had gone ten yards, the procession stopped short without any order or warning. A dreadful thing had happened—a dog, come goodness knows whence, had appeared in the yard. It came bounding among us with a loud volley of barks, and leapt round us wagging its whole body, wild with glee at finding so many human beings together. It was a large woolly dog, half Airedale, half pariah. For a moment it pranced round us, and then, before anyone could stop it, it had made a dash for the prisoner, and jumping up tried to lick his face. Everyone stood aghast, too taken aback even to grab at the dog.

"Who let that bloody brute in here?" said the superintendent angrily. "Catch it, someone!"

A warder, detached from the escort, charged clumsily after the dog, but it danced and gambolled just out of his reach, taking everything as part of the game. A young Eurasian jailer picked up a handful of gravel and tried to stone the dog away, but it dodged the stones and came after us again. Its yaps echoed from the jail walls. The prisoner, in the grasp of the two warders, looked on incuriously, as though this was another formality of the hanging. It was several minutes before someone managed to catch the dog. Then we put my handkerchief through its collar and moved off once more, with the dog still straining and whimpering.

It was about forty yards to the gallows. I watched the bare brown back of the prisoner marching in front of me. He walked clumsily with his bound arms, but quite steadily, with that bobbing gait of the Indian who never straightens his knees. At each step his muscles slid neatly into place, the lock of hair on his scalp danced up and down, his feet printed themselves on the wet gravel. And once, in spite of the men who gripped him by each shoulder, he stepped slightly aside to avoid a puddle on the path.

It is curious, but till that moment I had never realised what it means to destroy a healthy, conscious man. When I saw the prisoner step aside to avoid the puddle, I saw the mystery, the unspeakable wrongness, of cutting a life short when it is in full tide. This man was not dying, he was alive just as we were alive. All the organs of his body were working—bowels digesting food, skin renewing itself, nails growing, tissues forming—all toiling away in solemn foolery. His nails would still be growing when he stood on the drop, when he was falling through the air with a tenth of a second to live. His eyes saw the yellow gravel and the grey walls, and his brain still remembered, foresaw, reasoned—reasoned even about puddles. He and we were a party of men walking together, seeing, hearing, feeling, understanding the same world; and in two minutes, with a sudden snap, one of us would be gone—one mind less, one world less.

The gallows stood in a small yard, separate from the main grounds of the prison, and overgrown with tall prickly weeds. It was a brick erection like three sides of a shed, with planking on top, and above that two beams and a crossbar with the rope dangling. The hangman, a grey-haired convict in the white uniform of the prison, was waiting beside his machine. He greeted us with a servile crouch as we entered. At a word from Francis the two warders, gripping the prisoner more closely than ever, half led, half pushed him to the gallows and helped him clumsily up the ladder. Then the hangman climbed up and fixed the rope round the prisoner's neck.

We stood waiting, five yards away. The warders had formed in a rough circle round the gallows. And then, when the noose was fixed, the prisoner began crying out on his god. It was a high, reiterated cry of "Ram! Ram! Ram! Ram!", not urgent and fearful like a prayer or a cry for help, but steady, rhythmical, almost like the tolling of a bell. The dog answered the sound with a whine. The hangman, still standing on the gallows, produced a small cotton bag like a flour bag and drew it down over the prisoner's face. But the sound, muffled by the cloth, still persisted, over and over again: "Ram! Ram! Ram! Ram! Ram!"

The hangman climbed down and stood ready, holding the lever. Minutes seemed to pass. The steady, muffled crying from the prisoner went on and on, "Ram! Ram! Ram!" never faltering for an instant. The superintendent, his head on his chest, was slowly poking the ground with his stick; perhaps he was counting the cries, allowing the prisoner a fixed number—fifty, perhaps, or a hundred. Everyone had changed colour. The Indians had gone grey like bad coffee, and one or two of the bayonets were wavering. We looked at the lashed, hooded man on the drop, and listened to his cries—each cry another second of life; the same thought was in all our minds: oh, kill him quickly, get it over, stop that abominable noise!

Suddenly the superintendent made up his mind. Throwing up his head he made a swift motion with his stick. "Chalo!" he shouted almost fiercely.

There was a clanking noise, and then dead silence. The prisoner had vanished, and the rope was twisting on itself. I let go of the dog, and it galloped immediately to the back of the gallows; but when it got there it stopped short, barked, and then retreated into a corner of the yard, where it stood among the weeds, looking timorously out at us. We went round the gallows to inspect the prisoner's body. He was dangling with his toes pointed straight downwards, very slowly revolving, as dead as a stone.

The superintendent reached out with his stick and poked the bare body; it oscillated, slightly. "*He's* all right," said the superintendent. He backed out from under the gallows, and blew out a deep breath. The moody look had gone out of his face quite suddenly. He glanced at his wrist-watch. "Eight minutes past eight. Well, that's all for this morning, thank God."

The warders unfixed bayonets and marched away. The dog, sobered and conscious of having misbehaved itself, slipped after them. We walked out of the gallows yard, past the condemned cells with their waiting prisoners, into the big central yard of the prison. The convicts, under the command of warders armed with lathis, were already receiving their breakfast. They squatted in long rows, each man holding a tin pannikin, while two warders with buckets marched round ladling out rice; it seemed quite a homely, jolly scene, after the hanging. An enormous relief had come upon us now that the job was done. One felt an impulse to sing, to break into a run, to snigger. All at once everyone began chattering gaily.

The Eurasian boy walking beside me nodded towards the way we had come, with a knowing smile: "Do you know, sir, our friend (he meant the dead man), when he heard his appeal had been dismissed, he pissed on the floor of his cell. From fright.—Kindly take one of my cigarettes, sir. Do you not admire my new silver case, sir? From the boxwallah, two rupees eight annas. Classy European style."

Several people laughed—at what, nobody seemed certain.

Francis was walking by the superintendent, talking garrulously: "Well, sir, all hass passed off with the utmost satisfactoriness. It wass all finished—flick! like that. It iss not always so—oah, no! I have known cases where the doctor wass obliged to go beneath the gallows and pull the prisoner's legs to ensure decease. Most disagreeable!"

"Wriggling about, eh? That's bad," said the superintendent.

"Ach, sir, it iss worse when they become refractory! One man, I recall, clung to the bars of hiss cage when we went to take him out. You will scarcely credit, sir, that it took six warders to dislodge him, three pulling at each leg. We reasoned with him. 'My dear fellow,' we said, 'think of all the pain and trouble you are causing to us!' But no, he would not listen! Ach, he wass very troublesome!"

I found that I was laughing quite loudly. Everyone was laughing. Even the superintendent grinned in a tolerant way. "You'd better all come out and have a drink," he said quite genially. "I've got a bottle of whisky in the car. We could do with it."

We went through the big double gates of the prison, into the road. "Pulling at his legs!" exclaimed a Burmese magistrate suddenly, and burst into a loud chuckling. We all began laughing again. At that moment Francis's anecdote seemed extraordinarily funny. We all had a drink together, native and European alike, quite amicably. The dead man was a hundred yards away.

Rhetorical Analysis

1. There is biographical evidence that "A Hanging" may be fictional. Friends of Orwell twice reported that he told them "it was only a story."
   a. What details of this piece strike you as fictional, as made up?
   b. What rhetorical effects assist you in making that judgment—implausibility, inappropriateness, staginess? Remember that Orwell worked five years as a civil servant in Burma and knew the country well.
2. On the other hand, twice Orwell wrote that he had once "watched a man hanged." In one place he added, "it seemed to me worse than a thousand murders," and in the other, "There was no question that everybody concerned knew this to be a dreadful, unnatural action."
   a. Fiction is not falsehood, as the old proverb goes. Take one of Orwell's two comments as a truth that "A Hanging" intends to make the reader understand. How do the "fictional" parts you have identified (see above) serve to communicate that truth? *Rhetorically*, do they function any differently than those parts you feel are nonfictional?
   b. Fiction or nonfiction, the piece mainly operates on a purely descriptive level, *showing* events without *telling* the reader explicitly what they may mean. Take again one of Orwell's two comments quoted above as an implicit point, and analyze how he makes that point without doing so explicitly. What are the advantages in writing this way?
3. In ¶ 2, Orwell mentions films, and his essay moves rather cinematically: motion (starting and stopping) and color and setting are all realized, but the speaking voice is at a distance, observing.
   a. What is conditioning the essay to be built this way? Keep in mind that this essay is both a reminiscence and an act of discovery.
   b. Compare other essays of reminiscence (for example, those by Welty and Walker) to see if certain cinematic qualities affect meaning in similar ways.

Intellectual Analysis

1. The center of gravity in this essay is ¶ 10, where Orwell comes upon his own moral awareness.
   a. Examine the implications of that paragraph, paying particular attention to the last sentence; why "one world less"?
   b. What is the "unspeakable wrongness" which Orwell tries to articulate here? What does it tell us about his values?
   c. Orwell's central preception may be the miraculous difference between life and death. Consider that possibility (and you may want to compare a similar point in Eiseley's "Judgment of the Birds," or Dinesen's "The Iguana").
2. Many surprising and ironic developments cut across this somber procedure. Discuss the following.

a. The dog is conspicuous for his bounding about, his raw and friendly freedom. What else?
b. The commentary offered by "Francis, the head jailer" is strange in its tone and effect. What does his presence add to the meaning?
c. The completely ironic feeling of relief after the hanging has to be accounted for. How? Does Orwell give any clues?
d. Behind the whole essay, there may be a larger surprise: the irony of colonialism. Think of the phrase "Classy European style" in ¶ 18. Orwell says elsewhere that he left the Civil Service because he realized that colonialism was a "racket." Would that pertain here?
e. What other ironic details are there?

Suggestions for Writing

1. Recount a personal experience, as complete and as richly detailed as "A Hanging," crafting it so that it makes a point without ever explicitly telling the reader what the point is.
2. This writing assignment can be done only after you have finished Suggestion 1. Scrutinize your piece very carefully. Are parts of it fictional? Have you added anything, exaggerated, omitted, emphasized? The results of such scrutiny could well form the subject of another, perhaps shorter, essay.
3. At the end of "Politics and the English Language," Orwell gives six rules to be observed in good prose. Apply these terms for good writing to Orwell's own writing here. Does he meet his own standards?

AS I PLEASE

Miss Vera Brittain's pamphlet, *Seed of Chaos*, is an eloquent attack on indiscriminate or "obliteration" bombing. "Owing to the RAF raids," she says, "thousands of helpless and innocent people in German, Italian and German-occupied cities are being subjected to agonising forms of death and injury comparable to the worst tortures of the Middle Ages." Various well-known opponents of bombing, such as General Franco and Major-General Fuller, are brought out in support of this. Miss Brittain is not, however, taking the pacifist standpoint. She is willing and anxious to win the war, apparently. She merely wishes us to stick to "legitimate" methods of war and abandon civilian bombing, which she fears will blacken our reputation in the eyes of posterity. Her pamphlet is issued by the Bombing Restriction Committee, which has issued others with similar titles.

Now, no one in his senses regards bombing, or any other operation of war, with anything but disgust. On the other hand, no decent person cares tuppence for the opinion of posterity. And there is something very distasteful in accepting war as an instrument and at the same time wanting to dodge responsibility for its more obviously barbarous features. Pacifism is a tenable position, provided that you are willing to take the consequences. But all talk of "limiting" or "humanising" war is sheer humbug, based on the fact that the average human being never bothers to examine catchwords.

The catchwords used in this connection are "killing civilians", "massacre of women and children" and "destruction of our cultural heritage". It is tacitly assumed that air bombing does more of this kind of thing than ground warfare.

When you look a bit closer, the first question that strikes you is: Why is it worse to kill civilians than soldiers? Obviously one must not kill children if it is in any way avoidable, but it is only in propaganda pamphlets that every bomb drops on a school or an orphanage. A bomb kills a cross-section of the population; but not quite a representative selection, because the children and expectant mothers are usually the first to be evacuated, and some of the young men will be away in the army. Probably a disproportionately large number of bomb victims will be middle-aged. (Up to date, German bombs have killed between six and seven thousand children in this country. This is, I believe, less than the number killed in road accidents in the same period.) On the other hand, "normal" or "legitimate" warfare picks out and slaughters all the healthiest and bravest of the young male population. Every time a German submarine goes to the bottom about fifty young men of fine physique and good nerve are suffocated. Yet people who would hold up their hands at the very words "civilian bombing" will repeat with satisfaction such phrases as "We are winning the Battle of the Atlantic". Heaven knows how many people our blitz on Germany and the occupied countries has killed and will kill, but you can be quite certain it will never come anywhere near the slaughter that has happened on the Russian front.

War is not avoidable at this stage of history, and since it has to happen it does not seem to me a bad thing that others should be killed besides young men. I wrote in 1937: "Sometimes it is a comfort to me to think that the aeroplane is altering the conditions of war. Perhaps when the next great war comes we may see that sight unprecedented in all history, a jingo with a bullet hole in him." We haven't yet seen that (it is perhaps a contradiction in terms), but at any rate the suffering of this war has been shared out more evenly than the last one was. The immunity of the civilian, one of the things that have made war possible, has been shattered. Unlike Miss Brittain, I don't regret that. I can't feel that war is "humanised" by being confined to the slaughter of the young and becomes "barbarous" when the old get killed as well.

As to international agreements to "limit" war, they are never kept when it pays to break them. Long before the last war the nations had agreed not to use gas, but they used it all the same. This time they have refrained, merely because gas is comparatively ineffective in a war of movement, while its use against civilian populations would be sure to provoke reprisals in kind. Against an enemy who can't hit back, e.g. the Abyssinians, it is used readily enough. War is of its nature barbarous, it is better to admit that. If we see ourselves as the savages we are, some improvement is possible, or at least thinkable.

6

[May 19, 1944]

Rhetorical Analysis

1. Orwell's acquaintances remembered him, even in his teens, as being remarkably eager to listen to all sides of an issue. Where is that trait evident in "As I Please"?
    a. How does Orwell present the views of his intellectual adversary, Vera Brittain? Is his treatment of her position fair? He begins, for instance, by calling her pamphlet "eloquent." Does this compliment hinder or help his own argument?
    b. In ¶ 4 Orwell admits that "one must not kill children if it is any way avoidable," an important qualification of his major premise that everyone should bear the brunt of war. Find other hedges. Do these undercut or assist Orwell in persuading the reader?
2. "As I Please" was the title of Orwell's weekly column in the British newspaper *Tribune*. This selection offers straightforward argumentation, presenting the author very much as a public debater.
    a. A classic debate maneuver is refutation, in which one cites an opponent's assertion and proves it untrue or illogical. Which assertions of Vera Brittain does Orwell tackle, and how does he refute them?

b. Another classic debate maneuver is to base one's own assertions on accepted grounds of belief. Technically this is known as an "appeal." For instance, when Orwell argues in ¶ 5 that "the suffering of this war has been shared out more evenly than the last one was," his appeal is to custom, namely to the common assumption that burdens should be equally distributed. There are, of course, many different kinds of appeals—to emotion, to patriotism, to pragmatism, and so on. What kinds does Orwell choose? Why?

Intellectual Analysis

1. This essay is not so much a book review as a philosophical response to a pamphlet. (To appreciate the difference, compare this essay with Alice Walker's "Nuclear Madness.") Thus, Orwell's own ideas are more prominent than those of his adversary.
    a. Check closely the *assertions* in ¶ 2. How well grounded are these? Are they simply rapid-fire *opinions*? Are they valid *assumptions*?
    b. Throughout the essay there seem to be two underlying assumptions. Are they contradictory or complementary?
        (1) Orwell's position on pacificism: what is it? (See ¶s 2, 5, and 6.)
        (2) Orwell's acceptance of war: how does Orwell convey this? (See ¶s 2 and 4.)
2. Throughout the essay, Orwell also assumes *this* war to be different, largely due to the role of the airplane. Gather together his statements to this effect and discuss their implications for the role of technology in history. Bring his claim up to date.
3. Orwell's technique here is to "examine catchwords."
    a. During the rest of the essay, does he fulfill the bargain he implicitly makes in ¶ 3?
    b. Out of this focus on catchwords, a connection with Orwell's "Politics and the English Language" can be drawn. What is it?
4. On the surface, Orwell's argument and stance here seem an outrage. How does he then avoid being outrageous? Consider carefully the argument in ¶ 5 (making sure you know what "jingo" means). Is Orwell's position here, that the immunity of civilians helps make war possible, still true today?

Suggestions for Writing

1. This "As I Please" piece appeared during World War II (1944). Write a letter to the editor of your own newspaper in which you respond to it as though it appeared in yesterday's edition.
2. Orwell concludes this piece with the demand that we see ourselves as the savages we truly are, and that we must work for improvement. Elsewhere, he has written: "Man is not a Yahoo, but he is rather like a Yahoo and needs to be reminded of it

from time to time." Write a review of a news item in any good daily newspaper and make use of Orwell's contention. (Remember his direction in "Politics and the English Language" to the effect that we must write clearly enough so that if we say a stupid thing we will realize it to be stupid.)
3. Find an argument in print and write an essay opposing it, as vigorously as you can.

POLITICS AND THE ENGLISH LANGUAGE

*M*ost people who bother with the matter at all would admit that the English language is in a bad way, but it is generally assumed that we cannot by conscious action do anything about it. Our civilisation is decadent, and our language—so the argument runs—must inevitably share in the general collapse. It follows that any struggle against the abuse of language is a sentimental archaism, like preferring candles to electric light or hansom cabs to aeroplanes. Underneath this lies the half-conscious belief that language is a natural growth and not an instrument which we shape for our own purposes.

Now, it is clear that the decline of a language must ultimately have political and economic causes: it is not due simply to the bad influence of this or that individual writer. But an effect can become a cause, reinforcing the original cause and producing the same effect in an intensified form, and so on indefinitely. A man may take to drink because he feels himself to be a failure, and then fail all the more completely because he drinks. It is rather the same thing that is happening to the English language. It becomes ugly and inaccurate because our thoughts are foolish, but the slovenliness of our language makes it easier for us to have foolish thoughts. The point is that the process is reversible. Modern English, especially written English, is full of bad habits which spread by imitation and which can be avoided if one is willing to take the necessary trouble. If one gets rid of these habits one can think more clearly, and to think clearly is a necessary first step towards political regeneration: so that the fight against bad English is not frivolous and is not the exclusive concern of professional writers. I will come back to this presently, and I hope that by that time the meaning of what I have said here will have become clearer.

Meanwhile, here are five specimens of the English language as it is now habitually written.

These five passages haved not been picked out because they are especially bad—I could have quoted far worse if I had chosen—but because they illustrate various of the mental vices from which we now suffer. They are a little below the average, but are fairly representative samples. I number them so that I can refer back to them when necessary:

3

> 1. I am not, indeed, sure whether it is not true to say that the Milton who once seemed not unlike a seventeenth-century Shelley had not become, out of an experience ever more bitter in each year, more alien (sic) to the founder of that Jesuit sect which nothing could induce him to tolerate.
> Professor Harold Laski (Essay in *Freedom of Expression*).

> 2. Above all, we cannot play ducks and drakes with a native battery of idioms which prescribes such egregious collocations of vocables as the Basic *put up* for *tolerate* or *put at a loss* for *bewilder*.
> Professor Lancelot Hogben (*Interglossa*).

> 3. On the one side we have the free personality: by definition it is not neurotic, for it has neither conflict nor dream. Its desires, such as they are, are transparent, for they are just what institutional approval keeps in the forefront of consciousness; another institutional pattern would alter their number and intensity; there is little in them that is natural, irreducible, or culturally dangerous. But *on the other side*, the social bond itself is nothing but the mutual reflection of these self-secure integrities. Recall the definition of love. Is not this the very picture of a small academic? Where is there a place in this hall of mirrors for either personality or fraternity?
> Essay on psychology in *Politics* (New York).

> 4. All the "best people" from the gentlemen's clubs, and all the frantic Fascist captains, united in common hatred of Socialism and bestial horror of the rising tide of the mass revolutionary movement, have turned to acts of provocation, to foul incendiarism, to medieval legends of poisoned wells, to legalise their own destruction to proletarian orga-

nisations, and rouse the agitated petty-bourgeoisie to chauvinistic fervour on behalf of the fight against the revolutionary way out of the crisis.

Communist pamphlet.

5. If a new spirit *is* to be infused into this old country, there is one thorny and contentious reform which must be tackled, and that is the humanisation and galvanisation of the BBC. Timidity here will bespeak canker and atrophy of the soul. The heart of Britain may be sound and of strong beat, for instance, but the British lion's roar at present is like that of Bottom in Shakespeare's *Midsummer Night's Dream*—as gentle as any sucking dove. A virile new Britain cannot continue indefinitely to be traduced in the eyes, or rather ears, of the world by the effete languors of Langham Place, brazenly masquerading as "standard English". When the Voice of Britain is heard at nine o'clock, better far and infinitely less ludicrous to hear aitches honestly dropped than the present priggish, inflated, inhibited, school-ma'amish arch braying of blameless bashful mewing maidens!

Letter in *Tribune*.

Each of these passages has faults of its own, but, quite apart from avoidable ugliness, two qualities are common to all of them. The first is staleness of imagery: the other is lack of precision. The writer either has a meaning and cannot express it, or he inadvertently says something else, or he is almost indifferent as to whether his words mean anything or not. This mixture of vagueness and sheer incompetence is the most marked characteristic of modern English prose, and especially of any kind of political writing. As soon as certain topics are raised, the concrete melts into the abstract and no one seems able to think of turns of speech that are not hackneyed: prose consists less and less of *words* chosen for the sake of their meaning, and more of *phrases* tacked together like the sections of a prefabricated hen-house. I list below, with notes and examples, various of the tricks by means of which the work of prose construction is habitually dodged:

Dying metaphors. A newly invented metaphor assists thought by evoking a visual image, while on the other hand a metaphor which is technically "dead" (e.g. *iron resolution*) has in effect reverted to being an ordinary word and can generally be used without loss of vividness. But in between these two classes there is a huge dump of worn-out metaphors which have lost all evocative power and are merely used because they save people the trouble of inventing phrases for themselves. Examples are: *Ring the changes on, take up the cudgels for, toe the line, ride roughshod over, stand shoulder to shoulder with, play into the hands of, no axe to grind, grist to the mill, fishing in troubled waters, rift within the lute, on the order of the day, Achilles' heel, swan song, hotbed.* Many of these are used without knowledge of their meaning (what is a "rift", for instance?), and incompatible metaphors are frequently mixed, a sure sign that the writer is not interested in what he is saying. Some metaphors now current have been twisted out of their original meaning without those who use them even being aware of the fact. For example, *toe the line* is sometimes written *tow the line*. Another example is *the hammer and the anvil*, now always used with the implication that the anvil gets the worst of it. In real life it is always the anvil that breaks the hammer, never the other way about: a writer who stopped to think what he was saying would be aware of this, and would avoid perverting the original phrase.

Operators, or *verbal false limbs*. These save the trouble of picking out appropriate verbs and nouns, and at the same time pad each sentence with extra syllables which give it an appearance of symmetry. Characteristic phrases are: *render inoperative, militate against, prove unacceptable, make contact with, be subjected to, give rise to, give grounds for, have the effect of, play a leading part (rôle) in, make itself felt, take effect, exhibit a tendency to, serve the purpose of,* etc etc. The keynote is the elimination of simple verbs. Instead of being a single word, such as *break, stop, spoil, mend, kill,* a verb becomes a *phrase*, made up of a noun or adjective tacked on to some general-purposes verb such as *prove, serve, form, play, render*. In addition, the passive voice is wherever possible used in preference to the active, and noun constructions are used instead of gerunds (*by examination of* instead of *by examining*). The range of verbs is further cut down by means of the *-ise* and *de-* formations, and banal statements are given an appearance of profundity by means of the *not un-* formation. Simple conjunctions and prepositions are replaced by such phrases as *with respect to, having regard to, the fact that, by dint of, in view of, in the interests of, on the hypothesis that*; and the ends of sentences are saved from anticlimax by such resounding commonplaces as *greatly to be desired, cannot be left out of account, a development to be expected in the near future, deserving of serious consideration, brought to a satisfactory conclusion,* and so on and so forth.

6

Pretentious diction. Words like *phenomenon, element, individual* (as noun), *objective, categorical, effective, virtual, basic, primary, promote, constitute, exhibit, exploit, utilise, eliminate, liquidate,* are used to dress up simple statements and give an air of scientific impartiality to biassed judgements. Adjectives like *epoch-making, epic, historic, unforgettable, triumphant, age-old, inevitable, inexorable, veritable,* are used to dignify the sordid processes of international politics, while writing that aims at glorifying war usually takes on an archaic colour, its characteristic words being: *realm, throne, chariot, mailed fist, trident, sword, shield, buckler, banner, jackboot, clarion.* Foreign words and expressions such as *cul de sac, ancien régime, deus ex machina, mutatis mutandis, status quo, Gleichschaltung, Weltanschauung,* are used to give an air of culture and elegance. Except for the useful abbreviations *i.e., e.g.,* and *etc,* there is no real need for any of the hundreds of foreign phrases now current in English. Bad writers, and especially scientific, political and sociological writers, are nearly always haunted by the notion that Latin or Greek words are grander than Saxon ones, and unnecessary words like *expedite, ameliorate, predict, extraneous, deracinated, clandestine, sub-aqueous* and hundreds of others constantly gain ground from their Anglo-Saxon opposite numbers.[1] The jargon peculiar to Marxist writing (*hyena, hangman, cannibal, petty bourgeois, these gentry, lacquey, flunkey, mad dog, White Guard,* etc) consists largely of words and phrases translated from Russian, German or French; but the normal way of coining a new word is to use a Latin or Greek root with the appropriate affix and, where necessary, the *-ise* formation. It is often easier to make up words of this kind (*deregionalise, impermissible, extramarital, non-fragmentatory* and so forth) than to think up the English words that will cover one's meaning. The result, in general, is an increase in slovenliness and vagueness.

7

Meaningless words. In certain kinds of writing, particularly in art criticism and literary criticism, it is normal to come across long

8

---

1. An interesting illustration of this is the way in which the English flower names which were in use till very recently are being ousted by Greek ones, *snapdragon* becoming *antirrhinum, forget-me-not* becoming *myosotis,* etc. It is hard to see any practical reason for this change of fashion: it is probably due to an instinctive turning-away from the more homely word and a vague feeling that the Greek word is scientific. [Author's footnote.]

passages which are almost completely lacking in meaning.² Words like *romantic, plastic, values, human, dead, sentimental, natural, vitality*, as used in art criticism, are strictly meaningless, in the sense that they not only do not point to any discoverable object, but are hardly even expected to do so by the reader. When one critic writes, "The outstanding features of Mr. X's work is its living quality", while another writes, "The immediately striking thing about Mr. X's work is its peculiar deadness", the reader accepts this as a simple difference of opinion. If words like *black* and *white* were involved, instead of the jargon words *dead* and *living*, he would see at once that language was being used in an improper way. Many political words are similarly abused. The word *Fascism* has now no meaning except in so far as it signifies "something not desirable". The words *democracy, socialism, freedom, patriotic, realistic, justice*, have each of them several different meanings which cannot be reconciled with one another. In the case of a word like *democracy*, not only is there no agreed definition, but the attempt to make one is resisted from all sides. It is almost universally felt that when we call a country democratic we are praising it: consequently the defenders of every kind of régime claim that it is a democracy, and fear that they might have to stop using the word if it were tied down to any one meaning. Words of this kind are often used in a consciously dishonest way. That is, the person who uses them has his own private definition, but allows his hearer to think he means something quite different. Statements like *Marshal Pétain was a true patriot, The Soviet press is the freest in the world, The Catholic Church is opposed to persecution*, are almost always made with intent to deceive. Other words used in variable meanings, in most cases more or less dishonestly, are: *class, totalitarian, science, progressive, reactionary, bourgeois, equality*.

Now that I have made this catalogue of swindles and perversions, let me give another example of the kind of writing that they lead to. This time it must of its nature be an imaginary one. I am going to

---

2. Example: "Comfort's catholicity of perception and image, strangely Whitmanesque in range, almost the exact opposite in aesthetic compulsion, continues to evoke that trembling atmospheric accumulative hinting at a cruel, an inexorably serene timelessness ... Wrey Gardiner scores by aiming at simple bullseyes with precision. Only they are not so simple, and through this contented sadness runs more than the surface bitter-sweet of resignation." (*Poetry Quarterly*.) [Author's footnote.]

translate a passage of good English into modern English of the worst sort. Here is a well-known verse from *Ecclesiastes*:

> I returned, and saw under the sun, that the race is not to the swift, nor the battle to the strong, neither yet bread to the wise, nor yet riches to men of understanding, nor yet favour to men of skill; but time and chance happeneth to them all.

Here it is in modern English:

> Objective consideration of contemporary phenomena compels the conclusion that success or failure in competitive activities exhibits no tendency to be commensurate with innate capacity, but that a considerable element of the unpredictable must invariably be taken into account.

This is a parody, but not a very gross one. Exhibit 3, above, for instance, contains several patches of the same kind of English. It will be seen that I have not made a full translation. The beginning and ending of the sentence follow the original meaning fairly closely, but in the middle the concrete illustrations—race, battle, bread—dissolve into the vague phrase "success or failure in competitive activities". This had to be so, because no modern writer of the kind I am discussing—no one capable of using phrases like "objective consideration of contemporary phenomena"—would ever tabulate his thoughts in that precise and detailed way. The whole tendency of modern prose is away from concreteness. Now analyse these two sentences a little more closely. The first contains 49 words but only 60 syllables, and all its words are those of everyday life. The second contains 38 words of 90 syllables: 18 of its words are from Latin roots, and one from Greek. The first sentence contains six vivid images, and only one phrase ("time and chance") that could be called vague. The second contains not a single fresh, arresting phrase, and in spite of its 90 syllables it gives only a shortened version of the meaning contained in the first. Yet without a doubt it is the second kind of sentence that is gaining ground in modern English. I do not want to exaggerate. This kind of writing is not yet universal, and outcrops of simplicity will occur here and there in the worst-written page. Still, if you or I were told to write a few lines on the uncertainty of human fortunes, we should probably come much nearer to my imaginary sentence than to the one from *Ecclesiastes*.

As I have tried to show, modern writing at its worst does not consist in picking out words for the sake of their meaning and inventing images in order to make the meaning clearer. It consists in gumming together long strips of words which have already been set in order by someone else, and making the results presentable by sheer humbug. The attraction of this way of writing is that it is easy. It is easier—even quicker, once you have the habit—to say *In my opinion it is a not unjustifiable assumption that* than to say *I think*. If you use ready-made phrases, you not only don't have to hunt about for words; you also don't have to bother with the rhythms of your sentences, since these phrases are generally so arranged as to be more or less euphonious. When you are composing in a hurry—when you are dictating to a stenographer, for instance, or making a public speech—it is natural to fall into a pretentious, latinised style. Tags like *a consideration which we should do well to bear in mind* or *a conclusion to which all of us would readily assent* will save many a sentence from coming down with a bump. By using stale metaphors, similes and idioms, you save much mental effort, at the cost of leaving your meaning vague, not only for your reader but for yourself. This is the significance of mixed metaphors. The sole aim of a metaphor is to call up a visual image. When these images clash—as in *The Fascist octopus has sung its swan song, the jackboot is thrown into the melting-pot*—it can be taken as certain that the writer is not seeing a mental image of the objects he is naming; in other words he is not really thinking. Look again at the examples I gave at the beginning of this essay. Professor Laski (1) uses five negatives in 53 words. One of these is superfluous, making nonsense of the whole passage, and in addition there is the slip *alien* for akin, making further nonsense, and several avoidable pieces of clumsiness which increase the general vagueness. Professor Hogben (2) plays ducks and drakes with a battery which is able to write prescriptions, and, while disapproving of the everyday phrase *put up with*, is unwilling to look *egregious* up in the dictionary and see what it means. (3), if one takes an uncharitable attitude towards it, is simply meaningless: probably one could work out its intended meaning by reading the whole of the article in which it occurs. In (4) the writer knows more or less what he wants to say, but an accumulation of stale phrases chokes him like tea-leaves blocking a sink. In (5) words and meaning have almost parted company. People who write in this manner usually have a general emotional meaning—they dislike one thing and want to express solidarity with another—but they are not interested in the detail of what they are saying. A scrupulous writer, in every sentence that he writes, will ask himself at least four questions, thus: What am I trying to say? What words will express it? What image or idiom will make it clearer? Is this image fresh enough to have an effect? And he will probably ask himself two more: Could I put it more shortly? Have I said anything that is avoidably ugly? But you are not obliged to go to all this trouble. You can shirk it by simply throwing your mind open and letting the ready-made phrases come crowding in. They will construct your sentences for you—even think your thoughts for you, to a certain extent—and at need they will perform the important service of partially concealing your meaning even from yourself. It is at this point that the special connection between politics and the debasement of language becomes clear.

In our time it is broadly true that political writing is bad writing. Where it is not true, it will generally be found that the writer is some kind of rebel, expressing his private opinions, and not a "party line". Orthodoxy, of whatever colour, seems to demand a lifeless, imitative style. The political dialects to be found in pamphlets, leading articles, manifestos, White Papers and the speeches of Under-Secretaries do, of course, vary from party to party, but they are all alike in that one almost never finds in them a fresh, vivid, home-made turn of speech. When one watches some tired hack on the platform mechanically repeating the familiar phrases—*bestial atrocities, iron heel, bloodstained tyranny, free peoples of the world, stand shoulder to shoulder*—one often has a curious feeling that one is not watching a live human being but some kind of dummy: a feeling which suddenly becomes stronger at moments when the light catches the speaker's spectacles and turns them into blank discs which seem to have no eyes behind them. And this is not altogether fanciful. A speaker who uses that kind of phraseology has gone some distance towards turning himself into a machine. The appropriate noises are coming out of his larynx, but his brain is not involved as it would be if he were choosing his words for himself. If the speech he is making is one that he is accustomed to make over and over again, he may be almost unconscious of what he is saying, as one is when one utters the responses in church. And this reduced state of consciousness, if not indispensable, is at any rate favourable to political conformity.

In our time, political speech and writing are largely the defence of the indefensible. Things like the continuance of British rule in India, the Russian purges and deportations, the dropping of the atom bombs on Japan, can indeed be defended, but only by arguments which are too brutal for most people to face, and which do not square with the professed aims of political parties. Thus political language has to consist largely of euphemism, question-begging and sheer cloudy vagueness. Defenceless villages are bombarded from the air, the inhabitants driven out into the countryside, the cattle machine-gunned, the huts set on fire with incendiary bullets: this is called *pacification*. Millions of peasants are robbed of their farms and sent trudging along the roads with no more than they can carry: this is called *transfer of population* or *rectification of frontiers*. People are imprisoned for years without trial, or shot in the back of the neck or sent to die of scurvy in Arctic lumber camps: this is called *elimination of unreliable elements*. Such phraseology is needed if one wants to name things without calling up mental pictures of them. Consider for instance some comfortable English professor defending Russian totalitarianism. He cannot say outright, "I believe in killing off your opponents when you can get good results by doing so". Probably, therefore, he will say something like this:

> While freely conceding that the Soviet régime exhibits certain features which the humanitarian may be inclined to deplore, we must, I think, agree that a certain curtailment of the right to political opposition is an unavoidable concomitant of transitional periods, and that the rigours which the Russian people have been called upon to undergo have been amply justified in the sphere of concrete achievement.

The inflated style is itself a kind of euphemism. A mass of Latin words falls upon the facts like soft snow, blurring the outlines and covering up all the details. The great enemy of clear language is insincerity. When there is a gap between one's real and one's declared aims, one turns as it were instinctively to long words and exhausted idioms, like a cuttlefish squirting out ink. In our age there is no such thing as "keeping out of politics". All issues are political issues, and politics itself is a mass of lies, evasions, folly, hatred and schizophrenia. When the general atmosphere is bad, language must suffer. I should expect to find—this is a guess which I have not sufficient knowledge to verify—that the German, Russian and Italian languages have all deteriorated in the last ten or fifteen years, as a result of dictatorship.

But if thought corrupts language, language can also corrupt thought. A bad usage can spread by tradition and imitation, even among people who should and do know better. The debased language that I have been discussing is in some ways very convenient. Phrases like *a not unjustifiable assumption, leaves much to be desired, would serve no good purpose, a consideration which we should do well to bear in mind*, are a continuous temptation, a packet of aspirins always at one's elbow. Look back through this essay, and for certain you will find that I have again and again committed the very faults I am protesting against. By this morning's post I have received a pamphlet dealing with conditions in Germany. The author tells me that he "felt impelled" to write it. I open it at random, and here is almost the first sentence that I see: "(The Allies) have an opportunity not only of achieving a radical transformation of Germany's social and political structure in such a way as to avoid a nationalistic reaction in Germany itself, but at the same time of laying the foundations of a co-operative and unified Europe." You see, he "feels impelled" to write—feels, presumably, that he has something new to say—and yet his words, like cavalry horses answering the bugle, group themselves automatically into the familiar dreary pattern. This invasion of one's mind by ready-made phrases (*lay the foundations, achieve a radical transformation*) can only be prevented if one is constantly on guard against them, and every such phrase anaesthetises a portion of one's brain.

I said earlier that the decadence of our language is probably curable. Those who deny this would argue, if they produced an argument at all, that language merely reflects existing social conditions, and that we cannot influence its development by any direct tinkering with words and constructions. So far as the general tone or spirit of a language goes, this may be true, but it is not true in detail. Silly words and expressions have often disappeared, not through any evolutionary process but owing to the conscious action of a minority. Two recent examples were *explore every avenue* and *leave no stone unturned*, which were killed by the jeers of a few journalists. There is a long list of fly-blown metaphors which could similarly be got rid of if enough people would interest themselves in the job; and it should also be possible to laugh the *not un-* formation out of existence,[3] to reduce the amount of Latin and Greek in the average sentence, to drive out foreign phrases and strayed scientific words, and, in general, to make pretentiousness unfashionable. But all these are minor points. The defence of the English language implies more than this, and perhaps it is best to start by saying what it does *not* imply.

To begin with, it has nothing to do with archaism, with the salvaging of obsolete words and turns of speech, or with the setting-up of a "standard English" which must never be departed from. On the

---

3. One can cure oneself of the *not un-* formation by memorising this sentence: *A not unblack dog was chasing a not unsmall rabbit across a not ungreen field.* [Author's footnote.]

contrary, it is especially concerned with the scrapping of every word or idiom which has outworn its usefulness. It has nothing to do with correct grammar and syntax, which are of no importance so long as one makes one's meaning clear, or with the avoidance of Americanisms, or with having what is called a "good prose style". On the other hand it is not concerned with fake simplicity and the attempt to make written English colloquial. Nor does it even imply in every case preferring the Saxon word to the Latin one, though it does imply using the fewest and shortest words that will cover one's meaning. What is above all needed is to let the meaning choose the word, and not the other way about. In prose, the worst thing one can do with words is to surrender to them. When you think of a concrete object, you think wordlessly, and then, if you want to describe the thing you have been visualising, you probably hunt about till you find the exact words that seem to fit it. When you think of something abstract you are more inclined to use words from the start, and unless you make a conscious effort to prevent it, the existing dialect will come rushing in and do the job for you, at the expense of blurring or even changing your meaning. Probably it is better to put off using words as long as possible and get one's meaning as clear as one can through pictures or sensations. Afterwards one can choose—not simply *accept*—the phrases that will best cover the meaning, and then switch round and decide what impression one's words are likely to make on another person. This last effort of the mind cuts out all stale or mixed images, all prefabricated phrases, needless repetitions, and humbug and vagueness generally. But one can often be in doubt about the effect of a word or a phrase, and one needs rules that one can rely on when instinct fails. I think the following rules will cover most cases:

     i. Never use a metaphor, simile or other figure of speech which you are used to seeing in print.
    ii. Never use a long word where a short one will do.
   iii. If it is possible to cut a word out, always cut it out.
   iv. Never use the passive where you can use the active.
    v. Never use a foreign phrase, a scientific word or a jargon word if you can think of an everyday English equivalent.
   vi. Break any of these rules sooner than say anything outright barbarous.

These rules sound elementary, and so they are, but they demand a deep change of attitude in anyone who has grown used to writing in the style now fashionable. One could keep all of them and still write bad English, but one could not write the kind of stuff that I quoted in those five specimens at the beginning of this article.

I have not here been considering the literary use of language, but merely language as an instrument for expressing and not for concealing or preventing thought. Stuart Chase and others have come near to claiming that all abstract words are meaningless, and have used this as a pretext for advocating a kind of political quietism. Since you don't know what Fascism is, how can you struggle against Fascism? One need not swallow such absurdities as this, but one ought to recognise that the present political chaos is connected with the decay of language, and that one can probably bring about some improvement by starting at the verbal end. If you simplify your English, you are freed from the worst follies of orthodoxy. You cannot speak any of the necessary dialects, and when you make a stupid remark its stupidity will be obvious, even to yourself. Political language—and with variations this is true of all political parties, from Conservatives to Anarchists—is designed to make lies sound truthful and murder respectable, and to give an appearance of solidity to pure wind. One cannot change this all in a moment, but one can at least change one's own habits, and from time to time one can even, if one jeers loudly enough, send some worn-out and useless phrase—some *jackboot, Achilles' heel, hotbed, melting pot, acid test, veritable inferno* or other lump of verbal refuse—into the dustbin where it belongs.

19

Rhetorical Analysis

1. The "five specimens of the English language as it is now habitually written" that Orwell reprints are over forty years old. Find five contemporary specimens to replace them. Does Orwell's analysis of language still apply? Do present-day writers still habitually commit the same "mental vices"?
2. "Look back through this essay," Orwell says, "and for certain you will find that I have again and again committed the very faults I am protesting against." Select one of Orwell's paragraphs and judge it by his own standards. How well does he come off? Are Orwell's standards too demanding to be practicable?

Intellectual Analysis

1. One obvious and immediate question is, "How does Orwell get from one's personal language to politics?" You might wish to compare Russell's essay "Use-

less Knowledge" to this one; Russell's argument moves from one's personal knowledge to national and international tyranny. Note that the question of conformity, of sinking to the level of the lowest common denominator, arises in both essays.

2. In ¶ 12, Orwell makes an explicit connection between language and politics. Examine that paragraph carefully, and the four paragraphs following.
    a. How is it that "Orthodoxy, of whatever color, seems to demand a lifeless, imitative style"?
    b. Is it logical in Orwell's argument that a "reduced state of consciousness . . . is . . . favorable to political conformity"? What, exactly, does "reduced state of consciousness" mean?

3. Both quotations above suggest something about the nature of language. Public language, in Orwell's view, ought to be concrete rather than abstract. We build a metaphorical connection between ourselves and things, or ideas, by giving them concrete names. If we are both careful and honest, he implies, language will serve us as a reliable tool. The linguist, George Steiner, on the other hand, tells us that language in the twentieth century "no longer articulates . . . all major modes of action, thought, and sensibility." In other words, language has lost its authority to such other modes of expression as music and mathematics. Explore the implications of this conflict for the way you think about and respond to the world.

Suggestions for Writing

1. Write an essay exposing the "swindles and perversions" of a piece of contemporary prose. It might be an advertisement, the blurb on an LP album, a political speech (*The New York Times* often reprints entire speeches), a letter to the editor, or an editorial.

2. Turn back to an old piece of your own writing. Now rewrite it as "a scrupulous writer" should, according to Orwell: "A scrupulous writer, in every sentence that he writes, will ask himself at least four questions, thus: What am I trying to say? What words will express it? What image or idiom will make it clearer? Is this image fresh enough to have an effect? And he will probably ask himself two more: Could I put it more shortly? Have I said anything that is avoidably ugly?" If, after asking these questions, your piece does not seem to need rewriting, write an essay explaining why.

3. Find a passage of clear, simple prose and write a series of parodies on it, as Orwell parodies the passage from *Ecclesiastes*. Write it in the manner of a politician, government analyst, businessman, humanities teacher, sociologist, intellectual, and so on. There is a world of possibilities. You might even write it as you would have written it before you read Orwell's essay.

ALICE WALKER

Alice Walker was born the youngest of eight children to Willie Lee and Minnie Grant Walker, tenant farmers in Eatonton, Georgia, in February, 1944. For most writers such a bare listing of data would tell little; in the case of Alice Walker these facts are fundamental not only to her life but to her work, the work being a way to live her life. As a black, Southern writer, "as a natural right," she inherited "a sense of community." Such an inheritance, she goes on to say, is not easily come by any longer. Her life and work reflect a dual pattern of movement, both physical and intellectual, from this nurturing community: outward toward a larger community, and inward toward return and renewal.

In the early 1960s, Walker left Georgia to attend Sarah Lawrence College. She then made a trip to Africa from which she returned pregnant and depressed, contemplating suicide. "For three days," she writes, "I lay on the bed with a razor blade under my pillow." Partly as the result of a friend's devotion, instead of killing herself she wrote (in the space of a week) the poems that made up her first book, Once, published three years later in 1968. The poems are derived from her experiences in the Civil Rights Movement, her African visit, and her struggle with suicide, and as such they express simultaneously politics and personality.

Since Once, Walker's writings have continued to explore both realms. She has become increasingly preoccupied with the history of the black woman, especially as a creative figure in American society, a preoccupation which has surfaced recently in her novel, The Color Purple (1981), and in her book of essays, In Search of Our Mothers' Gardens (1983). Walker finds black women "fascinating" for the same reasons she is attracted to feminist authors, because they "search incessantly for a kind of salvation . . . envision a solution, an evolution to higher consciousness on the part of society, even when society cannot." That search for a solution, inextricably private and public, motivates all three essays reprinted below, whether their subject is the need to remember forgotten black women, or the need for nuclear disarmament, or the need to make peace with cultural standards of beauty.

"I believe in change," Walker said in a 1973 interview: "change personal, and change in society." Over the years the quality of Walker's writing has indeed changed. Her versatility has grown as her concerns have broadened. But her sense of heritage, of community as both earth and flower, of self as both individual and public, remains.

NUCLEAR MADNESS: WHAT YOU CAN DO

Nuclear Madness is a book you should read immediately. Before brushing your teeth. Before making love. Before lunch. Its author is Helen Caldicott (with the assistance of Nancy Herrington and Nahum Stiskin), a native Australian, pediatrician, and mother of three children. It is a short, serious book about the probability of nuclear catastrophe in our lifetime, eminently thoughtful, readable, and chilling, as a book written for nuclear nonexperts, as almost all Americans are, would have to be.

Caldicott was six years old when the atomic bomb was dropped on Hiroshima, and calls herself a child of the atomic age. She grew up, as many of us did, under the threat of nuclear war. She recalls the fifties, when students were taught to dive under their desks at the sound of the air-raid siren and Americans by the thousands built underground fallout shelters.

During the sixties, political assassinations, the Civil Rights Movement, and the Vietnam War turned many people away from concern about atomic weapons and toward problems they felt they could do something about. However, as Caldicott states, the Pentagon continued resolutely on its former course, making bigger and "better" bombs every year.

Sometime during the sixties Robert McNamara, then Secretary of Defense, said that between the United States and the Soviet Union there already existed some four hundred nuclear bombs, enough to kill millions of people on both sides, a viable "deterrent," in his opinion, to nuclear war. The Pentagon and the Kremlin, however, apparently assumed this was not enough, and so today between the two "superpowers" there are some *fifty thousand* bombs.

What this means is that the U.S. and the U.S.S.R. literally have more bombs than they know what to do with: so they have targeted every city in the Northern Hemisphere with a population of at least twenty-five thousand with the number of bombs formerly set aside to wipe out whole countries. So even as you squeeze out your toothpaste, kiss your lover's face, or bite into a turkey sandwich, you are on the superpowers' nuclear hit list, a hit list made up by people who have historically been unable to refrain from showing off every new and shameful horror that they make.

For several years Caldicott has been on leave from her work at the Harvard Medical Center, and spends all her time practicing what she calls "preventative medicine," traveling across the Earth attempting to make people aware of the dangers we face. Like most medicine, hers is bitter, but less bitter, she believes, than watching helplessly while her child patients suffer and die from cancer and genetic diseases that are directly caused by the chemical pollutants inevitably created in the production of nuclear energy.

The nuclear industry, powerful, profit-oriented, totally unconcerned about our health, aided and abetted by a government that is its twin, is murdering us and our children every day. And it is up to us, each one of us, to stop it. In the event of a nuclear war all life on the planet will face extinction, certainly human beings. But even if there is no war we will face the same end—unless we put an end to the nuclear-power industry itself—only it will be somewhat slower in coming, as the air, the water, and the soil become too poisoned from nuclear waste (for which there is no known safe disposal) to support life.

What can we do? Like Caldicott, but even more so, I do not believe we should waste any time looking for help from our legal system. Nor do I have faith in politicians, scientists, or "experts." I have great faith, however, in individual people: you with the toothbrush, you in the sack, and you there not letting any of this shit get between you and that turkey sandwich. If it comes down to it, I know one of us *individuals* (just think of Watergate) may have to tackle the killer who's running to push the catastrophe button, and I even hope said tackle will explain why so many of us are excellent football players. (Just as I hope *something* will soon illustrate for us what our brothers learned of protecting life in Vietnam.)

As individuals we must join others. No time to quibble about survival being "a white issue." No time to claim you don't live here, too. Massive demonstrations are vital. Massive civil disobedience. And, in fact, massive anything that's necessary to save our lives.

Talk with your family; organize your friends. Educate anybody you can get your mouth on. Raise money. Support those who go to jail. Write letters to those senators and congressmen who are making it easy for the nuclear-power industry to kill us: tell them if they don't change, "cullud" are going to invade their fallout shelters. In any case, this is the big one. We must save Earth, and relieve those who would destroy it of the power to do so. Join up with folks you don't even like, if you have to, so that we may all live to fight each other again.

But first, read Caldicott's book, and remember: the good news may be that Nature is phasing out the white man, but the bad news is that's who She thinks we all are.

Rhetorical Analysis

1. A book review summarizes and evaluates a book for people who have not read it. The review should give enough factual information about the book, together with an evaluation, to help us decide whether to read it. Is Walker's essay, then, a book review? Imagine yourself to be Helen Caldicott. Would you be satisfied with this essay as a review for the general reader?

2. This essay was originally published in *The Black Scholar*. Walker must have known that her audience, though small, would be North American, black, and well-educated. How does her awareness of her audience shape her essay and condition her strategies? Note especially ¶s 5, 8, 10, and 11.

3. Generally, Walker's essay accomplishes three purposes, each dependent on the previous:
    a. To provide facts about the subject (e.g., "Caldicott was six years old when the atomic bomb was dropped on Hiroshima").
    b. To judge those facts, by statement or implication, as good or bad (e.g., "the superpowers' nuclear hit list").
    c. To recommend action based on those judgments (e.g., "As individuals we must join others").

   Mark each paragraph according to which of the three aims it supports. Do you now find a rhetorical pattern in the essay as a whole?

Intellectual Analysis

1. Walker's style is different in this essay from her style in the other two selections: it is faster, less poetic, and more mundane in diction. What would cause Walker to alter her style and tone? And what effect does that alteration have on meaning? The urgency she feels can surely be felt by readers as well.
    a. Why mention brushing teeth, making love, and eating lunch, and then repeat these details twice?
    b. "Nuclear Madness" is, she says, "the big one," and before that subject all else pales. Such as what? Matters of race, for one thing. (Consider in fact all the references to racial issues here: what function do they serve?)
2. Why "madness"? Walker identifies two kinds of madness: that of the public on the one hand, and that of business and government (which are "twin") on the other.
    a. The general public, she implies, gets too distracted from facing the nuclear issue. How are they distracted and by what? Even football?
    b. Government and business deal in madness, too. How? And where? How does the term "hit list" function here?
3. What does this essay say about Americans generally, about their awareness, their folly? Consider, for example, the image of fall-out shelters, used twice in the essay. But consider, too, Walker's remarks about "individuals."

Suggestions for Writing

1. Try your hand at a book review, *especially* if you have recently read something about which you feel some urgency. Consider Virginia Woolf's remark in "Professions for Women" (¶ 3) that "you cannot review even a novel without having a mind of your own."
2. Write an essay in which you target an audience (probably students) and try to persuade them to do something; all else should be subordinate to your rhetorical attempt to "hit" that audience.

BEAUTY: WHEN THE OTHER DANCER IS THE SELF

*I*t is a bright summer day in 1947. My father, a fat, funny man with beautiful eyes and a subversive wit, is trying to decide which of his eight children he will take with him to the county fair. My mother, of course, will not go. She is knocked out from getting most of us ready: I hold my neck stiff against the pressure of her knuckles as she hastily completes the braiding and then beribboning of my hair.

My father is the driver for the rich old white lady up the road. Her name is Miss Mey. She owns all the land for miles around, as well as the house in which we live. All I remember about her is that she once offered to pay my mother thirty-five cents for cleaning her house, raking up piles of her magnolia leaves, and washing her family's clothes, and that my mother—she of no money, eight children, and a chronic earache—refused it. But I do not think of this in 1947. I am two and a half years old. I want to go everywhere my daddy goes. I am excited at the prospect of riding in a car. Someone has told me fairs are fun. That there is room in the car for only three of us doesn't faze me at all. Whirling happily in my starchy frock, showing off my biscuit-polished patent-leather shoes and lavender socks, tossing my head in a way that makes my ribbons bounce, I stand, hands on hips, before my father. "Take me, Daddy," I say with assurance; "I'm the prettiest!"

Later, it does not surprise me to find myself in Miss Mey's shiny black car, sharing the back seat with the other lucky ones. Does not surprise me that I thoroughly enjoy the fair. At home that night I tell the unlucky ones all I can remember about the merry-go-round, the man who eats live chickens, and the teddy bears, until they say: that's enough, baby Alice. Shut up now, and go to sleep.

It is Easter Sunday, 1950. I am dressed in a green, flocked, scalloped-hem dress (handmade by my adoring sister, Ruth) that has its own smooth satin petticoat and tiny hot-pink roses tucked into each scallop. My shoes, new T-strap patent leather, again highly biscuit-polished. I am six years old and have learned one of the longest Easter speeches to be heard that day, totally unlike the speech I said when I was two: "Easter lilies / pure and white / blossom in / the morning light." When I rise to give my speech I do so on a great wave of love and pride and expectation. People in the church stop rustling their new crinolines. They seem to hold their breath. I can tell they admire my dress, but it is my spirit, bordering on sassiness (womanishness), they secretly applaud.

"That girl's a little *mess*," they whisper to each other, pleased.

Naturally I say my speech without stammer or pause, unlike those who stutter, stammer, or, worst of all, forget. This is before the word "beautiful" exists in people's vocabulary, but "Oh, isn't she the *cutest* thing!" frequently floats my way. "And got so much sense!" they gratefully add . . . for which thoughtful addition I thank them to this day.

It was great fun being cute. But then, one day, it ended.

I am eight years old and a tomboy. I have a cowboy hat, cowboy boots, checkered shirt and pants, all red. My playmates are my brothers, two and four years older than I. Their colors are black and green, the only difference in the way we are dressed. On Saturday nights we all go to the picture show, even my mother; Westerns are her favorite kind of movie. Back home, "on the ranch," we pretend we are Tom Mix, Hopalong Cassidy, Lash LaRue (we've even named one of our dogs Lash LaRue); we chase each other for hours rustling cattle, being outlaws, delivering damsels from distress. Then my parents decide to buy my brothers guns. These are not "real" guns. They shoot "BBs," copper pellets my brothers say will kill birds. Because I am a girl, I do not get a gun. Instantly I am relegated to the position of Indian. Now there appears a great distance between us. They shoot and shoot at everything with their new guns. I try to keep up with my bow and arrows.

One day while I am standing on top of our makeshift "garage"—pieces of tin nailed across some poles—holding my bow and arrow and looking out toward the fields, I feel an incredible blow in my right eye. I look down just in time to see my brother lower his gun.

Both brothers rush to my side. My eye stings, and I cover it with my hand. "If you tell," they say, "we will get a whipping. You don't want that to happen, do you?" I do not. "Here is a piece of wire," says the older brother, picking it up from the roof; "say you stepped on one end of it and the other flew up and hit you." The pain is beginning to start. "Yes," I say. "Yes, I will say that is what happened." If I do not say this is what happened, I know my brothers will find ways to make me wish I had. But now I will say anything that gets me to my mother.

Confronted by our parents we stick to the lie agreed upon. They place me on a bench on the porch and I close my left eye while they examine the right. There is a tree growing from underneath the porch that climbs past the railing to the roof. It is the last thing my right eye sees. I watch as its trunk, its branches, and then its leaves are blotted out by the rising blood.

I am in shock. First there is intense fever, which my father tries to break using lily leaves bound around my head. Then there are chills: my mother tries to get me to eat soup. Eventually, I do not know how, my parents learn what has happened. A week after the "accident" they take me to see a doctor. "Why did you wait so long to come?" he asks, looking into my eye and shaking his head. "Eyes are sympathetic," he says. "If one is blind, the other will likely become blind too."

This comment of the doctor's terrifies me. But it is really how I look that bothers me most. Where the BB pellet struck there is a glob of whitish scar tissue, a hideous cataract, on my eye. Now when I stare at people—a favorite pastime, up to now—they will stare back. Not at the "cute" little girl, but at her scar. For six years I do not stare at anyone, because I do not raise my head.

Years later, in the throes of a mid-life crisis, I ask my mother and sister whether I changed after the "accident." "No," they say, puzzled. "What do you mean?"

What do I mean?

I am eight, and, for the first time, doing poorly in school, where I have been something of a whiz since I was four. We have just moved to the place where the "accident" occurred. We do not know any of the people around us because this is a different county. The only time I see the friends I knew is when we go back to our old church. The new school is the former state penitentiary. It is a large stone building, cold and drafty, crammed to overflowing with boisterous, ill-disciplined children. On the third floor there is a huge circular imprint of some partition that has been torn out.

"What used to be here?" I ask a sullen girl next to me on our way past it to lunch.

"The electric chair," says she.

At night I have nightmares about the electric chair, and about all the people reputedly "fried" in it. I am afraid of the school, where all the students seem to be budding criminals.

"What's the matter with your eye?" they ask, critically.

When I don't answer (I cannot decide whether it was an "accident" or not), they shove me, insist on a fight.

My brother, the one who created the story about the wire, comes to my rescue. But then brags so much about "protecting" me, I become sick.

After months of torture at the school, my parents decide to send me back to our old community, to my old school. I live with my grandparents and the teacher they board. But there is no room for Phoebe, my cat. By the time my grandparents decide there *is* room, and I ask for my cat, she cannot be found. Miss Yarborough, the boarding teacher, takes me under her wing, and begins to teach me to play the piano. But soon she marries an African—a "prince," she says—and is whisked away to his continent.

At my old school there is at least one teacher who loves me. She is the teacher who "knew me before I was born" and bought my first baby clothes. It is she who makes life bearable. It is her presence that finally helps me turn on the one child at the school who continually calls me "one-eyed bitch." One day I simply grab him by his coat and beat him until I am satisfied. It is my teacher who tells me my mother is ill.

My mother is lying in bed in the middle of the day, something I have never seen. She is in too much pain to speak. She has an abscess in her ear. I stand looking down on her, knowing that if she dies, I cannot live. She is being treated with warm oils and hot bricks held against her cheek. Finally a doctor comes. But I must go back to my grandparents' house. The weeks pass but I am hardly aware of it. All I know is that my mother might die, my father is not so jolly, my brothers still have their guns, and I am the one sent away from home.

"You did not change," they say.

Did I imagine the anguish of never looking up?

I am twelve. When relatives come to visit I hide in my room. My cousin Brenda, just my age, whose father works in the post office and whose mother is a nurse, comes to find me. "Hello," she says. And then she asks, looking at my recent school picture, which I did not want taken, and on which the "glob," as I think of it, is clearly visible, "You still can't see out of that eye?"

"No," I say, and flop back on the bed over my book.

That night, as I do almost every night, I abuse my eye. I rant and rave at it, in front of the mirror. I plead with it to clear up before morning. I tell it I hate and despise it. I do not pray for sight. I pray for beauty.

"You did not change," they say.

I am fourteen and baby-sitting for my brother Bill, who lives in Boston. He is my favorite brother and there is a strong bond between us. Understanding my feelings of shame and ugliness he and his wife take me to a local hospital, where the "glob" is removed by a doctor named O. Henry. There is still a small bluish crater where the scar tissue was, but the ugly white stuff is gone. Almost immediately I become a different person from the girl who does not raise her head. Or so I think. Now that I've raised my head I win the boyfriend of my dreams. Now that I've raised my head I have plenty of friends. Now that I've raised my head classwork comes from my lips as faultlessly as Easter speeches did, and I leave high school as valedictorian, most popular student, and *queen*, hardly believing my luck. Ironically, the girl who was voted most beautiful in our class (and was) was later shot twice through the chest by a male companion, using a "real" gun, while she was pregnant. But that's another story in itself. Or is it?

"You did not change," they say.

It is now thirty years since the "accident." A beautiful journalist comes to visit and to interview me. She is going to write a cover story for her magazine that focuses on my latest book. "Decide how you want to look on the cover," she says. "Glamorous, or whatever."

Never mind "glamorous," it is the "whatever" that I hear. Suddenly all I can think of is whether I will get enough sleep the night before the photography session: if I don't, my eye will be tired and wander, as blind eyes will.

At night in bed with my lover I think up reasons why I should not appear on the cover of a magazine. "My meanest critics will say I've sold out," I say. "My family will now realize I write scandalous books."

"But what's the real reason you don't want to do this?" he asks.

"Because in all probability," I say in a rush, "my eye won't be straight."

"It will be straight enough," he says. Then, "Besides, I thought you'd made your peace with that."

And I suddenly remember that I have.

I remember:

I am talking to my brother Jimmy, asking if he remembers anything unusual about the day I was shot. He does not know I consider that day the last time my father, with his sweet home remedy of cool lily leaves, chose me, and that I suffered and raged inside because of this. "Well," he says, "all I remember is standing by the side of the highway with Daddy, trying to flag down a car. A white man stopped, but when Daddy said he needed somebody to take his little girl to the doctor, he drove off."

I remember:

I am in the desert for the first time. I fall totally in love with it. I am so overwhelmed by its beauty, I confront for the first time, consciously, the meaning of the doctor's words years ago: "Eyes are sympathetic. If one is blind, the other will likely become blind too." I realize I have dashed about the world madly, looking at this, looking at that, storing up images against the fading of the light. *But I might have missed seeing the desert!* The shock of that possibility—and gratitude for over twenty-five years of sight—sends me literally to my knees. Poem after poem comes—which is perhaps how poets pray.

> ON SIGHT
>
> I am so thankful I have seen
> The Desert
> And the creatures in the desert
> And the desert Itself.
>
> The desert has its own moon
> Which I have seen
> With my own eye.
>
> There is no flag on it.
>
> Trees of the desert have arms
> All of which are always up
> That is because the moon is up
> The sun is up
> Also the sky
> The stars
> Clouds
> None with flags.

> If there *were* flags, I doubt
> the trees would point.
> Would you?

But mostly, I remember this:

I am twenty-seven, and my baby daughter is almost three. Since her birth I have worried about her discovery that her mother's eyes are different from other people's. Will she be embarrassed? I think. What will she say? Every day she watches a television program called "Big Blue Marble." It begins with a picture of the earth as it appears from the moon. It is bluish, a little battered-looking, but full of light, with whitish clouds swirling around it. Every time I see it I weep with love, as if it is a picture of Grandma's house. One day when I am putting Rebecca down for her nap, she suddenly focuses on my eye. Something inside me cringes, gets ready to try to protect myself. All children are cruel about physical differences, I know from experience, and that they don't always mean to be is another matter. I assume Rebecca will be the same.

But no-o-o-o. She studies my face intently as we stand, her inside and me outside her crib. She even holds my face maternally between her dimpled little hands. Then, looking every bit as serious and lawyerlike as her father, she says, as if it may just possibly have slipped my attention: "Mommy, there's a *world* in your eye." (As in, "Don't be alarmed, or do anything crazy.") And then, gently, but with great interest: "Mommy, where did you *get* that world in your eye?"

For the most part, the pain left then. (So what, if my brothers grew up to buy even more powerful pellet guns for their sons and to carry real guns themselves. So what, if a young "Morehouse man" once nearly fell off the steps of Trevor Arnett Library because he thought my eyes were blue.) Crying and laughing I ran to the bathroom, while Rebecca mumbled and sang herself off to sleep. Yes indeed, I realized, looking into the mirror. There *was* a world in my eye. And I saw that it was possible to love it: that in fact, for all it had taught me of shame and anger and inner vision, I *did* love it. Even to see it drifting out of orbit in boredom, or rolling up out of fatigue, not to mention floating back at attention in excitement (bearing witness, a friend has called it), deeply suitable to my personality, and even characteristic of me.

That night I dream I am dancing to Stevie Wonder's song "Always" (the name of the song is really "As," but I hear it as "Always").

As I dance, whirling and joyous, happier than I've ever been in my life, another bright-faced dancer joins me. We dance and kiss each other and hold each other through the night. The other dancer has obviously come through all right, as I have done. She is beautiful, whole and free. And she is also me.

Rhetorical Analysis

1. Walker uses an important technique of writings: facts or feelings highly charged with emotion are often best expressed with brief, understated, and controlled language. Consider the effect of sentence four in ¶ 11; the last sentence of ¶ 13; and the last sentence of ¶ 30. Find other instances.
2. Here are the main parts of this essay:
    ¶s 1–7
        8–13
        14–33
        34–end
    Rhetorically, how does Walker make the reader aware of these important divisions?
3. In Intellectual Analysis (following) we look at this essay as an act of exploration, as a review of past experiences to discover new meaning in them. This kind of exploratory essay has been popular especially in this century. Isak Dinesen's "The Iguana" and George Orwell's "The Hanging" belong to that genre. Essentially, the author recounts a personal moment of insight which carries some universal significance. Even if the insight is self-revealing, it applies to all people, not simply to the author.

    Several techniques peculiar to this genre may be easily illustrated by Walker's piece, and they are worth study.
    a. The ultimate insight, or at least its significance, is not divulged until near the end of the essay.
    b. The events are narrated fully and vividly so they carry the reader's interest until their final significance can be understood.
    c. Along the way, the reader is clued in to the presence of a personal drama in the process of being resolved (see, for example, ¶ 7).
    d. The final meaning is implied throughout (note, for instance, the stress on the word "beautiful" in ¶s 1 and 6).
    e. The meaning of the final revelation is not dwelt on. Instead readers are expected to gather the full meaning of the revelation from the richness of the event itself (study ¶s 48 and 49).

Intellectual Analysis

1. This essay is built step by step, or inductively, beginning with what at first seem to be arbitrary details and then moving toward a much more comprehensive statement. The essay's meaning is intimately involved with that very structure. How?
    a. Consider the parallel opening of many paragraphs (1, 4, and 7; and in a different way, 41, 43, and 45). What is the cumulative effect of those repeated patterns?
    b. This essay seems to be a radical exploration, or act of discovery, for the writer, even a "loop in time." The essay, as a whole, and in its parts, circles back to the writers' self and what she has discovered. How do form and meaning coalesce here? And what has she found at the end? To bolster this effect of exploration, Walker also gives a series of scenes, offered cinematically and in the present tense. In this process, the repeated question as to whether she changed after the "accident" becomes, at the end, a repeated assertion: "I remember."

    Thus, what she discovers becomes the subject of the piece.

2. The concern with change is bound up with the question of identity, and both are involved with beauty and self-hood. How do these relationships work?
    a. In different ways, her notion of beauty is tied to her self-acceptance and self-esteem. How? Is this connected with the two dancers mentioned in the title?
    b. There is a progression here having to do with perception: as a child, staring becomes the inability "to look up"; after her visit to the doctor, that theme turns into "looking out," and finally into a statement about the world we see and the world within us with which we see. In fact, the theme of perception is crucial all along. She must learn to see, as the poet William Blake wrote, "through the eye, not with it."

3. How does the poem function in the essay? For example, the fact that there is no flag on the moon has to do with there being no white "glob" on her eye. The nationalism suggested by the flag connects with the allusions to racial prejudice in the rest of the essay, which connect with the main subject of social attitudes toward physical appearance. How do all these connections hold together, reinforce each other, and finally cohere?

Suggestions for Writing

1. Explore your own experience in an essay of self-discovery, using the techniques listed above in the third suggestion for Rhetorical Analysis. Your essay will be, as Walker puts it in "In Search of Our Mothers' Gardens," "a personal account that is yet shared, in its theme and its meaning, by all of us."

2. Walker is able to write a unified essay that connects one of her earliest memories ("two and a half years old," ¶ 2) with an experience at Atlanta University ("the

steps of Trevor Lawrence Library," ¶ 48). Write an essay that pulls together and connects some equally distant events from your own life.

3. Ideals of physical appearance are not the only ways our culture may be implicated in individual "shame and anger and inner vision" (¶ 48). Write an essay discussing these other ways, or one of them.

4. The word "experience" comes from the Latin *ex* + *periculum*, through trial, and is thus cognate with the word "peril." If, as Walker argues, true knowledge is gained through troubles, what will happen to people who are blessed with an easy life? The question may suggest some good subjects to write about.

In Search of Our Mothers' Gardens

> *I described her own nature and temperament. Told how they needed a larger life for their expression. . . . I pointed out that in lieu of proper channels, her emotions had overflowed into paths that dissipated them. I talked, beautifully I thought, about an art that would be born, an art that would open the way for women the likes of her. I asked her to hope, and build up an inner life against the coming of that day. . . . I sang, with a strange quiver in my voice, a promise song.*
>
> —Jean Toomer, "Avey,"
> Cane

*T*he poet speaking to a prostitute who falls asleep while he's talking—

When the poet Jean Toomer walked through the South in the early twenties, he discovered a curious thing: black women whose spirituality was so intense, so deep, so *unconscious*, that they were themselves unaware of the richness they held. They stumbled blindly through their lives: creatures so abused and mutilated in body, so dimmed and confused by pain, that they considered themselves unworthy even of hope. In the selfless abstractions their bodies became to the men who used them, they became more than "sexual objects," more even than mere women: they became "Saints." Instead of being perceived as whole persons, their bodies became shrines: what was thought to be their minds became temples suitable for worship. These crazy Saints stared out at the world, wildly, like lunatics—or quietly, like suicides; and the "God" that was in their gaze was as mute as a great stone.

Who were these Saints? These crazy, loony, pitiful women?

Some of them, without a doubt, were our mothers and grandmothers.

In the still heat of the post-Reconstruction South, this is how they seemed to Jean Toomer: exquisite butterflies trapped in an evil honey, toiling away their lives in an era, a century, that did not acknowledge them, except as "the *mule* of the world." They dreamed dreams that no one knew—not even themselves, in any coherent fashion—and saw visions no one could understand. They wandered or sat about the countryside crooning lullabies to ghosts, and drawing the mother of Christ in charcoal on courthouse walls.

They forced their minds to desert their bodies and their striving spirits sought to rise, like frail whirlwinds from the hard red clay. And when those frail whirlwinds fell, in scattered particles, upon the ground, no one mourned. Instead, men lit candles to celebrate the emptiness that remained, as people do who enter a beautiful but vacant space to resurrect a God.

Our mothers and grandmothers, some of them: moving to music not yet written. And they waited.

They waited for a day when the unknown thing that was in them would be made known; but guessed, somehow in their darkness, that on the day of their revelation they would be long dead. Therefore to Toomer they walked, and even ran, in slow motion. For they were going nowhere immediate, and the future was not yet within their grasp. And men took our mothers and grandmothers, "but got no pleasure from it." So complex was their passion and their calm.

To Toomer, they lay vacant and fallow as autumn fields, with harvest time never in sight: and he saw them enter loveless marriages, without joy; and become prostitutes, without resistance; and become mothers of children, without fulfillment.

For these grandmothers and mothers of ours were not Saints, but Artists; driven to a numb and bleeding madness by the springs of creativity in them for which there was no release. They were Creators, who lived lives of spiritual waste, because they were so rich in spirituality—which is the basis of Art—that the strain of enduring their unused and unwanted talent drove them insane. Throwing away this spirituality was their pathetic attempt to lighten the soul to a weight their work-worn, sexually abused bodies could bear.

What did it mean for a black woman to be an artist in our grandmothers' time? In our great-grandmothers' day? It is a question with an answer cruel enough to stop the blood.

Did you have a genius of a great-great-grandmother who died under some ignorant and depraved white overseer's lash? Or was she required to bake biscuits for a lazy backwater tramp, when she cried out in her soul to paint watercolors of sunsets, or the rain falling on the green and peaceful pasturelands? Or was her body broken and forced to bear children (who were more often than not sold away from her)—eight, ten, fifteen, twenty children—when her one joy was the thought of modeling heroic figures of rebellion, in stone or clay?

How was the creativity of the black woman kept alive, year after year and century after century, when for most of the years black people have been in America, it was a punishable crime for a black person to read or write? And the freedom to paint, to sculpt, to expand the mind with action did not exist. Consider, if you can bear to imagine it, what might have been the result if singing, too, had been forbidden by law. Listen to the voices of Bessie Smith, Billie Holiday, Nina Simone, Roberta Flack, and Aretha Franklin, among others, and imagine those voices muzzled for life. Then you may begin to comprehend the lives of our "crazy," "Sainted" mothers and grandmothers. The agony of the lives of women who might have been Poets, Novelists, Essayists, and Short-Story Writers (over a period of centuries), who died with their real gifts stifled within them.

And, if this were the end of the story, we would have cause to cry out in my paraphrase of Okot p'Bitek's great poem:

> O, my clanswomen
> Let us all cry together!
> Come,
> Let us mourn the death of our mother,
> The death of a Queen
> The ash that was produced
> By a great fire!
> O, this homestead is utterly dead
> Close the gates
> With *lacari* thorns,
> For our mother
> The creator of the Stool is lost!

And all the young women
Have perished in the wilderness!

But this is not the end of the story, for all the young women—our mothers and grandmothers, *ourselves*—have not perished in the wilderness. And if we ask ourselves why, and search for and find the answer, we will know beyond all efforts to erase it from our minds, just exactly who, and of what, we black American women are.

One example, perhaps the most pathetic, most misunderstood one, can provide a backdrop for our mothers' work: Phillis Wheatley, a slave in the 1700s.

Virginia Woolf, in her book *A Room of One's Own*, wrote that in order for a woman to write fiction she must have two things, certainly: a room of her own (with key and lock) and enough money to support herself.

What then are we to make of Phillis Wheatley, a slave, who owned not even herself? This sickly, frail black girl who required a servant of her own at times—her health was so precarious—and who, had she been white, would have been easily considered the intellectual superior of all the women and most of the men in the society of her day.

Virginia Woolf wrote further, speaking of course not of our Phillis, that "any woman born with a great gift in the sixteenth century [insert "eighteenth century," insert "black woman," insert "born or made a slave"] would certainly have gone crazed, shot herself, or ended her days in some lonely cottage outside the village, half witch, half wizard [insert "Saint"], feared and mocked at. For it needs little skill and psychology to be sure that a highly gifted girl who had tried to use her gift for poetry would have been so thwarted and hindered by contrary instincts [add "chains, guns, the lash, the ownership of one's body by someone else, submission to an alien religion"], that she must have lost her health and sanity to a certainty."

The key words, as they relate to Phillis, are "contrary instincts." For when we read the poetry of Phillis Wheatley—as when we read the novels of Nella Larsen or the oddly false-sounding autobiography of that freest of all black women writers, Zora Hurston—evidence of "contrary instincts" is everywhere. Her loyalties were completely divided, as was, without question, her mind.

But how could this be otherwise? Captured at seven, a slave of wealthy, doting whites who instilled in her the "savagery" of the Africa they "rescued" her from . . . one wonders if she was even able to remember her homeland as she had known it, or as it really was.

Yet, because she did try to use her gift for poetry in a world that made her a slave, she was "so thwarted and hindered by . . . contrary instincts, that she . . . lost her health. . . ." In the last years of her brief life, burdened not only with the need to express her gift but also with a penniless, friendless "freedom" and several small children for whom she was forced to do strenuous work to feed, she lost her health, certainly. Suffering from malnutrition and neglect and who knows what mental agonies, Phillis Wheatley died.

So torn by "contrary instincts" was black, kidnapped, enslaved Phillis that her description of "the Goddess"—as she poetically called the Liberty she did not have—is ironically, cruelly humorous. And, in fact, has held Phillis up to ridicule for more than a century. It is usually read prior to hanging Phillis's memory as that of a fool. She wrote:

> The Goddess comes, she moves divinely fair,
> Olive and laurel binds her *golden* hair.
> Wherever shines this native of the skies,
> Unnumber'd charms and recent graces rise. [My italics]

It is obvious that Phillis, the slave, combed the "Goddess's" hair every morning; prior, perhaps, to bringing in the milk, or fixing her mistress's lunch. She took her imagery from the one thing she saw elevated above all others.

With the benefit of hindsight we ask, "How could she?"

But at last, Phillis, we understand. No more snickering when your stiff, struggling, ambivalent lines are forced on us. We know now that you were not an idiot or a traitor; only a sickly little black girl, snatched from your home and country and made a slave; a woman who still struggled to sing the song that was your gift, although in a land of barbarians who praised you for your bewildered tongue. It is not so much what you sang, as that you kept alive, in so many of our ancestors, *the notion of song.*

Black women are called, in the folklore that so aptly identifies one's status in society, "the *mule* of the world," because we have been handed the burdens that everyone else—*everyone* else—refused to carry. We have also been called "Matriarchs," "Superwomen," and "Mean and Evil Bitches." Not to mention "Castraters" and "Sapphire's Mama." When we have pleaded for understanding, our character has been distorted; when we have asked for simple caring, we have been handed empty inspirational appellations, then stuck in the farthest corner. When we have asked for love, we have been given children. In short, even our plainer gifts, our labors of fidelity and love, have been knocked down our throats. To be an artist and a black woman, even today, lowers our status in many respects, rather than raises it: and yet, artists we will be.

Therefore we must fearlessly pull out of ourselves and look at and identify with our lives the living creativity some of our great-grandmothers were not allowed to know. I stress *some* of them because it is well known that the majority of our great-grandmothers knew, even without "knowing" it, the reality of their spirituality, even if they didn't recognize it beyond what happened in the singing at church—and they never had any intention of giving it up.

How they did it—those millions of black women who were not Phillis Wheatley, or Lucy Terry or Frances Harper or Zora Hurston or Nella Larsen or Bessie Smith; or Elizabeth Catlett, or Katherine Dunham, either—brings me to the title of this essay, "In Search of Our Mothers' Gardens," which is a personal account that is yet shared, in its theme and its meaning, by all of us. I found, while thinking about the far-reaching world of the creative black woman, that often the truest answer to a question that really matters can be found very close.

In the late 1920s my mother ran away from home to marry my father. Marriage, if not running away, was expected of seventeen-year-old girls. By the time she was twenty, she had two children and was pregnant with a third. Five children later, I was born. And this is how I came to know my mother: she seemed a large, soft, loving-eyed woman who was rarely impatient in our home. Her quick, violent temper was on view only a few times a year, when she battled with the white landlord who had the misfortune to suggest to her that her children did not need to go to school.

She made all the clothes we wore, even my brothers' overalls. She made all the towels and sheets we used. She spent the summers canning vegetables and fruits. She spent the winter evenings making quilts enough to cover all our beds.

During the "working" day, she labored beside—not behind—my father in the fields. Her day began before sunup, and did not end until late at night. There was never a moment for her to sit down, undisturbed, to unravel her own private thoughts; never a time free from interruption—by work or the noisy inquiries of her many children. And yet, it is to my mother—and all our mothers who were not famous—that I went in search of the secret of what has fed that muzzled and often mutilated, but vibrant, creative spirit that the black woman has inherited, and that pops out in wild and unlikely places to this day.

But when, you will ask, did my overworked mother have time to know or care about feeding the creative spirit?

The answer is so simple that many of us have spent years discovering it. We have constantly looked high, when we should have looked high—and low.

For example: in the Smithsonian Institution in Washington, D.C., there hangs a quilt unlike any other in the world. In fanciful, inspired, and yet simple and identifiable figures, it portrays the story of the Crucifixion. It is considered rare, beyond price. Though it follows no known pattern of quilt-making, and though it is made of bits and pieces of worthless rags, it is obviously the work of a person of powerful imagination and deep spiritual feeling. Below this quilt I saw a note that says it was made by "an anonymous Black woman in Alabama, a hundred years ago."

If we could locate this "anonymous" black woman from Alabama, she would turn out to be one of our grandmothers—an artist who left her mark in the only materials she could afford, and in the only medium her position in society allowed her to use.

As Virginia Woolf wrote further, in *A Room of One's Own*:

> Yet genius of a sort must have existed among women as it must have existed among the working class. [Change this to "slaves" and "the wives and daughters of sharecroppers."] Now and again an Emily Brontë or a Robert Burns [change this to "a Zora Hurston or a Richard Wright"] blazes out and proves its presence. But certainly it never got itself on to paper. When, however, one reads of a witch being ducked, of a woman possessed by devils [or "Sainthood"], of a wise woman selling herbs [our root workers], or even a very remarkable man who had a mother, then I think we are on the track of a lost novelist, a suppressed poet, of some mute and inglorious Jane Austen.... Indeed, I would venture to guess that Anon, who wrote so many poems without signing them, was often a woman....

And so our mothers and grandmothers have, more often than not anonymously, handed on the creative spark, the seed of the flower they themselves never hoped to see: or like a sealed letter they could not plainly read.

And so it is, certainly, with my own mother. Unlike "Ma" Rainey's songs, which retained their creator's name even while blasting forth from Bessie Smith's mouth, no song or poem will bear my mother's name. Yet so many of the stories that I write, that we all write, are my mother's stories. Only recently did I fully realize this: that through years of listening to my mother's stories of her life, I have absorbed not only the stories themselves, but something of the manner in which she spoke, something of the urgency that involves the knowledge that her stories—like her life—must be recorded. It is probably for this reason that so much of what I have written is about characters whose counterparts in real life are so much older than I am.

But the telling of these stories, which came from my mother's lips as naturally as breathing, was not the only way my mother showed herself as an artist. For stories, too, were subject to being distracted, to dying without conclusion. Dinners must be started, and cotton must be gathered before the big rains. The artist that was and is my mother showed itself to me only after many years. This is what I finally noticed:

Like Mem, a character in *The Third Life of Grange Copeland*, my mother adorned with flowers whatever shabby house we were forced to live in. And not just your typical straggly country stand of zinnias, either. She planted ambitious gardens—and still does—with over fifty different varieties of plants that bloom profusely from early March until late November. Before she left home for the fields, she watered her flowers, chopped up the grass, and laid out new beds. When she returned from the fields she might divide clumps of bulbs, dig a cold pit, uproot and replant roses, or prune branches from her taller bushes or trees—until night came and it was too dark to see.

Whatever she planted grew as if by magic, and her fame as a grower of flowers spread over three counties. Because of her creativity with her flowers, even my memories of poverty are seen through a screen of blooms—sunflowers, petunias, roses, dahlias, forsythia, spirea, delphiniums, verbena . . . and on and on.

And I remember people coming to my mother's yard to be given cuttings from her flowers; I hear again the praise showered on her because whatever rocky soil she landed on, she turned into a garden. A garden so brilliant with colors, so original in its design, so magnificent with life and creativity, that to this day people drive by our house in Georgia—perfect strangers and imperfect strangers—and ask to stand or walk among my mother's art.

I notice that it is only when my mother is working in her flowers that she is radiant, almost to the point of being invisible—except as Creator: hand and eye. She is involved in work her soul must have. Ordering the universe in the image of her personal conception of Beauty.

Her face, as she prepares the Art that is her gift, is a legacy of respect she leaves to me, for all that illuminates and cherishes life. She has handed down respect for the possibilities—and the will to grasp them.

For her, so hindered and intruded upon in so many ways, being an artist has still been a daily part of her life. This ability to hold on, even in very simple ways, is work black women have done for a very long time.

This poem is not enough, but it is something, for the woman who literally covered the holes in our walls with sunflowers:

> They were women then
> My mama's generation
> Husky of voice—Stout of
> Step
> With fists as well as
> Hands
> How they battered down
> Doors
> And ironed
> Starched white
> Shirts
> How they led
> Armies
> Headragged Generals
> Across mined
> Fields
> Booby-trapped
> Kitchens
> To discover books
> Desks
> A place for us
> How they knew what we
> *Must* know
> Without knowing a page
> Of it
> Themselves.

Guided by my heritage of a love of beauty and a respect for strength—in search of my mother's garden, I found my own.

And perhaps in Africa over two hundred years ago, there was just such a mother; perhaps she painted vivid and daring decorations in oranges and yellows and greens on the walls of her hut; perhaps she sang—in a voice like Roberta Flack's—*sweetly* over the compounds of her village; perhaps she wove the most stunning mats or told the most ingenious stories of all the village storytellers. Perhaps she was herself a poet—though only her daughter's name is signed to the poems that we know. 49

Perhaps Phillis Wheatley's mother was also an artist. 50

Perhaps in more than Phillis Wheatley's biological life is her mother's signature made clear. 51

Rhetorical Analysis

1. As the title implies, this is an essay that searches for answers.
    a. Its structure takes the form of an intellectual investigation, where questions lead the investigator in certain directions and the answers found generate new questions to pursue.
    b. In following the steps of her inquiry, Walker does not shy from marking progress with actual questions. Skillful use of questions, in fact, is a rhetorical tactic of many good writers—though they must be careful, since too many questions, and especially rhetorical questions, put readers off. Study the questions Walker asks in ¶s 3, 11, 15 (indirect), 21, 25, and 33. Note especially that each is a new question and that each introduces a new stage in the search that frames the whole essay. Note also how such questioning is a fit expression for the inductive nature of that search.
2. Look at ¶ 29. Here is a place where the essay makes a major shift in direction. Walker observes a very important rhetorical principle: the more unexpected or difficult the logical turn, the more explicit the expression of that turn must be. Explain what that turn is in ¶ 29 and how Walker helps the reader make it.
3. The added spaces before and after ¶s 27 and 28 help identify the passage as a part to itself. The tone of these two paragraphs also changes from that of the preceding paragraphs. What part does this unit play and how is this tone appropriate to its role?

Intellectual Analysis

1. Walker's essay seems to pose two questions, one explicit and the other implied:
    a. "What did it mean for a black woman to be an artist in our grandmothers' time?" Here she discusses several important matters:
        (1) The life of black women in the past.
        (2) The immense importance of creativity, as she sees it.

(3) The likewise immense horror of repressed creativity.
(4) The connection between art and spirituality, and artist and saint.
  b. What does it mean to be a black female artist now? Here, too, Walker asserts several important ideas.
    (1) She offers "a personal account that is yet shared" (¶ 29). What does that mean?
    (2) She has inherited, she says, a respect for the possibilities of artistic expression and the "will to grasp them" (¶ 45).
    (3) She admires those who use the materials available, and whatever medium "social position" allows (¶ 36).
  These two questions become one at ¶ 28. How and why? For one thing, consider how both questions relate to the past, and how they relate to what is inherited. For another, consider Walker's claim that her mother was "Ordering the universe in the image of her personal conception of Beauty."
2. When Walker writes that the "striving spirits" of creative black women in the South "sought to rise, like frail whirlwinds from the hard red clay" (¶ 6), she alludes to the "whirlwind" out of which the Lord spoke to Job in the Bible (Job 38:1) and to the "whirlwind" in which Ezekiel saw his great spiritual vision (Ezek. 1:4). And the "red clay" may refer not only to the soil of the deep South but to a traditional etymology of the name Adam (from the Hebrew words for "redden" and "earth"). Why does Walker make these Biblical allusions in this section of her essay (see also "Saints" in ¶ 1 and "mother of Christ" in ¶ 5)?
3. Information about Okot p'Bitek, Phillis Wheatley, Bessie Smith, and the others mentioned in ¶s 14, 16, and 29, may be found in such reference works as the *Dictionary of American Negro Biography*, the *Afro-American Encyclopedia*, and the *Encyclopedia of World Literature in the 20th Century*. Is there a good reason why Walker herself does not explain more fully who these black artists are? Is she making a point implicitly by not identifying them?

Suggestions for Writing

1. "In Search of Our Mothers' Gardens" shows Walker using her writing as a means to examine her life as it is connected to the lives of others, identifying and selecting possible meanings and potential directions for future thinking and acting. Identify a person, place or event in your own life which has similar significance and write an essay in which you "search out" its implications.
2. Write an essay on the meaning of the word "garden" and the image of the garden in the whole context of this essay.
3. Evaluate Walker's essay as a feminist statement. You may wish to compare it to other feminist statements (Woolf's "Professions for Women," for example).
4. What is creativity? Do you place as much importance on it as Walker does, and do you feel as much a need for it in your life? Is creativity really necessary for a happy and useful life?

WILLIAM STYRON

There has always been something of the old-fashioned gentleman about William Styron. He was born in 1925 in Newport News, Virginia, and educated at Christchurch, a small preparatory school whose faculty, though "hideously underpaid drudges," were nevertheless both genial and bumblingly effective teachers. An indifferent scholar himself (his application to Hampden-Sydney College was refused because of four Fs in trigonometry—or physics, depending on which reminiscence you read), Styron managed to be admitted to Davidson College in North Carolina; then, after World War II, in which he served as a Marine, he graduated from Duke University. He was considered for a Rhodes Scholarship on the strength of his early fiction, but instead of going to Oxford, he headed to New York to work on his first novel. That book, Lie Down in Darkness (1951), established Styron as an important voice among a generation of promising talents, a generation which included J. D. Salinger, Leroi Jones, Norman Mailer, and Saul Bellow. In 1953 Styron went to Europe. While living in Paris, he helped found the Paris Review with George Plimpton, Peter Matthiesson, "two sinister-looking green bottles of absinthe," and an Algerian bistro owner named Paul (who loved Americans because of Edgar Allan Poe).

After returning to the United States, Styron has resided mainly in the North. Yet his Virginia roots remain, and he is essentially a Southern writer. In the second selection reprinted below, Styron describes the Virginia Tidewater landscape as resembling, topographically, America's "earliest configuration," and, in speech and architecture, its earliest social configuration as well. This terrain figures in all Styron's major novels, including Lie Down in Darkness, The Confessions of Nat Turner, and Sophie's Choice. Though the "region remains, ultimately, distinctly Southern, adumbrated by the memory of a tragic past," it is also where "the land and its people have achieved a certain harmony." Such a sense of the still-living possibilities of community, or region, bears a resemblance to a similar sense in both Walker and Welty, though Styron's uneasiness about the South troubles the verbal surface of his writings more than Welty's, and his reticence about it runs deeper than Walker's.

Thus, when we hear something of the old-fashioned Virginia gentleman in Styron's words, it is in the deepest sense of that designation: an urbane and deep fascination with history. The exploration of that Virginian topography—as in all three of the following essays—becomes the examination of the landscape of his own culture and psyche.

The Habit

*T*he lamentable history of the cigarette is that of a mortally corrupting addiction having been embraced by millions of people in the spirit of childlike innocence. It is a history which is also strikingly brief. Cigarettes began to be manufactured extensively around the turn of the century, but it was not until as recently as 1921 that cigarettes overtook chewing tobacco, as well as pipes and cigars, in per capita consumption, and the 1930s were well along before cigarette smoking became the accepted thing for ladies. 1

The popularity of cigarettes was inevitable and overwhelming. They were not offensive in close quarters, nor messy like pipes and cigars. They were easily portable. They did not look gross and unseemly in a lady's mouth. They were cheap to manufacture, and they were inhalable. Unlike the great majority of pipe and cigar smokers, whose pleasure is predominantly oral and contemplative, most cigarette smokers inhale deep into their lungs with bladelike, rhythmic sav- 2 agery, inflicting upon themselves in miniature a particularly abrasive form of air pollution. Further, the very fact of inhalation seems to enhance the cigarette's addictive power. Unhappily, few suspected the consequences in terms of health until long after cigarette smoking had gained its colossal momentum. That this type of auto-contamination is a major cause of lung cancer—that it is also a prime causative factor in deaths from coronary artery disease, bronchitis, asthma, emphysema, among other afflictions—was established, and for the first time well publicized, only a decade ago. The effect this knowledge has had upon the public consciousness may be suggested by the fact that sales this year reached the galactic sum of one-half trillion cigarettes—one hundred billion more than in 1953. There is something historically intimidating in the idea that cigarette smoking as a mass diversion and a raging increase in lung cancer have both come about during the lifetime of those who are now no more than fifty years old. It is the very *recentness* of the phenomenon which helps make it so shocking. The hard truth is that human beings have never in such a brief space of time, and in so grand and guileless a multitude, embraced a habit whose unwholesome effects not only would totally outweigh the meager satisfactions but would hasten the deaths of a large proportion of the people who indulged in it. Certainly (and there seems little doubt that the Surgeon General's report will make this clear) only nuclear fallout exceeds cigarette smoking in gravity as a public health problem.

3 For its lucid presentation of the medical evidence alone, *The Consumers Union Report on Smoking* would be a valuable document. "The conclusion is inescapable," the *Report* begins, "and even spokesmen for the cigarette industry rarely seek to escape it: we are living in the midst of a major lung cancer epidemic. This epidemic hit men first and hardest, but has affected women as well. It cannot be explained away by such factors as improved diagnosis. And there is reason to believe that the worst is yet to come." Yet despite this minatory beginning the tone throughout is one of caution and reasonableness, and the authors—who manage an accomplished prose style rare in such collective undertakings—marshal their facts with such efficiency and persuasion that it is hard to imagine anyone but a fool or a tobacco lobbyist denying the close association between smoking and lung cancer. Yet, of course, not only lung cancer. The *Report* quotes, for instance, data based on an extensive study of smokers and non-smokers among English physicians, where the death rate *from all*

causes was found to be doubled among heavy cigarette smokers in the group of men past 65, and quadrupled in the group 35 to 44. And the *Report* adds, with the modest and constructive irony that makes the book, if not exactly a joy, then agreeable to read: "These death rates among smokers are perhaps the least controversial of all the findings to date. For with respect to any particular disease there is always the possibility, however remote, that mistaken diagnosis and other conceivable errors may cast doubt on the statistics. But death is easily diagnosed."

In the end, however, what makes the *Report's* message supportable to those distracted souls among the millions of American smokers who may wish to kick the habit—or who, having kicked the habit, may wonder if it is not too late—is a kind of muted optimism. For all present evidence seems to indicate that the common cocktail party rationalization ("I've smoked too long to stop now, the damage is done") has no real basis in fact. In research carried out by the American Cancer Society, microscopic studies of the lung tissues of ex-smokers have shown a process in which precancerous cells are dying out instead of flourishing and reproducing as in the tissues of continuing smokers. Here the *Report* states, in regard to a carefully matched group composed in equal numbers of nonsmokers, ex-smokers and smokers: "Metaplastic cells with altered nuclei [i.e., precancerous cells] were found in 1.2 percent of the slides from the lungs of nonsmokers, as compared with 6.0 for ex-smokers—and *93.2 percent* for current smokers."

Certainly such evidence, combined with the fact that ex-smokers have a lung cancer death rate which ranges down to one fifth of that of smokers who continue to smoke, should be of the greatest practical interest to anyone who ponders whether it may be worthwhile abandoning what is, after all, a cheerless, grubby, fumbling addiction. (Only the passion of a convert could provoke these last words. The *Report* was an aid to my stopping a two-pack-a-day habit which commenced in early infancy. Of course, stopping smoking may be in itself a major problem, one of psychological complexity. For myself, after two or three days of great flaccidity of spirit, an aimless oral yearning, aching moments of hunger at the pit of the stomach, and an awful intermittent urge to burst into tears, the problem resolved itself, and in less than a week all craving vanished. Curiously, for the first time in my life, I developed a racking cough, but this, too, disappeared. A sense of smugness, a kind of fatness of soul, is the reward for such a struggle. The intensity of the addiction varies, however, and some people find the ordeal fearfully difficult, if not next to impossible. I do have an urgent suspicion, though, that the greatest barrier to a termination of the habit is the dread of some Faustian upheaval, when in fact that deprivation, while momentarily oppressive, is apt to prove not really cruel at all.)

But if the *Report* is splendidly effective as a caveat, it may be read for its sociological insights as well. Certainly the history of commerce has few instances of such shameful abdication of responsibility as that displayed by the cigarette industry when in 1952 the "health scare," as it is so winsomely known in the trade, brought about the crisis which will reach a head in this month's report by the Surgeon General. It seems clear that the industry, instead of trying to forestall the inevitable with its lies and evasions, might have acquitted itself with some honor had it made what the *Report* calls the only feasible choices: to have urged caution on smokers, to have given money to independent research organizations, to have avoided propaganda and controversy in favor of unbiased inquiry. At the very least the industry might have soft-pedaled or, indeed, silenced its pitch to young people. But panic and greed dominated the reaction, and during the decade since the smoking-lung cancer link was made public, the official position of the industry has been that, in the matter of lung cancer, the villain is any and everything *but* the cigarette. Even the American Cancer Society is in on the evil plot and, in the words of one industry spokesman, "relies almost wholly upon health scare propaganda to raise millions of dollars from a gullible public."

Meanwhile, $200 million was spent last year on cigarette ballyhoo, and during these last crucial ten years the annual advertising expenditure has increased 134 percent—a vast amount of it, of course, going to entice the very young. One million of these young people, according to the American Public Health Association, will die of smoking-induced lung cancer before they reach the age of seventy years. "Between the time a kid is eighteen and twenty-one, he's going to make the basic decision to smoke or not to smoke," says L. W. Bruff, advertising director of Liggett & Myers. "If he does decide to smoke, we want to get him." I have never met Mr. Bruff, but in my mind's eye I see him, poised like a cormorant above those doomed minnows, and I am amused by the refinement, the weight of conscience, the delicate interplay of intellectual and moral alternatives which go into the making of such a prodigious thought. As the report demonstrates, however, Mr. Bruff is only typical of the leaders of an industry which last year received a bounty of $7 billion from 63 million American smokers. Perhaps the tragic reality is that neither this estimable report nor that of the Surgeon General can measurably affect, much less really change, such awesome figures.

Rhetorical Analysis

1. One of the pleasures of writing is in finding the right word—the word that *fits*, that is especially graphic, startling, or apt. And the writer's pleasure transfers to the reader. When we read Styron's line about smokers inhaling deep "with bladelike, rhythmic savagery," we may sense his exultation in finding those three powerful words. Select and discuss other words or phrases you imagine must have given Styron pleasure in creating.
2. Styron says that he knows of many people who quit smoking after reading "The Habit": "more than anything I have written, it demonstrated the immediate way in which an opinion, if strongly enough expressed, can have produced results."
    a. Analyze how "The Habit" is "strongly . . . expressed." Consider not only diction, but irony, statistics, quotations, use of italics, and ordering of facts for emphasis.
    b. The danger with strong expression is that it may only convince the reader that the writer is too emotional to be objective. Besides the reliance on statistics—an obvious case—how does Styron convey both strong feelings and objectivity at the same time?
    c. Consider the repeated use of statistics. How does he keep them from palling? How does he make them clear?
3. What is the effect of the long parenthesis in ¶ 5? Why does Styron make it parenthetical at all?

Intellectual Analysis

1. Styron is particularly interested in the history of the smoking "habit."
    a. Track that interest through the essay. Where does he first introduce it, and why at that particular point?
    b. Does Styron's interest support his opinions about smoking? What is the nature of that interest, what emotions does it involve, and how do those emotions lead to his opinions?
    c. Evaluate his insistence on the "recentness of this phenomenon," an insistence which correlates with his focus on the huge number of people involved. What does he imply by that linkage? Has there ever been anything similar in history?

d. Styron is also taken with the "history of commerce" involved in the smoking issue. Where does this interest lead him? Toward what facts, what judgments, what arguments?
2. The final sentence qualifies the tone and the argument of the entire piece. What are the implications of that sentence?
   a. What would be the "tragic reality" Styron mentions? Would it involve something in human nature, in advertising, in the "habit" itself?
   b. Are the combined forces on one side too much for the truth to combat? What then are the implications?
3. Is this essay, first published in 1963, dated in any way? If so, how would you update it? What considerations might be added to it, new facts that were not available 25 or 30 years ago?

Suggestions for Writing

1. Other habits abound—alcohol, drugs, sugar, gambling, television, and so forth—and so do official reports on them. Select a recent governmental study and review its findings. Or read several reports, for a research paper. In any case, be objective yet clear about your opinions, as Styron is in "The Habit."
2. Styron's advice is straighforward and candid: if you smoke, quit; it you don't smoke, don't start. Write a piece of needed advice with similar directness that you hope will change people's ways.
3. Write on the morality of commercial interests that make money from bad habits—or good habits.

THE OLDEST AMERICA

George Washington, never so versatile and wide-ranging in his interests as Thomas Jefferson, was nonetheless a man of many parts who knew well how to employ his leisure time. Firmly implanted in the American mythology is Washington the solemn, taciturn soldier and statesman, the Rembrandt Peale portrait of the postage stamps; less well known is the pre-Revolutionary Virginia planter who was devoted equally to horse racing and the theater and who regularly traveled the hundred and fifty miles south from Mount Vernon across the somnolent Tidewater to Williamsburg—then the capital of the colony—where he placed bets on the horses by day, and by night attended performances of Shakespeare by troupes imported from London. If today one should wonder how that Tidewater countryside appeared to Washington's eyes, the answer is: much as it does now. For to a degree largely unmatched in America, the region resembles in topography its ancient, earliest configuration.

It is the oldest part of our country, and suffered its upheaval and exploitation not in the nineteenth century like New England nor in the present century like California, but decades before we became a nation. Recklessly overcultivated in tobacco for more than a century, the once rich bottomlands and green fields became fallow and depleted, so that even by the time of Washington's later years the abandoned farms and pastures were becoming reclaimed by new growths of woodland—oak and ash and sycamore and scrub pine. Long before the invention of the steam locomotive, much of the region—especially in the northern reaches, in the area just south of the Potomac and bordering on Chesapeake Bay—had subsided into the lazy sleep of a depopulated backwater, lacking either industry or productive agriculture, and for this reason (somewhat rare in the pattern of American regional growth), the absence of factories and railroads and great superhighways left the landscape mercifully unmarked. For this reason, too, the Tidewater has retained, generally speaking, a unique, unspoiled loveliness. Of course, architectural styles have changed the face of the landscape; shopping centers and split-level houses, indistinguishable from those elsewhere in America, have set their imprint here and there upon the land, and one should not visit the Tidewater in the expectation that each small town will yield a glimpse of something resembling Colonial Williamsburg or a Christopher Wren church. Also, the sprawling industrial and military complex that has grown up around Norfolk and Hampton Roads does not represent the quality of the Tidewater of which I speak.

Nevertheless, the old mansions and the eighteenth-century courthouses and churches still exist, their weathered brick rising out of the countryside from behind a grove of oaks in the most pleasantly disarming way. Such great old manor houses as Westover and Brandon and Carter's Grove still reign in lordly and stunning elegance along the banks of the James (these are the homes that H. L. Mencken, in outrage over the encroachment of all that was hideous in American architecture, described as the most perfectly proportioned dwellings ever fashioned by man).

Yet beyond all these noble relics of the past, there is the landscape itself, sometimes unspectacular and ordinary (cornfields, pine woods, country stores) but more often possessing a sorrowing beauty—everywhere lovelier and more mellow and melancholy and fledged with green than the hard-clay country that dominates the higher elevations of the Upper South. All this has to do, of course, with the rivers, the noble waterways that indent the face of the Tidewater and give the region so much of its character, including, indeed, its very name. Rarely here is one more than a few miles from a great brackish tideland stream, like the Rappahannock or the York or the James (and these are monumental rivers, too, in breadth if not in length: the James at its mouth is nearly six miles across, one of the widest estuaries in America), so that what is specifically Southern becomes commingled with the waterborne, the maritime. Thus the vistas of the solitary stands of pinewoods and barren cornfields, the sawmill in a remote clearing, the sudden immaculate and simple beauty of a freshly painted clapboard Negro church in a sunny grove are combined with a sense of broad, flat reaches of tidal shallows, mighty river estuaries, fish stakes and oyster boats, inlets and coves and bays, wild sudden squalls blowing out of the Chesapeake, the serene magnificence of sunrise coming up over the mouth of the Rappahannock, blood-red through the milk of morning mists. This is a low, drowsing, placid topography, literally half drowned. From the exhausted land the people have turned to the water for sustenance—river and estuary and bay. There is an odd truth in the remark that every native of the Tidewater is a skilled boatman, even if he is a farmer.

I love the place names of the Virginia Tidewater—that juxtaposition of the Indian and old England, which is more mellifluous and striking than any other place in America. The names of the counties alone are resonant with the past: Essex and Middlesex and York, Isle of Wight and Sussex, King William, Surry, Prince George, King and Queen. These are mingled with the ancestral names of the red men, who still exist in diminishing numbers, isolated on small reservations, where they make a modest living by fishing for the fat shad that still teem in the rivers bearing their tribal names: Pamunkey and Mattaponi, Chickahominy, Powhatan and Kecoughtan, Chuckatuck and Corotoman. Names like these have a lazy beauty, corresponding to the meandering pace of a bygone era.

Yet at the same time, no place of comparable area owns such an abundance of curiously or fancifully named hamlets and villages—Ark, Rescue, Ordinary, Naxera, Shadow, Zuni, Lively (the posted speed here is five miles an hour), Bumpass. These are often nothing more than a crossroads, a general store with a post office, and here one is most likely to hear the throaty, slurred Tidewater speech—beyond doubt the speech of the Father of His Country. Encapsulated in time and space, the natives of the remoter reaches of this part of Virginia still use the phonetic forms of a language spoken two and a half centuries ago by their ancestors, settlers from Devon and Dorset. Its quality cannot be fully savored unless heard, but it may be suggested by noting that in the Tidewater you never go out but "oot," and that "house" rhymes less directly with "mouse" than with "noose." Still occasionally heard is the "yar" sound, in which "garden" becomes "gyarden," "far" turns into "fyah," and that old family name of Carter, one of Virginia's most illustrious, is transmuted into "Cyatah." This locution was, in my childhood, largely the property of old ladies fragrant with lavender—usually Daughters of the Confederacy—and still hovers in my memory as the quintessential sound of Southern womanhood and good breeding. Alas, it is dying out and will soon be gone forever, absorbed into the flattened-out tonality of Basic American.

Neither the Tidewater nor the rest of Virginia is, of course, the Deep South, but the underlying quality of the region remains, ultimately, distinctly Southern, adumbrated by the memory of a tragic past. Some of the bloodiest battles of the Civil War were fought on this soil, the selfsame soil to which there was brought for the first time—at Jamestown, in 1619, in the form of a handful of African slaves—the institution that became, in large part, the basis for that awful conflict. The legacy still remains. A majority of the Tidewater counties is heavily populated by Negroes; in many counties Negroes outnumber whites in a ratio resembling parts of Alabama and Mississippi. Here, as elsewhere in the South (and the North), there are grievous inequities; it is not in order to minimize those inequities that I reflect on the fact that no part of the South where such a racial composition is found has been so free of friction or strife. The Ku Klux Klan has never found a welcome here; the reign of terror that swept the South in the 1920s and 1930s—the decades of blazing crosses and lynchings—would have been unthinkable in the Tidewater.

I suggest that over the reach of decades a certain way of life may produce attitudes—a sense of fair play, an abhorrence of violence, a respect for the dignity of men—that supersede all other considerations and come to dominate moral conduct. However strongly it may be argued that this is not enough, it remains a tradition to be reckoned with, and the Virginia Tidewater lays justifiable claim to such a heritage. The region possesses the shortcomings common to all places, but the land and its people have achieved a certain harmony. Perhaps more than in any other comparable part of America, men have learned to get along with one another. It would be a pleasant irony if the land where the American dilemma began—close by the shores of the tranquil and lovely James, with its memory of black chained cargoes—should by its way of life come to embody an answer to that same dilemma.

Rhetorical Analysis

1. By any standards Styron's sentences are long, but they are not difficult to follow because he builds them with familiar logical structures. Here are four typical structures, all well worth study and imitation.
    a. *Specification of a more general term:* "new growths of woodland—oak and ash and sycamore and scrub pine" (¶ 2).
    b. *Synecdoche*, where a part or example serves for the whole: "the sawmill in a remote clearing" (¶ 4).
    c. *Reservation*: "Neither the Tidewater nor the rest of Virginia is, of course, the Deep South, but . . ." (¶ 7).
    d. *Explanation by negation*: "[The Tidewater] suffered its upheaval and exploitation not in the nineteenth century . . . but decades before we became a nation" (¶ 2).
   There are at least two other instances of each one of these four constructions in Styron's essay. Find one more of each. Can you identify other common logical structures?
2. Another way to appreciate Styron's sentences is to take a few of the longest and carefully analyze them. Besides logical patterning, what other special devices does he use—punctuation, parallel syntax, word choice?
3. This essay seems to be purely descriptive, but it does contain an argument (see the second suggestion for Intellectual Analysis). Rhetorically, how does Styron signal the presence of this argument? Look especially at ¶s 7 and 8.

Intellectual Analysis

1. Styron's central idea, that landscape affects morality, is highly debatable. How might you argue against it? How does Styron qualify his claim?
2. The argument embedded in Styron's essay is basically inductive. Locate the

generalization which results from induction. How else can you tell that the essay is built inductively?
3. Styron's title operates in the way a title ought to: it is part of the essay it adroitly introduces.
   a. Styron implies in the title that from our very beginnings at Jamestown in 1609, the problem of racial inequity has been with us. Where, in the essay, do you find that implication? And what effect does this have on his meaning?
   b. Styron insists that within the "oldest America" lies an answer to the central problem of racial injustice. What are we to infer? What is he saying about the burden of history, about the relationship of past, present, and future?
4. Styron's answer to all of the above might be labelled "harmony" (notice the word in ¶ 8): if so, harmony of what?
   a. Several pairs of opposites are mentioned throughout the essay (Indian and English, for example); isolate these pairs, and evaluate their importance. This should lead you to awareness of the complex theme in this very urbane essay.
   b. What has George Washington to do with Styron's themes here—especially the idea of harmony?

Suggestions for Writing

1. Styron asserts that geography—in its broadest sense, as the land and the people living on it—can affect "moral conduct." Argue for or against this proposition.
2. Select a region like the Tidewater that you know well and describe—just as Styron has done here—the "certain harmony" it has, the harmony of land, people, and history.

THIS QUIET DUST

> You mought be rich as cream
> And drive you coach and four-horse team,
> But you can't keep de world from moverin' round
> Nor Nat Turner from gainin' ground.
>
> And your name it mought be Caesar sure
> And got you cannon can shoot a mile or more,
> But you can't keep de world from moverin' round
> Nor Nat Turner from gainin' ground.
>
> —OLD-TIME NEGRO SONG

My native state of Virginia is, of course, more than ordinarily conscious of its past, even for the South. When I was learning my lessons in the mid-1930s at a grammar school on the banks of the James River, one of the required texts was a history of Virginia—a book I can recall far more vividly than any history of the United States or of Europe I studied at a later time. It was in this work that I first encountered the name Nat Turner. The reference to Nat was brief; as a matter of fact, I do not think it unlikely that it was the very brevity of the allusion—amounting almost to a quality of haste—which captured my attention and stung my curiosity. I can no longer quote the passage exactly, but I remember that it went something like this: "In 1831, a fanatical Negro slave named Nat Turner led a terrible insurrection in Southampton County, murdering many white people. The insurrection was immediately put down, and for their cruel deeds Nat Turner and most of the other Negroes involved in the rebellion were hanged." Give or take a few harsh adjectives, this was all the information on Nat Turner supplied by that forgotten historian, who hustled on to matters of greater consequence.

I must have first read this passage when I was ten or eleven years old. At that time my home was not far from Southampton County, where the rebellion took place, in a section of the Virginia Tidewater which is generally considered part of the Black Belt because of the predominance of Negroes in the population. (When I speak of the South and Southerners here, I speak of *this* South, where Deep South attitudes prevail; it would include parts of Maryland and East Texas.) My boyhood experience was the typically ambivalent one of most native Southerners, for whom the Negro is simultaneously taken for granted and as an object of unending concern. On the one hand, Negroes are simply a part of the landscape, an unexceptional feature of the local scenery, yet as central to its character as the pinewoods and sawmills and mule teams and sleepy river estuaries that give such color and tone to the Southern geography. Unnoticed by white people, the Negroes blend with the land and somehow melt and fade into it, so that only when one reflects upon their possible absence, some magical disappearance, does one realize how unimaginable this absence would be: it would be easier to visualize a South without trees, without *any* people, without life at all. Thus, at the same time, ignored by white people, Negroes impinge upon their collective subconscious to such a degree that it may be rightly said that they become the focus of an incessant preoccupation, somewhat like a monstrous, recurring dream populated by identical faces wearing expressions of inquietude and vague reproach. "Southern whites cannot walk, talk, sing, conceive of laws or justice, think of sex, love, the family, or freedom without responding to the presence of Negroes." The words are those of Ralph Ellison, and, of course, he is right.

Yet there are many Souths, and the experience of each Southerner is modified by the subtlest conditions of self and family and environment and God knows what else, and I have wondered if it has ever properly been taken into account how various this response to the presence of the Negroes can be. I cannot tell how typical my own awareness of Negroes was, for instance, as I grew up near my birthplace—a small seaside city about equally divided between black and white. My feelings seem to have been confused and blurred, tinged with sentimentality, colored by a great deal of folklore, and wobbling always between a patronizing affection, fostered by my elders, and downright hostility. Most importantly, my feelings were completely uninformed by that intimate knowledge of black people which Southerners claim as their special patent; indeed, they were based upon an almost total ignorance.

For one thing, from the standpoint of attitudes toward race, my upbringing was hardly unusual: it derived from the simple conviction that Negroes were in every respect inferior to white people and should be made to stay in their proper order in the scheme of things. At the same time, by certain Southern standards my family was enlightened: although my mother taught me firmly that the use of "lady" instead of "woman" in referring to a Negro female was quite improper, she writhed at the sight of the extremes of Negro poverty and would certainly have thrashed me had she ever heard me use the word "nigger." Yet outside the confines of family, in the lower-middle-class school world I inhabited every day, this was a word I commonly used. School segregation, which was an ordinary fact of life for me, is devastatingly effective in accomplishing something that it was only peripherally designed to do: it prevents the awareness even of the existence of another race. Thus, whatever hostility I bore toward the Negroes was based almost entirely upon hearsay.

And so the word "nigger," which like all my schoolmates I uttered so freely and so often, had even then an idle and listless ring. How could that dull epithet carry meaning and conviction when it was applied to a people so diligently isolated from us that they barely existed except as shadows which came daily to labor in the kitchen, to haul away garbage, to rake up leaves? An unremarked paradox of

Southern life is that its racial animosity is really grounded not upon friction and propinquity, but upon an almost complete lack of contact. Surrounded by a sea of Negroes, I cannot recall more than once—and then briefly, when I was five or six—ever having played with a Negro child, or ever having spoken to a Negro, except in trifling talk with the cook, or in some forlorn and crippled conversation with a dotty old grandfather angling for hardshell crabs on a lonesome Sunday afternoon many years ago. Nor was I by any means uniquely sheltered. Whatever knowledge I gained in my youth about Negroes I gained from a distance, as if I had been watching actors in an all-black puppet show.

Such an experience has made me distrust any easy generalizations about the South, whether they are made by white sociologists or Negro playwrights, Southern politicians or Northern editors. I have come to understand at least as much about the Negro after having lived in the North. One of the most egregious of the Southern myths—one in this case propagated solely by Southerners—is that of the Southern white's boast that he "knows" the Negro. Certainly in many rural areas of the South the cultural climate has been such as to allow a mutual understanding, and even a kind of intimacy, to spring up between the races, at least in some individual instances. But my own boyhood surroundings, which were semi-urban (I suppose suburban is the best description, though the green little village on the city's outskirts where I grew up was a far cry from Levittown), and which have become the youthful environment for vast numbers of Southerners, tended almost totally to preclude any contact between black and white, especially when that contact was so sedulously proscribed by law.

Yet if white Southerners cannot "know" the Negro, it is for this very reason that the entire sexual myth needs to be re-examined. Surely a certain amount of sexual tension between the races does continue to exist, and the Southern white man's fear of sexual aggression on the part of the Negro male is still too evident to be ignored. But the nature of the growth of the urban, modern South has been such as to impose ever more effective walls between the races. While it cannot be denied that slavery times produced an enormous amount of interbreeding (with all of its totalitarianism, this was a free-for-all atmosphere far less self-conscious about carnal mingling than the Jim Crow era which began in the 1890s) and while even now there must logically take place occasional sexual contacts between the races—especially in rural areas where a degree of casual familiarity has always obtained—the monolithic nature of segregation has raised such an effective barrier between whites and Negroes that it is impossible not to believe that theories involving a perpetual sexual "tension" have been badly inflated. Nor is it possible to feel that a desire to taste forbidden fruit has ever really caused this barrier to be breached. From the standpoint of the Negro, there is indifference or uncomplicated fear; from that of the white—segregation, the law and, finally, indifference too. When I was growing up, the older boys might crack wan jokes about visiting the Negro whorehouse street (patronized entirely, I later discovered, by Negroes plus a few Scandinavian sailors), but to my knowledge none of them ever really went there. Like Negroes in general, Negro girls were to white men phantoms, shadows. To assume that anything more than a rare and sporadic intimacy on any level has existed in the modern South between whites and Negroes is simply to deny, with a truly willful contempt for logic, the monstrous effectiveness of that apartheid which has been the Southern way of life for almost three quarters of a century.

I have lingered on this matter only to try to underline a truth about Southern life which has been too often taken for granted, and which has therefore been overlooked or misinterpreted. Most Southern white people *cannot* know or touch black people and this is because of the deadly intimidation of a universal law. Certainly one feels the presence of this gulf even in the work of a writer as supremely knowledgeable about the South as William Faulkner, who confessed a hesitancy about attempting to "think Negro," and whose Negro characters, as marvelously portrayed as most of them are, seem nevertheless to be meticulously *observed* rather than *lived*. Thus, in *The Sound and the Fury*, Faulkner's magnificent Dilsey comes richly alive, yet in retrospect one feels this is a result of countless mornings, hours, days Faulkner had spent watching and listening to old Negro servants, and not because Dilsey herself is a being created from a sense of withinness: at the last moment Faulkner draws back, and it is no mere happenstance that Dilsey, alone among the four central figures from whose points of view the story is told, is seen from the outside rather than from that intensely "inner" vantage point, the interior monologue.

Innumerable white Southerners have grown up as free of knowledge of the Negro character and soul as a person whose background is rural Wisconsin or Maine. Yet, of course, there is a difference, and it is a profound one, defining the white Southerner's attitudes and causing him to be, for better or for worse, whatever it is he is to be. For the Negro is *there*. And he is there in a way he never is in the North, no matter how great his numbers. In the South he is a perpetual and immutable part of history itself, a piece of the vast fabric so integral and necessary that without him the fabric dissolves; his voice, his black or brown face passing on a city street, the sound of his cry rising from a wagonload of flowers, his numberless procession down dusty country roads, the neat white church he has built in some pine grove with its air of grace and benison and tranquillity, his silhouette behind a mule team far off in some spring field, the wail of his blues blaring from some jukebox in a backwoods roadhouse, the sad wet faces of nurse-maids and cooks waiting in the evening at city bus stops in pouring rain—the Negro is always *there*.

No wonder then, as Ellison says, the white Southerner can do virtually nothing without responding to the presence of Negroes. No wonder the white man so often grows cranky, fanciful, freakish, loony, violent: how else respond to a paradox which requires, with the full majesty of law behind it, that he deny the very reality of a people whose multitude approaches and often exceeds his own; that he disclaim the existence of those whose human presence has marked every acre of the land, every hamlet and crossroad and city and town, and whose humanity, however inflexibly denied, is daily evidenced to him like a heartbeat in loyalty and wickedness, madness and hilarity and mayhem and pride and love? The Negro may feel that it is too late to be known, and that the desire to know him reeks of outrageous conde-scension. But to break down the old law, to come to *know* the Negro, has become the moral imperative of every white Southerner.

II

I suspect that my search for Nat Turner, my own private attempt as a novelist to re-create and bring alive that dim and prodigious black man, has been at least a partial fulfillment of this mandate, although the problem has long since resolved itself into an artistic one—which is as it should be. In the late 1940s, having finished college in North Carolina and come to New York, I found myself again haunted by that name I had first seen in the Virginia history textbook. I had learned something more of Southern history since then, and I had become fascinated by the subject of Negro slavery. One of the most striking aspects of the institution is the fact that in the two hundred and fifty years of its existence in America, it was singularly free of organized uprisings, plots and rebellions. (It is curious that as recently as the late 1940s, scholarly insights were lagging, and I could only have suspected then what has since been made convincing by such historians as Frank Tannenbaum and Stanley Elkins:* that American Negro slavery, unique in its psychological oppressiveness—the worst the world has ever known—was simply so despotic and emasculating as to render organized revolt next to impossible.) There were three exceptions: a conspiracy by the slave Gabriel Prosser and his followers near Richmond in the year 1800, the plot betrayed, the conspirators hanged; a similar conspiracy in 1822, in Charleston, South Carolina, led by a free Negro named Denmark Vesey, who also was betrayed before he could carry out his plans, and who was executed along with other members of the plot.

The last exception, of course, was Nat Turner, and he alone in the entire annals of American slavery—alone among all those "many thousand gone"—achieved a kind of triumph.

Even today, many otherwise well-informed people have never heard the name Nat Turner, and there are several plausible reasons for such an ignorance. One of these, of course, is that the study of our history—and not alone in the South—has been tendentious in the extreme and has often avoided even an allusion to a figure like Nat, who inconveniently disturbs our notion of a slave system which, though morally wrong, was conducted with such charity and restraint that any organized act of insurrectory and murderous violence would be unthinkable. But a general ignorance about Nat Turner is even more understandable in view of the fact that so little is left of the actual record. Southampton County, which even now is off the beaten track, was at that period the remotest backwater imaginable. The relativity of time allows us elastic definitions: 1831 was yesterday. Yet the year 1831, in the presidency of Andrew Jackson, lay in the very dawn of our modern history, three years before a railroad ever touched the soil of Virginia, a full fifteen years before the use of the telegraph. The rebellion itself was of such a cataclysmic nature as practically to guarantee confusion of the news, distortion, wild rumors, lies and,

---

*. . . Elkins' work has undergone such severe revision by other historians as to make my own responses to his theories appear perhaps a bit simplistic. Nonetheless, his work remains important and most of his insights are still valid.—W. S. (1982)

finally, great areas of darkness and suppression; all of these have contributed to Nat's obscurity.

As for the contemporary documents themselves, only one survives: "The Confessions of Nat Turner," a brief pamphlet of some five thousand words, transcribed from Nat's lips as he awaited trial, by a somewhat enigmatic lawyer named Thomas Gray, who published the "Confessions" in Baltimore and then vanished from sight. There are several discrepancies in Gray's transcript but it was taken down in haste, and in all major respects it seems completely honest and reliable. Those few newspaper accounts of the time, from Richmond and Norfolk, are sketchy, remote, filled with conjecture, and are thus virtually worthless. The existing county court records of Southampton remain brief and unilluminating, dull lists, a dry catalogue of names in fading ink: the white people slain, the Negroes tried and transported south, or acquitted, or convicted and hanged.

Roughly seventy years after the rebellion (in 1900, which by coincidence was the year Virginia formally adopted its first Jim Crow laws), the single scholarly book ever to be written on the affair was published—*The Southampton Insurrection*, by a Johns Hopkins Ph.D. candidate named William S. Drewry, who was an unreconstructed Virginian of decidedly pro-slavery leanings and a man so quaintly committed to the *ancien régime* that, in the midst of a description of the ghastliest part of the uprising, he was able to reflect that "slavery in Virginia was not such to arouse rebellion, but was an institution which nourished the strongest affection and piety in slave and owner, as well as moral qualities worthy of any age of civilization." For Drewry, Nat Turner was some sort of inexplicable aberration, like a man from Mars. Drewry was close enough to the event in time, however, to be able to interview quite a few of the survivors, and since he also possessed a bloodthirsty relish for detail, it was possible for him to reconstruct the chronology of the insurrection with what appears to be considerable accuracy. Drewry's book (it is of course long out of print) and Nat's "Confessions" remain the only significant sources about the insurrection. Of Nat himself, his background and early years, very little can be known. This is not disadvantageous to a novelist, since it allows him to speculate—with a freedom not accorded the historian—upon all the intermingled miseries, ambitions, frustrations, hopes, rages and desires which caused this extraordinary black man to rise up out of those early mists of our history and strike down his oppressors with a fury of retribution unequaled before or since.

He was born in 1800, which would have made him at the time of the insurrection thirty-one years old—exactly the age of so many great revolutionaries at the decisive moment of their insurgency: Martin Luther,* Robespierre, Danton, Fidel Castro. Thomas Gray, in a footnote to the "Confessions," describes him as having the "true Negro face" (an offhand way of forestalling an assumption that he might have possessed any white blood), and he adds that "for natural intelligence and quickness of apprehension he is surpassed by few men I have ever seen"—a lofty tribute indeed at that inflammatory instant, with antebellum racism at its most hysteric pitch. Although little is known for certain of Nat's childhood and youth, there can be no doubt that he was very precocious and that he not only learned to read and write with ease—an illustrious achievement in itself, when learning to read and write was forbidden to Negroes by law—but at an early age acquired a knowledge of astronomy, and later on experimented in making paper and gunpowder. (The resemblance here to the knowledge of the ancient Chinese is almost too odd to be true, but I can find no reason to doubt it.)

16

The early decades of the nineteenth century were years of declining prosperity for the Virginia Tidewater, largely because of the ruination of the land through greedy cultivation of tobacco—a crop which had gradually disappeared from the region, causing the breakup of many of the big old plantations and the development of subsistence farming on small holdings. It was in these surroundings—a flat pastoral land of modest farms and even more modest homesteads, where it was rare to find a white man prosperous enough to own more than half a dozen Negroes, and where two or three slaves to a family was the general rule—that Nat was born and brought up, and in these surroundings he prepared himself for the apocalyptic role he was to play in history. Because of the failing economic conditions it was not remarkable that Nat was purchased and sold several times by various owners (in a sense, he was fortunate in not having been sold off to the deadly cotton and rice plantations of South Carolina and Georgia, which was the lot of many Virginia Negroes of the period); and

17

---

*See Erik Erikson's *Young Man Luther* for a brilliant study of the development of the revolutionary impulse in a young man, and the relationship of this impulse to the father figure. Although it is best to be wary of any heavy psychoanalytical emphasis, one cannot help believing that Nat Turner's relationship with his father (or his surrogate father, his master) was tormented and complicated, like Luther's.

although we do not know much about any of these masters, the evidence does not appear to be that Nat was ill-treated, and in fact one of these owners (Samuel Turner, brother of the man whose property Nat was born) developed so strong a paternal feeling for the boy and such regard for Nat's abilities that he took the fateful step of encouraging him in the beginnings of an education.

The atmosphere of the time and place was fundamentalist and devout to a passionate degree, and at some time during his twenties Nat, who had always been a godly person—"never owning a dollar, never uttering an oath, never drinking intoxicating liquors, and never committing a theft"—became a Baptist preacher. Compared to the Deep South, Virginia slave life was not so rigorous; Nat must have been given considerable latitude and found many opportunities to preach and exhort the Negroes. His gifts for preaching, for prophecy, and his own magnetism seem to have been so extraordinary that he grew into a rather celebrated figure among the Negroes of the county, his influence even extending to the whites, one of whom—a poor, half-cracked overseer named Brantley—he converted to the faith and baptized in a millpond in the sight of a multitude of the curious, both black and white. (After this no one would have anything to do with Brantley, and he left the county in disgrace.)

At about this time Nat began to withdraw into himself, fasting and praying, spending long hours in the woods or in the swamp, where he communed with the Spirit and where there came over him, urgently now, intimations that he was being prepared for some great purpose. His fanaticism grew in intensity, and during these lonely vigils in the forest he began to see apparitions:

> I saw white spirits and black spirits engaged in battle, and the sun was darkened; the thunder rolled in the heavens and blood flowed in streams . . . I wondered greatly at these miracles, and prayed to be informed of a certainty of the meaning thereof; and shortly afterwards, while laboring in the fields, I discovered drops of blood on the corn as though it were dew from heaven. For as the blood of Christ had been shed on this earth, and had ascended to heaven for the salvation of sinners, it was now returning to earth again in the form of dew . . . On the twelfth day of May, 1828, I heard a loud noise in the heavens, and the Spirit instantly appeared to me and said the Serpent was loosened, and Christ had laid down the yoke he had borne for the sins of men, and that I should

take it on and fight against the Serpent, for the time was fast approaching when the first should be last and the last should be first . . .

Like all revolutions, that of Nat Turner underwent many worrisome hesitations, false starts, procrastinations, delays (with appropriate irony, Independence Day 1830 had been one of the original dates selected, but Nat fell sick and the moment was put off again); finally, however, on the night of Sunday, August 21, 1831, Nat, together with five other Negroes in whom he had placed his confidence and trust, assembled in the woods near the home of his owner of the time, a carriage maker named Joseph Travis, and commenced to carry out a plan of total annihilation. The penultimate goal was the capture of the county seat, then called Jerusalem (a connotation certainly not lost on Nat, who, with the words of the prophets roaring in his ears, must have felt like Gideon himself before the extermination of the Midianites); there were guns and ammunition in Jerusalem, and with these captured it was then Nat's purpose to sweep thirty miles eastward, gathering black recruits on the way until the Great Dismal Swamp was reached—a snake-filled and gloomy fastness in which, Nat believed, with probable justification, only Negroes could survive and no white man's army could penetrate. The immediate objective, however, was the destruction of every white man, woman and child on the ten-mile route to Jerusalem; no one was to be spared; tender infancy and feeble old age alike were to perish by the axe and the sword. The command, of course, was that of God Almighty, through the voice of His prophet Ezekiel: *Son of Man, prophesy and say, Thus saith the Lord; Say, a sword, a sword is sharpened, and also furbished: it is sharpened to make a sore slaughter . . . Slay utterly old and young, both maids, and little children, and women* . . . It was a scheme so wild and daring that it could only have been the product of the most wretched desperation and frustrate misery of soul; and of course it was doomed to catastrophe not only for whites but for Negroes—and for black men in ways which from the vantage point of history now seem almost unthinkable.

20

They did their job rapidly and with merciless and methodical determination. Beginning at the home of Travis—where five people, including a six-month-old infant, were slain in their beds—they marched from house to house on an eastward route, pillaging, murdering, sparing no one. Lacking guns—at least to begin with—they

21

employed axes, hatchets and swords as their tools of destruction, and swift decapitation was their usual method of dispatch. (It is interesting that the Negroes did not resort to torture, nor were they ever accused of rape. Nat's attitude toward sex was Christian and high-minded, and he had said: "We will not do to their women what they have done to ours.")

On through the first day they marched, across the hot August fields, gaining guns and ammunition, horses and a number of willing recruits. That the insurrection was not purely racial but perhaps obscurely pre-Marxist may be seen in the fact that a number of dwellings belonging to poor white people were pointedly passed by. At midday on Monday their force had more than tripled, to the number of nineteen, and nearly thirty white people lay dead. By this time the alarm had been sounded throughout the county, and while the momentum of the insurgent band was considerable, many of the whites had fled in panic to the woods, and some of the farmers had begun to resist, setting up barricades from which they could fire back at Nat's forces. Furthermore, quite a few of the rebels had broken into the brandy cellars of the houses they had attacked and had gotten roaring drunk—an eventuality Nat had feared and had warned against. Nevertheless, the Negroes—augmented now by forty more volunteers—pressed on toward Jerusalem, continuing the attack into the next night and all through the following day, when at last obstinate resistance by the aroused whites and the appearance of a mounted force of militia troops (also, it must be suspected, continued attrition by the apple brandy) caused the rebels to be dispersed, only a mile or so from Jerusalem.

Almost every one of the Negroes was rounded up and brought to trial—a legalistic nicety characteristic of a time in which it was necessary for one to determine whether *his* slave, property, after all, worth eight or nine hundred dollars, was really guilty and deserving of the gallows. Nat disappeared immediately after the insurrection and hid in the woods for over two months, when near-starvation and the onset of autumnal cold drove him from his cave and forced him to surrender to a lone farmer with a shotgun. Then he, too, was brought to trial in Jerusalem—early in November 1831—for fomenting a rebellion in which sixty white people had perished.

The immediate consequences of the insurrection were exceedingly grim. The killing of so many white people was in itself an act of futility. It has never been determined with any accuracy how many black people, not connected with the rebellion, were slain at the hands of rampaging bands of white men who swarmed all over Southampton in the week following the uprising, seeking reprisal and vengeance. A contemporary estimate by a Richmond newspaper, which deplored this retaliation, put the number at close to two hundred Negroes, many of them free, and many of them tortured in ways unimaginably horrible. But even more important was the effect that Nat Turner's insurrection had upon the institution of slavery at large. News of the revolt spread among Southern whites with great speed: the impossible, the unspeakable had at last taken place after two hundred years of the ministrations of sweet old mammies and softly murmured "Yassuh's" and docile compliance—and a shock wave of anguish and terror ran through the entire South. If such a nightmarish calamity happened there, would it not happen *here*—here in Tennessee, in Augusta, in Vicksburg, in these bayous of Louisiana? Had Nat lived to see the consequences of his rebellion, surely it would have been for him the cruelest irony that his bold and desperate bid for liberty had caused only the most tyrannical new controls to be imposed upon Negroes everywhere—the establishment of patrols, further restrictions upon movement, education, assembly, and the beginning of other severe and crippling restraints which persisted throughout the slave-holding states until the Civil War. Virginia had been edging close to emancipation, and it seems reasonable to believe that the example of Nat's rebellion, stampeding many moderates in the legislature into a conviction that the Negroes could not be safely freed, was a decisive factor in the ultimate victory of the pro-slavery forces. Had Virginia, with its enormous prestige among the states, emancipated its slaves, the effect upon our history would be awesome to contemplate.

    Nat brought cold, paralyzing fear to the South, a fear that never departed. If white men had sown the wind with chattel slavery, in Nat Turner they had reaped the whirlwind for white and black alike.

    Nat was executed, along with sixteen other Negroes who had figured large in the insurrection. Most of the others were transported south, to the steaming fields of rice and cotton. On November 11, 1831, Nat was hanged from a live-oak tree in the town square of Jerusalem. He went to his death with great dignity and courage. "The bodies of those executed," wrote Drewry, "with one exception, were buried in a decent and becoming manner. That of Nat Turner was delivered to the doctors, who skinned it and made grease of the flesh."

III

Not long ago, in the spring of the year, when I was visiting my family in Virginia, I decided to go down for the day to Southampton County, which is a drive of an hour or so by car from the town where I was born and raised. Nat Turner was of course the reason for this trip, although I had nothing particular or urgent in mind. What research it was possible to do on the event I had long since done. The Southampton court records, I had already been reliably informed, would prove unrewarding. It was not a question, then, of digging out more facts, but simply a matter of wanting to savor the mood and atmosphere of a landscape I had not seen for quite a few years, since the times when as a boy I used to pass through Southampton on the way to my father's family home in North Carolina. I thought also that there might be a chance of visiting some of the historic sites connected with the insurrection, and even of retracing part of the route of the uprising through the help of one of those handsomely produced guidebooks for which the Association for the Preservation of Virginia Antiquities is famous—guides indispensable for a trip to such Old Dominion shrines as Jamestown and Appomattox and Monticello. I became even more eager to go when one of my in-laws put me in touch by telephone with a cousin of his. This man, whom I shall call Dan Seward, lived near Franklin, the main town of Southampton, and he assured me in those broad cheery Southern tones which are like a warm embrace—and which, after long years in the chill North, are to me always so familiar, reminiscent, and therefore so unsettling, sweet and curiously painful—that he would like nothing better than to aid me in my exploration in whatever way he could.

Dan Seward is a farmer and prosperous grower of peanuts in a prosperous agricultural region where the peanut is the unquestioned monarch. A combination of sandy loam soil and a long growing season has made Southampton ideal for the cultivation of peanuts; over 30,000 acres are planted annually, and the crop is processed and marketed in Franklin—a thriving little town of 7,000 people—or in Suffolk and Portsmouth, where it is rendered into Planters cooking oil and stock feed and Skippy peanut butter. There are other money-making crops—corn and soybeans and cotton. The county is at the northernmost edge of the Cotton Belt, and thirty years ago cotton was a major source of income. Cotton has declined in importance but the average yield per acre is still among the highest in the South, and the single gin left in the country in the little village of Drewryville processes each year several thousand bales, which are trucked to market down in North Carolina. Lumbering is also very profitable, owing mainly to an abundance of the loblolly pines valuable in the production of kraft wood pulp; and the Union Bag-Camp Paper Company's plant on the Blackwater River in Franklin is a huge enterprise employing over 1,600 people. But it is peanuts—the harvested vines in autumn piled up mile after mile in dumpy brown stacks like hay—that have brought money to Southampton, and a sheen of prosperity that can be seen in the freshly painted farmhouses along the monotonously flat state highway which leads into Franklin, and the new-model Dodges and Buicks parked slantwise against the curb of some crossroads hamlet, and the gaudy, eye-catching signs that advise the wisdom of a bank savings account for all those surplus funds.

The county has very much the look of the New South about it, with its airport and its shiny new motels, its insistent billboards advertising space for industrial sites, the sprinkling of housing developments with television antennas gleaming from every rooftop, its supermarkets and shopping centers and its flavor of go-getting commercialism. This is the New South, where agriculture still prevails but has joined in a vigorous union with industry, so that even the peanut when it goes to market is ground up in some rumbling engine of commerce and becomes metamorphosed into wood stain or soap or cattle feed. The Negroes, too, have partaken of this abundance—some of it, at least—for they own television sets also, and if not new-model Buicks (the Southern white man's strictures against Negro ostentation remain intimidating), then decent late-model used Fords; while in the streets of Franklin the Negro women shopping seemed on the day of my visit very proud and well-dressed compared to the shabby, stooped figures I recalled from the Depression years when I was a boy. It would certainly appear that Negroes deserve some of this abundance, if only because they make up so large a part of the work force. Since Nat Turner's day the balance of population in Southampton—almost 60 percent Negro—has hardly altered by a hair.

"I don't know anywhere that a Negro is treated better than around here," Mr. Seward was saying to the three of us, on the spring morning I visited him with my wife and my father. "You take your average person from up North, he just doesn't *know* the Negro like we do. Now, for instance, I have a Negro who's worked for me for years, name of Ernest. He knows if he breaks his arm—like he did a while ago, fell off a tractor—he knows he can come to me and I'll see that he's taken care of, hospital expenses and all, and I'll take care of him and his family while he's unable to work, right on down the line. I don't ask him to pay back a cent, either, that's for sure. We have a wonderful relationship, that Negro and myself. By God, I'd die for that Negro and he knows it, and he'd do the same for me. But Ernest doesn't want to sit down at my table, here in this house, and have supper with me—and he wouldn't want me in *his* house. And Ernest's got kids like I do, and he doesn't want them to go to school with my Bobby, any more than Bobby wants to go to school with *his* kids. It works both ways. People up North don't seem to be able to understand a simple fact like that."

Mr. Seward was a solidly fleshed, somewhat rangy, big-shouldered man in his early forties with an open, cheerful manner which surely did nothing to betray the friendliness with which he had spoken on the telephone. He had greeted us—total strangers, really—with an animation and uncomplicated good will that would have shamed an Eskimo; and for a moment I realized that after years amid the granite outcroppings of New England, I had forgotten that this *was* the passionate, generous, outgoing nature of the South, no artificial display but a social gesture as natural as breathing.

Mr. Seward had just finished rebuilding his farmhouse on the outskirts of town, and he had shown us around with a pride I found understandable: there was a sparkling electric kitchen worthy of an advertisement in *Life* magazine, some handsome modern furniture and several downstairs rooms paneled beautifully in the prodigal and lustrous hardwood of the region. It was altogether a fine, tasteful house, resembling more one of the prettier medium-priced homes in the Long Island suburbs than the house one might contemplate for a Tidewater farmer. Upstairs, we had inspected his son Bobby's room, a kid's room with books like *Pinocchio* and *The Black Arrow* and *The Swiss Family Robinson*, and here there was a huge paper banner spread across one entire wall with the crayon inscription: *"Two . . . four . . . six . . . eight! We Don't Want to Integrate!"* It was a sign which so overwhelmingly dominated the room that it could not help provoking comment, and it was this that eventually had led to Mr. Seward's reflections about *knowing* Negroes.

There might have been something vaguely defensive in his remarks but not a trace of hostility. His tone was matter-of-fact and good-natured, and he pronounced the word Negro as *"nigra,"* which most Southerners do with utter naturalness while intending no disrespect whatsoever, in fact quite the opposite—the mean epithet, of course, is *"nigger."* I had the feeling that Mr. Seward had begun amiably to regard us as sympathetic but ill-informed outsiders, non-Southern, despite his knowledge of my Tidewater background and my father's own accent, which is thick as grits. Moreover, the fact that I had admitted to having lived in the North for fifteen years caused me, I fear, to appear alien in his eyes, *déraciné,* especially when my acculturation to Northern ways has made me adopt the long "e" and say "Negro." The racial misery, at any rate, is within inches of driving us mad: how can I explain that with all my silent disagreement with Mr. Seward's paternalism, I knew that when he said, "By God, I'd die for that Negro," he meant it?

Perhaps I should not have been surprised that Mr. Seward seemed to know very little about Nat Turner. When we got around to the subject, it developed that he had always thought that the insurrection occurred way back in the eighteenth century. Affably, he described seeing in his boyhood the "Hanging Tree," the live oak from which Nat had been hanged in Courtland (Jerusalem had undergone this change of name after the Civil War), and which had died and been cut down some thirty years ago; as for any other landmarks, he regretted that he did not know of a single one. No, so far as he knew, there just wasn't anything.

For me, it was the beginning of disappointments which grew with every hour. Had I *really* been so ingenuous as to believe that I would unearth some shrine, some home preserved after the manner of Colonial Williamsburg, a relic of the insurrection at whose portal I would discover a lady in billowing satin and crinoline who for fifty cents would shepherd me about the rooms with a gentle drawl indicating the spot where a good mistress fell at the hands of the murderous darky? The native Virginian, despite himself, is cursed with a suffocating sense of history, and I do not think it impossible that I actually suspected some such monument. Nevertheless, confident that there would be something to look at, I took heart when Mr. Seward suggested that after lunch we all drive over to Courtland, ten miles to the west. He had already spoken to a friend of his, the sheriff of the county, who knew all the obscure byways and odd corners of Southampton, mainly because of his endless search for illegal stills; if there was a solitary person alive who might be able to locate some landmark or could help retrace part of Nat Turner's march, it was the sheriff. This gave me hope. For I had brought along Drewry's book and its map, which showed the general route of the uprising, marking the houses by name. In the sixty years since Drewry, there would have been many changes in the landscape. But with this map oriented against the sheriff's detailed county map, I should easily be able to pick up the trail and thus experience, however briefly, a sense of the light and shadow that played over that scene of slaughter and retribution a hundred and thirty-four years ago.

Yet it was as if Nat Turner had never existed, and as the day lengthened and afternoon wore on, and as we searched Nat's part of the county—five of us now, riding in the sheriff's car with its huge star emblazoned on the doors, and its radio blatting out hoarse intermittent messages, and its riot gun protectively nuzzling the backs of our necks over the edge of the rear seat—I had the sensation from time to time that this Negro, who had so long occupied my thoughts, who indeed had so obsessed my imagination that he had acquired larger spirit and flesh than most of the living people I encountered day in and day out, had been merely a crazy figment of my mind, a phantom no more real than some half-recollected image from a fairy tale. For here in the back country, this horizontal land of woods and meadows where he had roamed, only a few people had heard of Nat Turner, and of those who had—among the people we stopped to make inquiries of, both white and black, along dusty country roads, at farms, at filling stations, at crossroad stores—most of them confused him, I think, with something spectral, mythic, a black Paul Bunyan who had perpetrated mysterious and nameless deeds in millennia past. They were neither facetious nor evasive, simply unaware. Others confounded him with the Civil War—a Negro general. One young Negro field hand, lounging at an Esso station, figured he was a white man. A white man, heavy-lidded, and paunchy, slow-witted, an idler at a rickety store, thought him an illustrious race horse of bygone days.

The sheriff, a smallish, soft-speaking ruminative man, with a whisper of a smile frozen on his face as if he were perpetually enjoying a good joke, knew full well who Nat Turner was, and I could tell he relished our frustrating charade. He was a shrewd person, quick and sharp with countrified wisdom, and he soon became quite as fascinated as I with the idea of tracking down some relic of the uprising (although he said that Drewry's map was hopelessly out of date, the roads of that time now abandoned to the fields and woods, the homes burned down or gone to ruin); the country people's ignorance he found irresistible and I think it tickled him to perplex their foolish heads, white or black, with the same old leading question: "You heard about old Nat Turner, ain't you?" But few of them had heard, even though I was sure that many had plowed the same fields that Nat had crossed, lived on land that he had passed by; and as for dwellings still standing which might have been connected with the rebellion, not one of these back-country people could offer the faintest hint or clue. As effectively as a monstrous and unbearable dream, Nat had been erased from memory.

It was late afternoon when, with a sense of deep fatigue and frustration, I suggested to Mr. Seward and the sheriff that maybe we had better go back to Courtland and call it a day. They were agreeable—relieved, I felt, to be freed of this tedious and fruitless search—and as we headed east down a straight unpaved road, the conversation became desultory, general. We spoke of the North. The sheriff was interested to learn that I often traveled to New York. He went there occasionally himself, he said; indeed, he had been there only the month before—"to pick up a nigger," a fugitive from custody who had been awaiting trial for killing his wife. New York was a fine place to spend the night, said the sheriff, but he wouldn't want to live there.

As he spoke I had been gazing out of the window, and now suddenly something caught my eye—something familiar, a brief flickering passage of a distant outline, a silhouette against the sun-splashed woods—and I asked the sheriff to stop the car. He did, and as we backed up slowly through a cloud of dust I recognized a house standing perhaps a quarter of a mile off the road, from this distance only a lopsided oblong sheltered by an enormous oak, but the whole tableau—the house and the glorious hovering tree and the stretch of woods beyond—so familiar to me that it might have been some home I passed every day. And of course now as recognition came flooding back I knew whose house it was. For in *The Southampton Insurrection*, the indefatigable Drewry had included many photographs—amateurish, doubtless taken by himself, and suffering from the fuzzy offset reproduction of 1900. But they were clear enough to provide an unmistakable guide to the dwellings in question, and now as I again consulted the book I could see that this house—the monumental oak above it grown scant inches, it seemed, in sixty years—was the one referred to by Drewry as having belonged to Mrs. Catherine Whitehead. From this distance, in the soft clear light of a spring afternoon, it seemed most tranquil, but few houses have come to know such a multitude of violent deaths. There in the late afternoon of Monday, August 22, Nat Turner and his band had appeared, and they set upon and killed "Mrs. Catherine Whitehead, son Richard, and four daughters, and grandchild."

The approach to the house was by a rutted lane long ago abandoned and overgrown with lush weeds, which made a soft, crushed, rasping sound as we rolled over them. Dogwood, white and pink, grew on either side of the lane, quite wild and wanton in lovely pastel splashes. Not far from the house a pole fence interrupted our way; the sheriff stopped the car and we got out and stood there for a moment, looking at the place. It was quiet and still—so quiet that the sudden chant of a mockingbird in the woods was almost frightening—and we realized then that no one lived in the house. Scoured by weather, paintless, worn down to the wintry gray of bone and with all the old mortar gone from between the timbers, it stood alone and desolate above its blasted, sagging front porch, the ancient door ajar like an open wound. Although never a manor house, it had once been a spacious and comfortable country home; now in near-ruin it sagged, finished, a shell, possessing only the most fragile profile of itself. As we drew closer still, we could see that the entire house, from its upper story to the cellar, was filled with thousands of shucked ears of corn—feed for the malevolent-looking razorback pigs which suddenly appeared in a tribe at the edge of the house, eying us, grunting. Mr. Seward sent them scampering with a shied stick and a farmer's sharp "Whoo!" I looked up at the house, trying to recollect its particular role in Nat's destiny, and then I remembered.

There was something baffling, secret, irrational about Nat's own participation in the uprising. He was unable to kill. Time and time again in his confession one discovers him saying (in an offhand tone; one must dig for the implications): "I could not give the death blow, the hatchet glanced from his head," or, "I struck her several blows over the head, but I was unable to kill her, as the sword was dull . . ." It is too much to believe, over and over again: the glancing hatchet, the dull sword. It smacks rather, as in *Hamlet*, of rationalization, ghastly fear, an access of guilt, a shrinking from violence, and fatal irresolution. Alone here at this house, turned now into a huge corncrib around which pigs rooted and snorted in the silence of a spring afternoon, here alone was Nat finally able—or was he forced?—to commit a murder, and this upon a girl of eighteen named Margaret Whitehead, described by Drewry in terms perhaps not so romantic or far-fetched, after all, as "the belle of the county." The scene is apocalyptic—afternoon bedlam in wild harsh sunlight and August heat.

> I returned to commence the work of death, but those whom I left had not been idle; all the family were already murdered but Mrs. Whitehead and her daughter Margaret. As I came around the door I saw Will pulling Mrs. Whitehead out of the house and at the step he nearly severed her head from her body with his axe. Miss Margaret, when I discovered her, had concealed herself in the corner formed by the projection of the cellar cap from the house; on my approach she fled into the field but was soon overtaken and after repeated blows with a sword, I killed her by a blow on the head with a fence rail.

It is Nat's only murder. Why, from this point on, does the momentum of the uprising diminish, the drive and tension sag? Why, from this moment in the "Confessions," does one sense in Nat something dispirited, listless, as if all life and juice had been drained from him, so that never again through the course of the rebellion is he even on the scene when a murder is committed? What happened to Nat in this place? Did he discover his humanity here, or did he lose it? 42

I lifted myself up into the house, clambering through a doorway without steps, pushing myself over the crumbling sill. The house had a faint yeasty fragrance, like flat beer. Dust from the mountains of corn lay everywhere in the deserted rooms, years and decades of dust, dust an inch thick in some places, lying in a fine gray powder like sooty fallen snow. Off in some room amid the piles of corn I could hear a delicate scrabbling and a plaintive squeaking of mice. Again it was very still, the shadow of the prodigious old oak casting a dark pattern of leaves, checkered with bright sunlight, aslant through the gaping door. As in those chilling lines of Emily Dickinson, even this lustrous and golden day seemed to find its only resonance in the memory, and perhaps a premonition, of death. 43

> This quiet Dust was Gentlemen and Ladies,
> And Lads and Girls;
> Was laughter and ability and sighing,
> And frocks and curls.

Outside, the sheriff was calling in on his car radio, his voice blurred and indistinct; then the return call from the county seat, loud, a dozen incomprehensible words in an uproar of static. Suddenly it was quiet again, the only sound my father's soft voice as he chatted with Mr. Seward.

I leaned against the rotting frame of the door, gazing out past the great tree and into that far meadow where Nat had brought down and slain Miss Margaret Whitehead. For an instant, in the silence, I thought I could hear a mad rustle of taffeta, and rushing feet, and a shrill girlish piping of terror; then that day and this day seemed to meet and melt together, becoming almost one, and for a long moment indistinguishable.

Rhetorical Analysis

1. The first paragraph of "This Quiet Dust" is a long one; it sets up the subject and focus of the essay, and establishes its tone. One might argue that both topic and tone are firmly established by the end of the first sentence, and that the rest of the paragraph is mere elaboration. Copy down the first sentence on a sheet of paper and show how the rest of the paragraph is derived from it. How does Styron use parenthetical phrases to help establish his tone? What is the function of the quotation in the paragraph?

2. Styron divides his essay into three parts, each relatively distinct in content and in expression.
    a. What is the effect of this three-part structure? Could the parts have been switched around with equal or greater effect?
    b. How does the three-part structure strengthen the final sentence: "that day and this day seemed to meet and melt together . . ."?
    c. The structure of the whole finally achieves a unity; analyze what that unity implies. What is implied about Styron? about the nature of history? about Turner and what he represents?

3. Why does Styron refuse to make his meaning lucid to the reader in his conclusion? What does he gain by beginning the essay with a clear presentation of ideas, and then concluding it with a series of detailed descriptions (of Southampton, of Dan Seward, of the ride with the sheriff), a statement of Nat Turner's "baffling"

inability to murder, an unglossed quotation from Turner's *Confessions*, a paragraph of unanswered questions, and finally a description, again without comment, of the author's experience at a moment of time? What are we to make of this winding down and how does it work as a rhetorical device?

Intellectual Analysis

1. Consider a sentence at the end of Part I: "But to break down the old law, to come to *know* the Negro, has become the moral imperative of every white Southerner."
    a. Is this the real thesis of "This Quiet Dust"? If so, how does the rest of the essay hinge on it?
    b. This idea of breaking down the old law blends with Styron's statement (¶ 5) that racial animosity in the South is "grounded not upon friction and propinquity, but upon an almost complete lack of contact." Styron wants us to rethink several assumptions, myths, and notions about race and the South which follow. Consider Styron's comments about the sexual myth, his comments about "deadly intimidation of a universal law," and a paradox which has behind it "the full majesty of the law." Analyze these in light of what Styron sees as the underlying cause of racial tension.
2. In Part II, Styron links several details which, on reflection, deserve further analysis: Turner's age at the time (31); his preparation of himself "for the apocalyptic role he was to play"; his withdrawal and fasting; his supposed madness, and vision; the reaction after his capture (including the tree from which he was hanged). What are we to infer from these details? Analyze them carefully. Styron himself speculates on at least one detail.
3. In Part III, Styron seems inordinately taken with Turner's "only murder." But, as noted above, Styron raises more questions than he answers. Why? You should take into account not only Turner, white Southern reaction, and Styron himself, but broader questions about civil insurrection, tyranny of the majority, the failure of the judicial system, and the political consequences of a failed revolution.

Suggestions for Writing

1. Develop an essay on the aptness and meaning of the title, "This Quiet Dust." Look at the Emily Dickinson poem below from which the title is taken.

> This quiet Dust was Gentlemen and Ladies
> And Lads and Girls—
> Was laughter and ability and Sighing
> And Frocks and Curls.

> This Passive Place a Summer's nimble mansion
> Where Bloom and Bees
> Exists an Oriental Circuit
> Then cease, like these—

2. Write an essay divided into two or three parts, each part written entirely in a different mode. You might, for example, begin with narration, followed by two sections of exposition. However, the whole ought to be unified by a single theme.

E. M. Forster

It is something of a surprise that after the appearance in 1924 of his most famous novel, A Passage to India, Forster wrote no more novels. But he did not stop writing altogether. Travel books, essays, and criticism appeared regularly, if occasionally. Indeed, Forster might be regarded as the last of a nineteenth-century type, the English Man of Letters, writing when he had something to say, then saying it quietly with a wry, though somewhat distant, irony born of unhurried days in the country and measured by ample dinners taken with imported claret.

Yet Edward Morgan Forster (1879–1970) ranks among the foremost of twentieth-century novelists. Educated at Kings College, Cambridge, he was for a time associated with the brilliant Bloomsbury group, traveled for several months in India, and lived briefly in Alexandria, Egypt. During World War II, he worked as a propaganda broadcaster for the BBC; many of those talks, rewritten, became essays in Two Cheers for Democracy, published in 1951. As a result of these broadcasts, he was placed on the famous Nazi blacklist, alongside politicians, military men, and other "subversives." In later years he lived quietly in his house in the country parish of Abinger, which provided him with the title of his first book of essays, Abinger Harvest (1936).

One may say of Forster, at least as a writer, what he himself said of Voltaire as a man: humanity "to him was not a platform gesture. He got down to brass tacks over it." The most characteristic tone of Forster's essays is a bemused irony, engendered by a persistent refusal to give the third cheer. His lifelong insistence that the English needed to feel more passion more deeply more often was tempered by the conviction that one must have "tolerance" for the passions of others, however eccentric they may seem.

Regarded as a spokesman for old-fashioned liberal humanism, Forster might better be seen as a conservative in the eighteenth-century sense of that term—as conserving the hard won, "brass-tacks" values of a civilization in its place in the natural world. In a pageant written for performance at Abinger in the thirties, Forster assigned himself the role of "the Woodman" (caretaker of the estate), and, looking out over the present state of England, said: "Look into your hearts and look into the past, and remember that all this beauty is a gift which you can never replace, which no money can buy, which no cleverness can refashion. You can make a town, you can make a desert, you can even make a garden; but you can never, never make the country, because it was made by time."

My Wood

A few years ago I wrote a book which dealt in part with the difficulties of the English in India. Feeling that they would have had no difficulties in India themselves, the Americans read the book freely. The more they read it the better it made them feel, and a cheque to the author was the result. I bought a wood with the cheque. It is not a large wood—it contains scarcely any trees, and it is intersected, blast it, by a public footpath. Still, it is the first property that I have owned, so it is right that other people should participate in my shame, and should ask themselves, in accents that will vary in horror, this very important question: What is the effect of property upon the character? Don't let's touch economics; the effect of private ownership upon the community as a whole is another question—a more important question, perhaps, but another one. Let's keep to psychology. If you own things, what's their effect on you? What's the effect on me of my wood?

In the first place, it makes me feel heavy. Property does have this effect. Property produces men of weight, and it was a man of weight

1

2

who failed to get into the Kingdom of Heaven. He was not wicked, that unfortunate millionaire in the parable, he was only stout; he stuck out in front, not to mention behind, and as he wedged himself this way and that in the crystalline entrance and bruised his well-fed flanks, he saw beneath him a comparatively slim camel passing through the eye of a needle and being woven into the robe of God. The Gospels all through couple stoutness and slowness. They point out what is perfectly obvious, yet seldom realized: that if you have a lot of things you cannot move about a lot, that furniture requires dusting, dusters require servants, servants require insurance stamps, and the whole tangle of them makes you think twice before you accept an invitation to dinner or go for a bathe in the Jordan. Sometimes the Gospels proceed further and say with Tolstoy that property is sinful; they approach the difficult ground of asceticism here, where I cannot follow them. But as to the immediate effects of property on people, they just show straightforward logic. It produces men of weight. Men of weight cannot, by definition, move like the lightning from the East unto the West, and the ascent of a fourteen-stone bishop into a pulpit is thus the exact antithesis of the coming of the Son of Man. My wood makes me feel heavy.

In the second place, it makes me feel it ought to be larger. 3

The other day I heard a twig snap in it. I was annoyed at first, for 4
I thought that someone was blackberrying, and depreciating the value of the undergrowth. On coming nearer, I saw it was not a man who had trodden on the twig and snapped it, but a bird, and I felt pleased. My bird. The bird was not equally pleased. Ignoring the relation between us, it took fright as soon as it saw the shape of my face, and flew straight over the boundary hedge into a field, the property of Mrs. Henessy, where it sat down with a loud squawk. It had become Mrs. Henessy's bird. Something seemed grossly amiss here, something that would not have occurred had the wood been larger. I could not afford to buy Mrs. Henessy out, I dared not murder her, and limitations of this sort beset me on every side. Ahab did not want that vineyard—he only needed it to round off his property, preparatory to plotting a new curve—and all the land around my wood has become necessary to me in order to round off the wood. A boundary protects. But—poor little thing—the boundary ought in its turn to be protected. Noises on the edge of it. Children throw stones. A little more, and then a little more, until we reach the sea. Happy Canute! Happier Alexander! And after all, why should even the world be the limit of possession? A rocket containing a Union Jack, will, it is hoped, be shortly fired at the moon.

Mars. Sirius. Beyond which . . . But these immensities ended by saddening me. I could not suppose that my wood was the destined nucleus of universal dominion—it is so very small and contains no mineral wealth beyond the blackberries. Nor was I comforted when Mrs. Henessy's bird took alarm for the second time and flew clean away from us all, under the belief that it belonged to itself.

In the third place, property makes its owner feel that he ought to do something to it. Yet he isn't sure what. A restlessness comes over him, a vague sense that he has a personality to express—the same sense which, without any vagueness, leads the artist to an act of creation. Sometimes I think I will cut down such trees as remain in the wood, at other times I want to fill up the gaps between them with new trees. Both impulses are pretentious and empty. They are not honest movements towards money-making or beauty. They spring from a foolish desire to express myself and from an inability to enjoy what I have got. Creation, property, enjoyment form a sinister trinity in the human mind. Creation and enjoyment are both very, very good, yet they are often unattainable without a material basis, and at such moments property pushes itself in as a substitute, saying, "Accept me instead—I'm good enough for all three." It is not enough. It is, as Shakespeare said of lust, "The expense of spirit in a waste of shame": it is "Before, a joy proposed; behind, a dream." Yet we don't know how to shun it. It is forced on us by our economic system as the alternative to starvation. It is also forced on us by an internal defect in the soul, by the feeling that in property may lie the germs of self-development and of exquisite or heroic deeds. Our life on earth is, and ought to be, material and carnal. But we have not yet learned to manage our materialism and carnality properly; they are still entangled with the desire for ownership, where (in the words of Dante) "Possession is one with loss."

And this brings us to our fourth and final point: the blackberries.

Blackberries are not plentiful in this meagre grove, but they are easily seen from the public footpath which traverses it, and all too easily gathered. Foxgloves, too—people will pull up the foxgloves, and ladies of an educational tendency even grub for toadstools to show them on the Monday in class. Other ladies, less educated, roll down the bracken in the arms of their gentlemen friends. There is paper, there are tins. Pray, does my wood belong to me or doesn't it? And, if it does, should I not own it best by allowing no one else to walk there? There is a wood near Lyme Regis, also cursed by a public footpath, where the owner has not hesitated on this point. He had built high stone walls each side of the path, and has spanned it by bridges, so that the public circulate like termites while he gorges on the blackberries unseen. He really does own his wood, this able chap. Dives in Hell did pretty well, but the gulf dividing him from Lazarus could be traversed by vision, and nothing traverses it here. And perhaps I shall come to this in time. I shall wall in and fence out until I really taste the sweets of property. Enormously stout, endlessly avaricious, pseudo-creative, intensely selfish, I shall weave upon my forehead the quadruple crown of possession until those nasty Bolshies come and take it off again and thrust me aside into the outer darkness.

Rhetorical Analysis

1. A good way to write a bad essay is to follow the formula sometimes prescribed by high-school English teachers. End your introductory paragraph with a question which the rest of the essay answers. Divide your answer into three or four parts, devote one paragraph to each part, and begin each paragraph with a clear transition, "In the first place," "In the second place," and so on. Finally, restate in your conclusion the parts of your answer. It is hard to imagine an essay organized in this fashion that would not be clumsy, stilted, boring. Yet this is exactly what Forster has done in "My Wood." How does he get by with it? Does his subject or his method of dealing with his subject lend itself especially to this organization? (Forster's essay on "Anonymity" similarly proceeds in an obvious way.)

2. *Lead into your topic in an entertaining way. Restrict your topic.* These are two pieces of advice you again may have heard in high-school composition courses but, this time, they are also techniques which professional writers use over and over. Forster accomplishes both in his first paragraph, with great skill. Analyze very carefully how he does so.

3. Humor is notoriously hard to analyze. In a writer as sophisticated as Forster, it is especially elusive. But for the beginning writer, a good deal can be learned by spending a few minutes with a piece such as "My Wood," simply looking for the source of humorous points without attempting to generalize. You will be surprised at the variety of ways Forster can be witty in a short space.

Intellectual Analysis

1. In the opening paragraph, Forster announces his topic clearly: "What is the effect of property on the character," psychologically speaking. And he divides his comments into four parts, all likewise clearly signaled:

"It makes me feel heavy."
"It makes me feel it ought to be larger."
"It makes its owner feel he ought to do something to it."
". . . the blackberries."
Is there any progression among these four points?

2. Forster speaks with urbanity and with detached, ironic wit: yet he uses this tone to speak of something important. Why? What thematic or intellectual advantage does he gain by his wit?

3. Forster refers to the Biblical simile of the needle's eye (Matt. 19:24), and the story of the rich man and Lazarus, the beggar (Luke 16:19), together with Shakespeare's sonnet (No. 129) and a sentence from Dante: "Possession is one with loss." You will find it invigorating to compare and evaluate either of the Biblical references or the Shakespeare sonnet with the essay. As for the quote from Dante, what do you think it means, and what implications are involved? Can we ever really possess anything? If there are things we are able to possess and have, what are they? (Take a look once again at the first lines of the essay!)

Suggestions for Writing

1. Take any one of the four principal ideas Forster maps out, and develop an essay—perhaps of a speculative sort—on that point.
2. Consider the sentence, "A little more, then a little more, until we reach the sea," and develop an essay on its meaning, using the perspective of Forster's essay.
3. Write an essay on your possessions. What significance do they have to you? What were your very first possessions? What significance does the word "mine" have, especially to a child?

TOLERANCE

*E*verybody is talking about reconstruction. Our enemies have their schemes for a new order in Europe, maintained by their secret police, and we on our side talk of rebuilding London or England, or western civilization, and we make plans how this is to be done. Which is all very well, but when I hear such talk, and see the architects sharpening their pencils and the contractors getting out their estimates, and the statesmen marking out their spheres of influence, and everyone getting down to the job, a very famous text occurs to me: "Except the Lord build the house, they labour in vain that build it." Beneath the poetic imagery of these words lies a hard scientific truth, namely, unless you have a sound attitude of mind, a right psychology, you cannot construct or reconstruct anything that will endure. The text is true, not only for religious people, but for workers whatever their outlook, and it is significant that one of our historians, Dr. Arnold Toynbee, should have chosen it to preface his great study of the growth and decay of civilizations. Surely the only sound foundation for a civilization is a sound state of mind. Architects, contractors, international commissioners, marketing boards, broadcasting corporations will never, by themselves, build a new world. They must be inspired by the proper spirit, and there must be the proper spirit in the people for whom they are working. For instance, we shall never have a beautiful new London until people refuse to live in ugly houses. At present, they don't mind; they demand more comfort, but are indifferent to civic beauty; indeed they have no taste. I live myself in a hideous block of flats, but I can't say it worries me, and until we are worried all schemes for reconstructing London beautifully must automatically fail.

What, though, is the proper spirit? We agree that the basic problem is psychological, that the Lord must build if the work is to stand, that there must be a sound state of mind before diplomacy or economics or trade conferences can function. But what state of mind is sound? Here we may differ. Most people, when asked what spiritual quality is needed to rebuild civilization, will reply "Love". Men must love one another, they say; nations must do likewise, and then the series of cataclysms which is threatening to destroy us will be checked. 2

Respectfully but firmly, I disagree. Love is a great force in private life; it is indeed the greatest of all things; but love in public affairs does not work. It has been tried again and again: by the Christian civilizations of the Middle Ages, and also by the French Revolution, a secular movement which reasserted the Brotherhood of Man. And it has always failed. The idea that nations should love one another, or that business concerns or marketing boards should love one another, or that a man in Portugal should love a man in Peru of whom he has never heard—it is absurd, unreal, dangerous. It leads us into perilous and vague sentimentalism. "Love is what is needed," we chant, and then sit back and the world goes on as before. The fact is, we can only love what we know personally. And we cannot know much. In public affairs, in the rebuilding of civilization, something much less dramatic and emotional is needed, namely tolerance. Tolerance is a very dull 3 virtue. It is boring. Unlike love, it has always had a bad press. It is negative. It merely means putting up with people, being able to stand things. No one has ever written an ode to tolerance, or raised a statue to her. Yet this is the quality which will be most needed after the war. This is the sound state of mind which we are looking for. This is the only force which will enable different races and classes and interests to settle down together to the work of reconstruction.

4   The world is very full of people—appallingly full; it has never been so full before—and they are all tumbling over each other. Most of these people one doesn't know and some of them one doesn't like; doesn't like the colour of their skins, say, or the shapes of their noses, or the way they blow them or don't blow them, or the way they talk, or their smell, or their clothes, or their fondness for jazz or their dislike of jazz, and so on. Well, what is one to do? There are two solutions. One of them is the Nazi solution. If you don't like people, kill them, banish them, segregate them, and then strut up and down proclaiming that you are the salt of the earth. The other way is much less thrilling, but it is on the whole the way of the democracies, and I prefer it. If you don't like people, put up with them as well as you can. Don't try to love them; you can't, you'll only strain yourself. But try to tolerate them. On the basis of that tolerance a civilized future may be built. Certainly I can see no other foundation for the post-war world.

5   For what it will most need is the negative virtues: not being huffy, touchy, irritable, revengeful. I have lost all faith in positive militant ideals; they can so seldom be carried out without thousands of human beings getting maimed or imprisoned. Phrases like "I will purge this nation", "I will clean up this city", terrify and disgust me. They might not have mattered when the world was emptier; they are horrifying now, when one nation is mixed up with another, when one city cannot be organically separated from its neighbours. And another point: reconstruction is unlikely to be rapid. I do not believe that we are psychologically fit for it, plan the architects never so wisely. In the long run, yes, perhaps; the history of our race justifies that hope. But civilization has its mysterious regressions, and it seems to me that we are fated now to be in one of them, and must recognize this and behave accordingly. Tolerance, I believe, will be imperative after the establishment of peace. It's always useful to take a concrete instance; and I have been asking myself how I should behave if, after peace was signed, I met Germans who had been fighting against us. I shouldn't try to love them; I shouldn't feel inclined. They have broken a window in my little ugly flat for one thing. But I shall try to tolerate them,

because it is common sense, because in the post-war world we shall have to live with Germans. We can't exterminate them, any more than they have succeeded in exterminating the Jews. We shall have to put up with them, not for any lofty reason, but because it is the next thing that will have to be done.

I don't then, regard tolerance as a great eternally established divine principle, though I might perhaps quote "In my Father's house are many mansions" in support of such a view. It is just a makeshift, suitable for an overcrowded and overheated planet. It carries on when love gives out, and love generally gives out as soon as we move away from our home and our friends, and stand among strangers in a queue for potatoes. Tolerance is wanted in the queue; otherwise we think, "Why will people be so slow?"; it is wanted in the tube, or "Why will people be so fat?"; it is wanted at the telephone, or "Why are they so deaf?" or, conversely, "Why do they mumble?" It is wanted in the street, in the office, at the factory, and it is wanted above all between classes, races and nations. It's dull. And yet it entails imagination. For you have all the time to be putting yourself in someone else's place. Which is a desirable spiritual exercise.

This ceaseless effort to put up with other people seems tame, almost ignoble, so that it sometimes repels generous natures, and I don't recall many great men who have recommended tolerance. St. Paul certainly did not. Nor did Dante. However, a few names occur. Going back over two thousand years, and to India, there is the great Buddhist Emperor Asoka, who set up inscriptions recording not his own exploits but the need for mercy and mutual understanding and peace. Going back about four hundred years, to Holland, there is the Dutch scholar Erasmus, who stood apart from the religious fanaticism of the Reformation and was abused by both parties in consequence. In the same century there was the Frenchman Montaigne, subtle, intelligent, witty, who lived in his quiet country house and wrote essays which still delight and confirm the civilized. And England: there was John Locke, the philosopher; there was Sydney Smith, the Liberal and liberalizing divine; there was Lowes Dickinson, writer of *A Modern Symposium*, which might be called the Bible of Tolerance. And Germany—yes, Germany: there was Goethe. All these men testify to the creed which I have been trying to express: a negative creed, but necessary for the salvation of this crowded jostling modern world.

Two more remarks. First, it is very easy to see fanaticism in other people, but difficult to spot in oneself. Take the evil of racial prejudice. We can easily detect it in the Nazis; their conduct has been infamous ever since they rose to power. But we ourselves—are we guiltless? We are far less guilty than they are. Yet is there no racial prejudice in the British Empire? Is there no colour question? I ask you to consider that, those of you to whom tolerance is more than a pious word. My other remark is to forestall a criticism. Tolerance is not the same as weakness. Putting up with people does not mean giving in to them. This complicates the problem. But the rebuilding of civilization is bound to be complicated. I only feel certain that unless the Lord builds the house they will labour in vain who build it. Perhaps, when the house is completed, love will enter it, and the greatest force in our private lives will also rule in public life.

Rhetorical Analysis

1. Good writers are always conscious of the real-world conditions under which their writing will be read.
    a. Forster wrote "Tolerance" in 1941 for an England that had experienced nearly two years of full war with Nazi Germany, and had suffered many months of the blitz. How does Forster make use of these circumstances?
    b. Forster also wrote the piece as a public address. He knew, then, that his audience would have only one chance to gather his meaning. Stylistically, how does he meet the requirements of this rhetorical situation?
2. Research into the way people write has shown that students tend to construct more sentences of the same length than do experienced writers. What advantages does a writer gain by varying sentence length? Study of Forster's paragraphs in this essay will suggest a number of different advantages.
3. Is tolerance not only the subject of this essay but a quality that is also reflected in its style? Consider the frequent qualifications, the admissions of doubt, the entertainment of alternatives, the civilized pleasantries ("Respectfully but firmly, I disagree"), the overall urbanity of tone. Forster's style—much admired—is difficult to describe. Can you suggest qualities other than tolerance that better explain its compelling nature?

Intellectual Analysis

1. Though its title is "Tolerance," the immediate impulse for the writing of this essay is the subject of European reconstruction after the Second World War. Several questions immediately occur.
    a. What does "reconstruction" mean, and what has it to do with tolerance?

b. The date of this piece is important; the war was a long way from being over, and the outcome was far from certain. (The Allies, for example, might have lost the war in 1942, given certain setbacks.) How do those circumstances affect Forster's meaning when he talks about the such abstractions as love, justice, and so forth?
2. What is Forster's opinion, in this essay, of love?
   a. In a single paragraph he claims that "it is indeed the greatest of all things," and "it is absurd, unreal, dangerous" (¶ 3). How may such statements be reconciled?
   b. Love and population have more in common than the crude fact that an increase in the practice of one often leads to an increase in the other. How, in Forster's thinking, does the latter weaken the former as a force for true reconstruction?
3. Why does Forster continually undercut tolerance, the very virtue about which he wants to instruct his audience? Or does he?
   a. In ¶ 3, he says, "Tolerance is a very dull virtue," and in ¶ 6 that "It is just a makeshift" virtue. What is his intended meaning in such pejorative expressions?
   b. Forster also makes some grander claims for tolerance: for example, it is clearly not passive, it involves imagination, and ends as a "spiritual exercise" (¶ 6). Finally he insists that it is not "the same as weakness" (¶ 8).
Evaluate these two opposed sets of statements. Why would he put tolerance down, only to build it up? What does this tension add to his meaning?
4. Forster links his plea for tolerance with some great thinkers—first with Arnold Toynbee (whose 12-volume *A Study of History* is one of the monuments of twentieth-century scholarship) and toward the end with Erasmus, Montaigne, Goethe, and others.
   a. Is this appeal to authority a legitimate way to support his argument?
   b. Is there a connection between tolerance and the vocations of these men: historians, leaders, philosophers, theologians, artists? What are some ways these vocations require tolerance?

Suggestions for Writing

1. Attempts at reconstruction were made after the American Civil War and after both World Wars. If you are studying any of these periods, develop a research essay on the effects of such "reconstructions."
2. Pick another "dull" virtue such as honesty, frugality, or industriousness and write a lively essay in support of it.
3. Compare "Tolerance" with "Mottoes of My Life," "Decline and Validity of the Idea of Progress," and "Professions for Women," which were also speeches when first presented to the public.

Anonymity: An Enquiry

Do you like to know who a book's by?

The question is more profound than may appear. A poem, for example: do we gain more or less pleasure from it when we know the name of the poet? The "Ballad of Sir Patrick Spens", for example. No one knows who wrote "Sir Patrick Spens". It comes to us out of the northern void like a breath of ice. Set beside it another ballad whose author is known—"The Rime of the Ancient Mariner". That, too, contains a tragic voyage and the breath of ice, but it is signed by Samuel Taylor Coleridge, and we know a certain amount about this Coleridge. Coleridge signed other poems and knew other poets; he ran away from Cambridge; he enlisted as a dragoon under the name of Trooper Comberbache, but fell so constantly from his horse that it had to be withdrawn from beneath him permanently; he was employed instead upon matters relating to sanitation; he married Southey's sister, and gave lectures; he became stout, pious and dishonest, took opium and died. With such information in our heads, we speak of "The Ancient Mariner" as "a poem by Coleridge", but of "Sir Patrick Spens" as "a poem". What difference, if any, does this difference between them make upon our minds? And in the case of novels and plays—does ignorance or knowledge of their authorship signify? And newspaper articles—do they impress more when they are signed or unsigned? Thus—rather vaguely—let us begin our quest.

Books are composed of words, and words have two functions to perform: they give information or they create an atmosphere. Often they do both, for the two functions are not incompatible, but our enquiry shall keep them distinct. Let us turn for our next example to public notices. There is a word that is sometimes hung up at the edge of a tramline: the word "Stop". Written on a metal label by the side of the line, it means that a tram should stop here presently. It is an example of pure information. It creates no atmosphere—at least, not in my mind. I stand close to the label and wait and wait for the tram. If the tram comes, the information is correct; if it doesn't come, the information is incorrect; but in either case it remains information, and the notice is an excellent instance of one of the uses of words.

Compare it with another public notice which is sometimes exhibited in the darker cities of England: "Beware of pickpockets, male and female." Here, again, there is information. A pickpocket may come along presently, just like a tram, and we take our measures accordingly. But there is something else besides. Atmosphere is created. Who can see those words without a slight sinking feeling at the heart? All the people around look so honest and nice, but they are not, some of them are pickpockets, male or female. They hustle old gentlemen, the old gentleman glances down, his watch is gone. They steal up behind an old lady and cut out the back breadth of her beautiful sealskin jacket with sharp and noiseless pairs of scissors. Observe that happy little child running to buy sweets. Why does he suddenly burst into tears? A pickpocket, male or female, has jerked his halfpenny out of his hand. All this, and perhaps much more, occurs to us when we read the notice in question. We suspect our fellows of dishonesty, we observe them suspecting us. We have been reminded of several disquieting truths, of the general insecurity of life, human frailty, the violence of the poor, and the fatuous trustfulness of the rich, who always expect to be popular without having done anything to deserve it. It is a sort of *memento mori*, set up in the midst of Vanity Fair. By taking the form of a warning it has made us afraid, although nothing is gained by fear; all we need to do is to protect our precious purses, and fear will not help us to do this. Besides conveying information it has created an atmosphere, and to that extent is literature. "Beware of pickpockets, male and female" is not good literature, and it is unconscious. But the words are performing two functions, whereas the word "Stop" only performed one, and this is an important difference, and the first step in our journey.

Next step. Let us now collect together all the printed matter of the world into a single heap: poetry books, exercise books, plays, newspapers, advertisements, street notices, everything. Let us arrange the contents of the heap into a line, with the works that convey pure information at one end, and the works that create pure atmosphere at the other end, and the works that do both in their intermediate positions, the whole line being graded so that we pass from one attitude to another. We shall find that at the end of pure information stands the tramway notice "Stop", and that at the extreme other end is lyric poetry. Lyric poetry is absolutely no use. It is the exact antithesis of a street notice, for it conveys no information of any kind. What's the use of "A slumber did my spirt seal" or "Whether on Ida's shady brow" or "So, we'll go no more a roving" or "Far in a western brookland"? They do not tell us where the tram will stop or even whether it exists. And, passing from lyric poetry to ballad, we are still deprived of information. It is true that "The Ancient Mariner" describes an Antarctic expedition, but in such a muddled way that it is no real help to the explorer, the accounts of the polar currents and winds being hopelessly inaccurate. It is true that the "Ballad of Sir Patrick Spens" refers to the bringing home of the Maid of Norway in the year 1285, but the reference is so vague and confused that the historians turn from it in despair. Lyric poetry is absolutely no use, and poetry generally is almost no use.

But when, proceeding down the line, we leave poetry behind and arrive at the drama, and particularly at those plays that purport to contain normal human beings, we find a change. Uselessness still predominates, but we begin to get information as well. *Julius Caesar* contains some reliable information about Rome. And when we pass from the drama to the novel the change is still more marked. Information abounds. What a lot we learn from *Tom Jones* about the west countryside! And from *Northanger Abbey* about the same countryside fifty years later! In psychology too the novelist teaches us much. How carefully has Henry James explored certain selected recesses of the human mind! What an analysis of a country rectory in *The Way of All Flesh*! The instincts of Emily Brontë—they illuminate passion. And Proust—how amazingly does Proust describe not only French society, not only the working of his characters, but the personal equipment of the reader, so that one keeps stopping with a gasp to say, "Oh! how did he find that out about me? I didn't even know it myself until he informed me, but it is so!" The novel, whatever else it may be, is partly a noticeboard. And that is why many men who do not care for poetry or even for the drama enjoy novels and are well qualified to criticize them.

Beyond the novel we come to works whose avowed aim is information, works of learning, history, sociology, philosophy, psychology, science, etc. Uselessness is now subsidiary, though it still may persist as it does in the *Decline and Fall* or *The Stones of Venice*. And next come those works that give, or profess to give, us information about contemporary events: the newspapers. (Newspapers are so important and so peculiar that I shall return to them later, but mention them here in their place in the procession of printed matter.) And then come advertisements, timetables, the price list inside a taxi, and public notices: the notice warning us against pickpockets, which incidentally produced an atmosphere though its aim was information, and the pure information contained in the announcement "Stop". It is a long journey from lyric poetry to a placard beside a tramline, but it is a journey in which there are no breaks. Words are all of one family, and do not become different because some are printed in a book and others on a metal disc. It is their functions that differentiate them. They have two functions, and the combination of those functions is infinite. If there is on earth a house with many mansions, it is the house of words.

Looking at this line of printed matter, let us again ask ourselves: Do I want to know who wrote that? Ought it to be signed or not? The question is becoming more interesting. Clearly, in so far as words convey information, they ought to be signed. Information is supposed to be true. That is its only reason for existing, and the man who gives it ought to sign his name, so that he may be called to account if he has told a lie. When I have waited for several hours beneath the notice "Stop", I have the right to suggest that it be taken down, and I cannot do this unless I know who put it up. Make your statement, sign your name. That's common sense. But as we approach the other function of words—the creation of atmosphere—the question of signature surely loses its importance. It does not matter who wrote "A slumber did my spirit seal", because the poem itself does not matter. Ascribe it to Ella Wheeler Wilcox and the trams will run as usual. It does not matter much who wrote *Julius Caesar* and *Tom Jones*. They contain descriptions of ancient Rome and eighteenth-century England, and to that extent we wish them signed, for we can judge from the author's name whether the description is likely to be reliable; but beyond that the guarantee of Shakespeare or Fielding might just as well be Charles Garvice's. So we come to the conclusion, firstly, that what is information ought to be signed; and, secondly, that what is not information need not be signed.

The question can now be carried a step further.

What is this element in words that is not information? I have called it "atmosphere", but it requires stricter definition than that. It resides not in any particular word, but in the order in which words are arranged—that is to say, in style. It is the power that words have to raise our emotions or quicken our blood. It is also something else, and to define that other thing would be to explain the secret of the universe. This "something else" in words is undefinable. It is their power to create not only atmosphere, but a world, which, while it lasts, seems more real and solid than this daily existence of pickpockets and trams. Before we begin to read "The Ancient Mariner" we know that the Polar Seas are not inhabited by spirits, and that if a man shoots an albatross he is not a criminal but a sportsman, and that if he stuffs the albatross afterwards he becomes a naturalist also. All this is common knowledge. But when we are reading "The Ancient Mariner", or remembering it intensely, common knowledge disappears and uncommon knowledge takes its place. We have entered a universe that only answers to its own laws, supports itself, internally coheres, and has a new standard of truth. Information is true if it is accurate. A poem is true if it hangs together. Information points to something else. A poem points to nothing but itself. Information is relative. A poem is absolute. The world created by words exists neither in space nor time though it has semblances of both, it is eternal and indestructible, and yet its action is no stronger than a flower; it is adamant, yet it is also what one of its practitioners thought it to be, namely the shadow of a shadow. We can best define it by negations. It is not this world, its laws are not the laws of science or logic, its conclusions not those of common sense. And it causes us to suspend our ordinary judgements.

Now comes the crucial point. While we are reading "The Ancient Mariner" we forget our astronomy and geography and daily ethics. Do we not also forget the author? Does not Samuel Taylor Coleridge, lecturer, opium-eater and dragoon, disappear with the rest of the world of information? We remember him before we begin the poem and after we finish it, but during the poem nothing exists but the poem. Consequently while we read "The Ancient Mariner" a change takes place in it. It becomes anonymous, like the "Ballad of Sir Patrick Spens". And here is the point I would support: that all literature tends towards a condition of anonymity, and that, so far as words are creative, a signature merely distracts us from their true significance. I do not say literature "ought" not to be signed, because literature is alive, and consequently "ought" is the wrong word to use. It wants not to be signed. That puts my point. It is always tugging in that direction and saying in effect: "I, not my author, exist really." So do the trees, flowers and human beings say, "I really exist, not God," and continue to say so despite the admonitions to the contrary addressed to them by clergymen and scientists. To forget its Creator is one of the functions of a Creation. To remember him is to forget the days of one's youth. Literature does not want to remember. It is alive—not in a vague complementary sense—but alive tenaciously, and it is always covering up the tracks that connect it with the laboratory.

It may here be objected that literature expresses personality, that it is the result of the author's individual outlook, that we are right in asking for his name. It is his property—he ought to have the credit.

An important objection; also a modern one, for in the past 13
neither writers nor readers attached the high importance to personality that they do today. It did not trouble Homer or the various people who were Homer. It did not trouble the writers in the Greek Anthology, who would write and rewrite the same poem in almost identical language, their notion being that the poem, not the poet, is the important thing, and that by continuous rehandling the perfect expression natural to the poem may be attained. It did not trouble the medieval balladists, who, like the cathedral-builders, left their works unsigned. It troubled neither the composers nor the translators of the Bible. The Book of Genesis today contains at least three different elements—Jahvist, Elohist and Priestly—which were combined into a single account by a committee who lived under King Josiah at Jerusalem and translated into English by another committee who lived under King James I at London. And yet the Book of Genesis is literature. These earlier writers and readers knew that the words a man writes express him, but they did not make a cult of expression as we do today. Surely they were right, and modern critics go too far in their insistence on personality.

They go too far because they do not reflect what personality is. 14
Just as words have two functions—information and creation—so each human mind has two personalities, one on the surface, one deeper down. The upper personality has a name. It is called S. T. Coleridge, or William Shakespeare, or Mrs. Humphry Ward. It is conscious and alert, it does things like dining out, answering letters, etc., and it differs vividly and amusingly from other personalities. The lower personality is a very queer affair. In many ways it is a perfect fool, but without it there is no literature, because unless a man dips a bucket down into it occasionally he cannot produce first-class work. There is something general about it. Although it is inside S. T. Coleridge, it cannot be labelled with his name. It has something in common with all other deeper personalities, and the mystic will assert that the common quality is God, and that here, in the obscure recesses of our being, we near the gates of the Divine. It is in any case the force that makes for anonymity. As it came from the depths, so it soars to the heights, out of local questionings; as it is general to all men, so the works it inspires have something general about them, namely beauty. The poet wrote the poem, no doubt, but he forgot himself while he wrote it, and we forget him while we read. What is so wonderful about great literature is that it transforms the man who reads it towards the condition of the man who wrote, and brings to birth in us also the creative impulse.

Lost in the beauty where he was lost, we find more than we ever threw away, we reach what seems to be our spiritual home, and remember that it was not the speaker who was in the beginning but the Word.

If we glance at one or two writers who are not first-class this point will be illustrated. Charles Lamb and R. L. Stevenson will serve. Here are two gifted, sensitive, fanciful, tolerant, humorous fellows, but they always write with their surface-personalities and never let down buckets into their underworld. Lamb did not try: bbbbuckets, he would have said, are bbeyond me, and he is the pleasanter writer in consequence. Stevenson was always trying oh ever so hard, but the bucket either stuck or else came up again full of the R.L.S. who let it down, full of the mannerisms, the self-consciousness, the sentimentality, the quaintness which he was hoping to avoid. He and Lamb append their names in full to every sentence they write. They pursue us page after page, always to the exclusion of higher joy. They are letter-writers, not creative artists, and it is no coincidence that each of them did write charming letters. A letter comes off the surface: it deals with the events of the day or with plans: it is naturally signed. Literature tries to be unsigned. And the proof is that, whereas we are always exclaiming "How like Lamb!" or "How typical of Stevenson!" we never say "How like Shakespeare!" or "How typical of Dante!" We are conscious only of the world they have created, and we are in a sense co-partners in it. Coleridge, in his smaller domain, makes us co-partners too. We forget for ten minutes his name and our own, and I contend that this temporary forgetfulness, this momentary and mutual anonymity, is sure evidence of good stuff. The demand that literature should express personality is far too insistent in these days, and I look back with longing to the earlier modes of criticism where a poem was not an expression but a discovery, and was sometimes supposed to have been shown to the poet by God.

The personality of a writer does become important after we have read his book and begin to study it. When the glamour of creation ceases, when the leaves of the divine tree are silent, when the co-partnership is over, then a book changes its nature, and we can ask ourselves questions about it such as "What is the author's name?", "Where did he live?", "Was he married?" and "Which was his favourite flower?" Then we are no longer reading the book, we are studying it and making it subserve our desire for information. "Study" has a very solemn sound. "I am studying Dante" sounds much more than "I am reading Dante". It is really much less. Study is only a serious form of gossip. It teaches us everything about the book except the central thing, and between that and us it raises a circular barrier which only the wings of the spirit can cross. The study of science, history, etc., is necessary and proper, for they are subjects that belong to the domain of information, but a creative subject like literature—to study that is excessively dangerous, and should never be attempted by the immature. Modern education promotes the unmitigated study of literature and concentrates our attention on the relation between a writer's life—his surface life—and his work. That is one reason why it is such a curse. There are no questions to be asked about literature while we read it because "la paix succède à la pensée", in the words of Paul Claudel. An examination paper could not be set on "The Ancient Mariner" as it speaks to the heart of the reader, and it was to speak to the heart that it was written, and otherwise it would not have been written. Questions only occur when we cease to realize what it was about and become inquisitive and methodical.

A word in conclusion on the newspapers—for they raise an interesting contributory issue. We have already defined a newspaper as something which conveys, or is supposed to convey, information about passing events. It is true, not to itself like a poem, but to the facts it purports to relate—like the tram notice. When the morning paper arrives it lies upon the breakfast table simply steaming with truth in regard to something else. Truth, truth, and nothing but truth. Unsated by the banquet, we sally forth in the afternoon to buy an evening paper, which is published at midday as the name implies, and feast anew. At the end of the week we buy a weekly, or a Sunday paper, which as the name implies has been written on the Saturday, and at the end of the month we buy a monthly. Thus do we keep in touch with the world of events as practical men should. 17

And who is keeping us in touch? Who gives us this information upon which our judgements depend, and which must ultimately influence our characters? Curious to relate, we seldom know. Newspapers are for the most part anonymous. Statements are made and no signature appended. Suppose we read in a paper that the Emperor of Guatemala is dead. Our first feeling is one of mild consternation; out of snobbery we regret what has happened, although the Emperor didn't play much part in our lives, and if ladies we say to one another, "I feel so sorry for the poor Empress." But presently we learn that the Emperor cannot have died, because Guatemala is a Republic, and the Empress cannot be a widow, because she does not exist. If the state- 18 ment was signed, and we know the name of the goose who made it, we shall discount anything he tells us in the future. If—which is more probable—it is unsigned or signed "Our Special Correspondent", we remain defenceless against future misstatements. The Guatemala lad may be turned on to write about the Fall of the Franc and mislead us over that.

It seems paradoxical that an article should impress us more if it is unsigned than if it is signed. But it does, owing to the weakness of our psychology. Anonymous statements have, as we have seen, a universal air about them. Absolute truth, the collected wisdom of the universe, seems to be speaking, not the feeble voice of a man. The modern newspaper has taken advantage of this. It is a pernicious caricature of literature. It has usurped that divine tendency towards anonymity. It has claimed for information what only belongs to creation. And it will claim it as long as we allow it to claim it, and to exploit the defects of our psychology. "The High Mission of the Press." Poor Press! As if it were in a position to have a mission! It is we who have a mission to it. To cure a man through the newspapers or through propaganda of any sort is impossible; you merely alter the symptoms of his disease. We shall only be cured by purging our minds of confusion. The papers trick us not so much by their lies as by their exploitation of our weakness. They are always confusing the two functions of words and insinuating that "The Emperor of Guatemala is dead" and "A slumber did my spirit seal" belong to the same category. They are always usurping the privileges that only uselessness may claim, and they will do this as long as we allow them to do it.

This ends our enquiry. The question "Ought things to be signed?" seemed, if not an easy question, at all events an isolated one, but we could not answer it without considering what words are, and disentangling the two functions they perform. We decided pretty easily that information ought to be signed; common sense leads to this conclusion, and newspapers which are largely unsigned have gained by that device their undesirable influence over civilization. Creation—that we found a more difficult matter. "Literature wants not to be signed," I suggested. Creation comes from the depths—the mystic will say from God. The signature, the name, belongs to the surface-personality, and pertains to the world of information, it is a ticket, not the spirit of life. While the author wrote he forgot his name; while we read him we forget both his name and our own. When we have finished reading we begin to ask questions, and to study the book and the author, we drag them into the realm of information. Now we learn a thousand things, but we have lost the pearl of great price, and in the chatter of question and answer, in the torrents of gossip and examination papers, we forget the purpose for which creation was performed. I am not asking for reverence. Reverence is fatal to literature. My plea is for something more vital: imagination. "Imagination is as the immortal God which should assume flesh for the redemption of mortal passion" (Shelley). Imagination is our only guide into the world created by words. Whether those words are signed or unsigned becomes, as soon as the imagination redeems us, a matter of no importance, because we have approximated to the state in which they were written, and there are no names down there, no personality as we understand personality, no marrying or giving in marriage. What there is down there—ah, that is another enquiry, and may the clergymen and the scientists pursue it more successfully in the future than they have in the past.

Rhetorical Analysis

1. In "Anonymity: An Enquiry," Forster finds two functions of language: to inform and to generate a mood. We can divide the functions of language another way, into language which refers to the world outside the text, and language which refers to the text itself. An example of the second function is summary material, in which authors refer to their own text (see ¶ 20). Other statements do not refer back but instead look ahead, or *anticipate* text that is to come. The first sentence of ¶ 11 is an example of such an anticipatory statement: "Now comes the crucial point." Find at least six more examples in this essay.
    a. What are the rhetorical benefits of anticipatory language?
    b. Where does Forster tend to place such language? Why in those places?
    c. As for summary statements, find and analyze the instances other than the rather formal summation of ¶ 20.
2. Patient analysis of good writers helps dispel some common beliefs about "incorrect" writing—or at least to temper them. Outstanding writers do not break the rules. The "rules" are simply inadequate descriptions of reality. For example:
    a. Do not join two independent clauses with a comma. Forster does this twice in ¶ 4.
    b. Do not write sentence fragments. There are two in ¶ 17 and three in a row in ¶ 19.

     c. Do not begin a sentence with "and," "or," or "but." Check ¶s 18 and 19.
     d. Do not end a sentence with a preposition. See the opening sentence of the essay.

   Can you argue, in each instance, that Forster has chosen the most elegant and effective (rather than simply incorrect) expression? What, then, about the rules? Are they to be disobeyed at will? Or do we need another set of rules?

3. Paragraphs 17, 18, and 19 form a unit that has a special relationship to the rest of the essay. What is it, and why does Forster place that unit where he does? (The final paragraph of "Tolerance" has the same relationship to that essay.)

Intellectual Analysis

1. Forster cites a number of works without naming their authors. In order, the authors are William Wordsworth, William Blake, Lord Byron, A.E. Housman (¶ 5), Edward Gibbon and John Ruskin (¶ 7), Shakespeare and Joseph Fielding (¶ 8). Plato is alluded to in ¶ 10 ("one of its practitioners"), and in ¶ 20 we encounter unattributed quotations from Shakespeare's *Othello* ("the pearl of great price") and the Bible ("no marrying or giving in marriage"). Finally, in ¶ 15 Forster leaves unstated the fact that Charles Lamb was a stutterer and that Robert Louis Stevenson often referred to himself by his initials. How does this treatment of literary giants fit in with the argument of the essay?

2. Forster's essay comprehends a number of issues and ideas. One way to find a center is to come to grips with exactly what Forster is campaigning for and what against.
     a. For example, Forster is convinced of the "uselessness" of literature, the mystery of its creation, even its self-referential quality. Given these beliefs, what, according to Forster, is the proper function of literature in society?
     b. At the same time, Forster is strongly opposed to the formal *study* of literature. How does he maintain that position in the face of his deep love of literature?
     c. Forster clearly values information, too, yet he takes an impassioned stand against certain practices of newspapers. Why? Here it is worth noting that reviews written by Forster were published by *The Listener* without a by-line, contrary to his wishes.
     d. Out of such discussion and analysis should emerge some sense of Forster's subject, which is not anonymity, really. What is it, then?

3. Consider the great impertinence of this essay, both in its style and content. Here are, for example, three striking statements from the essay:
   "To forget its Creator is one of the functions of a Creation" (¶ 11).
   "Study is only a serious form of gossip" (¶ 16).
   "Poor Press! As if it were in a position to have a mission" (¶ 19).
   Are these and other remarks snide? condescending? intended merely to startle?

What is Forster's intended effect? Is this part of his campaign? If so, again, against whom or what?

4. What implicit statement does Forster make about writers, their supposed commitment, their proper reward, their legitimate relationship to their work? "It does not so much matter who wrote *Julius Caesar* or *Tom Jones*," Forster blithely claims (¶ 8).

Suggestions for Writing

1. Besides the allusion to Christ's answer to the Sadducees (see above), there are other unglossed quotations from the Bible here. A concordance of the Bible will help you identify them. Take Forster's use of the Bible in this essay—or in all three of the essays reprinted here—as the subject of an essay of your own.
2. Forster's inquiry into the curious phenomenon of anonymity does not close off the issue, but rather opens it up. Write an essay continuing the inquiry. What about anonymity in advertising, in political speeches (ghost writing), in student essays (plagiarism), in graffiti, in gift-giving, etc.?
3. Should academic work be submitted anonymously for teacher or peer evaluation? Write an essay debating that deceptively simple question.

Virginia Woolf

Daughter of one well-known English scholar, wife to another, Virginia Woolf's fame had eclipsed that of both of these men by the time she drowned herself in the River Ouse in 1941. That act, as well as her membership in the British avant-garde, her pioneering and intellectual feminism, her love affair with Vita Sackville-West, all contributed to the making of a legend of Virginia Woolf that often obscured the actual writer.

Woolf fascinated many who seemed intent on encapsulating her in a phrase or anecdote, clever quips which often got added to the legend. Her nephew, Quentin Bell, said of her that her imagination was "furnished with an accelerator but no brakes." Rosamond Lehmann described her as "a spirit balanced at a pitch of intensity impossible to sustain without collapse." Once, recovering from the recurrent mental illness which finally drove her to suicide, she heard the birds singing Greek and the King of England muttering obscenities outside her window. Yet it is also characteristic of Woolf's presence of mind that she calmly continued her game of lawn bowls as the Battle of Britain erupted in the skies over her head, with Spitfires and Messerschmitts whining and diving about her.

Despite the legend, and despite the anecdotes and epigrams which have kept her more in the public eye than have novels like To the Lighthouse and Mrs. Dalloway, or the essays and reviews,

Virginia Woolf possessed an extremely sensitive, acute, nervous mind, but a mind balanced and sane. She saw phantoms, indeed, and she struggled with them and she ultimately gave way. But as the result of that struggle she cast a steady light into shadowy corners.

It is in her essays that the suppleness and clarity of her sensibility is most evident. Of essays she wrote that they should be "pure like water or pure like wine, but pure from dullness, deadness and deposits of extraneous matter." Whatever may be the difficulties of reading her essays, they certainly are purified of dullness and deadness.

OLD MRS. GREY

There are moments even in England, now, when even the busiest, most contented suddenly let fall what they hold—it may be the week's washing. Sheets and pyjamas crumble and dissolve in their hands, because, though they do not state this in so many words, it seems silly to take the washing round to Mrs. Peel when out there over the fields over the hills, there is no washing; no pinning of clothes to lines; mangling and ironing; no work at all, but boundless rest. Stainless and boundless rest; space unlimited; untrodden grass; wild birds flying; hills whose smooth uprise continue that wild flight.

Of all this however only seven foot by four could be seen from Mrs. Grey's corner. That was the size of her front door which stood wide open, though there was a fire burning in the grate. The fire looked like a small spot of dusty light feebly trying to escape from the embarrassing pressure of the pouring sunshine.

Mrs. Grey sat on a hard chair in the corner looking—but at what? Apparently at nothing. She did not change the focus of her eyes when visitors came in. Her eyes had ceased to focus themselves; it may be that they had lost the power. They were aged eyes, blue, unspectacled. They could see, but without looking. She had never used her eyes on anything minute and difficult; merely upon faces, and dishes and fields. And now at the age of ninety-two they saw nothing but a zigzag of pain wriggling across the door, pain that twisted her legs as it wriggled; jerked her body to and fro like a marionette. Her body was wrapped round the pain as a damp sheet is folded over a wire. The wire was spasmodically jerked by a cruel invisible hand. She flung out a foot, a hand. Then it stopped. She sat still for a moment.

In that pause she saw herself in the past at ten, at twenty, at twenty-five. She was running in and out of a cottage with eleven brothers and sisters. The line jerked. She was thrown forward in her chair.

"All dead. All dead," she mumbled. "My brothers and sisters. And my husband gone. My daughter too. But I go on. Every morning I pray God to let me pass."

The morning spread seven foot by four green and sunny. Like a fling of grain the birds settled on the land. She was jerked again by another tweak of the tormenting hand.

"I'm an ignorant old woman. I can't read or write, and every morning when I crawls down stairs, I say I wish it were night; and every night, when I crawls up to bed, I say, I wish it were day. I'm only an ignorant old woman. But I prays to God: O let me pass. I'm an ignorant old woman—I can't read or write."

So when the colour went out of the doorway, she could not see the other page which is then lit up; or hear the voices that have argued, sung, talked for hundreds of years.

The jerked limbs were still again.

"The doctor comes every week. The parish doctor now. Since my daughter went, we can't afford Dr. Nicholls. But he's a good man. He says he wonders I don't go. He says my heart's nothing but wind and water. Yet I don't seem able to die."

So we—humanity—insist that the body shall still cling to the wire. We put out the eyes and the ears; but we pinion it there, with a bottle of medicine, a cup of tea, a dying fire, like a rook on a barn door; but a rook that still lives, even with a nail through it.

Rhetorical Analysis

1. Notice how often Woolf forces a delay between our reading of a word or phrase and our full understanding of it. We do not learn that "now" in the first line of "Old Mrs. Grey" refers to sunny springtime until the end of the paragraph; nor that "seven foot by four" in the first sentence of ¶ 2 refers to the "size of her front door" until the second sentence.

    a. Woolf's tactic should be seen as a kind of suspense—a suspense in exposi-

tory prose not unlike the suspense in mystery novels or James Bond movies. What other examples of suspense can you find in "Old Mrs. Grey"?
   b. No matter in which genre it appears, suspense seems to run contrary to the assumption that writing should always be clear and direct. How can you justify use of suspense in expository writing?
2. What is the effect of the three passages of verbatim quotation from Mrs. Grey? Consider how differently Woolf would have had to write had she elected to convey that same *content* through paraphrase.
3. On reading "Old Mrs. Grey" for the first time, readers often comment on its powerfulness. Yet the essay is very brief. How does Woolf convey so much energy in so short a piece?

Intellectual Analysis

1. The subject of this essay is death, but death in at least three senses. Each of these warrants careful discussion.
   a. Paragraph 5 suggests that death is a release. From what and to what?
   b. But death is also viewed ironically at various places in the essay. For example, the birds settling "on the land" do not seem troubled about it (¶ 6).
   c. In the last paragraph, death is denial: we cling to life and expect "Old Mrs. Grey" to cling to it as well. What do you infer from Woolf's mention of the doctor's visits?
   d. A further implication might be implied in the very first sentence. What life event other than death causes even the "most contented suddenly [to] let fall what they hold"?
2. As usual with Woolf's essays, the imagery in "Old Mrs. Grey" is rich in implication. Here are four striking images to discuss:
   a. "Stainless and boundless rest" (¶ 1).
   b. The "seven foot by four" of Mrs. Grey's door (¶ 2).
   c. The "damp sheet folded over a wire" (¶ 3).
   d. The "rook" in the last paragraph (recollect that a rook is quite like an American crow, black, raucous, and prone to nest on or near buildings).
   Find some other images worth exploring.
3. How are the physical senses regarded in this essay? They certainly have much to do with the life and quality of the mind. You will need to study ¶ 8 carefully until you are sure of its meaning.
   a. What of old Mrs. Grey's eyes and ears, both now and in the past? Also, how have the rest of us "put out the eyes and ears" of Mrs. Grey?
   b. What does the life of the senses mean to the author, the voice speaking in the essay?
   c. How do reading and ignorance figure in Woolf's meaning?

Suggestions for Writing

1. Write an essay, especially if you have specific knowledge of the matter, on the aged in our society. Do we behave as Woolf implies we do with our elderly? Amplify the issues involved as far as you can.
2. Compare and contrast "Old Mrs. Grey" with Welty's treatment of her grandfather in "My Grandmother's House."
3. Describe the death of a friend or loved one—your feelings and your grieving process.

Professions for Women

When your secretary invited me to come here, she told me that your Society is concerned with the employment of women and she suggested that I might tell you something about my own professional experiences. It is true I am a woman; it is true I am employed; but what professional experiences have I had? It is difficult to say. My profession is literature; and in that profession there are fewer experiences for women than in any other, with the exception of the stage—fewer, I mean, that are peculiar to women. For the road was cut many years ago—by Fanny Burney, by Aphra Behn, by Harriet Martineau, by Jane Austen, by George Eliot—many famous women, and many more unknown and forgotten, have been before me, making the path smooth, and regulating my steps. Thus, when I came to write, there were very few material obstacles in my way. Writing was a reputable and harmless occupation. The family peace was not broken by the scratching of a pen. No demand was made upon the family purse. For ten and sixpence one can buy paper enough to write all the plays of Shakespeare—if one has a mind that way. Pianos and models, Paris, Vienna and Berlin, masters and mistresses, are not needed by a writer. The cheapness of writing paper is, of course, the reason why women have succeeded as writers before they have succeeded in the other professions. 1

But to tell you my story—it is a simple one. You have only got to figure to yourselves a girl in a bedroom with a pen in her hand. She had only to move that pen from left to right—from ten o'clock to one. Then 2 it occurred to her to do what is simple and cheap enough after all—to slip a few of those pages into an envelope, fix a penny stamp in the corner, and drop the envelope into the red box at the corner. It was thus that I became a journalist; and my effort was rewarded on the first day of the following month—a very glorious day it was for me—by a letter from an editor containing a cheque for one pound ten shillings and sixpence. But to show you how little I deserve to be called a professional woman, how little I know of the struggles and difficulties of such lives, I have to admit that instead of spending that sum upon bread and butter, rent, shoes and stockings, or butcher's bills, I went out and bought a cat—a beautiful cat, a Persian cat, which very soon involved me in bitter disputes with my neighbours.

    What could be easier than to write articles and to buy Persian cats with the profits? But wait a moment. Articles have to be about something. Mine, I seem to remember, was about a novel by a famous man. And while I was writing this review, I discovered that if I were going to review books I should need to do battle with a certain phantom. And the phantom was a woman, and when I came to know her better I called her after the heroine of a famous poem, The Angel in the House. It was she who used to come between me and my paper when I was writing reviews. It was she who bothered me and wasted my time and so tormented me that at last I killed her. You who come of a younger and happier generation may not have heard of her—you may not know what I mean by the Angel in the House. I will describe her as shortly as I can. She was intensely sympathetic. She was immensely charming. She was utterly unselfish. She excelled in the difficult arts of family life. She sacrificed herself daily. If there was chicken, she took the leg; if there was a draught she sat in it—in short she was so constituted that she never had a mind or a wish of her own, but preferred to sympathize always with the minds and wishes of others. Above all—I need not say it—she was pure. Her purity was supposed to be her chief beauty—her blushes, her great grace. In those days—the last of Queen Victoria—every house had its Angel. And when I came to write I encountered her with the very first words. The shadow of her wings fell on my page; I heard the rustling of her skirts in the room. Directly, that is to say, I took my pen in my hand to review that novel by a famous man, she slipped behind me and whispered: "My dear, you are a young woman. You are writing about a book that has been written by a man. Be sympathetic; be tender; flatter; deceive; use all the arts and wiles of our sex. Never let anybody guess that you have a mind of your own. Above all, be pure." And she made as if to guide my pen. I now record the one act for which I take some credit to myself, though the credit rightly belongs to some excellent ancestors of mine who left me a certain sum of money—shall we say five hundred pounds a year?—so that it was not necessary for me to depend solely on charm for my living. I turned upon her and caught her by the throat. I did my best to kill her. My excuse, if I were to be had up in a court of law, would be that I acted in self-defence. Had I not killed her she would have killed me. She would have plucked the heart out of my writing. For, as I found, directly I put pen to paper, you cannot review even a novel without having a mind of your own, without expressing what you think to be the truth about human relations, morality, sex. And all these questions, according to the Angel of the House, cannot be dealt with freely and openly by women; they must charm, they must conciliate, they must—to put it bluntly—tell lies if they are to succeed. Thus, whenever I felt the shadow of her wing or the radiance of her halo upon my page, I took up the inkpot and flung it at her. She died hard. Her fictitious nature was of great assistance to her. It is far harder to kill a phantom than a reality. She was always creeping back when I thought I had despatched her. Though I flatter myself that I killed her in the end, the struggle was severe; it took much time that had better have been spent upon learning Greek grammar; or in roaming the world in search of adventures. But it was a real experience; it was an experience that was bound to befall all women writers at that time. Killing the Angel in the House was part of the occupation of a woman writer.

But to continue my story. The Angel was dead; what then remained? You may say that what remained was a simple and common object—a young woman in a bedroom with an inkpot. In other words, now that she had rid herself of falsehood, that young woman had only to be herself. Ah, but what is "herself"? I mean, what is a woman? I assure you, I do not know. I do not believe that you know. I do not believe that anybody can know until she has expressed herself in all the arts and professions open to human skill. That indeed is one of the reasons why I have come here—out of respect for you, who are in process of showing us by your experiments what a woman is, who are in process of providing us, by your failures and successes, with that extremely important piece of information.

But to continue the story of my professional experiences. I made one pound ten and six by my first review; and I bought a Persian cat with the proceeds. Then I grew ambitious. A Persian cat is all very well, I said; but a Persian cat is not enough. I must have a motor car. And it was thus that I became a novelist—for it is a very strange thing that people will give you a motor car if you will tell them a story. It is a still stranger thing that there is nothing so delightful in the world as telling stories. It is far pleasanter than writing reviews of famous novels. And yet, if I am to obey your secretary and tell you my professional experiences as a novelist, I must tell you about a very strange experience that befell me as a novelist. And to understand it you must try first to imagine a novelist's state of mind. I hope I am not giving away professional secrets if I say that a novelist's chief desire is to be as unconscious as possible. He has to induce in himself a state of perpetual lethargy. He wants life to proceed with the utmost quiet and regularity. He wants to see the same faces, to read the same books, to do the same things day after day, month after month, while he is writing, so that nothing may break the illusion in which he is living—so that nothing may disturb or disquiet the mysterious nosings about, feelings round, darts, dashes and sudden discoveries of that very shy and illusive spirit, the imagination. I suspect that this state is the same both for men and women. Be that as it may, I want you to imagine me writing a novel in a state of trance. I want you to figure to yourselves a girl sitting with a pen in her hand, which for minutes, and indeed for hours, she never dips into the inkpot. The image that comes to my mind when I think of this girl is the image of a fisherman lying sunk in dreams on the verge of a deep lake with a rod held out over the water. She was letting her imagination sweep unchecked round every rock and cranny of the world that lies submerged in the depths of our unconscious being. Now came the experience, the experience that I believe to be far commoner with women writers than with men. The line raced through the girl's fingers. Her imagination had rushed away. It had sought the pools, the depths, the dark places where the largest fish slumber. And then there was a smash. There was an explosion. There was foam and confusion. The imagination had dashed itself against something hard. The girl was roused from her dream. She was indeed in a state of the most acute and difficult distress. To speak without figure she had thought of something, something about the body, about the passions which it was unfitting for her as a woman to say. Men, her reason told her, would be shocked. The consciousness of what men will say of a woman who speaks the truth about her passions had roused her from her artist's state of unconsciousness. She could write no more. The trance was over. Her imagination could work no longer. This I believe to be a very common experience with women writers—they are impeded by the extreme conventionality of the other sex. For though men sensibly allow themselves great freedom in these respects, I doubt that they realize or can control the extreme severity with which they condemn such freedom in women.

These then were two very genuine experiences of my own. These were two of the adventures of my professional life. The first—killing the Angel in the House—I think I solved. She died. But the second, telling the truth about my own experiences as a body, I do not think I solved. I doubt that any woman has solved it yet. The obstacles against her are still immensely powerful—and yet they are very difficult to define. Outwardly, what is simpler than to write books? Outwardly, what obstacles are there for a woman rather than for a man? Inwardly, I think, the case is very different; she has still many ghosts to fight, many prejudices to overcome. Indeed it will be a long time still, I think, before a woman can sit down to write a book without finding a phantom to be slain, a rock to be dashed against. And if this is so in literature, the freest of all professions for women, how is it in the new professions which you are now for the first time entering?

Those are the questions that I should like, had I time, to ask you. And indeed, if I have laid stress upon these professional experiences of mine, it is because I believe that they are, though in different forms, yours also. Even when the path is nominally open—when there is nothing to prevent a woman from being a doctor, a lawyer, a civil servant—there are many phantoms and obstacles, as I believe, looming in her way. To discuss and define them is I think of great value and importance; for thus only can the labour be shared, the difficulties be solved. But besides this, it is necessary also to discuss the ends and the aims for which we are fighting, for which we are doing battle with these formidable obstacles. Those aims cannot be taken for granted; they must be perpetually questioned and examined. The whole position, as I see it—here in this hall surrounded by women practising for the first time in history I know not how many different professions—is one of extraordinary interest and importance. You have won rooms of your own in the house hitherto exclusively owned by men. You are able, though not without great labour and effort, to pay the rent. You are earning your five hundred pounds a year. But this freedom is only a beginning; the room is your own, but it is still bare. It has to be furnished; it has to be decorated; it has to be shared. How are you going to furnish it, how are you going to decorate it? With whom are you going to share it, and upon what terms? These, I think, are questions of the utmost importance and interest. For the first time in history you are able to ask them; for the first time you are able to decide for yourselves what the answers should be. Willingly would I stay and discuss those questions and answers—but not to-night. My time is up; and I must cease.

Rhetorical Analysis

1. What ingredients go to make up Virginia Woolf's style? It is a famous one and very distinct, not too hard to account for. Consider elements such as punctuation, diction, metaphoric language, sentence length and type, wit, and humor.
2. Like Dinesen's "On Mottoes of My Life" and Forster's "Tolerance," "Professions for Women" was originally written as a talk in 1931. What allowances does Woolf make to fit those circumstances? Note that Woolf was speaking to The Women's Service League, a lay audience consisting of very few professional writers. How does Woolf accommodate to this fact? Study especially ¶s 2, 5, 6, and 7.
3. Remember that when a text is read aloud, paragraphing disappears. That is, the textual sign for a new paragraph, the indentation, is not pronounced aloud as a word is. This fact may explain the unusually bulky paragraphs in this printed version of "Professions for Women."
    a. A manuscript editor would probably say that ¶s 3 and 5 are too long; the lengthy stretches of unbroken text tire the eye. Without changing the text, indicate with a paragraph mark (¶) where you would begin new paragraphs in these two passages. Explain your decision.
    b. Despite the above, Woolf herself edited this printed version. Six times she elected to begin a new paragraph. Study each decision and explain what you believe was her rationale in each case.

Intellectual Analysis

1. "Professions for Women" springs from a simple, recurrent image: that of a woman in a room of her own, with pen and inkpot and paper.
    a. That image is the only prop Woolf needs to tell her story, which is a "simple one," she says. Trace through the essay the appearances of this image, variants of it, or extensions. You will discover that the image of a woman writing alone in her room becomes both a structural and a thematic device.
    b. In ¶ 3, this image connects, by allusion, to a well-known story about Martin

Luther (1483–1546), who once writing alone in his study saw the Devil coming up the stairs and threw an inkpot at him. How was Luther's position as founder of the Protestant Reformation comparable to Woolf's as a gifted woman writer working in the twilight of the British Empire (on which, it used to be said, "the sun never sets")?

2. What is involved in Woolf's "simple story" is, of course, not so simple, but complex, profound, and important (see ¶ 7).

    a. Woolf speaks of "two very genuine experiences of my own" (¶ 6). The first experience is killing the "Angel of the House." What are we to make of this "phantom"? Why does Woolf mention (¶ 3) "In those days—the last of Queen Victoria"? Do we gain anything from the historical reference? What values do you suppose this phantom represents?

    b. The second experience involves writing a novel. For a woman, writes Woolf, this poses the question of finding her own identity:

        (1) First she proceeds to discuss the self-ness of novelists generally, but in striking terms. Their aim is to be "as unconscious as possible." Does that not seem paradoxical? Don't we expect our writers to be more "conscious" than anyone else? What does that imply? (You may be able to draw some analogies with Forster's comments on literary writers in "Anonymity: An Enquiry.")

        (2) Woolf moves on to the difficulties of women novelists: "They are impeded by the extreme conventionality of the other sex" (¶ 5). What does she mean by such a statement, and do you think it a legitimate claim?

3. The depth of these two experiences is sounded in ¶s 6–7. What is at stake? Here are some possibilities:

The identity and consciousness of women.

Obstacles to women in entering the various professions.

The burden of history and of traditional ways of thinking and acting.

Suggestions for Writing

1. "It is far harder to kill a phantom," writes Woolf, "than a reality" (¶ 3). Write an essay describing, perhaps even slaying, those phantoms that bedevil you when you sit down to write—or when you converse with friends, or make academic decisions, or communicate with the opposite sex.

2. Women have the chance to develop freely, Woolf says, "for the first time in history." Explore the implications of Woolf's claim.

3. *A Room of One's Own* is a longer and very famous work by Woolf, that expands on many of the ideas in "Professions for Women." Write an essay comparing these two expressions of her ideas. Which of the two seems more prophetic?

4. Woolf's essay, "Professions for Women," might be said to sum up the interior face

of the late British Empire. Strangely, Orwell's "A Hanging" may sum up its exterior face. Both essays involve putting someone to death—an angel in one case, a criminal in the other. There is a bedroom in one case, a cell in the other. The prisoner passes from consciousness into unconsciousness, the writer from unconsciousness into consciousness. Other common features are the fish, the doctor, the road, and the time of day. Compare and contrast the elements and the significance of these two essays.

GAS

*I*t is not necessary, perhaps, to dwell upon the circumstances. There can be few people who have not at one time or another had a tooth out under gas. The dentist stands very clean and impersonal in his long white overcoat. He tells one not to cross one's legs and arranges a bit under one's chin. Then the anaesthetist comes in with his bag as clean and impersonal as the dentist and only as black as the other is white. Both seem to wear uniform and to belong to some separate order of humanity, some third sex. The ordinary conventions lapse, for in ordinary life one does not after shaking hands with an unknown man at once open one's mouth and show him a broken tooth. The new relation with the third sex is stony, statuesque, colourless, but nevertheless humane. These are the people who manage the embarcations and disembarcations of the human spirit; these are they who stand on the border line between life and death forwarding the spirit from one to the other with clean impersonal antiseptic hands. Very well, I resign myself to your charge, one says, uncrossing one's legs; and at your command I cease to breathe through the mouth and breathe through the nose; breathe deep, breathe quietly, and your assurance that one is doing it very nicely is a parting salute, a farewell from the officer who presides over the ritual of disembarcation. Soon one is beyond his care. 1

With each breath one draws in confusion; one draws in darkness, falling, scattering, like a cloud of falling soot flakes. And also one puts out to sea; with every breath one leaves the shore, one cleaves the hot waves of some new sulphurous dark existence in which one flounders without support, attended only by strange relics of old memories, elongated, stretched out, so that they seem to parody the 2 world from which one brought them, with which one tries to keep still in touch by their means; as the curved glass at a fair makes the body seem tapering and then bloated. And as we plunge deeper and deeper away from shore, we seem to be drawn on in the wake of some fast flying always disappearing black object, drawn rapidly ahead of us. We become aware of something that we could never see in the other world; something that we have been sent in search of. All the old certainties become smudged and dispersed, because in comparison with this they are unimportant, like old garments crumpled up and dropped in a heap, because one needs to be naked, for this chase, this pursuit; all our most cherished beliefs and certainties and loves become like that. Scudding under a low dark sky we fly on the trail of this truth by which, if we could grasp it, we should be for ever illuminated. And we rush faster and faster and the whole world becomes spiral and like wheels and circles about us, pressing closer and closer until it seems by its pressure to force us through a central hole, very narrow through which it hurts us, squeezing us with its pressure on the head, to pass. Indeed we seem to be crushed between the upper world and the lower world and then suddenly the pressure is lessened; the whole aperture widens up; we pass through a gorge, emerge into daylight, and behold a glass dish and hear a voice saying, "Rinse the mouth. Rinse the mouth," while a trickle of warm blood runs from between the lips. So we are received back by the officials. The truth that was being drawn so fast ahead of us vanishes.

Such is a very common experience. Everybody goes through it. But it seems to explain something that one observes very often in a third-class railway carriage for example. For it is impossible not to ask some questions as one looks down the long narrow compartment where so many different people sit facing each other. If they begin originally like that, one muses, looking at a child of three, what is the process that turns them into that? And here one looks at a heavy old man with a despatch box; or at an overdressed red-faced woman. What has made that extraordinary change? What sights, what experiences? For except in some very rare cases it seems as if the passing of sixty or seventy years had inflicted a most terrible punishment on the smooth pink face, had imparted some very strange piece of information, so that, however the features differ, the eyes of old people always have the same expression. 3

And what is that piece of information? one asks. Is it probably that all these people have been several times under gas? Gradually they have been made to think that what passes before them has very little substance. They know that they can be rid of it for a small sum. They can then see another thing, more important, perhaps drawn through the water. But what hardly any of them knows is whether he or she wishes to be rid of it. There they sit, the plumber with his leaden coil, the man with his despatch box, the middle-class woman with her parcel from Selfridges, revolving often unconsciously the question whether there is any meaning in this world compared with the other, and what the truth is that dashed ahead through the water. They woke before they had seized it. And the other world vanished. And perhaps to forget it, to cover it over, they went to the public house, they went to Oxford Street and bought a hat. As one looks down the third-class carriage, one sees that all the men and women over twenty have often been under gas; it is this that has done more than anything to change the expression of the face. An unchanged face would look almost idiotic. But, of course, there are a few faces which look as if they had caught the thing that dashes through the water.

Rhetorical Analysis

1. It is not unusual for contemporary American readers to have difficulty comprehending some of the details in "Gas" which are specific to the time and place. Find or figure out the meanings of the following: "tooth out under gas" (¶ 1), "falling soot flakes" (¶ 2), "sit facing each other" and "despatch box" (¶ 3), "leaden coil" and "Selfridges" and "public house" and "Oxford Street" (¶ 4). Now the question: would this essay be better or worse had the author not written anything a reader fifty years later would have trouble understanding?

2. Woolf wants to convince us of an insight of both universal and evanescent truth to describe a reality that is equally pervasive yet hard to grasp as air (which is technically a gas!).
    a. Woolf locates this universal experience in particular events the reader can visualize. What are those events?
    b. How does she embody this spiritual truth in concrete images the reader can grasp?

3. "Gas" seems to have neither a formal introduction nor a conclusion. How does Woolf get away without a "hello" or a "good-bye"?

Intellectual Analysis

1. This very difficult essay is chiseled into two parts: ¶s 1–3, and ¶s 3–4. Each part is governed by one major image: gas and the third-class train carriage.
   a. What do gas and the train carriage have to do with each other? Study the first three sentences of ¶ 3 for the connections. What other sentences in ¶s 3–4 make connections between these two sections?
   b. Both sections have to do with an "it" and a "thing": check carefully Woolf's use of these most indefinite words, and try to determine what she is referring to.
2. Now study the image of "gas" and ¶s 1 and 2.
   a. Woolf has had a vision, thanks to an anesthetic, of something of great value, "something we have been sent in search of" (¶ 2). What do you take this to be? We have the whole kaleidoscopic experience described in a number of ways, but we can be sure only that Woolf envisions a "truth by which, if we could grasp it, we should be for ever illuminated" (¶ 2). Examine ¶ 2 with great care, noting especially the apparent contradictions:
      (1) The truth is both *exciting* and *terrifying*; how can that be so?
      (2) It is both *birth* and *death*; what sense does that make?
      (3) It is both *within* and *without*; what does that mean? (The literal meaning of "ecstasy" might be applicable here.)
   b. Then Woolf is very suddenly jerked back to reality (if we may call it that!). Why are we left with nothing at the end? Why can't this moment be recaptured or reconstructed?
3. Now for the railway carriage, and ¶s 3 and 4.
   a. The people she describes are all unhappy. From what details can we derive that?
   b. They have not literally "often been under gas," thus Woolf's experience can occur under other circumstances. What can that mean?
   c. The train, as an image, implies a great deal: for one thing, Woolf herself is on it, too. Are the rest of us also on it? Is this train carriage a microcosm of society?
   d. What do you make of the "few faces" who seem to have caught "the thing"?

Suggestions for Writing

1. If you have had a memorable experience while under anesthetic, attempt a description of it.
2. Riding a train, plane, bus, or even an elevator is often a visceral experience. Attempt a description of what you feel when a machine is moving you from one place to another.

Stephen Jay Gould

Stephen Jay Gould, Professor of Geology and Zoology and Curator of Invertebrate Paleontology at the Museum of Comparative Zoology at Harvard University, has been, for several years, at the center of a storm as fierce as any in American intellectual history. In 1972 Gould collaborated with another paleontologist, Niles Eldredge, on a scientific paper in which they introduced a theory amending Darwin's theory of evolution. "Punctuated equilibrium" attempts to explain the lack of fossil evidence for transitional forms between species which Darwin predicted paleontologists would eventually find. To date, paleontologists have not found them. So Gould and Eldredge have proposed that they simply are not there, and that evolution actually occurs as the result of (relatively) sudden transformations. Orthodox Darwinians immediately counterattacked; and Creationists leaped gleefully into the breach, exploiting the confusion, even, to his chagrin, using Gould as a weapon against scientific Darwinism.

That Gould should have spawned such a controversy is not surprising to anyone who has read even a few of his essays. His irreverence, his wit, and the bracing vitality of his thought, while they may invigorate a disinterested reader, often infuriate those who are the targets of his criticisms. Even more troubling to Gould's adversaries is that people enjoy reading him. Thus, for many years he has written a popular column for Natural History magazine. These columns he periodically gathers into such books as The Panda's Thumb (1980) and Hen's Teeth and Horse's Toes (1983), which sell steadily and bring him literary prizes.

Gould harmonizes apparently incongruous traits easily and gracefully. An emender of Darwin, he is a passionate Darwinian; although a rigorous scientist, he quotes poets and novelists with the facility of a humanist; although a synthesizer of knowledge across several disciplines, he is the foremost specialist in a small, Bahamian land snail, genus Cerion.

A Biological Homage to Mickey Mouse

Age often turns fire to placidity. Lytton Strachey, in his incisive portrait of Florence Nightingale, writes of her declining years:

> Destiny, having waited very patiently, played a queer trick on Miss Nightingale. The benevolence and public spirit of that long life had only been equalled by its acerbity. Her virtue had dwelt in hardness. . . . And now the sarcastic years brought the proud woman her punishment. She was not to die as she had lived. The sting was to be taken out of her; she was to be made soft; she was to be reduced to compliance and complacency.

I was therefore not surprised—although the analogy may strike some people as sacrilegious—to discover that the creature who gave his name as a synonym for insipidity had a gutsier youth. Mickey Mouse turned a respectable fifty last year. To mark the occasion, many theaters replayed his debut performance in *Steamboat Willie* (1928). The original Mickey was a rambunctious, even slightly sadistic fellow. In a remarkable sequence, exploiting the exciting new development of sound, Mickey and Minnie pummel, squeeze, and twist the animals on board to produce a rousing chorus of "Turkey in the Straw." They honk a duck with a tight embrace, crank a goat's tail, tweak a pig's nipples, bang a cow's teeth as a stand-in xylophone, and play bagpipe on her udder.

1

2

Christopher Finch, in his semiofficial pictorial history of Disney's work, comments: "The Mickey Mouse who hit the movie houses in the late twenties was not quite the well-behaved character most of us are familiar with today. He was mischievous, to say the least, and even displayed a streak of cruelty." But Mickey soon cleaned up his act, leaving to gossip and speculation only his unresolved relationship with Minnie and the status of Morty and Ferdie. Finch continues: "Mickey . . . had become virtually a national symbol, and as such he was expected to behave properly at all times. If he occasionally stepped out of line, any number of letters would arrive at the Studio from citizens and organizations who felt that the nation's moral well-being was in their hands. . . . Eventually he would be pressured into the role of straight man."

As Mickey's personality softened, his appearance changed. Many Disney fans are aware of this transformation through time, but few (I suspect) have recognized the coordinating theme behind all the alterations—in fact, I am not sure that the Disney artists themselves explicitly realized what they were doing, since the changes appeared in such a halting and piecemeal fashion. In short, the blander and inoffensive Mickey became progressively more juvenile in appearance. (Since Mickey's chronological age never altered—like most cartoon characters he stands impervious to the ravages of time—this change in appearance at a constant age is a true evolutionary transformation. Progressive juvenilization as an evolutionary phenomenon is called neoteny. More on this later.)

The characteristic changes of form during human growth have inspired a substantial biological literature. Since the head-end of an

Mickey's evolution during 50 years (left to right). As Mickey became increasingly well behaved over the years, his appearance became more youthful. Measurements of three stages in his development revealed a larger relative head size, larger eyes, and an enlarged cranium—all traits of juvenility. © Walt Disney Productions embryo differentiates first and grows more rapidly in utero than the foot-end (an antero-posterior gradient, in technical language), a newborn child possesses a relatively large head attached to a medium-sized body with diminutive legs and feet. This gradient is reversed through growth as legs and feet overtake the front end. Heads continue to grow but so much more slowly than the rest of the body that relative head size decreases.

In addition, a suite of changes pervades the head itself during human growth. The brain grows very slowly after age three, and the bulbous cranium of a young child gives way to the more slanted, lower-browed configuration of adulthood. The eyes scarcely grow at all and relative eye size declines precipitously. But the jaw gets bigger and bigger. Children, compared with adults, have larger heads and eyes, smaller jaws, a more prominent, bulging cranium, and smaller, pudgier legs and feet. Adult heads are altogether more apish, I'm sorry to say.

Mickey, however, has traveled this ontogenetic pathway in reverse during his fifty years among us. He has assumed an ever more childlike appearance as the ratty character of *Steamboat Willie* became the cute and inoffensive host to a magic kingdom. By 1940, the former tweaker of pig's nipples gets a kick in the ass for insubordination (as the *Sorcerer's Apprentice* in *Fantasia*). By 1953, his last cartoon, he has gone fishing and cannot even subdue a squirting clam.

The Disney artists transformed Mickey in clever silence, often using suggestive devices that mimic nature's own changes by different routes. To give him the shorter and pudgier legs of youth, they lowered his pants line and covered his spindly legs with a baggy outfit. (His arms and legs also thickened substantially—and acquired joints for a floppier appearance.) His head grew relatively larger and its features more youthful. The length of Mickey's snout has not altered, but decreasing protrusion is more subtly suggested by a pronounced thickening. Mickey's eye has grown in two modes: first, by a major, discontinuous evolutionary shift as the entire eye of ancestral Mickey became the pupil of his descendants, and second, by gradual increase thereafter.

Mickey's improvement in cranial bulging followed an interesting path since his evolution has always been constrained by the unaltered convention of representing his head as a circle with appended ears and an oblong snout. The circle's form could not be altered to provide a bulging cranium directly. Instead, Mickey's ears moved back, increasing the distance between nose and ears, and giving him a rounded, rather than a sloping, forehead.

To give these observations the cachet of quantitative science, I applied my best pair of dial calipers to three stages of the official phylogeny—the thin-nosed, ears-forward figure of the early 1930s (stage 1), the latter-day Jack of Mickey and the Beanstalk (1947, stage 2), and the modern mouse (stage 3). I measured three signs of Mickey's creeping juvenility: increasing eye size (maximum height) as a percentage of head length (base of the nose to top of rear ear); increasing head length as a percentage of body length; and increasing cranial vault size measured by rearward displacement of the front ear (base of the nose to top of front ear as a percentage of base of the nose to top of rear ear).

All three percentages increased steadily—eye size from 27 to 42 percent of head length; head length from 42.7 to 48.1 percent of body length; and nose to front ear from 71.7 to a whopping 95.6 percent of nose to rear ear. For comparison, I measured Mickey's young "nephew" Morty Mouse. In each case, Mickey has clearly been evolving toward youthful stages of his stock, although he still has a way to go for head length.

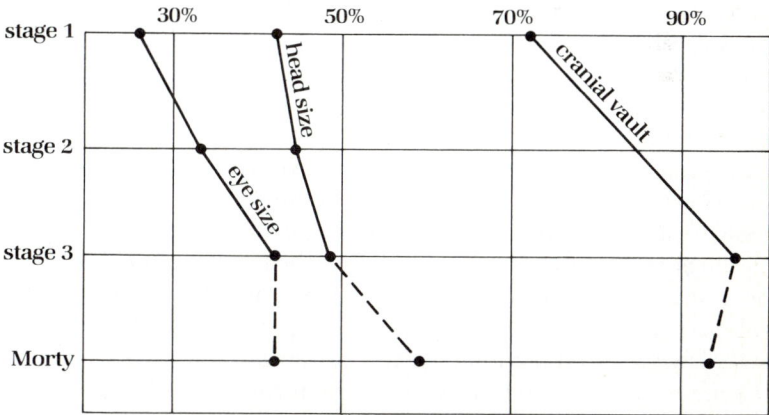

The "Evolution" of Mickey Mouse At an early stage in his evolution, Mickey had a smaller head, cranial vault, and eyes. He evolved toward the characteristics of his young nephew Morty (connected to Mickey by a dotted line).

You may, indeed, now ask what an at least marginally respectable scientist has been doing with a mouse like that. In part, fiddling around and having fun, of course. (I still prefer *Pinocchio* to *Citizen Kane*.) But I do have a serious point—two, in fact—to make. We must first ask why Disney chose to change his most famous character so gradually and persistently in the same direction? National symbols are not altered capriciously and market researchers (for the doll industry in particular) have spent a good deal of time and practical effort learning what features appeal to people as cute and friendly. Biologists also have spent a great deal of time studying a similar subject in a wide range of animals.

In one of his most famous articles, Konrad Lorenz argues that humans use the characteristic differences in form between babies and adults as important behavioral cues. He believes that features of juvenility trigger "innate releasing mechanisms" for affection and nurturing in adult humans. When we see a living creature with babyish features, we feel an automatic surge of disarming tenderness. The adaptive value of this response can scarcely be questioned, for we must nurture our babies. Lorenz, by the way, lists among his releasers the very features of babyhood that Disney affixed progressively to Mickey: "a relatively large head, predominance of the brain capsule, large and low-lying eyes, bulging cheek region, short and thick extremities, a springy elastic consistency, and clumsy movements." (I propose to leave aside for this article the contentious issue of whether or not our affectionate response to babyish features is truly innate and inherited directly from ancestral primates—as Lorenz argues—or whether it is simply learned from our immediate experience with babies and grafted upon an evolutionary predisposition for attaching ties of affection to certain learned signals. My argument works equally well in either case for I only claim that babyish features tend to elicit strong feelings of affection in adult humans, whether the biological basis be direct programming or the capacity to learn and fix upon signals. I also treat as collateral to my point the major thesis of Lorenz's article—that we respond not to the totality or *Gestalt*, but to a set of specific features acting as releasers. This argument is important to Lorenz because he wants to argue for evolutionary identity in modes of behavior between other vertebrates and humans, and we know that many birds, for example, often respond to abstract features rather than *Gestalten*. Lorenz's article, published in 1950, bears the title *Ganzheit und Teil in der tierischen und menschlichen Gemeinschaft*—"Entirety and part in animal and human society." Disney's piecemeal change of

Mickey's appearance does make sense in this context—he operated in sequential fashion upon Lorenz's primary releasers.)

Lorenz emphasizes the power that juvenile features hold over us, and the abstract quality of their influence, by pointing out that we judge other animals by the same criteria—although the judgment may be utterly inappropriate in an evolutionary context. We are, in short, fooled by an evolved response to our own babies, and we transfer our reaction to the same set of features in other animals.

Many animals, for reasons having nothing to do with the inspiration of affection in humans, possess some features also shared by human babies but not by human adults—large eyes and a bulging forehead with retreating chin, in particular. We are drawn to them, we cultivate them as pets, we stop and admire them in the wild—while we reject their small-eyed, long-snouted relatives who might make more affectionate companions or objects of admiration. Lorenz points out that the German names of many animals with features mimicking

Humans feel affection for animals with juvenile features: large eyes, bulging craniums, retreating chins (left column). Small-eyed, long-snouted animals (right column) do not elicit the same response. From *Studies in Animal and Human Behavior*, vol. II, by Konrad Lorenz, 1971. Methuen & Co. Ltd.

human babies end in the diminutive suffix *chen*, even though the animals are often larger than close relatives without such features—*Rotkehlchen* (robin), *Eichhörnchen* (squirrel), and *Kaninchen* (rabbit), for example.

In a fascinating section, Lorenz then enlarges upon our capacity for biologically inappropriate response to other animals, or even to inanimate objects that mimic human features. "The most amazing objects can acquire remarkable, highly specific emotional values by 'experiential attachment' of human properties. . . . Steeply rising, somewhat overhanging cliff faces or dark storm-clouds piling up have the same, immediate display value as a human being who is standing at full height and leaning slightly forwards"—that is, threatening.

We cannot help regarding a camel as aloof and unfriendly because it mimics, quite unwittingly and for other reasons, the "gesture of haughty rejection" common to so many human cultures. In this gesture, we raise our heads, placing our nose above our eyes. We then half-close our eyes and blow out through our nose—the "harumph" of the stereotyped upperclass Englishman or his well-trained servant. "All this," Lorenz argues quite cogently, "symbolizes resistance against all sensory modalities emanating from the disdained counterpart." But the poor camel cannot help carrying its nose above its elongate eyes, with mouth drawn down. As Lorenz reminds us, if you wish to know whether a camel will eat out of your hand or spit, look at its ears, not the rest of its face.

In his important book *Expression of the Emotions in Man and Animals*, published in 1872, Charles Darwin traced the evolutionary basis of many common gestures to originally adaptive actions in animals later internalized as symbols in humans. Thus, he argued for evolutionary continuity of emotion, not only of form. We snarl and raise our upper lip in fierce anger—to expose our nonexistent fighting canine tooth. Our gesture of disgust repeats the facial actions associated with the highly adaptive act of vomiting in necessary circumstances. Darwin concluded, much to the distress of many Victorian contemporaries: "With mankind some expressions, such as the bristling of the hair under the influence of extreme terror, or the uncovering of the teeth under that of furious rage, can hardly be understood, except on the belief that man once existed in a much lower and animal-like condition."

In any case, the abstract features of human childhood elicit powerful emotional responses in us, even when they occur in other animals. I submit that Mickey Mouse's evolutionary road down the course of his own growth in reverse reflects the unconscious discovery of this biological principle by Disney and his artists. In fact, the emotional status of most Disney characters rests on the same set of distinctions. To this extent, the magic kingdom trades on a biological illusion—our ability to abstract and our propensity to transfer inappropriately to other animals the fitting responses we make to changing form in the growth of our own bodies.

Donald Duck also adopts more juvenile features through time. His elongated beak recedes and his eyes enlarge; he converges on Huey, Louie, and Dewey as surely as Mickey approaches Morty. But Donald, having inherited the mantle of Mickey's original misbehavior, remains more adult in form with his projecting beak and more sloping forehead.

Mouse villains or sharpies, contrasted with Mickey, are always more adult in appearance, although they often share Mickey's chronological age. In 1936, for example, Disney made a short entitled *Mickey's Rival*. Mortimer, a dandy in a yellow sports car, intrudes

Dandified, disreputable Mortimer (here stealing Minnie's affections) has strikingly more adult features than Mickey. His head is smaller in proportion to body length; his nose is a full 80 percent of head length. © Walt Disney Productions

upon Mickey and Minnie's quiet country picnic. The thoroughly disreputable Mortimer has a head only 29 percent of body length, to Mickey's 45, and a snout 80 percent of head length, compared with Mickey's 49. (Nonetheless, and was it ever different, Minnie transfers her affection until an obliging bull from a neighboring field dispatches Mickey's rival.) Consider also the exaggerated adult features of other Disney characters—the swaggering bully Peg-leg Pete or the simple, if lovable, dolt Goofy.

As a second, serious biological comment on Mickey's odyssey in form, I note that his path to eternal youth repeats, in epitome, our own evolutionary story. For humans are neotenic. We have evolved by retaining to adulthood the originally juvenile features of our ancestors. Our australopithecine forebears, like Mickey in *Steamboat Willie*, had projecting jaws and low vaulted craniums.

Our embryonic skulls scarcely differ from those of chimpanzees. And we follow the same path of changing form through growth: relative decrease of the cranial vault since brains grow so much more slowly than bodies after birth, and continuous relative increase of the jaw. But while chimps accentuate these changes, producing an adult strikingly different in form from a baby, we proceed much more slowly down the same path and never get nearly so far. Thus, as adults, we retain juvenile features. To be sure, we change enough to produce a notable difference between baby and adult, but our alteration is far smaller than that experienced by chimps and other primates.

A marked slowdown of developmental rates has triggered our neoteny. Primates are slow developers among mammals, but we have accentuated the trend to a degree matched by no other mammal. We have very long periods of gestation, markedly extended childhoods, and the longest life span of any mammal. The morphological features of eternal youth have served us well. Our enlarged brain is, at least in part, a result of extending rapid prenatal growth rates to later ages. (In all mammals, the brain grows rapidly in utero but often very little after birth. We have extended this fetal phase into postnatal life.)

But the changes in timing themselves have been just as important. We are preeminently learning animals, and our extended childhood permits the transference of culture by education. Many animals display flexibility and play in childhood but follow rigidly programmed patterns as adults. Lorenz writes, in the same article cited above: "The characteristic which is so vital for the human peculiarity of the true man—that of always remaining in a state of development—

Cartoon villains are not the only Disney characters with exaggerated adult features. Goofy, like Mortimer, has a small head relative to body length and a prominent snout. © Walt Disney Productions

is quite certainly a gift which we owe to the neotenous nature of mankind."

In short, we, like Mickey, never grow up although we, alas, do grow old. Best wishes to you, Mickey, for your next half-century. May we stay as young as you, but grow a bit wiser.

26

Rhetorical Analysis

1. Lively verbs account for much of the color and vigor of Gould's writing. He avoids bland verbs such as *is* and *have*—although any writer, and especially scientists with their need to describe, cannot avoid them entirely.
    a. Choose any paragraph and circle the main verbs (not the helping verbs). Make a list of what you find. Compare that list to a similar list you could prepare by analyzing one paragraph from the dullest textbook on your shelf. Notice the vigor and interest of active, colorful verbs.

b. Rewrite some sentences, replacing the main verbs with forms of *is* and *have*. For instance, you might revise the first sentence of the essay to say, "Placidity is often the substitution for fire in old age." Where Gould already has *is* or *have* as a main verb, replace it with a more active one. Do your revisions improve or disfigure the originals? Why?
2. A logical sequence that Gould often uses begins with a description of a puzzling situation, continues with a theory to explain it, and ends with facts which support the theory. That sequence is used by many writers to organize both long and short stretches of discourse, and bears study.
   a. The first part of "A Biological Homage" follows that three-part sequence:
      Puzzle: The curious softening of Mickey Mouse's personality over the years (¶s 2–4).
      Theory: The changes consistently make Mickey's appearance more and more juvenile (¶s 4–6).
      Confirmation: Comparison and even measurement of Mickey at three stages mark biological growth traits (¶s 7–11).
   What transitions does Gould use to help the reader follow this sequence? Which logical elements of the sequence does he emphasize to add persuasive power to his writing?
   b. Where else in the essay does Gould use this sequence?
   c. ¶ 12 uses the sequence as the first step of a different kind of progression. What progression is that?
3. Editorial style books emphasize that illustrations should be attractive and self-explanatory. The reader should not have to consult the text to make sense of them.
   a. Why should illustrations be independent of the text?
   b. Consider the captions of the five illustrations in "A Biological Homage." How has Gould made the pictures self-explanatory? What do they add to the argument of the text?

Intellectual Analysis

1. The first section of this essay describes the changes in the physical image of Mickey Mouse over time.
   a. Why is this topic striking? For one thing, we think of cartoon characters as fixed, as durable. But consider one of Gould's comments: "National symbols are not altered capriciously" (¶ 12). Evaluate the implications of that statement carefully.
   b. Why is this material entertaining (even with the measurements and percentages)? Are we amused simply because the subject is Mickey? Consider some other factors, such as Gould's tone, language, and playfulness.
2. "But I do have a serious point—two, in fact—to make," Gould says at ¶ 12. Try to formulate both points, boiled down to the plainest terms.
   a. Gould relies here on the theoretical writing of Konrad Lorenz.

(1) The first point is that "features of juvenility trigger 'innate releasing mechanisms'" (¶ 13). What are these mechanisms and what have they to do with Mickey?

(2) What other factors are there of importance in "the power that juvenile features hold over us" (¶ 14)? Why, for instance, does Gould mention our reactions to animals?

b. Why mention Darwin in ¶ 18? What does this evidence add, and what position does it support?

c. Paragraph 19 contains a masterful summary of the first of Gould's "important" points. Examine it carefully.

3. Gould moves on to his second and more startling point in ¶ 22: Mickey's "path to eternal youth repeats, in epitome, our own evolutionary story."

a. What is the point of Gould's elaborate comparison between human beings and chimps? Does this comparison lend support to Lorenz's position, or Darwin's, or neither?

b. What are the implications of our neotenic nature? Do they have any evolutionary or cultural consequence? Are they hopeful for us, or merely interesting?

Suggestions for Writing

1. The classic method of experimental science is to find a phenomenon in need of satisfactory explanation, to hypothesize a reasonable explanation, to construct a test to confirm the explanation, to run the test, and then to judge how well the results support the hypothesis. Gould follows that method in "A Biological Homage." Like Gould, test a hypothesis of your own (perhaps in conjunction with a science course), and report on the results.

2. A number of writers besides Gould have argued that our culture worships "juvenility". Find support for, or against, this argument.

3. A good library will make it possible for you to compare a similar evolution of other popular and long-lasting comic-strip characters, like Dick Tracy, Skeezix (*Gasoline Alley*), or Dagwood (*Blondie*). Do some research and write an essay giving your own interpretation of subtle changes in style over the years.

THE NONSCIENCE OF HUMAN NATURE

When a group of girls suffered simultaneous seizures in the presence of an accused witch, the justices of seventeenth century Salem could offer no explanation other than true demonic possession. When the followers of Charlie Manson attributed occult powers to their leader, no judge took them seriously. In nearly three hundred years separating the two incidents, we have learned quite a bit about social, economic, and psychological determinants of group behavior. A crudely literal interpretation of such events now seems ridiculous.

An equally crude literalism used to prevail in interpreting human nature and the differences among human groups. Human behavior was attributed to innate biology; we do what we do because we are made that way. The first lesson of an eighteenth-century primer stated the position succinctly: In Adam's fall, we sinned all. A movement away from this biological determinism has been a major trend in twentieth-century science and culture. We have come to see ourselves as a learning animal; we have come to believe that the influences of class and culture far outweigh the weaker predispositions of our genetic constitution.

Nonetheless, we have been deluged during the past decade by a resurgent biological determinism, ranging from "pop ethology" to outright racism.

With Konrad Lorenz as godfather, Robert Ardrey as dramatist, and Desmond Morris as raconteur, we are presented with man, "the naked ape," descended from an African carnivore, innately aggressive and inherently territorial.

Lionel Tiger and Robin Fox try to find a biological basis for outmoded Western ideals of aggressive, outreaching men and docile, restricted women. In discussing cross-cultural differences between men and women, they propose a hormonal chemistry inherited from the requirements of our supposed primal roles as group hunters and child rearers.

Carleton Coon offered a prelude of events to come with his claim (*The Origin of Races*, 1962) that five major human races evolved independently from *Homo erectus* ("Java" and "Peking" man) to *Homo sapiens*, with black people making the transition last. More recently, the IQ test has been (mis)used to infer genetic differences in intelligence among races (Arthur Jensen and William Shockley) and classes (Richard Herrnstein)—always, I must note, to the benefit of the particular group to which the author happens to belong (see next essay).

All these views have been ably criticized on an individual basis; yet they have rarely been treated together as expressions of a common philosophy—a crude biological determinism. One can, of course, accept a specific claim and reject the others. A belief in the innate nature of human violence does not brand anyone a racist. Yet all these claims have a common underpinning in postulating a direct genetic basis for our most fundamental traits. If we are programmed to be what we are, then these traits are ineluctable. We may, at best, channel them, but we cannot change them, either by will, education, or culture.

If we accept the usual platitudes about "scientific method" at face value, then the coordinated resurgence of biological determinism must be attributed to new information that refutes the earlier findings of twentieth-century science. Science, we are told, progresses by accumulating new information and using it to improve or replace old theories. But the new biological determinism rests upon no recent fund of information and can cite in its behalf not a single unambiguous fact. Its renewed support must have some other basis, most likely social or political in nature.

Science is always influenced by society, but it operates under a strong constraint of fact as well. The Church eventually made its peace with Galileo because, after all, the earth does go around the sun. In studying the genetic components of such complex human traits as intelligence and aggressiveness, however, we are freed from the constraint of fact, for we know practically nothing. In these questions, "science" follows (and exposes) the social and political influences acting upon it.

What then, are the nonscientific reasons that have fostered the resurgence of biological determinism? They range, I believe, from pedestrian pursuits of high royalties for best sellers to pernicious attempts to reintroduce racism as respectable science. Their common denominator must lie in our current malaise. How satisfying it is to fob off the responsibility for war and violence upon our presumably carnivorous ancestors. How convenient to blame the poor and the hungry for their own condition—lest we be forced to blame our economic system or our government for an abject failure to secure a decent life for all people. And how convenient an argument for those who control government and, by the way, provide the money that science requires for its very existence.

Deterministic arguments divide neatly into two groups—those based on the supposed nature of our species in general and those that invoke presumed differences among "racial groups" of *Homo sapiens*. I discuss the first subject here and treat the second in my next essay.

Summarized briefly, mainstream pop ethology contends that two lineages of hominids inhabited Pleistocene Africa. One, a small, territorial carnivore, evolved into us; the other, a larger, presumably gentle herbivore, became extinct. Some carry the analogy of Cain and Abel to its full conclusion and accuse our ancestors of fratricide. The "predatory transition" to hunting established a pattern of innate violence and engendered our territorial urges: "With the coming of the hunting life to the emerging hominid came the dedication to territory" (Ardrey, *The Territorial Imperative*). We may be clothed, citified, and civilized, but we carry deep within us the genetic patterns of behavior that served our ancestor, the "killer ape." In *Africa Genesis* Ardrey champions Raymond Dart's contention that "the predatory transition and the weapons fixation explained man's bloody history, his eternal aggression, his irrational, self-destroying, inexorable pursuit of death for death's sake."

Tiger and Fox extend the theme of group hunting to proclaim a biological basis for the differences between men and women that Western cultures have traditionally valued. Men did the hunting; women stayed home with the kids. Men are aggressive and combative, but they also form strong bonds among themselves that reflect the ancient need for cooperation in the killing of big game and now find expression in touch football and rotary clubs. Women are docile and devoted to their own children. They do not form intense bonds among themselves because their ancestors needed none to tend their homes and their men: sisterhood is an illusion. "We are wired for hunting.... We remain Upper Paleolithic hunters, fine-honed machines designed for the efficient pursuit of game" (Tiger and Fox, *The Imperial Animal*).

The story of pop ethology has been built on two lines of supposed evidence, both highly disputable:

1. Analogies with the behavior of other animals (abundant but imperfect data). No one doubts that many animals (including some, but not all, primates) display innate patterns of aggression and territorial behavior. Since we exhibit similar behavior, can we not infer a similar cause? The fallacy of this assumption reflects a basic issue in evolutionary theory. Evolutionists divide the similarities between two species into *homologous* features shared by common descent and a common genetic constitution, and *analogous* traits evolved separately.

Comparisons between humans and other animals lead to causal assertions about the genetics of our behavior only if they are based on homologous traits. But how can we know whether similarities are homologous or analogous? It is hard to differentiate even when we deal with concrete structures, such as muscles and bones. In fact, most classical arguments in the study of phylogeny involve the confusion of homology and analogy, for analogous structures can be strikingly similar (we call this phenomenon evolutionary convergence). How much harder it is to tell when similar features are only the outward motions of behavior! Baboons may be territorial; their males may be organized into a dominance hierarchy—but is our quest for Lebensraum and the hierarchy of our armies an expression of the same genetic makeup or merely an analogous pattern that might be purely cultural in origin? And when Lorenz compares us with geese and fish, we stray even further into pure conjecture; baboons, at least, are second cousins.

2. Evidence from hominid fossils (scrappy but direct data). Ardrey's claims for territoriality rest upon the assumption that our African ancestor *Australopithecus africanus*, was a carnivore. He derives his "evidence" from accumulations of bones and tools at the South African cave sites and the size and shape of teeth. The bone piles are no longer seriously considered; they are more likely the work of hyenas than of hominids.

Teeth are granted more prominence, but I believe that the evidence is equally poor if not absolutely contradictory. The argument rests upon relative size of grinding teeth (premolars and molars). Herbivores need more surface area to grind their gritty and abundant food. *A. robustus*, the supposed gentle herbivore, possessed grinding teeth relatively larger than those of its carnivorous relative, our ancestor *A. africanus*.

But *A. robustus* was a larger creature than *A. africanus*. As size increases, an animal must feed a body growing as the cube of length by chewing with tooth areas that increase only as the square of length if they maintain the same relative size (see essays of section 6). This will not do, and larger mammals must have differentially larger teeth than smaller relatives. I have tested this assertion by measuring tooth areas and body sizes for species in several groups of mammals (rodents, piglike herbivores, deer, and several groups of primates). Invariably, I find that larger animals have relatively larger teeth—not because they eat different foods, but simply because they are larger.

Moreover, the "small" teeth of *A. africanus* are not at all diminutive. They are *absolutely larger* than ours (although we are three times as heavy), and they are about as big as those of gorillas weighing nearly ten times as much! The evidence of tooth size indicates to me that *A. africanus* was primarily herbivorous.

The issue of biological determinism is not an abstract matter to be debated within academic cloisters. These ideas have important consequences, and they have already permeated our mass media. Ardrey's dubious theory is a prominent theme in Stanley Kubrick's film *2001*. The bone tool of our apelike ancestor first smashes a tapir's skull and then twirls about to transform into a space station of our next evolutionary stage—as the superman theme of Richard Strauss' *Zarathustra* yields to Johann's *Blue Danube*. Kubrick's next film, *Clockwork Orange*, continues the theme and explores the dilemma inspired by claims of innate human violence. (Shall we accept totalitarian controls for mass deprogramming or remain nasty and vicious within a democracy?) But the most immediate impact will be felt as male privilege girds its loins to battle a growing women's movement. As Kate Millett remarks in *Sexual Politics*: "Patriarchy has a tenacious or powerful hold through its successful habit of passing itself off as nature."   21

Rhetorical Analysis

1. Gould published "The Nonscience of Human Nature" first in *Natural History* magazine (April 1974), and later in his book, *Ever Since Darwin* (1977). Gould revised the essay in the three years between the magazine appearance and the book's publication. We have reprinted the later version, but a comparison with the earlier allows a rare look at the rewriting technique of a professional writer.
    a. The first paragraph of the earlier *Natural History* version reads:
    > When in the seventeenth century a group of girls simultaneously suffered seizures in the presence of an accused witch, the justices of Salem explained the girls' behavior as demonic possession. In 1971, when the followers of Charles Manson attributed occult powers to their leader, no judge took them seriously. During the nearly 300 years separating the two incidents, we have learned quite a bit about the psychological determinants of group behavior. A crudely literal interpretation of such events now seems ridiculous.

    Compare this text with the later text. Where the two texts differ, speculate on Gould's rationale.
    b. Gould also altered the paragraphing. The original version began a fresh paragraph with the fifth sentence of ¶ 12 and with the sixth sentence of ¶ 16. In the later version of the essay, why did Gould combine paragraphs at these two spots?

c. Here are some other revised passages. We quote the *Natural History* version first, the later version second.
- (1) Human behavior was simply attributed . . . / Human behavior was attributed . . . (¶ 2, sentence 2).
- (2) . . . not a single fact . . . / . . . not a single unambiguous fact . . . (¶ 8, sentence 3).
- (3) The church eventually made its peace with Galilean cosmology / The church eventually made its peace with Galileo because, after all, the earth does go around the sun (¶ 9, sentence 2).
- (4) . . . of fact, for we are sure of practically nothing about these traits / . . . of fact, for we know practically nothing (¶ 9, sentence 3).
- (5) The pop ethology story has . . . / The story of pop ethology has . . . (¶ 14, sentence 1).
- (6) Comparison between human beings and other animals can yield causal . . . / Comparisons between humans and other animals lead to casual . . . (¶ 16, sentence 1).
- (7) The relative size of grinding teeth (premolars and molars) is the basis of the argument / The argument rests upon relative size of grinding teeth (premolars and molars) (¶ 18, sentence 2).
- (8) . . . next evolutionary stage. Kubrick's next film . . . / . . . next evolutionary stage—as the theme of Richard Strauss' *Zarathustra* yields to Johann's *Blue Danube*. Kubrick's next film . . . (¶ 21, sentence 4).

What did Gould add, what did he delete, and why?

d. Finally, the original version contained the following paragraph between ¶s 7 and 8. Why do you think Gould eliminated it?

> In various guises, the political function of biological determinism has been to serve the supporters of class, sex, and race distinctions at home and of conquest or domination of supposedly inferior peoples abroad. In the context of Western history, this means that biological determinism has served as a tool of state and commercial power.

Intellectual Analysis

1. The structure of this entire essay follows the pattern we suggest for the opening of "Mickey Mouse": puzzle, theory, confirmation. Find the paragraphs—all clearly signalled by Gould—which mark these three parts. Can you now see the form of this essay whole?

2. One of Gould's major questions is, What is wrong with "resurgent biological determinism" (¶ 3)? What issues are raised? (Paragraphs 7–10 are important for both this item and the next.)
    a. Biological determinists assume there is a genetic basis for "our most basic traits"; what repercussions does genetic determinism have on evolutionary theory as applied to humans?
    b. Does determinism leave any room for "free will"?

c. Does genetic determinism deny that we are shaped in any way by environmental forces, economic or social or geographical or whatever? (For instance, does free will or the environment have nothing to do with poverty?)
   d. At the societal level, does determinism rob human beings of responsibility for their actions?
3. Gould is cryptic about "our current malaise," but since that phrase is crucial to his argument, we have to use his cues, and invent the rest.
   a. Science ought to operate under "constraint of fact," he says, and in that way lead society "to improve or replace old theories" (¶ 9). Besides Galileo, what other examples of science operating properly can you think of?
   b. But when there is an absence of reliable facts, sometimes science instead "follows (and exposes) the social and political influences acting upon it" (¶ 9). What does this essay expose about the current state of affairs? What does the state of science show about the influence of economics? What does it show about confusion in society? About complexity? About fear?
4. Deterministic arguments are of two sorts, Gould says, but in this essay he is interested only in theories "based on the supposed nature of our species in general" (¶ 11).
   a. "Pop ethology," Gould's expression for this sort of theory, has progressed along two lines of "supposed evidence." The terms you need for the *first* are "homology" and "analogy": discuss these terms and how they become confused (¶ 16).
   b. The *second* kind is fossil evidence. This is the strongest part of Gould's "confirmation" of his claims. Discuss the evidence of teeth.

Suggestions for Writing

1. Read the essay following this one (published in *Ever Since Darwin*), to which this essay is linked, and write an essay analyzing the questions it raises. Does the second essay complete this one? Should the two be read together?
2. Write a study of Gould's rewriting techniques. For this, you will need copies of his book and access to the magazine, *Natural History*.

CRAZY OLD RANDOLPH KIRKPATRICK

Oblivion, not infamy, is the usual fate of a crackpot. I shall be more than mildly surprised if any reader (who is not a professional taxonomist with a special attachment to sponges) can identify Randolph Kirkpatrick.

On the surface, Kirkpatrick fit the stereotype of a self-effacing, mild-mannered, dedicated, but slightly eccentric British natural historian. He was the assistant keeper of "lower" invertebrates at the British Museum from 1886 until his retirement in 1927. (I have always admired the English penchant for simple, literal terms—lifts and flats for our elevators and apartments, for example. We use the Latin *curator* for guardians of museum collections; the British call them "keepers." We, however, have done better in retaining "fall" for their "autumn.") Kirkpatrick trained as a medical student, but decided on a "less strenuous career" in natural history after several bouts with illness. He chose well, for he traveled all over the world searching for specimens and lived to be eighty-seven. In the last months of his life, in 1950, he continued to pedal his bicycle through London's busiest streets.

Early in his career, Kirkpatrick published some sound taxonomic work on sponges, but his name rarely appears in scientific journals after the First World War. In an obituary note, his successor attributed this halt in mid-career to Kirkpatrick's behavior as "an ideal public servant." "Unassuming to a fault, courteous and generous, he would spare no effort to help either a colleague or a visiting student. It was in all probability his extreme willingness to interrupt whatever he was doing to help others that prevented his completing his work."

Kirkpatrick's story, however, is by no means so simple and conventionally spotless. He did not stop publishing in 1915; instead, he shifted to private printing for a series of works that he knew no scientific journal would touch. Kirkpatrick spent the rest of his career developing what has to be the nuttiest of crackpot theories developed in this century by a professional natural historian (and keeper at the staid British Museum, no less). I do not challenge this usual assessment of his "nummulosphere" theory, but I will stoutly defend Kirkpatrick.

In 1912, Kirkpatrick was collecting sponges off the island of Porto Santo in the Madeira group, west of Morocco. One day, a friend brought him some volcanic rocks collected on a peak 1,000 feet above sea level. Kirkpatrick described his great discovery: "I examined them carefully under my binocular microscope and found to my amazement traces of nummulitic disks in all of them. Next day I visited the place whence the fragments had come."

Now *Nummulites* is one of the largest forams that ever lived (forams are single-celled creatures related to amoebas, but they secrete shells and are commonly preserved as fossils). *Nummulites* looks like the object that provided its name: a coin. Its shell is a flat disk up to an inch or two in diameter. The disk is built of individual chambers, one following the next and all wound tightly into a single coil. (The shell looks much like a coil of rope, appropriately scaled down.) Nummulites were so abundant in early Tertiary times (about 50 million years ago) that some rocks are composed almost entirely of their shells; these are called "nummulitic limestones." Nummulites litter the ground around Cairo; the Greek geographer Strabo identified them as petrified lentils left over from rations doled out to slaves who had built the Great Pyramids.

Kirkpatrick then returned to Madeira and "discovered" nummulites in the igneous rocks there as well. I can scarcely imagine a more radical claim about the earth's structure. Igneous rocks are the products of volcanic eruption or the cooling of molten magmas within the earth; they cannot contain fossils. But Kirkpatrick argued that the igneous rocks of Madeira and Porto Santo not only included nummulites but were actually made of them. Therefore, "igneous" rocks must be sediments deposited at the ocean bottom, not the products of molten material from the earth's interior. Kirkpatrick wrote:

> After the discovery of the nummulitic nature of nearly the whole island of Porto Santo, of the buildings, wine presses, soil, etc., the name *Eozoon portosantum* seemed a fitting one for the fossils. [*Eozoon* means "dawn animal," more on it in a moment.] When the igneous rocks of Madeira were likewise found to be nummulitic, *Eozoon atlanticum* seemed a more fitting name.

Nothing could stop Kirkpatrick now. He returned to London, itching to examine igneous rocks from other areas of the world. All were made of nummulites! "I annexed in one morning for *Eozoon* volcanic rocks of the Arctic and in the afternoon of the same day those of the Pacific, Indian and Atlantic oceans. The designation *Eozoon orbis-terrarum* then suggested itself." Finally, he looked at meteorites and, yes, you guessed it, all nummulites.

> If *Eozoon*, after taking in the world, had sighed for more worlds to conquer, its fortunes would have surpassed those of Alexander, for its desires would have been realized. When the empire of the nummulites was found to extend to space a final alteration of name to *Eozoon universum* apparently became necessary.

Kirkpatrick did not shy away from the evident conclusion:—all rocks on the earth's surface (including the influx from space) are made of fossils: "The original organic nature of these rocks is to me self-evident, because I can see the Foraminiferal structure in them, and often very clearly indeed." Kirkpatrick claimed that he could see the nummulites with a low-power hand lens, although no one ever agreed with him. "My views on igneous and certain other rocks," he wrote, "have been received with a good deal of skepticism, and this is not surprising."

I hope I will not be dismissed as an establishment dogmatist if I state with some assurance that Kirkpatrick had somehow managed to delude himself. By his own admission, he often had to work very hard in toeing his own line: "Sometimes I have found it necessary to examine a fragment of rock with the closest scrutiny for hours before convincing myself that I have seen all the above-mentioned details."

But what version of the earth's history would yield a crust made entirely of nummulites? Kirkpatrick proposed that nummulites had arisen early in the history of life as the first creatures with shells. Hence, he adopted for them the name *Eozoon*, first proposed in the 1850s by the great Canadian geologist Sir J. W. Dawson for a supposed fossil from some of the earth's oldest rocks. (We now know that *Eozoon* is an inorganic structure, made of alternating white and green layers of the minerals calcite and serpentine—see essay 23.)

In these early times, Kirkpatrick speculated, the ocean bottom must have accumulated a deep deposit of nummulitic shells over its entire surface, for the seas contained no predators to digest them. Heat from the earth's interior fused them together and injected them with silica (thus solving the vexatious problem of why igneous rocks are silicates, while true nummulites are made of calcium carbonate). As the nummulites were squeezed and fused, some were pushed upward and tossed out into space, later to descend as nummulitic meteorites.

> Rocks are sometimes classified as fossiliferous and unfossiliferous, but all are fossiliferous. . . . Really, then, there is, broadly speaking, one rock. . . . The lithosphere is veritably a silicated nummulosphere.

Kirkpatrick still was not satisfied. He thought he had discovered something even more fundamental. Not content with the earth's crust and its meteorites, he began to see the coiled form of nummulites as an expression of life's essence, as the architecture of life itself. Finally, he broadened his claim to its limit: we should not say that the rocks are nummulites; rather, the rocks and the nummulites and everything else alive are expressions of "the fundamental structure of living matter," the spiral form of all existence.

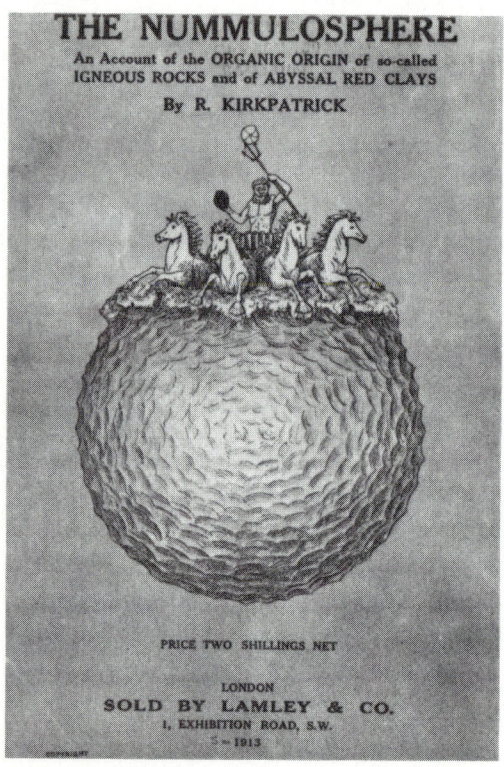

The cover to Kirkpatrick's privately published Nummulosphere. Of it, he writes: "The design on the cover represents Neptune on the globe of waters. On one of the prongs of his trident is a piece of volcanic rock in the shape of a nummulitic disk, and in his hand is a meteorite. These emblems signify that Neptune's domain is enlarged not only at the expense of nether Jove, but also at that of high Jove whose supposed emblem of sovereignty—the thunderbolt—really belongs to the Sea God . . . Neptune's bolt is poised ready to be hurled at rash and ignorant mortals of the type of the a priori would-be refuter, daring to dispute the validity of his title-deeds."

Nutty, yes (unless you feel that he had intuited the double helix). Inspired, surely. A method to his madness, yes, again—and this is the crucial point. In framing his nummulosphere theory, Kirkpatrick followed the procedure that motivated all his scientific work. He had an uncritical passion for synthesis and an imagination that compelled him to gather truly disparate things together. He consistently sought similarities of geometric form among objects conventionally classified in different categories, while ignoring the ancient truth that similarity of form need not designate common cause. He also constructed similarities out of his hopes, rather than his observations.

Still, an uncautious search for synthesis may uncover real connections that would never occur to a sober scientist (although he may be jostled to reflect upon them once someone else makes the initial suggestion). Scientists like Kirkpatrick pay a heavy price, for they are usually wrong. But when they are right, they may be so outstandingly right that their insights beggar the honest work of many scientific lifetimes in conventional channels.

Let us return then to Kirkpatrick and ask why he was on Madeira and Porto Santo in the first place when he made his fateful discovery in 1912. "In September 1912," he writes, "I journeyed to Porto Santo via Madeira, in order to complete my investigation of that strange organism, the sponge-alga *Merlia normani*." In 1900, a taxonomist named J. J. Lister had discovered a peculiar sponge on the Pacific islands of Lifu and Funafuti. It contained spicules of silica, but had an additional calcareous skeleton bearing a striking resemblance to some corals (spicules are the small, needle-like elements forming the skeleton of most sponges). A sober man, Lister could not accept the "hybrid" of silica and calcite; he conjectured that the spicules had entered the sponge from elsewhere. But Kirkpatrick collected more specimens and correctly concluded that the sponge secretes the spicules. Then, in 1910, Kirkpatrick found *Merlia normani* on Madeira, a second sponge with siliceous spicules and a supplementary calcareous skeleton.

Inevitably, Kirkpatrick unleashed his passion for synthesis upon *Merlia*. He noticed that its calcareous skeleton resembled several problematic groups of fossils usually classified among the corals—the stromatoporoids and the chaetetid tabulates in particular. (This may seem like a small issue to many, but I assure you that it is a major concern of all professional paleontologists. Stromatoporoids and chaetetids are very common as fossils; they form reefs in some ancient deposits. Their status lies among the classical mysteries of my field, and many distinguished paleontologists have spent entire careers devoted to their study.) Kirkpatrick decided that these and other enigmatic fossils must be sponges. He set out to find spicules in them, a sure sign of affinity with sponges. Sure enough, they all contained spicules. We may be quite sure that Kirkpatrick had deluded himself again in some cases, for he included among his "sponges" the undoubted bryozoan *Monticulipora*. In any case, Kirkpatrick soon became preoccupied with his nummulosphere theory. He never published the major treatise that he had planned on *Merlia*. The nummulosphere made him a scientific pariah, and his work on coralline sponges was pretty much forgotten.

Kirkpatrick worked the same way in studying both nummulospheres and coralline sponges: he invoked a similarity of abstract, geometric form to infer a common source for objects that no one had thought to unite, and he followed his theory with such passion that he eventually "saw" the expected form, even where it manifestly did not exist. Yet, I must note one major difference between the two studies: Kirkpatrick was right about the sponges.

During the 1960s, Thomas Goreau, late of the Discovery Bay Marine Laboratory in Jamaica, began to explore the cryptic environments of West Indian reefs. These cracks, crevices, and caves contain a major fauna, previously undetected. In one of the most exciting zoological discoveries of the last twenty years, Goreau and his colleagues Jeremy Jackson and Willard Hartman showed that these habitats contain numerous "living fossils." This cryptic community seems to represent an entire ecosystem literally overshadowed by the evolution of more modern forms. The community may be cryptic, but its members are neither moribund nor uncommon. The linings of caves and crevices form a major part of modern reefs. Before the advent of scuba diving, scientists could not gain access to these areas.

Two elements dominate this cryptic fauna: brachiopods and Kirkpatrick's coralline sponges. Goreau and Hartman described six species of coralline sponges from the fore-reef slope of Jamaica's reef. These species form the basis for an entire new class of sponges, the Sclerospongiae. In the course of their work, they rediscovered Kirkpatrick's papers and studied his opinion on the relationship between coralline sponges and the enigmatic fossil stromatoporoids and chaetetids. "Kirkpatrick's comments," they write, "have led us to compare the coralline sponges described above with representatives of several groups of organisms known from the fossil record." They have shown, quite convincingly I think, that these fossils are indeed sponges. A major zoological discovery has solved an outstanding problem in paleontology. And crazy old Randolph Kirkpatrick had known it all along.

When I wrote to Hartman to inquire about Kirkpatrick, he cautioned me not to judge the man too harshly on his nummulosphere, for his taxonomic work on sponges had been sound. But I respect Kirkpatrick both for his sponges and for his numinous nummulosphere. It is easy to dismiss a crazy theory with laughter that debars any attempt to understand a man's motivation—and the nummulosphere is a crazy theory. I find that few men of imagination are not worth my attention. Their ideas may be wrong, even foolish, but their methods often repay a close study. Few honest passions are not based upon some valid perception of unity or some anomaly worthy of note. The different drummer often beats a fruitful tempo.

Rhetorical Analysis

1. The modern philosopher Jean-Paul Sartre argues that the essential relationship between reader and writer is *freedom*. This means, in part, that readers are free to stop reading any time they have reason to. And since the most common reason is boredom or lack of interest, the writer must be constantly concerned to maintain that interest.
    a. A little analysis of "Crazy Old Randolph Kirkpatrick" shows a lot about how Gould exploits our in-born curiosity. "Crazy" in the title piques us enough to read the first paragraph. And there, the word "crackpot," plus the suggestion that Kirkpatrick is unknown but still *worth* knowing, encourages us to read the second paragraph. Continue the analysis on through the essay. What are some different ways Gould holds our interest, that is, keeps us reading?
    b. Paragraphs 4, 15, and 18 mark key points where Gould seems especially concerned about arousing the reader's curiosity. Why *these* points?
2. The organization of this essay may be seen as follows:
    ¶ 1
    ¶s 2–3
    ¶s 4–13
    ¶s 14–17
    ¶s 18–20
    ¶ 21

Identify the role of each of these sections in the essay as a whole. What one plan organizes the whole essay?

3. Stephen Jay Gould shares the goal of a number of fine contemporary writers, to make the theories and findings of science understandable to nonscientists. What has Gould done to simplify, clarify, explain, and interpret science in "Crazy Old Randolph Kirkpatrick"? How well does he achieve these aims for you?

Intellectual Analysis

1. Thematically this essay divides into two parts, the first recounting Kirkpatrick's crazy theory of the "nummulosphere," the second his brilliant investigations of "coralline sponges." How and where are the two parts joined? Why does Gould construct the essay in two parts? The answer brings one to the real subject of the essay, the reason why Gould "will stoutly defend Kirkpatrick" (¶ 4).
   a. In ¶ 14, Gould mentions "the crucial point"; examine it carefully.
   b. In ¶ 15, Gould begins with, "Still an uncautious search . . . may uncover real connections," and he proceeds to make a serious statement about scientific research. What is implied by this statement?
   c. In ¶ 16, the scene shifts once again to Porto Santo; here, surely, is a clear hinge to the two parts of the essay. What point is there in signaling it?
   d. Finally, in ¶ 18, Gould gathers together an important thematic statement on Kirkpatrick's work. Evaluate that statement.

   It may be that the entire midsection of the essay is its hinge: look again at ¶s 14–18. The common denominator in both halves may well be the consistency or integrity of Kirkpatrick's method. Analyze Gould's treatment of that method, here and at the end of the essay.

2. What does Gould's essay say about progress in science, about scientific method, and about the relationship between research and personality?
   a. Consider the implications here about objectivity.
   b. What does Gould imply about our ability to hypothesize?

Suggestions for Writing

1. "Few honest passions are not based upon some valid perception." Write an essay defending or attacking that assertion. Or write an essay defining and evaluating honest and dishonest passions.

2. Compare this essay to other character sketches in this anthology (for example, "Pooran Singh" and "In Search of Our Mothers' Gardens"). You may know people who, like Randolph Kirkpatrick, are unlikely combinations of nuttiness and brilliance. Write a character sketch of one.

3. Note the epigrammatic quality of the first and last sentences of this essay, and the use Gould makes of them. The last sentence, in fact, is a paraphrase of a famous line from Thoreau's *Walden*. In the reference area of your library, find a collection of quotations or proverbs, read through it until you find an epigram that suggests a topic for an essay you would like to write, and then use that epigram in either the opening or closing of the essay.

JAMES BALDWIN

James Baldwin was born in 1924 in New York City's black neighborhood of Harlem. By his mid teens he had already abandoned one promising career as a child evangelist and had despaired of entering the second—the profession of writing. Baldwin's lack of formal education and the color of his skin, he knew, worked against him. But in 1946 he met the painter Beauford Delaney, who showed him by example that a black man could survive as an artist in American society. Their meeting was critical, for Baldwin then resolved to persist as a writer: he began his apprenticeship by doing book reviews for The New Leader, a periodical edited by Saul Levitas. In 1948, partly through the influence of his mentor, the novelist Richard Wright, Baldwin was awarded a literary fellowship which he used to travel to Europe. He lived in Paris as an expatriate for several years.

In 1952 Baldwin accompanied a friend to Switzerland, shut himself up in a chalet in a small village, and there, to the accompaniment of Bessie Smith recordings, wrote Go Tell It on the Mountain. That novel, a fictionalized account of his own conflict with his father, was published the next year to critical acclaim and popular success. It was soon followed by Giovanni's Room (1956), Another Country (1962), and other novels, as well as plays, stories, essays and articles.

Though he has done important work

as a novelist, Baldwin's best writing, like Woolf's, may be in the essay genre. The critic John Henrik Clarke has written that "more than any other writer of our times [Baldwin] has succeeded in restoring the personal essay to its place as a form of creative literature." This success may be attributed partly to genius, partly to circumstance. Baldwin returned in 1957 from his expatriation in Europe to an America on the verge of racial revolution. His polemical gifts, his profound sense of his special role in American history, and his urgency coupled with his passionate fingering of the racial wound in his own psyche, were best expressed in the essay form. His early career as a child evangelist may have contributed something, too, for his essays are often jeremiads, or sermons.

As a novelist, Baldwin demands that America live up to its national ideals as expressed in the Constitution and other founding documents. Knowing it will not, he wonders aloud why it does not try. That wondering aloud, honed to a very sharp edge, results in his essays, which must be read as open letters to all Americans.

Notes of a Native Son

On the twenty-ninth of July, in 1943, my father died. On the same day, a few hours later, his last child was born. Over a month before this, while all our energies were concentrated in waiting for these events, there had been, in Detroit, one of the bloodiest race riots of the century. A few hours after my father's funeral, while he lay in state in the undertaker's chapel, a race riot broke out in Harlem. On the morning of the third of August, we drove my father to the graveyard through a wilderness of smashed plate glass.

The day of my father's funeral had also been my nineteenth birthday. As we drove him to the graveyard, the spoils of injustice, anarchy, discontent, and hatred were all around us. It seemed to me that God himself had devised, to mark my father's end, the most sustained and brutally dissonant of codas. And it seemed to me, too, that the violence which rose all about us as my father left the world had been devised as a corrective for the pride of his eldest son. I had declined to believe in that apocalypse which had been central to my father's vision; very well, life seemed to be saying, here is something that will certainly pass for an apocalypse until the real thing comes along. I had inclined to be contemptuous of my father for the conditions of his life, for the conditions of our lives. When his life had ended I began to wonder about that life and also, in a new way, to be apprehensive about my own.

I had not known my father very well. We had got on badly, partly because we shared, in our different fashions, the vice of stubborn pride. When he was dead I realized that I had hardly ever spoken to him. When he had been dead a long time I began to wish I had. It seems to be typical of life in America, where opportunities, real and fancied, are thicker than anywhere else on the globe, that the second generation has no time to talk to the first. No one, including my father, seems to have known exactly how old he was, but his mother had been born during slavery. He was of the first generation of free men. He, along with thousands of other Negroes, came North after 1919 and I was part of that generation which had never seen the landscape of what Negroes sometimes call the Old Country.

He had been born in New Orleans and had been a quite young man there during the time that Louis Armstrong, a boy, was running errands for the dives and honky-tonks of what was always presented to me as one of the most wicked of cities—to this day, whenever I think of New Orleans, I also helplessly think of Sodom and Gomorrah. My father never mentioned Louis Armstrong, except to forbid us to play his records; but there was a picture of him on our wall for a long time. One of my father's strong-willed female relatives had placed it there and forbade my father to take it down. He never did, but he eventually maneuvered her out of the house and when, some years later, she was in trouble and near death, he refused to do anything to help her.

He was, I think, very handsome. I gather this from photographs and from my own memories of him, dressed in his Sunday best and on his way to preach a sermon somewhere, when I was little. Handsome, proud, and ingrown, "like a toenail," somebody said. But he looked to me, as I grew older, like pictures I had seen of African tribal chieftains: he really should have been naked, with warpaint on and barbaric mementos, standing among spears. He could be chilling in the pulpit and indescribably cruel in his personal life and he was certainly the most bitter man I have ever met; yet it must be said that there was something else in him, buried in him, which lent him his tremendous power and, even, a rather crushing charm. It had something to do with his blackness, I think—he was very black—with his blackness and his beauty, and with the fact that he knew that he was black but did not know that he was beautiful. He claimed to be proud of his blackness but it had also been the cause of much humiliation and it had fixed bleak boundaries to his life. He was not a young man when we were growing up and he had already suffered many kinds of ruin; in his outrageously demanding and protective way he loved his children, who were black like him and menaced, like him; and all these things sometimes showed in his face when he tried, never to my knowledge with any success, to establish contact with any of us. When he took one of his children on his knee to play, the child always became fretful and began to cry; when he tried to help one of us with our homework the absolutely unabating tension which emanated from him caused our minds and our tongues to become paralyzed, so that he, scarcely knowing why, flew into a rage and the child, not knowing why, was punished. If it ever entered his head to bring a surprise home for his children, it was, almost unfailingly, the wrong surprise and even the big watermelons he often brought home on his back in the summertime led to the most appalling scenes. I do not remember, in all those years, that one of his children was ever glad to see him come home. From what I was able to gather of his early life, it seemed that this inability to establish contact with other people had always marked him and had been one of the things which had driven him out of New Orleans. There was something in him, therefore, groping and tentative, which was never expressed and which was buried with him. One saw it most clearly when he was facing new people and hoping to impress them. But he never did, not for long. We went from church to smaller and more improbable church, he found himself in less and less demand as a minister, and by the time he died none of his friends had come to see him for a long time. He had lived and died in an intolerable bitterness of spirit and it frightened me, as we drove him to the graveyard through those unquiet, ruined streets, to see how powerful and overflowing this bitterness could be and to realize that this bitterness now was mine.

When he died I had been away from home for a little over a year. In that year I had had time to become aware of the meaning of all my father's bitter warnings, had discovered the secret of his proudly pursed lips and rigid carriage: I had discovered the weight of white people in the world. I saw that this had been for my ancestors and now would be for me an awful thing to live with and that the bitterness which had helped to kill my father could also kill me.

He had been ill a long time—in the mind, as we now realized, reliving instances of his fantastic intransigence in the new light of his affliction and endeavoring to feel a sorrow for him which never, quite, came true. We had not known that he was being eaten up by paranoia, and the discovery that his cruelty, to our bodies and our minds, had been one of the symptoms of his illness was not, then, enough to enable us to forgive him. The younger children felt, quite simply, relief that he would not be coming home anymore. My mother's observation that it was he, after all, who had kept them alive all these years meant nothing because the problems of keeping children alive are not real for children. The older children felt, with my father gone, that they could invite their friends to the house without fear that their friends would be insulted or, as had sometimes happened with me, being told that their friends were in league with the devil and intended to rob our family of everything we owned. (I didn't fail to wonder, and it made me hate him, what on earth we owned that anybody else would want.)

His illness was beyond all hope of healing before anyone realized that he was ill. He had always been so strange and had lived, like a prophet, in such unimaginably close communion with the Lord that his long silences which were punctuated by moans and hallelujahs and snatches of old songs while he sat at the living-room window never seemed odd to us. It was not until he refused to eat because, he said, his family was trying to poison him that my mother was forced to accept as a fact what had, until then, been only an unwilling suspicion. When he was committed, it was discovered that he had tuberculosis and, as it turned out, the disease of his mind allowed the disease of his body to destroy him. For the doctors could not force him to eat, either, and, though he was fed intravenously, it was clear from the beginning that there was no hope for him.

In my mind's eye I could see him, sitting at the window, locked up in his terrors; hating and fearing every living soul including his children who had betrayed him, too, by reaching toward the world which had despised him. There were nine of us. I began to wonder what it could have felt like for such a man to have had nine children whom he could barely feed. He used to make little jokes about our poverty, which never, of course, seemed very funny to us; they could not have seemed very funny to him, either, or else our all too feeble response to them would never have caused such rages. He spent great energy and achieved, to our chagrin, no small amount of success in keeping us away from the people who surrounded us, people who had all-night rent parties to which we listened when we should have been sleeping, people who cursed and drank and flashed razor blades on Lenox Avenue. He could not understand why, if they had so much energy to spare, they could not use it to make their lives better. He treated almost everybody on our block with a most uncharitable asperity and neither they, nor, of course, their children were slow to reciprocate.

The only white people who came to our house were welfare workers and bill collectors. It was almost always my mother who dealt with them, for my father's temper, which was at the mercy of his pride, was never to be trusted. It was clear that he felt their very presence in his home to be a violation: this was conveyed by his carriage, almost ludicrously stiff, and by his voice, harsh and vindictively polite. When I was around nine or ten I wrote a play which was directed by a young, white schoolteacher, a woman, who then took an interest in me, and gave me books to read and, in order to corroborate my theatrical bent, decided to take me to see what she somewhat tactlessly referred to as "real" plays. Theater-going was forbidden in our house, but, with the really cruel intuitiveness of a child, I suspected that the color of this woman's skin would carry the day for me. When, at school, she suggested taking me to the theater, I did not, as I might have done if she had been a Negro, find a way of discouraging her, but agreed that she should pick me up at my house one evening. I then, very cleverly, left all the rest to my mother, who suggested to my father, as I knew she would, that it would not be very nice to let such a kind woman make the trip for nothing. Also, since it was a schoolteacher, I imagine that my mother countered the idea of sin with the idea of "education," which word, even with my father, carried a kind of bitter weight.

Before the teacher came my father took me aside to ask *why* she was coming, what *interest* she could possibly have in our house, in a boy like me. I said I didn't know but I, too, suggested that it had something to do with education. And I understood that my father was waiting for me to say something—I didn't quite know what; perhaps that I wanted his protection against this teacher and her "education." I said none of these things and the teacher came and we went out. It was clear, during the brief interview in our living room, that my father was agreeing very much against his will and that he would have refused permission if he had dared. The fact that he did not dare caused me to despise him: I had no way of knowing that he was facing in that living room a wholly unprecedented and frightening situation.

Later, when my father had been laid off from his job, this woman became very important to us. She was really a very sweet and generous woman and went to a great deal of trouble to be of help to us, particularly during one awful winter. My mother called her by the highest name she knew: she said she was a "christian." My father could scarcely disagree but during the four or five years of our relatively close association he never trusted her and was always trying to surprise in her open, Midwestern face the genuine, cunningly hidden, and hideous motivation. In later years, particularly when it began to be clear that this "education" of mine was going to lead me to perdition, he became more explicit and warned me that my white friends in high school were not really my friends and that I would see, when I was older, how white people would do anything to keep a Negro down. Some of them could be nice, he admitted, but none of them were to be trusted and most of them were not even nice. The best thing was to have as little to do with them as possible. I did not feel this way and I was certain, in my innocence, that I never would.

But the year which preceded my father's death had made a great change in my life. I had been living in New Jersey, working in defense plants, working and living among southerners, white and black. I knew about the South, of course, and about how southerners treated Negroes and how they expected them to behave, but it had never entered my mind that anyone would look at me and expect *me* to behave that way. I learned in New Jersey that to be a Negro meant, precisely, that one was never looked at but was simply at the mercy of the reflexes the color of one's skin caused in other people. I acted in New Jersey as I had always acted, that is as though I thought a great deal of myself—I had to *act* that way—with results that were, simply, unbelievable. I had scarcely arrived before I had earned the enmity, which was extraordinarily ingenious, of all my superiors and nearly all my co-workers. In the beginning, to make matters worse, I simply did not know what was happening. I did not know what I had done, and I shortly began to wonder what *anyone* could possibly do, to bring about such unanimous, active, and unbearably vocal hostility. I knew about jim crow but I had never experienced it. I went to the same self-service restaurant three times and stood with all the Princeton boys before the counter, waiting for a hamburger and coffee; it was always an extraordinarily long time before anything was set before me; but it was not until the fourth visit that I learned that, in fact, nothing had ever been set before me: I had simply picked something up. Negroes were not served there, I was told, and they had been waiting for me to realize that I was always the only Negro present. Once I was told this, I determined to go there all the time. But now they were ready for me and, though some dreadful scenes were subsequently enacted in that restaurant, I never ate there again.

It was the same story all over New Jersey, in bars, bowling alleys, diners, places to live. I was always being forced to leave, silently, or with mutual imprecations. I very shortly became notorious and children giggled behind me when I passed and their elders whispered or shouted—they really believed that I was mad. And it did begin to work on my mind, of course; I began to be afraid to go anywhere and to compensate for this I went places to which I really should not have gone and where, God knows, I had no desire to be. My reputation in town naturally enhanced my reputation at work and my working day became one long series of acrobatics designed to keep me out of trouble. I cannot say that these acrobatics succeeded. It began to seem that the machinery of the organization I worked for was turning over, day and night, with but one aim: to eject me. I was fired once, and contrived, with the aid of a friend from New York, to get back on the payroll; was fired again, and bounced back again. It took a while to fire me for the third time, but the third time took. There were no loopholes anywhere. There was not even any way of getting back inside the gates.

That year in New Jersey lives in my mind as though it were the year during which, having an unsuspected predilection for it, I first contracted some dread, chronic disease, the unfailing symptom of which is a kind of blind fever, a pounding in the skull and fire in the bowels. Once this disease is contracted, one can never be really carefree again, for the fever, without an instant's warning, can recur at any moment. It can wreck more important things than race relations. There is not a Negro alive who does not have this rage in his blood— one has the choice, merely, of living with it consciously or surrendering to it. As for me, this fever has recurred in me, and does, and will until the day I die.

My last night in New Jersey, a white friend from New York took me to the nearest big town, Trenton, to go to the movies and have a few drinks. As it turned out, he also saved me from, at the very least, a violent whipping. Almost every detail of that night stands out very clearly in my memory. I even remember the name of the movie we saw because its title impressed me as being so patly ironical. It was a movie about the German occupation of France, starring Maureen O'Hara and Charles Laughton and called *This Land Is Mine*. I remember the name of the diner we walked into when the movie ended: it was the "American Diner." When we walked in the counterman asked what we wanted and I remember answering with the casual sharpness which had become my habit: "We want a hamburger and a cup of coffee, what do you think we want?" I do not know why, after a year of such rebuffs, I so completely failed to anticipate his answer, which was, of course, "we don't serve Negroes here." This reply failed to discompose me, at least for the moment. I made some sardonic comment about the name of the diner and we walked out into the streets.

This was the time of what was called the "brownout," when the lights in all American cities were very dim. When we reentered the streets something happened to me which had the force of an optical illusion, or a nightmare. The streets were very crowded and I was facing north. People were moving in every direction but it seemed to me, in that instant, that all of the people I could see, and many more than that, were moving toward me, against me, and that everyone was white. I remember how their faces gleamed. And I felt, like a physical sensation, a *click* at the nape of my neck as though some interior string connecting my head to my body had been cut. I began to walk. I heard my friend call after me, but I ignored him. Heaven only knows what was going on in his mind, but he had the good sense not to touch me—I don't know what would have happened if he had—and to keep me in sight. I don't know what was going on in my mind, either; I certainly had no conscious plan. I wanted to do something to crush these white faces, which were crushing me. I walked for perhaps a block or two until I came to an enormous, glittering, and fashionable restaurant in which I knew not even the intercession of the Virgin would cause me to be served. I pushed through the doors and took the first vacant seat I saw, at a table for two, and waited.

I do not know how long I waited and I rather wonder, until today, what I could possibly have looked like. Whatever I looked like, I frightened the waitress who shortly appeared, and the moment she appeared all of my fury flowed toward her. I hated her for her white face, and for her great, astounded, frightened eyes. I felt that if she found a black man so frightening I would make her fright worthwhile.

She did not ask me what I wanted, but repeated, as though she had learned it somewhere, "We don't serve Negroes here." She did not say it with the blunt, derisive hostility to which I had grown so accustomed, but, rather, with a note of apology in her voice, and fear. This made me colder and more murderous than ever. I felt I had to do something with my hands. I wanted her to come close enough for me to get her neck between my hands.

So I pretended not to have understood her, hoping to draw her closer. And she did step a very short step closer, with her pencil poised incongruously over her pad, and repeated the formula: ". . . don't serve Negroes here."

Somehow, with the repetition of that phrase, which was already ringing in my head like a thousand bells of a nightmare, I realized that she would never come any closer and that I would have to strike from a distance. There was nothing on the table but an ordinary watermug half full of water, and I picked this up and hurled it with all my strength at her. She ducked and it missed her and shattered against the mirror behind the bar. And, with that sound, my frozen blood abruptly thawed, I returned from wherever I had been, I *saw*, for the first time, the restaurant, the people with their mouths open, already, as it seemed to me, rising as one man, and I realized what I had done, and where I was, and I was frightened. I rose and began running for the door. A round, potbellied man grabbed me by the nape of the neck just as I reached the doors and began to beat me about the face. I kicked him and got loose and ran into the streets. My friend whispered, "*Run!*" and I ran.

My friend stayed outside the restaurant long enough to misdirect my pursuers and the police, who arrived, he told me, at once. I do not know what I said to him when he came to my room that night. I could not have said much. I felt, in the oddest, most awful way, that I had somehow betrayed him. I lived it over and over and over again, the way one relives an automobile accident after it has happened and one finds oneself alone and safe. I could not get over two facts, both equally difficult for the imagination to grasp, and one was that I could have been murdered. But the other was that I had been ready to commit murder. I saw nothing very clearly but I did see this: that my life, my *real* life, was in danger, and not from anything other people might do but from the hatred I carried in my own heart.

II

I had returned home around the second week in June—in great haste because it seemed that my father's death and my mother's confinement were both but a matter of hours. In the case of my mother, it soon became clear that she had simply made a miscalculation. This had always been her tendency and I don't believe that a single one of us arrived in the world, or has since arrived anywhere else, on time. But none of us dawdled so intolerably about the business of being born as did my baby sister. We sometimes amused ourselves, during those endless, stifling weeks, by picturing the baby sitting within in the safe, warm dark, bitterly regretting the necessity of becoming a part of our chaos and stubbornly putting it off as long as possible. I understood her perfectly and congratulated her on showing such good sense so soon. Death, however, sat as purposefully at my father's bedside as life stirred within my mother's womb and it was harder to understand why he so lingered in that long shadow. It seemed that he had bent, and for a long time, too, all of his energies toward dying. Now death was ready for him but my father held back.

All of Harlem, indeed, seemed to be infected by waiting. I had never before known it to be so violently still. Racial tensions throughout this country were exacerbated during the early years of the war, partly because the labor market brought together hundreds of thousands of ill-prepared people and partly because Negro soldiers, regardless of where they were born, received their military training in the south. What happened in defense plants and army camps had repercussions, naturally, in every Negro ghetto. The situation in Harlem had grown bad enough for clergymen, policemen, educators, politicians, and social workers to assert in one breath that there was no "crime wave" and to offer, in the very next breath, suggestions as to how to combat it. These suggestions always seemed to involve playgrounds, despite the fact that racial skirmishes were occurring in the playgrounds, too. Playground or not, crime wave or not, the Harlem police force had been augmented in March, and the unrest grew—perhaps, in fact, partly as a result of the ghetto's instinctive hatred of policemen. Perhaps the most revealing news item, out of the steady parade of reports of muggings, stabbings, shootings, assaults, gang wars, and accusations of police brutality, is the item concerning six Negro girls who set upon a white girl in the subway because, as they all too accurately put it, she was stepping on their toes. Indeed she was, all over the nation.

I had never before been so aware of policemen, on foot, on horseback, on corners, everywhere, always two by two. Nor had I ever been so aware of small knots of people. They were on stoops and on corners and in doorways, and what was striking about them, I think, was that they did not seem to be talking. Never, when I passed these groups, did the usual sound of a curse or a laugh ring out and neither did there seem to be any hum of gossip. There was certainly, on the other hand, occurring between them communication extraordinarily intense. Another thing that was striking was the unexpected diversity of the people who made up these groups. Usually, for example, one would see a group of sharpies standing on the street corner, jiving the passing chicks; or a group of older men, usually, for some reason, in the vicinity of a barber shop, discussing baseball scores, or the numbers, or making rather chilling observations about women they had known. Women, in a general way, tended to be seen less often together—unless they were church women, or very young girls, or prostitutes met together for an unprofessional instant. But that summer I saw the strangest combinations: large, respectable, churchly matrons standing on the stoops or the corners with their hair tied up, together with a girl in sleazy satin whose face bore the marks of gin and the razor, or heavy-set, abrupt, no-nonsense older men, in company with the most disreputable and fanatical "race" men, or these same "race" men with the sharpies, or these sharpies with the churchly women. Seventh Day Adventists and Methodists and Spiritualists seemed to be hobnobbing with Holyrollers and they were all, alike, entangled with the most flagrant disbelievers; something heavy in their stance seemed to indicate that they had all, incredibly, seen a common vision, and on each face there seemed to be the same strange, bitter shadow.

The churchly women and the matter-of-fact, no-nonsense men had children in the Army. The sleazy girls they talked to had lovers there, the sharpies and the "race" men had friends and brothers there. It would have demanded an unquestioning patriotism, happily as uncommon in this country as it is undesirable, for these people not to have been disturbed by the bitter letters they received, by the newspaper stories they read, not to have been enraged by the posters, then to be found all over New York, which described the Japanese as "yellow-bellied Japs." It was only the "race" men, to be sure, who spoke ceaselessly of being revenged—how this vengeance was to be exacted was not clear—for the indignities and dangers suffered by Negro boys in uniform; but everybody felt a directionless, hopeless bitterness, as well as that panic which can scarcely be suppressed when one knows that a human being one loves is beyond one's reach, and in danger.

This helplessness and this gnawing uneasiness does something, at length, to even the toughest mind. Perhaps the best way to sum all this up is to say that the people I knew felt, mainly, a peculiar kind of relief when they knew that their boys were being shipped out of the south, to do battle overseas. It was, perhaps, like feeling that the most dangerous part of a dangerous journey had been passed and that now, even if death should come, it would come with honor and without the complicity of their countrymen. Such a death would be, in short, a fact with which one could hope to live.

It was on the twenty-eighth of July, which I believe was a Wednesday, that I visited my father for the first time during his illness and for the last time in his life. The moment I saw him I knew why I had put off this visit so long. I had told my mother that I did not want to see him because I hated him. But this was not true. It was only that I *had* hated him and I wanted to hold on to this hatred. I did not want to look on him as a ruin: it was not a ruin I had hated. I imagine that one of the reasons people cling to their hates so stubbornly is because they sense, once hate is gone, that they will be forced to deal with pain.

We traveled out to him, his older sister and myself, to what seemed to be the very end of a very Long Island. It was hot and dusty and we wrangled, my aunt and I, all the way out, over the fact that I had recently begun to smoke and, as she said, to give myself airs. But I knew that she wrangled with me because she could not bear to face the fact of her brother's dying. Neither could I endure the reality of her despair, her unstated bafflement as to what had happened to her brother's life, and her own. So we wrangled and I smoked and from time to time she fell into a heavy reverie. Covertly, I watched her face, which was the face of an old woman; it had fallen in, the eyes were sunken and lightless; soon she would be dying, too.

In my childhood—it had not been so long ago—I had thought her beautiful. She had been quick-witted and quick-moving and very generous with all the children and each of her visits had been an event. At one time one of my brothers and myself had thought of running away to live with her. Now she could no longer produce out of her handbag some unexpected and yet familiar delight. She made me feel pity and revulsion and fear. It was awful to realize that she no longer caused me to feel affection. The closer we came to the hospital the more querulous she became and at the same time, naturally, grew more dependent on me. Between pity and guilt and fear I began to feel that there was another me trapped in my skull like a jack-in-the-box who might escape my control at any moment and fill the air with screaming.

She began to cry the moment we entered the room and she saw him lying there, all shriveled and still, like a little black monkey. The great, gleaming apparatus which fed him and would have compelled him to be still even if he had been able to move brought to mind, not beneficence, but torture; the tubes entering his arm made me think of pictures I had seen when a child, of Gulliver, tied down by the pygmies on that island. My aunt wept and wept, there was a whistling sound in my father's throat; nothing was said; he could not speak. I wanted to take his hand, to say something. But I do not know what I could have said, even if he could have heard me. He was not really in that room with us, he had at last really embarked on his journey; and though my aunt told me that he said he was going to meet Jesus, I did not hear anything except that whistling in his throat. The doctor came back and we left, into that unbearable train again, and home. In the morning came the telegram saying that he was dead. Then the house was suddenly full of relatives, friends, hysteria, and confusion and I quickly left my mother and the children to the care of those impressive women, who, in Negro communities at least, automatically appear at times of bereavement armed with lotions, proverbs, and patience, and an ability to cook. I went downtown. By the time I returned, later the same day, my mother had been carried to the hospital and the baby had been born.

III

For my father's funeral I had nothing black to wear and this posed a nagging problem all day long. It was one of those problems, simple, or impossible of solution, to which the mind insanely clings in order to avoid the mind's real trouble. I spent most of that day at the downtown apartment of a girl I knew, celebrating my birthday with whisky and wondering what to wear that night. When planning a birthday celebration one naturally does not expect that it will be up against competition from a funeral and this girl had anticipated taking me out that night, for a big dinner and a night club afterwards. Sometime during the course of that long day we decided that we would go out anyway, when my father's funeral service was over. I imagine I decided it, since, as the funeral hour approached, it became clearer and clearer to me that I would not know what to do with myself when it was over. The girl, stifling her very lively concern as to the possible effects of the whisky on one of my father's chief mourners, concentrated on being conciliatory and practically helpful. She found a black shirt for me somewhere and ironed it and, dressed in the darkest pants and jacket I owned, and slightly drunk, I made my way to my father's funeral.

32   The chapel was full, but not packed, and very quiet. There were, mainly, my father's relatives, and his children, and here and there I saw faces I had not seen since childhood, the faces of my father's one-time friends. They were very dark and solemn now, seeming somehow to suggest that they had known all along that something like this would happen. Chief among the mourners was my aunt, who had quarreled with my father all his life; by which I do not mean to suggest that her mourning was insincere or that she had not loved him. I suppose that she was one of the few people in the world who had, and their incessant quarreling proved precisely the strength of the tie that bound them. The only other person in the world, as far as I knew, whose relationship to my father rivaled my aunt's in depth was my mother, who was not there.

33   It seemed to me, of course, that it was a very long funeral. But it was, if anything, a rather shorter funeral than most, nor, since there were no overwhelming, uncontrollable expressions of grief, could it be called—if I dare to use the word—successful. The minister who preached my father's funeral sermon was one of the few my father had still been seeing as he neared his end. He presented to us in his sermon a man whom none of us had ever seen—a man thoughtful, patient, and forbearing, a Christian inspiration to all who knew him, and a model for his children. And no doubt the children, in their disturbed and guilty state, were almost ready to believe this; he had been remote enough to be anything and, anyway, the shock of the incontrovertible, that it was really our father lying up there in that casket, prepared the mind for anything. His sister moaned and this grief-stricken moaning was taken as corroboration. The other faces held a dark, noncommittal thoughtfulness. This was not the man they had known, but they had scarcely expected to be confronted with *him*; this was, in a sense deeper than questions of fact, the man they had not known, and the man they had not known may have been the real one. The real man, whoever he had been, had suffered and now he was dead: this was all that was sure and all that mattered now. Every man in the chapel

hoped that when his hour came he, too, would be eulogized, which is to say forgiven, and that all of his lapses, greeds, errors, and strayings from the truth would be invested with coherence and looked upon with charity. This was perhaps the last thing human beings could give each other and it was what they demanded, after all, of the Lord. Only the Lord saw the midnight tears, only He was present when one of His children, moaning and wringing hands, paced up and down the room. When one slapped one's child in anger the recoil in the heart reverberated through heaven and became part of the pain of the universe. And when the children were hungry and sullen and distrustful and one watched them, daily, growing wilder, and further away, and running headlong into danger, it was the Lord who knew what the charged heart endured as the strap was laid to the backside; the Lord alone who knew what one *would* have said if one had had, like the Lord, the gift of the living word. It was the Lord who knew of the impossibility every parent in that room faced: how to prepare the child for the day when the child would be despised and how to *create* in the child—by what means?—a stronger antidote to this poison than one had found for oneself. The avenues, side streets, bars, billiard halls, hospitals, police stations, and even the playgrounds of Harlem—not to mention the houses of correction, the jails, and the morgue—testified to the potency of the poison while remaining silent as to the efficacy of whatever antidote, irresistibly raising the question of whether or not such an antidote existed; raising, which was worse, the question of whether or not an antidote was desirable; perhaps poison should be fought with poison. With these several schisms in the mind and with more terrors in the heart than could be named, it was better not to judge the man who had gone down under an impossible burden. It was better to remember: *Thou knowest this man's fall; but thou knowest not his wrassling.*

While the preacher talked and I watched the children—years of changing their diapers, scrubbing them, slapping them, taking them to school, and scolding them had had the perhaps inevitable result of making me love them, though I am not sure I knew this then—my mind was busily breaking out with a rash of disconnected impressions. Snatches of popular songs, indecent jokes, bits of books I had read, movie sequences, faces, voices, political issues—I thought I was going mad; all these impressions suspended, as it were, in the solution of the faint nausea produced in me by the heat and liquor. For a moment I had the impression that my alcoholic breath, inefficiently disguised with chewing gum, filled the entire chapel. Then someone began singing one of my father's favorite songs and, abruptly, I was with him, sitting on his knee, in the hot, enormous, crowded church which was the first church we attended. It was the Abyssinian Baptist Church on 138th Street. We had not gone there long. With this image, a host of others came. I had forgotten, in the rage of my growing up, how proud my father had been of me when I was little. Apparently, I had had a voice and my father had liked to show me off before the members of the church. I had forgotten what he had looked like when he was pleased but now I remembered that he had always been grinning with pleasure when my solos ended. I even remembered certain expressions on his face when he teased my mother—had he loved her? I would never know. And when had it all begun to change? For now it seemed that he had not always been cruel. I remembered being taken for a haircut and scraping my knee on the footrest of the barber's chair and I remembered my father's face as he soothed my crying and applied the stinging iodine. Then I remembered our fights, fights which had been of the worst possible kind because my technique had been silence.

35 I remembered the one time in all our life together when we had really spoken to each other.

36 It was on a Sunday and it must have been shortly before I left home. We were walking, just the two of us, in our usual silence, to or from church. I was in high school and had been doing a lot of writing and I was, at about this time, the editor of the high school magazine. But I had also been a Young Minister and had been preaching from the pulpit. Lately, I had been taking fewer engagements and preached as rarely as possible. It was said in the church, quite truthfully, that I was "cooling off."

37 My father asked me abruptly, "You'd rather write than preach, wouldn't you?"

38 I was astonished at his question—because it was a real question. I answered, "Yes."

39 That was all we said. It was awful to remember that that was all we had *ever* said.

40 The casket now was opened and the mourners were being led up the aisle to look for the last time on the deceased. The assumption was that the family was too overcome with grief to be allowed to make this journey alone and I watched while my aunt was led to the casket and, muffled in black, and shaking, led back to her seat. I disapproved of

forcing the children to look on their dead father, considering that the shock of his death, or, more truthfully, the shock of death as a reality, was already a little more than a child could bear, but my judgment in this matter had been overruled and there they were, bewildered and frightened and very small, being led, one by one, to the casket. But there is also something very gallant about children at such moments. It has something to do with their silence and gravity and with the fact that one cannot help them. Their legs, somehow, seem *exposed*, so that it is at once incredible and terribly clear that their legs are all they have to hold them up.

I had not wanted to go to the casket myself and I certainly had not wished to be led there, but there was no way of avoiding either of these forms. One of the deacons led me up and I looked on my father's face. I cannot say that it looked like him at all. His blackness had been equivocated by powder and there was no suggestion in that casket of what his power had or could have been. He was simply an old man dead, and it was hard to believe that he had ever given anyone either joy or pain. Yet, his life filled that room. Further up the avenue his wife was holding his newborn child. Life and death so close together, and love and hatred, and right and wrong, said something to me which I did not want to hear concerning man, concerning the life of man. 41

After the funeral, while I was downtown desperately celebrating my birthday, a Negro soldier, in the lobby of the Hotel Braddock, got into a fight with a white policeman over a Negro girl. Negro girls, white policemen, in or out of uniform, and Negro males—in or out of uniform—were part of the furniture of the lobby of the Hotel Braddock and this was certainly not the first time such an incident had occurred. It was destined, however, to receive an unprecedented publicity, for the fight between the policeman and the soldier ended with the shooting of the soldier. Rumor, flowing immediately to the streets outside, stated that the soldier had been shot in the back, an instantaneous and revealing invention, and that the soldier had died protecting a Negro woman. The facts were somewhat different—for example, the soldier had not been shot in the back, and was not dead, and the girl seems to have been as dubious a symbol of womanhood as her white counterpart in Georgia usually is, but no one was interested in the facts. They preferred the invention because this invention expressed and corroborated their hates and fears so perfectly. It is just as well to remember that people are always doing this. Perhaps many of those legends, including Christianity, to which the world clings began 42 their conquest of the world with just some such concerted surrender to distortion. The effect, in Harlem, of this particular legend was like the effect of a lit match in a tin of gasoline. The mob gathered before the doors of the Hotel Braddock simply began to swell and to spread in every direction, and Harlem exploded.

43   The mob did not cross the ghetto lines. It would have been easy, for example, to have gone over Morningside Park on the west side or to have crossed the Grand Central railroad tracks at 125th Street on the east side, to wreak havoc in white neighborhoods. The mob seems to have been mainly interested in something more potent and real than the white face, that is, in white power, and the principal damage done during the riot of the summer of 1943 was to white business establishments in Harlem. It might have been a far bloodier story, of course, if, at the hour the riot began, these establishments had still been open. From the Hotel Braddock the mob fanned out, east and west along 125th Street, and for the entire length of Lenox, Seventh, and Eighth Avenues. Along each of these avenues, and along each major side street—116th, 125th, 135th, and so on—bars, stores, pawnshops, restaurants, even little luncheonettes had been smashed open and entered and looted—looted, it might be added, with more haste than efficiency. The shelves really looked as though a bomb had struck them. Cans of beans and soup and dog food, along with toilet paper, corn flakes, sardines and milk tumbled every which way, and abandoned cash registers and cases of beer leaned crazily out of the splintered windows and were strewn along the avenues. Sheets, blankets, and clothing of every description formed a kind of path, as though people had dropped them while running. I truly had not realized that Harlem *had* so many stores until I saw them all smashed open; the first time the word *wealth* ever entered my mind in relation to Harlem was when I saw it scattered in the streets. But one's first, incongruous impression of plenty was countered immediately by an impression of waste. None of this was doing anybody any good. It would have been better to have left the plate glass as it had been and the goods lying in the stores.

44   It would have been better, but it would also have been intolerable, for Harlem had needed something to smash. To smash something is the ghetto's chronic need. Most of the time it is the members of the ghetto who smash each other, and themselves. But as long as the ghetto walls are standing there will always come a moment when these outlets do not work. That summer, for example, it was not

enough to get into a fight on Lenox Avenue, or curse out one's cronies in the barber shops. If ever, indeed, the violence which fills Harlem's churches, pool halls, and bars erupts outward in a more direct fashion, Harlem and its citizens are likely to vanish in an apocalyptic flood. That this is not likely to happen is due to a great many reasons, most hidden and powerful among them the Negro's real relation to the white American. This relation prohibits, simply, anything as uncomplicated and satisfactory as pure hatred. In order really to hate white people, one has to blot so much out of the mind—and the heart—that this hatred itself becomes an exhausting and self-destructive pose. But this does not mean, on the other hand, that love comes easily: the white world is too powerful, too complacent, too ready with gratuitous humiliation, and, above all, too ignorant and too innocent for that. One is absolutely forced to make perpetual qualifications and one's own reactions are always canceling each other out. It is this, really, which has driven so many people mad, both white and black. One is always in the position of having to decide between amputation and gangrene. Amputation is swift but time may prove that the amputation was not necessary—or one may delay the amputation too long. Gangrene is slow, but it is impossible to be sure that one is reading one's symptoms right. The idea of going through life as a cripple is more than one can bear, and equally unbearable is the risk of swelling up slowly, in agony, with poison. And the trouble, finally, is that the risks are real even if the choices do not exist.

"But as for me and my house," my father had said, "we will serve the Lord." I wondered, as we drove him to his resting place, what this line had meant for him. I had heard him preach it many times. I had preached it once myself, proudly giving it an interpretation different from my father's. Now the whole thing came back to me, as though my father and I were on our way to Sunday school and I were memorizing the golden text: *And if it seem evil unto you to serve the Lord, choose you this day whom you will serve; whether the gods which your fathers served that were on the other side of the flood, or the gods of the Amorites, in whose land ye dwell: but as for me and my house, we will serve the Lord.* I suspected in these familiar lines a meaning which had never been there for me before. All of my father's texts and songs, which I had decided were meaningless, were arranged before me at his death like empty bottles, waiting to hold the meaning which life would give them for me. This was his legacy: nothing is ever escaped. That bleakly memorable morning I hated the unbelievable streets and the Negroes and whites who had, equally, made them that way. But I knew that it was folly, as my father would have said, this bitterness was folly. It was necessary to hold on to the things that mattered. The dead man mattered, the new life mattered; blackness and whiteness did not matter; to believe that they did was to acquiesce in one's own destruction. Hatred, which could destroy so much, never failed to destroy the man who hated and this was an immutable law.

It began to seem that one would have to hold in the mind forever two ideas which seemed to be in opposition. The first idea was acceptance, the acceptance, totally without rancor, of life as it is, and men as they are: in the light of this idea, it goes without saying that injustice is a commonplace. But this did not mean that one could be complacent, for the second idea was of equal power: that one must never, in one's own life, accept these injustices as commonplace but must fight them with all one's strength. This fight begins, however, in the heart and it now had been laid to my charge to keep my own heart free of hatred and despair. This intimation made my heart heavy and, now that my father was irrecoverable, I wished that he had been beside me so that I could have searched his face for the answers which only the future would give me now. 46

Rhetorical Analysis

1. If readers could foresee at every point in a piece of writing what was going to be said next, they would have no reason to read on. This means, of course, that regardless of what else makes writing good, one necessary ingredient is *surprise*—surprise in its most basic sense as the emotion one feels on coming across something unexpected.
    a. In the essay as a whole, how does Baldwin arrange the sequence of events so that the element of surprise is maintained? Note that events *are* carefully and strategically arranged. Baldwin elects to mention a few details from the total run of events, and he departs from a strict chronological listing of those events he does choose.
    b. How does Baldwin create local effect of surprise through syntax and diction within sentences? Look at any paragraph, sentence by sentence, and you will probably be surprised by how easily you can find answers to this question.

Note the difference between surprising readers with unexpected facts and surprising them with an unexpected turn of language. For example, in ¶ 26 Baldwin does not write, "I saw my father once during his illness, and he died before I could see him again," but instead: "I visited my father for the first time during his illness and for the last time in his life."

2. Consider the sentence just quoted from ¶ 27. The words could not be simpler. The entire essay is written with a diction of enviable directness and simplicity. How does this simple and direct style fit the larger purposes of the writer? Note that this essay does not represent Baldwin's only style (see "An Open Letter to Angela Davis" for a comparison).

3. Look at the openings and closings of the three sections of the essay. How well do they work, for each part and for the whole?

Intellectual Analysis

1. While "Notes of a Native Son" begins and ends with the funeral of Baldwin's father, many other subjects are framed within that simple recollection. For instance, a few of the major themes which can be traced through the whole essay include World War II, black soldiers, racial tensions at home, fathers and sons, growing up, leaving home, returning home, and so forth. What other themes run through the essay?

2. A major concern of the essay is hatred; in fact, it is so constant and powerful a theme that it overwhelms everything else.
    a. What of Baldwin's hatred for his father? Trace this deep animosity through the essay, paying particular attention to ¶s 23 and 27. What relationship is there between hatred of father and hatred of country? Further, what does hatred have to do with repression, whether psychological or social? Are people *unable* or *unwilling* to stop hating? Why?
    b. The subject of hatred is connected to repeated images and words having to do with sickness. For example, hatred and sickness are specifically linked in ¶ 15, and again in ¶ 44 where both are linked to "madness." Finally, both hatred and sickness infect the society as a whole. Analyze this theme carefully. The conclusion will lead you to the very heart of the essay.
    c. In summing up his father, Baldwin is forced to merge love and hatred in a complex and uncomfortable synthesis. That synthesis is the underlying subject of the first and last paragraphs. What other opposites have to be held in uneasy tension throughout this essay?

3. Do you think this essay was psychologically important for Baldwin to write? There are several ways of getting at such a question, but here are three possible lines of analysis.
    a. First, find and analyze places where Baldwin struggles (or "wrestles," to use one of his words) to be accurate, fair, and honest (accurate, fair, and honest to *whom* or *what*?).

    b. Second, notice the universality of this very individual experience. Baldwin sees the experience of his father's death against what kinds of backdrop?
    c. Third, try to discover what connection there is between Baldwin's writing this essay and his inability to talk to his father.

Suggestions for Writing

1. "Notes of a Native Son" is another in the genre of reminiscence. Compare Baldwin's technique in this essay with that of Welty or Orwell, and make that comparison the subject of an essay.
2. Baldwin took his title from Richard Wright's novel, *Native Son*; "Notes of a Native Son" is both a tribute to his mentor and an ironic play on words. Write a paper in which you discuss those ironies. For a longer essay, you might wish to read Baldwin's essay on Wright, "Alas, Poor Richard" (reprinted in *Nobody Knows My Name*), which would give you more information about the relationship of these two native sons.

AN OPEN LETTER TO MY SISTER, MISS ANGELA DAVIS

November 19, 1970

Dear Sister:

    One might have hoped that, by this hour, the very sight of chains on black flesh, or the very sight of chains, would be so intolerable a sight for the American people, and so unbearable a memory, that they would themselves spontaneously rise up and strike off the manacles. But, no, they appear to glory in their chains; now, more than ever, they appear to measure their safety in chains and corpses. And so, *Newsweek*, civilized defender of the indefensible, attempts to drown you in a sea of crocodile tears ("it remained to be seen what sort of personal liberation she had achieved") and puts you on its cover, chained.

    You look exceedingly alone—as alone, say, as the Jewish housewife in the boxcar headed for Dachau, or as any one of our ancestors, chained together in the name of Jesus, headed for a Christian land.

Well. Since we live in an age in which silence is not only criminal but suicidal, I have been making as much noise as I can, here in Europe, on radio and television—in fact, have just returned from a land, Germany, which was made notorious by a silent majority not so very long ago. I was asked to speak on the case of Miss Angela Davis, and did so. Very probably an exercise in futility, but one must let no opportunity slide.

I am something like twenty years older than you, of that generation, therefore, of which George Jackson ventures that "there are no healthy brothers—*none at all.*" I am in no way equipped to dispute this speculation (not, anyway, without descending into what, at the moment, would be irrelevant subtleties) for I know too well what he means. My own state of health is certainly precarious enough. In considering you, and Huey, and George and (especially) Jonathan Jackson, I began to apprehend what you may have had in mind when you spoke of the uses to which we could put the experience of the slave. What has happened, it seems to me, and to put it far too simply, is that a whole new generation of people have assessed and absorbed their history, and, in that tremendous action, have freed themselves of it and will never be victims again. This may seem an odd, indefensibly impertinent and insensitive thing to say to a sister in prison, battling for her life—for all our lives. Yet, I dare to say, for I think that you will perhaps not misunderstand me, and I do not say it, after all, from the position of a spectator.

I am trying to suggest that you—for example—do not appear to be your father's daughter in the same way that I am my father's son. At bottom, my father's expectations and mine were the same, the expectations of his generation and mine were the same; and neither the immense difference in our ages nor the move from the South to the North could alter these expectations or make our lives more viable. For, in fact, to use the brutal parlance of that hour, the interior language of that despair, he was just a nigger—a nigger laborer preacher, and so was I. I jumped the track but that's of no more importance here, in itself, than the fact that *some* poor Spaniards become rich bull fighters, or that *some* poor black boys become rich—boxers, for example. That's rarely, if ever, afforded the people more than a great emotional catharsis, though I don't mean to be condescending about that, either. But when Cassius Clay became

Muhammad Ali and refused to put on that uniform (and sacrificed all that money!) a very different impact was made on the people and a very different kind of instruction had begun.

The American triumph—in which the American tragedy has always been implicit—was to make black people despise themselves. When I was little I despised myself, I did not know any better. And this meant, albeit unconsciously, or against my will, or in great pain, that I also despised my father. *And* my mother. *And* my brothers. *And* my sisters. Black people were killing each other every Saturday night out on Lenox Avenue, when I was growing up; and no one explained to them, or to me, that it was *intended* that they should; that they were penned where they were, like animals, in order that they should consider themselves no better than animals. Everything supported this sense of reality, nothing denied it: and so one was ready, when it came time to go to work, to be treated as a slave. So one was ready, when human terrors came, to bow before a white God and beg Jesus for salvation—this same white God who was unable to raise a finger to do so little as to help you pay your rent, unable to be awakened in time to help you save your child!

There is always, of course, more to any picture than can speedily be perceived and in all of this—groaning and moaning, watching, calculating, clowning, surviving, and outwitting, some tremendous strength was nevertheless being forged, which is part of our legacy today. But that particular aspect of our journey now begins to be behind us. The secret is out: we are men!

But the blunt, open articulation of this secret has frightened the nation to death. I wish I could say, "to life," but that is much to demand of a disparate collection of displaced people still cowering in their wagon trains and singing "Onward Christian Soldiers." The nation, *if* America is a nation, is not in the least prepared for this day. It is a day which the Americans never expected or desired to see, however piously they may declare their belief in "progress and democracy." These words, now, on American lips, have become a kind of universal obscenity: for this most unhappy people, strong believers in arithmetic, never expected to be confronted with the algebra of their history.

One way of gauging a nation's health, or of discerning what it really considers to be its interests—or to what extent it can be considered as a nation as distinguished from a coalition of special interests—is to examine those people it elects to represent or protect it. One glance at the American leaders (or figure-heads) conveys that America is on the edge of absolute chaos, and also suggests the future to which American interests, if not the bulk of the American people, appear willing to consign the blacks. (Indeed, one look at our past conveys that.) It is clear that for the bulk of our (nominal) countrymen, we are all expendable. And Messrs. Nixon, Agnew, Mitchell, and Hoover, to say nothing, of course, of the *Kings' Row* basket case, the winning Ronnie Reagan, will not hesitate for an instant to carry out what they insist is the will of the people.

But what, in America, is the will of the people? And who, for the above-named, *are* the people? The people, whoever they may be, know as much about the forces which have placed the above-named gentlemen in power as they do about the forces responsible for the slaughter in Vietnam. The will of the people, in America, has always been at the mercy of an ignorance not merely phenomenal, but sacred, and sacredly cultivated: the better to be used by a carnivorous economy which democratically slaughters and victimizes whites and blacks alike. But most white Americans do not dare admit this (though they suspect it) and this fact contains mortal danger for the blacks and tragedy for the nation.

Or, to put it another way, as long as white Americans take refuge in their whiteness—for so long as they are unable to walk out of this most monstrous of traps—they will allow millions of people to be slaughtered in their name, and will be manipulated into and surrender themselves to what they will think of—and justify—as a racial war. They will never, so long as their whiteness puts so sinister a distance between themselves and their own experience and the experience of others, feel themselves sufficiently human, *sufficiently worthwhile*, to become responsible for themselves, their leaders, their country, their children, or their fate. They will perish (as we once put it in our black church) in their sins—that is, in their delusions. And this is happening, needless to say, already, all around us.

Only a handful of the millions of people in this vast place are aware that the fate intended for you, Sister Angela, and for George Jackson, and for the numberless prisoners in our concentration camps—for that is what they are—is a fate which is about to engulf them, too. White lives, for the forces which rule in this country, are no more sacred than black ones, as many and many a student is discovering, as the white American corpses in Vietnam prove. If the American people are unable to contend with their elected leaders for the redemption of their own honor and the lives of their own children, we, the blacks, the most rejected of the Western children, can expect very little help at their hands: which, after all, is nothing new. What the Americans do not realize is that a war between brothers, in the same cities, on the same soil, is not a *racial* war but a *civil* war. But the American delusion is not only that their brothers all are white but that the whites are all their brothers.

So be it. We cannot awaken this sleeper, and God knows we have tried. We must do what we can do, and fortify and save each other— *we* are not drowning in an apathetic self-contempt, we *do* feel ourselves sufficiently worthwhile to contend even with inexorable forces in order to change our fate and the fate of our children and the condition of the world! We know that a man is not a thing and is not to be placed at the mercy of things. We know that air and water belong to all mankind and not merely to industrialists. We know that a baby does not come into the world merely to be the instrument of someone else's profit. We know that democracy does not mean the coercion of all into a deadly—and, finally, wicked—mediocrity but the liberty for all to aspire to the best that is in him, or that has ever been.

We know that we, the blacks, and not only we, the blacks, have been, and are, the victims of a system whose only fuel is greed, whose only god is profit. We know that the fruits of this system have been ignorance, despair, and death, and we know that the system is doomed because the world can no longer afford it—if, indeed, it ever could have. And we know that, for the perpetuation of this system, we have all been mercilessly brutalized, and have been told nothing but lies, lies about ourselves and our kinsmen and our past, and about love, life, and death, so that both soul and body have been bound in hell.

The enormous revolution in black consciousness which has occurred in your generation, my dear sister, means the beginning or the end of America. Some of us, white and black, know how great a price has already been paid to bring into existence a new consciousness, a new people, an unprecedented nation. If we know, and do nothing, we are worse than the murderers hired in our name.

If we know, then we must fight for your life as though it were our own—which it is—and render impassable with our bodies the corridor to the gas chamber. For, if they take you in the morning, they will be coming for us that night.

Therefore: peace.

Brother James

Rhetorical Analysis

1. "An Open Letter to My Sister, Miss Angela Davis" comes out of the tense political atmosphere in the United States during the Nixon years (1968–1974). In fall of 1970, when Baldwin wrote this piece, Huey Newton (¶ 4), cofounder of the Black Panther Party, was in jail for allegedly killing a policeman. Another young black, Jonathan Jackson, had been killed in August of that year in a courtroom shootout to free his brother, George Jackson, from San Quentin Prison. Angela Davis, a black professor of philosophy at UCLA and an avowed Marxist, had been apprehended by the FBI in flight to avoid prosecution for allegedly buying guns used by Jonathan Jackson.
    a. What is the dominant emotion of the letter? How does Baldwin convey it?
    b. What are the ways Baldwin makes the reader *respect* his emotion?
2. This is a "letter," addressed to "Sister" and signed "Brother." Yet it is also "open," meaning it has been deliberately made public—in this case published in the *New York Review of Books*. What persuasive effects does Baldwin encourage by setting up two very different audiences, one private, the other public? The question of audience is unusually complicated in this case.
3. Even the most detached and objective forms of discourse express, and use, elements that can only be called dramatic. Behind the laboratory or research report lies the shout of "Eureka!" Behind police blotter reports in the local newspaper are many shouts, cries, and whispers. What dramatic scenes lie behind "An Open Letter to Angela Davis"? For instance, what about:
    a. The public exposure of misconduct (the finger pointed in scorn)?
    b. The gesture of solidarity to the comrade being taken into prison?
    c. The giving over of the battle long fought ("So be it. We cannot awaken this sleeper, and God knows we have tried")?
    d. The letter to a stranger being written in secret admiration?
    e. The worldly wise elder giving a talk to a member of a younger generation ("I am something like twenty years older than you")?
    f. The Jeremiah preaching to a people about their own sins?

Analyze and discuss these situations. What other dramatic scenes does this letter convey?

Intellectual Analysis

1. One of Baldwin's concerns in this "Open Letter to Miss Angela Davis" is a historic change in consciousness among blacks. The first question must be to determine exactly what the change is he has in mind.
    a. Baldwin says to Angela Davis, "you—for example—do not appear to be your father's daughter in the same way that I am my father's son" (¶ 5). What does that mean for Baldwin, for Davis, and for blacks generally?
    b. Baldwin's conceptions of history and "a whole new generation" play a part in his argument (for example, ¶ 4). What is Baldwin's point? How do the two interact?
    c. Muhammad Ali becomes a symbol of the change (¶ 5): how politically did Ali come to symbolize so much?
    d. Baldwin says (in ¶ 7), a "journey now begins to be behind us," and a "secret is out." Both statements are striking. How do they figure in his overall theme?
2. Another major theme—but hardly separable from the first—arises out of an image.
    a. In ¶s 1 and 2, notice the vocabulary: "chains" occurs 4 times, "chained" twice, "manacles" once. Why would Baldwin hammer so incessantly on jailhouse images? And, through the rest of the essay, how does his language continue that image (for example, "traps" in ¶ 11)?
        (1) The chains of the slave-past is the most obvious connection, but there is much more to it than that. Even in ¶ 1, "their chains" refers implicitly to all Americans!
        (2) To what else are blacks and whites chained? Words such as "profit" and "money," and expressions such as "believers in arithmetic" (¶ 8) and "carnivorous economy" (¶ 10) suggest another kind of oppression.
    b. The concept of "self-esteem" lies behind some images of the letter. For example, in ¶ 6, Baldwin speaks of how blacks "despise themselves" and other blacks; but whites, as long as they "take refuge" (¶ 11) in their "whiteness," cannot see themselves as "sufficiently worthwhile" (a phrase repeated in ¶ 13). Discuss such a theme.
3. All the above issues have to do with Baldwin's concern about the future of America. He sees a need for solidarity among Americans. Yet he also sees, on the one hand, the "algebra" of history (¶ 8), and on the other the "absolute chaos" (¶ 9) we now face and which is "about to engulf" us (¶ 12). Analyze and evaluate this complex matter.

Suggestions for Writing

1. The October 26, 1970, issue of *Newsweek* has a striking cover photo of Angela Davis in handcuffs on courthouse steps. Read the cover story and write an essay comparing the two assessments of her situations—*Newsweek*'s and Baldwin's. (For further balance, read the reports in the *New York Times* dated October 14th and 15th, 1970, the editorial page for the 16th, and the "Week in Review" section in the Sunday *Times*, October 18, 1970.)
2. In ¶ 9, Baldwin comments harshly on American political leaders (in 1970 Ronald Reagan had just been elected to a second term as governor of California; years earlier, he had played an amputee in the movie "King's Row"). Write an essay "gauging the nation's health," giving your evaluation of the quality of its elected leaders today.
3. Select a public figure about whom you have strong feelings and write an "open" letter to her or him. Send the letter to your local newspaper or to some other outlet.

IF BLACK ENGLISH ISN'T A LANGUAGE, THEN TELL ME, WHAT IS?

The argument concerning the use, or the status, or the reality, of black English is rooted in American history and has absolutely nothing to do with the question the argument supposes itself to be posing. The argument has nothing to do with language itself but with the role of language. Language, incontestably, reveals the speaker. Language, also, far more dubiously, is meant to define the other—and, in this case, the other is refusing to be defined by a language that has never been able to recognize him.

People evolve a language in order to describe and thus control their circumstances or in order not to be submerged by a situation that they cannot articulate. (And if they cannot articulate it, they are submerged.) A Frenchman living in Paris speaks a subtly and crucially different language from that of the man living in Marseilles; neither sounds very much like a man living in Quebec; and they would all have great difficulty in apprehending what the man from Guadeloupe, or Martinique, is saying, to say nothing of the man from Senegal—although the "common" language of all these areas is French. But each has paid, and is paying, a different price for this "common" language, in which, as it turns out, they are not saying, and cannot be saying, the same things: They each have very different realities to articulate, or control.

What joins all languages, and all men, is the necessity to confront life, in order, not inconceivably, to outwit death: The price for this is the acceptance, and achievement, of one's temporal identity. So that, for example, though it is not taught in the schools (and this has the potential of becoming a political issue) the south of France still clings to its ancient and musical Provençal, which resists being described as a "dialect." And much of the tension in the Basque countries, and in Wales, is due to the Basque and Welsh determination not to allow their languages to be destroyed. This determination also feeds the flames in Ireland for among the many indignities the Irish have been forced to undergo at English hands is the English contempt for their language.

It goes without saying, then, that language is also a political instrument, means, and proof of power. It is the most vivid and crucial key to identity: It reveals the private identity, and connects one with, or divorces one from, the larger, public, or communal identity. There have been, and are, times and places, when to speak a certain language could be dangerous, even fatal. Or, one may speak the same language, but in such a way that one's antecedents are revealed, or (one hopes) hidden. This is true in France, and is absolutely true in England: The range (and reign) of accents on that damp little island make England coherent for the English and totally incomprehensible for everyone else. To open your mouth in England is (if I may use black English) to "put your business in the street." You have confessed your parents, your youth, your school, your salary, your self-esteem, and, alas, your future.

Now, I do not know what white Americans would sound like if there had never been any black people in the United States, but they would not sound the way they sound. *Jazz*, for example, is a very specific sexual term, as in *jazz me, baby*, but white people purified it into the Jazz Age. *Sock it to me*, which means, roughly, the same thing, has been adopted by Nathaniel Hawthorne's descendants with no qualms or hesitations at all, along with *let it all hang out* and *right on! Beat to his socks*, which was once the black's most total and despairing image of poverty, was transformed into a thing called the Beat Generation, which phenomenon was, largely, composed of *uptight*, middle-class white people, imitating poverty, trying to *get down*, to get *with it*, doing their *thing*, doing their despairing best to be *funky*, which we, the blacks, never dreamed of doing—we were funky, baby, like *funk* was going out of style.

Now, no one can eat his cake, and have it, too, and it is late in the day to attempt to penalize black people for having created a language that permits the nation its only glimpse of reality, a language without which the nation would be even more *whipped* than it is.

I say that the present skirmish is rooted in American history, and it is. Black English is the creation of the black diaspora. Blacks came to the United States chained to each other, but from different tribes. Neither could speak the other's language. If two black people, at that bitter hour of the world's history, had been able to speak to each other, the institution of chattel slavery could never have lasted as long as it did. Subsequently, the slave was given, under the eye, and the gun, of his master, Congo Square, and the Bible—or, in other words, and under those conditions, the slave began the formation of the black church, and it is within this unprecedented tabernacle that black English began to be formed. This was not, merely, as in the European example, the adoption of a foreign tongue, but an alchemy that transformed ancient elements into a new language: *A language comes into existence by means of brutal necessity, and the rules of the language are dictated by what the language must convey.*

There was a moment, in time, and in this place, when my brother, or my mother, or my father, or my sister, had to convey to me, for example, the danger in which I was standing from the white man standing just behind me, and to convey this with a speed and in a language, that the white man could not possibly understand, and that, indeed, he cannot understand, until today. He cannot afford to understand it. This understanding would reveal to him too much about himself and smash that mirror before which he has been frozen for so long.

Now, if this passion, this skill, this (to quote Toni Morrison) "sheer intelligence," this incredible music, the mighty achievement of having brought a people utterly unknown to, or despised by "history"—to have brought this people to their present, troubled, troubling, and unassailable and unanswerable place—if this absolutely unprecedented journey does not indicate that black English is a language, I am curious to know what definition of languages is to be trusted.

A people at the center of the western world, and in the midst of so hostile a population, has not endured and transcended by means of what is patronizingly called a "dialect." We, the blacks, are in trouble, certainly, but we are not inarticulate because we are not compelled to defend a morality that we know to be a lie.

The brutal truth is that the bulk of the white people in America never had any interest in educating black people, except as this could serve white purposes. It is not the black child's language that is despised. It is his experience. A child cannot be taught by anyone who despises him, and a child cannot afford to be fooled. A child cannot be taught by anyone whose demand, essentially, is that the child repudiate his experience, and all that gives him sustenance, and enter a limbo in which he will no longer be black, and in which he knows that he can never become white. Black people have lost too many black children that way.

And, after all, finally, in a country with standards so untrustworthy, a country that makes heroes of so many criminal mediocrities, a country unable to face why so many of the nonwhite are in prison, or on the needle, or standing, futureless, in the streets—it may very well be that both the child, and his elder, have concluded that they have nothing whatever to learn from the people of a country that has managed to learn so little.

Rhetorical Analysis

1. The first sentence of "If Black English Isn't a Language, Then Tell Me, What Is?" assumes that the reader knows something about the controversy surrounding black English: should black children be taught "standard English" and untaught their native habits of speech ("use"); are language habits of blacks wrong or inferior to those of whites' ("status"); and is black English a derivative of standard English, or a language in its own right ("reality")? Would the essay have been any stronger if Baldwin explained all this?
2. Whatever the language of choice, Baldwin's essay illustrates an essential quality of sophisticated discourse: precision. By precision we mean the degree to which ideas are expressed both cogently and compactly. Look at these three italicized phrases from Baldwin's essay:
    a. "The argument concerning *the use, or the status, or the reality* of black English" (¶ 1).

    b. "People evolve a language in order *to describe and thus control* their circumstances" (¶ 2).
    c. "A Frenchman living in Paris speaks *a subtly and crucially different* language from that of the man living in Marseilles" (¶ 2).

In each case, elements are distinct and the logical relationship between them clear and valid; and the ideas could not be expressed more economically without changing the meaning. That is what we mean by precision. At random, pick sentences from the essay. Are they ever imprecise, or is there even any uncertainty in your mind about Baldwin's meaning?

3. The argument of Baldwin's essay is carefully and simply laid out. The author defines language in general, describes black and white English in particular, and then shows how black English satisfies the definition: it must therefore be a language. Review this classic argumentative sequence (argument by definition and example) step by step. How persuasive is it? Does it convince you of its conclusion? If you accept that the definition and the facts presented are true, are you obliged to accept the conclusion which flows from the other statements?

Intellectual Analysis

1. As Baldwin says, the "argument" over black language "is rooted in American history," referring to the forcible suppression of African speech by slave owners, on the one hand, and the strictures against literacy among slaves, on the other.
    a. Given this history, how does Baldwin arrive at the distinction between "language itself" and "the role of language"?
    b. Why does Baldwin insist on calling black English a "language" when many would refer to it simply as a "dialect"?
    c. By suggesting that to "open your mouth in England" is to "put your business in the street," (that is, to confess "your parents, your youth," and so forth), Baldwin relates language not only to history but also to power politics. Do you think Baldwin stretches the point too far?
2. In ¶ 7 Baldwin writes that "black English is the creation of black diaspora," or scattering. Black English, he says, was forged out of need, and blacks depended on it for survival. Congo Square, which Baldwin mentions along with the Bible, was a section of New Orleans where blacks in the nineteenth century gathered to dance and celebrate holidays.
    a. What are the connections in ¶ 7 between the Bible, Congo Square, and the master's gun? What do these have to do with the development of black language?
    b. How do the following two paragraphs (¶s 8 and 9) develop and extend the images of Bible, Square, and gun?

Suggestions for Writing

1. Research the effort on the state and national levels to make English the "official" language of the United States. There is a similar move to exclude black English and other ethnic languages, as well as Spanish, as languages of instruction in the public schools. Give these issues some thought; discuss them with your classmates. Then write an essay in which you take a position, pro or con, on the issue.
2. Baldwin says that language is an exceptionally powerful political tool. Evaluate that statement.

Joan Didion

In many ways writing is the act of saying *I*, of imposing oneself upon other people, of saying *listen to me, see it my way, change your mind*. It's an aggressive, even hostile act. You can disguise its aggressiveness all you want with veils of subordinate clauses and qualifiers and tentative subjunctives, with ellipses and evasions—with the whole manner of intimating rather than claiming, of alluding rather than stating—but there's no getting around the fact that setting words on paper is the tactic of a secret bully, an invasion, an imposition of the writer's sensibility on the reader's most private space.

These words, whether or not one accepts them as definitive for all acts of writing, certainly characterize with precision Joan Didion's writing acts. We deliberately use that somewhat awkward phrase, "writing act," because Didion treats writing as not removed from action, from life, but as life lived to its utmost.

Didion has often described herself—in her essays—as shy and awkward. The essays themselves exhibit a sensibility exactly the opposite. Two collections especially, Slouching Toward Bethlehem *(1968) and* The White Album *(1979), abound with sentences that are at once laconic and sinuous, and they occur in essays that are both reticent and impulsively confessional.*

Born in Sacramento, California, in 1934, she attended high school there, and then went to the University of California, Berkeley, where she majored in English literature. Though she lived in New York for several years (she was appointed staff writer for Vogue magazine after winning Vogue's Prix de Paris contest for young writers), she returned with her husband, writer John Gregory Dunne, to Los Angeles in 1964, and has remained there ever since. As a writer she has become identified with a California which is as much a state of mind as it is a place: the California of freeways, of sun-drenched anguish, of lives both mobile and empty. Her vision at its most grim is presented in a novel, Play It As It Lays (1970), which became a best seller and was nominated for the prestigious National Book Award.

Her particular vision is characterized by an emotional and intellectual toughness combined with an acute sensitivity to particulars and to, as she puts it, "the underside of the tapestry." She mistrusts the grand gesture, the public pronouncement, the officially sanctioned. Speaking of herself as a member of the "silent generation" of young adults in the 1950s, she wrote: "We were silent because the exhilaration of social action seemed to many of us just one more way of escaping the personal, of masking for a while that dread of the meaninglessness which was man's fate." Her writings, for the most part, mean to tear away that mask, to face the nothingness, the immense loss of confidence and permanence which so many Americans—and perhaps the culture itself—seem to feel.

ON KEEPING A NOTEBOOK

*T*hat woman Estelle,' " the note reads, " 'is partly the reason why George Sharp and I are separated today.' *Dirty crepe-de-Chine wrapper, hotel bar, Wilmington RR, 9:45 a.m. August Monday morning.*"

Since the note is in my notebook, it presumably has some meaning to me. I study it for a long while. At first I have only the most general notion of what I was doing on an August Monday morning in the bar of the hotel across from the Pennsylvania Railroad station in Wilmington, Delaware (waiting for a train? missing one? 1960? 1961? why Wilmington?), but I do remember being there. The woman in the dirty crepe-de-Chine wrapper had come down from her room for a beer, and the bartender had heard before the reason why George Sharp and she were separated today. "Sure," he said, and went on mopping the floor. "You told me." At the other end of the bar is a girl. She is talking, pointedly, not to the man beside her but to a cat lying in the triangle of sunlight cast through the open door. She is wearing a plaid silk dress from Peck & Peck, and the hem is coming down.

Here is what it is: the girl has been on the Eastern Shore, and now she is going back to the city, leaving the man beside her, and all she can see ahead are the viscous summer sidewalks and the 3 a.m. long-distance calls that will make her lie awake and then sleep drugged through all the steaming mornings left in August (1960? 1961?). Because she must go directly from the train to lunch in New York, she wishes that she had a safety pin for the hem of the plaid silk dress, and she also wishes that she could forget about the hem and the lunch and stay in the cool bar that smells of disinfectant and malt and make friends with the woman in the crepe-de-Chine wrapper. She is afflicted by a little self-pity, and she wants to compare Estelles. That is what that was all about.

Why did I write it down? In order to remember, of course, but exactly what was it I wanted to remember? How much of it actually happened? Did any of it? Why do I keep a notebook at all? It is easy to deceive oneself on all those scores. The impulse to write things down is a peculiarly compulsive one, inexplicable to those who do not share it, useful only accidentally, only secondarily, in the way that any compulsion tries to justify itself. I suppose that it begins or does not begin in the cradle. Although I have felt compelled to write things down since I was five years old, I doubt that my daughter ever will, for she is a singularly blessed and accepting child, delighted with life exactly as life presents itself to her, unafraid to go to sleep and unafraid to wake up. Keepers of private notebooks are a different breed altogether, lonely and resistant rearrangers of things, anxious malcontents, children afflicted apparently at birth with some presentiment of loss.

My first notebook was a Big Five tablet, given to me by my mother with the sensible suggestion that I stop whining and learn to amuse myself by writing down my thoughts. She returned the tablet to me a few years ago; the first entry is an account of a woman who believed herself to be freezing to death in the Arctic night, only to find, when day broke, that she had stumbled onto the Sahara Desert, where she would die of the heat before lunch. I have no idea what turn of a five-year-old's mind could have prompted so insistently "ironic" and exotic a story, but it does reveal a certain predilection for the extreme which has dogged me into adult life; perhaps if I were analytically inclined I would find it a truer story than any I might have told about

Donald Johnson's birthday party or the day my cousin Brenda put Kitty Litter in the aquarium.

    So the point of my keeping a notebook has never been, nor is it now, to have an accurate factual record of what I have been doing or thinking. That would be a different impulse entirely, an instinct for reality which I sometimes envy but do not possess. At no point have I ever been able successfully to keep a diary; my approach to daily life ranges from the grossly negligent to the merely absent, and on those few occasions when I have tried dutifully to record a day's events, boredom has so overcome me that the results are mysterious at best. What is this business about "shopping, typing piece, dinner with E, depressed"? Shopping for what? Typing what piece? Who is E? Was this "E" depressed, or was I depressed? Who cares?

    In fact I have abandoned altogether that kind of pointless entry; instead I tell what some would call lies. "That's simply not true," the members of my family frequently tell me when they come up against my memory of a shared event. "The party was *not* for you, the spider was *not* a black widow, *it wasn't that way at all.*" Very likely they are right, for not only have I always had trouble distinguishing between what happened and what merely might have happened, but I remain unconvinced that the distinction, for my purposes, matters. The cracked crab that I recall having for lunch the day my father came home from Detroit in 1945 must certainly be embroidery, worked into the day's pattern to lend verisimilitude; I was ten years old and would not now remember the cracked crab. The day's events did not turn on cracked crab. And yet it is precisely that fictitious crab that makes me see the afternoon all over again, a home movie run all too often, the father bearing gifts, the child weeping, an exercise in family love and guilt. Or that is what it was to me. Similarly, perhaps it never did snow that August in Vermont; perhaps there never were flurries in the night wind, and maybe no one else felt the ground hardening and summer already dead even as we pretended to bask in it, but that was how it felt to me, and it might as well have snowed, could have snowed, did snow.

    How it felt to me: that is getting closer to the truth about a notebook. I sometimes delude myself about why I keep a notebook, imagine that some thrifty virtue derives from preserving everything observed. See enough and write it down, I tell myself, and then some morning when the world seems drained of wonder, some day when I am only going through the motions of doing what I am supposed to do, which is write—on that bankrupt morning I will simply open my notebook and there it will all be, a forgotten account with accumulated interest, paid passage back to the world out there: dialogue overheard in hotels and elevators and at the hat-check counter in Pavillon (one middle-aged man shows his hat check to another and says, "That's my old football number"); impressions of Bettina Aptheker and Benjamin Sonnenberg and Teddy ("Mr. Acapulco") Stauffer; careful *aperçus* about tennis bums and failed fashion models and Greek shipping heiresses, one of whom taught me a significant lesson (a lesson I could have learned from F. Scott Fitzgerald, but perhaps we all must meet the very rich for ourselves) by asking, when I arrived to interview her in her orchid-filled sitting room on the second day of a paralyzing New York blizzard, whether it was snowing outside.

I imagine, in other words, that the notebook is about other people. But of course it is not. I have no real business with what one stranger said to another at the hat-check counter in Pavillon; in fact I suspect that the line "That's my old football number" touched not my own imagination at all, but merely some memory of something once read, probably "The Eighty-Yard Run." Nor is my concern with a woman in a dirty crepe-de-Chine wrapper in a Wilmington bar. My stake is always, of course, in the unmentioned girl in the plaid silk dress. *Remember what it was to be me*: that is always the point.

It is a difficult point to admit. We are brought up in the ethic that others, any others, all others, are by definition more interesting than ourselves; taught to be diffident, just this side of self-effacing. ("You're the least important person in the room and don't forget it," Jessica Mitford's governess would hiss in her ear on the advent of any social occasion; I copied that into my notebook because it is only recently that I have been able to enter a room without hearing some such phrase in my inner ear.) Only the very young and the very old may recount their dreams at breakfast, dwell upon self, interrupt with memories of beach picnics and favorite Liberty lawn dresses and the rainbow trout in a creek near Colorado Springs. The rest of us are expected, rightly, to affect absorption in other people's favorite dresses, other people's trout.

And so we do. But our notebooks give us away, for however dutifully we record what we see around us, the common denominator of all we see is always, transparently, shamelessly, the implacable "I."

We are not talking here about the kind of notebook that is patently for public consumption, a structural conceit for binding together a series of graceful *pensées*; we are talking about something private, about bits of the mind's string too short to use, an indiscriminate and erratic assemblage with meaning only for its maker.

And sometimes even the maker has difficulty with the meaning. There does not seem to be, for example, any point in my knowing for the rest of my life that, during 1964, 720 tons of soot fell on every square mile of New York City, yet there it is in my notebook, labeled "FACT." Nor do I really need to remember that Ambrose Bierce liked to spell Leland Stanford's name "£eland $tanford" or that "smart women almost always wear black in Cuba," a fashion hint without much potential for practical application. And does not the relevance of these notes seem marginal at best?:

> In the basement museum of the Inyo County Courthouse in Independence, California, sign pinned to a mandarin coat: "This MANDARIN COAT was often worn by Mrs. Minnie S. Brooks when giving lectures on her TEAPOT COLLECTION."
>
> Redhead getting out of car in front of Beverly Wilshire Hotel, chinchilla stole, Vuitton bags with tags reading:
>
> MRS LOU FOX
> HOTEL SAHARA
> VEGAS

Well, perhaps not entirely marginal. As a matter of fact, Mrs. Minnie S. Brooks and her MANDARIN COAT pull me back into my own childhood, for although I never knew Mrs. Brooks and did not visit Inyo County until I was thirty, I grew up in just such a world, in houses cluttered with Indian relics and bits of gold ore and ambergris and the souvenirs my Aunt Mercy Farnsworth brought back from the Orient. It is a long way from that world to Mrs. Lou Fox's world, where we all live now, and is it not just as well to remember that? Might not Mrs. Minnie S. Brooks help me to remember what I am? Might not Mrs. Lou Fox help me to remember what I am not?

But sometimes the point is harder to discern. What exactly did I have in mind when I noted down that it cost the father of someone I know $650 a month to light the place on the Hudson in which he lived before the Crash? What use was I planning to make of this line by Jimmy Hoffa: "I may have my faults, but being wrong ain't one of them"? And although I think it interesting to know where the girls who travel with the Syndicate have their hair done when they find themselves on the West Coast, will I ever make suitable use of it? Might I not be better off just passing it on to John O'Hara? What is a recipe for sauerkraut doing in my notebook? What kind of magpie keeps this notebook? *"He was born the night the Titanic went down."* That seems a nice enough line, and I even recall who said it, but is it not really a better line in life than it could ever be in fiction?

But of course that is exactly it: not that I should ever use the line, but that I should remember the woman who said it and the afternoon I heard it. We were on her terrace by the sea, and we were finishing the wine left from lunch, trying to get what sun there was, a California winter sun. The woman whose husband was born the night the *Titanic* went down wanted to rent her house, wanted to go back to her children in Paris. I remember wishing that I could afford the house, which cost $1,000 a month. "Someday you will," she said lazily. "Someday it all comes." There in the sun on her terrace it seemed easy to believe in someday, but later I had a low-grade afternoon hangover and ran over a black snake on the way to the supermarket and was flooded with inexplicable fear when I heard the checkout clerk explaining to the man ahead of me why she was finally divorcing her husband. "He left me no choice," she said over and over as she punched the register. "He has a little seven-month-old baby by her, he left me no choice." I would like to believe that my dread then was for the human condition, but of course it was for me, because I wanted a baby and did not then have one and because I wanted to own the house that cost $1,000 a month to rent and because I had a hangover.

It all comes back. Perhaps it is difficult to see the value in having one's self back in that kind of mood, but I do see it; I think we are well advised to keep on nodding terms with the people we used to be, whether we find them attractive company or not. Otherwise they turn up unannounced and surprise us, come hammering on the mind's door at 4 a.m. of a bad night and demand to know who deserted them, who betrayed them, who is going to make amends. We forget all too soon the things we thought we could never forget. We forget the loves and the betrayals alike, forget what we whispered and what we screamed, forget who we were. I have already lost touch with a couple of people I used to be; one of them, a seventeen-year-old, presents little threat, although it would be of some interest to me to know again what it feels like to sit on a river levee drinking vodka-and-orange-juice and listening to Les Paul and Mary Ford and their echoes sing "How High the Moon" on the car radio. (You see I still have the scenes, but I no longer perceive myself among those present, no longer could even improvise the dialogue.) The other one, a twenty-three-year-old, bothers me more. She was always a good deal of trouble, and I suspect she will reappear when I least want to see her, skirts too long, shy to the point of aggravation, always the injured party, full of recriminations and little hurts and stories I do not want to hear again, at once saddening me and angering me with her vulnerability and ignorance, an apparition all the more insistent for being so long banished.

It is a good idea, then, to keep in touch, and I suppose that keeping in touch is what notebooks are all about. And we are all on our own when it comes to keeping those lines open to ourselves: your notebook will never help me, nor mine you. "*So what's new in the whiskey business?*" What could that possibly mean to you? To me it means a blonde in a Pucci bathing suit sitting with a couple of fat men by the pool at the Beverly Hills Hotel. Another man approaches, and they all regard one another in silence for a while. "So what's new in the whiskey business?" one of the fat men finally says by way of welcome, and the blonde stands up, arches one foot and dips it in the pool, looking all the while at the cabaña where Baby Pignatari is talking on the telephone. That is all there is to that, except that several years later I saw the blonde coming out of Saks Fifth Avenue in New York with her California complexion and a voluminous mink coat. In the harsh wind that day she looked old and irrevocably tired to me, and even the skins in the mink coat were not worked the way they were doing them that year, not the way she would have wanted them done, and there is the point of my story. For a while after that I did not like to look in the mirror, and my eyes would skim the newspapers and pick out only the deaths, the cancer victims, the premature coronaries, the suicides, and I stopped riding the Lexington Avenue IRT because I noticed for the first time that all the strangers I had seen for years—the man with the seeing-eye dog, the spinster who read the classified pages every day, the fat girl who always got off with me at Grand Central—looked older than they once had.

17

It all comes back. Even that recipe for sauerkraut: even that brings it back. I was on Fire Island when I first made that sauerkraut, and it was raining, and we drank a lot of bourbon and ate the sauerkraut and went to bed at ten, and I listened to the rain and the Atlantic and felt safe. I made the sauerkraut again last night and it did not make me feel any safer, but that is, as they say, another story. 18

Rhetorical Analysis

1. Watching Joan Didion write, as distinct from reading her, is a lesson in how a good writer constantly maneuvers in language to achieve special effects, both great and small.
    a. Here are some of Didion's quicker moves. Why does she
        (1) say "the note" instead of "my notebook entry" in ¶ 1?
        (2) not clearly identify "a girl" in ¶ 2 as referring to herself until the end of ¶ 9?
        (3) construct ¶ 6 nearly all in negatives (¶ 9 as well)?
        (4) leave unexplained "Bettina Aptheker and Benjamin Sonnenberg and Teddy ('Mr. Acapulco') Stauffer" (¶ 8)?
        (5) not say that "The Eighty-Yard Run" was written by Irwin Shaw (¶ 9)?
        (6) put "Remember what it was to be me" in italics (¶ 9)?
        (7) say "pensées" instead of the English "thoughts" (¶ 11)?
        (8) end ¶ 13, and that section of the essay, with two unanswered questions?
        (9) construct the next paragraph almost entirely of unanswered questions?
        (10) begin ¶ 16 (and many other paragraphs) with such a short sentence?
        (11) use the word "forget" five times in two sentences (¶ 16)?
        (12) end the essay with a reference, unexplained, to "another story" (¶ 18)?
    b. Here are some larger moves she makes; what reason can you imagine for them?
        (1) Notice the fragmentary, broken, even jerky rhythm of this essay: Didion seems deliberately to avoid smooth development.
        (2) Examine her paragraphing and the sometimes oblique or missing transitions, or the way some paragraphs are closely linked. To what end?
2. The play with language and structure noted above has a second motive. Playwright John Mortimer writes, "The only rule I have found to have any validity in

writing is not to bore yourself." Where else in this essay do you see playfulness—evidence that Didion may have been writing not only to engage the reader but also to entertain herself?

Intellectual Analysis

1. Didion distinguishes three kinds of notebooks, the first two of which she rejects: the kind in which events and facts are recorded (¶ 6), another which is written for "public consumption" (¶ 11), and the kind she keeps.
   a. At the end of ¶ 9, she arrives at a definitional point, and answers the question the first 9 paragraphs set up: Why keep a notebook? *"Remember what it was to be me.* That is always the point." Evaluate that statement, and trace it through the rest of the piece.
   b. In ¶ 11, Didion can refine that purpose more clearly. The importance of the notebook is "the implacable 'I.' " Why is this "I" so important?
2. Didion then goes on in the rest of the essay to explore this idea of "the implacable 'I.' "
   a. At ¶ 16, Didion announces, "I think we are all well-advised to keep on nodding terms with the people we used to be." What is the significance of such an assertion, and how does she develop it?
   b. She emphasizes, in ¶ 17, that "we are all on our own when it comes to keeping those lines open to ourselves." What kind of resonance does that statement have—in this essay and beyond it. In this connection, consider the very fragmentary nature of this essay.
   c. In fact, notice the various pronouns by which Didion refers to herself (see especially ¶ 16).

Suggestions for Writing

1. "We are brought up in the ethic that others, any others, all others, are by definition more interesting than ourselves; taught to be diffident, just this side of self-effacing," Didion asserts. Write an essay exploring that statement, its truth or falsehood, its effect on our lives.
2. Teachers of composition often ask that students keep a "journal." Using Didion's terms, or your own, write an essay in which you discuss the value of such an assignment.
3. Look over old class notes, a journal, or letters and, based on what you can observe about your own writing habits, assemble an essay built like Didion's.
4. Compare Didion's reasons for keeping a notebook with Alice Walker's comments on writing in "In Search of Our Mother's Gardens."

Bureaucrats

The closed door upstairs at 120 South Spring Street in downtown Los Angeles is marked OPERATIONS CENTER. In the windowless room beyond the closed door a reverential hush prevails. From six A.M. until seven P.M. in this windowless room men sit at consoles watching a huge board flash colored lights. "There's the heart attack," someone will murmur, or "we're getting the gawk effect." 120 South Spring is the Los Angeles office of Caltrans, or the California Department of Transportation, and the Operations Center is where Caltrans engineers monitor what they call "the 42-Mile Loop." The 42-Mile Loop is simply the rough triangle formed by the intersections of the Santa Monica, the San Diego and the Harbor freeways, and 42 miles represents less than ten per cent of freeway mileage in Los Angeles County alone, but these particular 42 miles are regarded around 120 South Spring with a special veneration. The Loop is a "demonstration system," a phrase much favored by everyone at Caltrans, and is part of a "pilot project," another two words carrying totemic weight on South Spring.

The Loop has electronic sensors embedded every half-mile out there in the pavement itself, each sensor counting the crossing cars every twenty seconds. The Loop has its own mind, a Xerox Sigma V computer which prints out, all day and night, twenty-second readings on what is and is not moving in each of the Loop's eight lanes. It is the Xerox Sigma V that makes the big board flash red when traffic out there drops below fifteen miles an hour. It is the Xerox Sigma V that tells the Operations crew when they have an "incident" out there. An "incident" is the heart attack on the San Diego, the jackknifed truck on the Harbor, the Camaro just now tearing out the Cyclone fence on the Santa Monica. "Out there" is where incidents happen. The windowless room at 120 South Spring is where incidents get "verified." "Incident verification" is turning on the closed-circuit TV on the console and watching the traffic slow down to see (this is "the gawk effect") where the Camaro tore out the fence.

As a matter of fact there is a certain closed-circuit aspect to the entire mood of the Operations Center. "Verifying" the incident does not after all "prevent" the incident, which lends the enterprise a kind of tranced distance, and on the day recently when I visited 120 South Spring it took considerable effort to remember what I had come to talk about, which was that particular part of the Loop called the Santa

Monica Freeway. The Santa Monica Freeway is 16.2 miles long, runs from the Pacific Ocean to downtown Los Angeles through what is referred to at Caltrans as "the East-West Corridor," carries more traffic every day than any other freeway in California, has what connoisseurs of freeways concede to be the most beautiful access ramps in the world, and appeared to have been transformed by Caltrans, during the several weeks before I went downtown to talk about it, into a 16.2-mile parking lot.

The problem seemed to be another Caltrans "demonstration," or "pilot," a foray into bureaucratic terrorism they were calling "The Diamond Lane" in their promotional literature and "The Project" among themselves. That the promotional literature consisted largely of schedules for buses (or "Diamond Lane Expresses") and invitations to join a car pool via computer ("Commuter Computer") made clear not only the putative point of The Project, which was to encourage travel by car pool and bus, but also the actual point, which was to eradicate a central Southern California illusion, that of individual mobility, without anyone really noticing. This had not exactly worked out. "FREEWAY FIASCO," the *Los Angeles Times* was headlining page-one stories. "THE DIAMOND LANE: ANOTHER BUST BY CALTRANS." "CALTRANS PILOT EFFORT ANOTHER IN LONG LIST OF FAILURES." "OFFICIAL DIAMOND LANE STANCE: LET THEM HOWL."

All "The Diamond Lane" theoretically involved was reserving the fast inside lanes on the Santa Monica for vehicles carrying three or more people, but in practice this meant that 25 per cent of the freeway was reserved for 3 per cent of the cars, and there were other odd wrinkles here and there suggesting that Caltrans had dedicated itself to making all movement around Los Angeles as arduous as possible. There was for example the matter of surface streets. A "surface street" is anything around Los Angeles that is not a freeway ("going surface" from one part of town to another is generally regarded as idiosyncratic), and surface streets do not fall directly within the Caltrans domain, but now the engineer in charge of surface streets was accusing Caltrans of threatening and intimidating him. It appeared that Caltrans wanted him to create a "confused and congested situation" on his surface streets, so as to force drivers back to the freeway, where they would meet a still more confused and congested situation and decide to stay home, or take a bus. "We are beginning a process of deliberately making it harder for drivers to use freeways," a Caltrans director had in fact said at a transit conference some months before. "We are prepared to endure considerable public outcry in order to pry John Q. Public out of his car. . . . I would emphasize that this is a political decision, and one that can be reversed if the public gets sufficiently enraged to throw us rascals out."

6 Of course this political decision was in the name of the greater good, was in the interests of "environmental improvement" and "conservation of resources," but even there the figures had about them a certain Caltrans opacity. The Santa Monica normally carried 240,000 cars and trucks every day. These 240,000 cars and trucks normally carried 260,000 people. What Caltrans described as its ultimate goal on the Santa Monica was to carry the same 260,000 people, "but in 7,800 fewer, or 232,200 vehicles." The figure "232,200" had a visionary precision to it that did not automatically create confidence, especially since the only effect so far had been to disrupt traffic throughout the Los Angeles basin, triple the number of daily accidents on the Santa Monica, prompt the initiation of two lawsuits against Caltrans, and cause large numbers of Los Angeles County residents to behave, most uncharacteristically, as an ignited and conscious proletariat. Citizen guerrillas splashed paint and scattered nails in the Diamond Lanes. Diamond Lane maintenance crews expressed fear of hurled objects. Down at 120 South Spring the architects of the Diamond Lane had taken to regarding "the media" as the architects of their embarrassment, and Caltrans statements in the press had been cryptic and contradictory, reminiscent only of old communiqués out of Vietnam.

7 To understand what was going on it is perhaps necessary to have participated in the freeway experience, which is the only secular communion Los Angeles has. Mere driving on the freeway is in no way the same as participating in it. Anyone can "drive" on the freeway, and many people with no vocation for it do, hesitating here and resisting there, losing the rhythm of the lane change, thinking about where they came from and where they are going. Actual participants think only about where they are. Actual participation requires a total surrender, a concentration so intense as to seem a kind of narcosis, a rapture-of-the-freeway. The mind goes clean. The rhythm takes over. A distortion of time occurs, the same distortion that characterizes the instant before an accident. It takes only a few seconds to get off the Santa Monica Freeway at National-Overland, which is a difficult exit requiring the driver to cross two new lanes of traffic streamed in from the San Diego Freeway, but those few seconds always seem to me the longest part of the trip. The moment is dangerous. The exhilaration is in doing it. "As

you acquire the special skills involved," Reyner Banham observed in an extraordinary chapter about the freeways in his 1971 *Los Angeles: The Architecture of Four Ecologies*, "the freeways become a special way of being alive . . . the extreme concentration required in Los Angeles seems to bring on a state of heightened awareness that some locals find mystical."

Indeed some locals do, and some nonlocals too. Reducing the number of lone souls careering around the East-West Corridor in a state of mechanized rapture may or may not have seemed socially desirable, but what it was definitely not going to seem was easy. "We're only seeing an initial period of unfamiliarity," I was assured the day I visited Caltrans. I was talking to a woman named Eleanor Wood and she was thoroughly and professionally grounded in the diction of "planning" and it did not seem likely that I could interest her in considering the freeway as regional mystery. "Any time you try to rearrange people's daily habits, they're apt to react impetuously. All this project requires is a certain rearrangement of people's daily planning. That's really all we want."

It occurred to me that a certain rearrangement of people's daily planning might seem, in less rarefied air than is breathed at 120 South Spring, rather a great deal to want, but so impenetrable was the sense of higher social purpose there in the Operations Center that I did not express this reservation. Instead I changed the subject, mentioned an earlier "pilot project" on the Santa Monica: the big electronic message boards that Caltrans had installed a year or two before. The idea was that traffic information transmitted from the Santa Monica to the Xerox Sigma V could be translated, here in the Operations Center, into suggestions to the driver, and flashed right back out to the Santa Monica. This operation, in that it involved telling drivers electronically what they already knew empirically, had the rather spectral circularity that seemed to mark a great many Caltrans schemes, and I was interested in how Caltrans thought it worked.

"Actually the message boards were part of a larger pilot project," Mrs. Wood said. "An ongoing project in incident management. With the message boards we hoped to learn if motorists would modify their behavior according to what we told them on the boards."

I asked if the motorists had.

"Actually no," Mrs. Wood said finally. "They didn't react to the signs exactly as we'd hypothesized they would, no. *But*. If we'd *known* what the motorist would do . . . then we wouldn't have needed a pilot project in the first place, would we."

The circle seemed intact. Mrs. Wood and I smiled, and shook   13
hands. I watched the big board until all lights turned green on the
Santa Monica and then I left and drove home on it, all 16.2 miles of it.
All the way I remembered that I was watched by the Xerox Sigma V.
All the way the message boards gave me the number to call for CAR
POOL INFO. As I left the freeway it occurred to me that they might
have their own rapture down at 120 South Spring, and it could be
called Perpetuating the Department. Today the California Highway
Patrol reported that, during the first six weeks of the Diamond Lane,
accidents on the Santa Monica, which normally range between 49 and
72 during a six-week period, totaled 204. Yesterday plans were
announced to extend the Diamond Lane to other freeways at a cost of
$42,500,000.

Rhetorical Analysis

1. Critics tend to characterize Didion's journalistic prose with words such as "barbed," "trenchant," and "fine-honed"—which suggest a razor-sharp intelligence. She fosters this impression not only with sharp-edged commentary ("bureaucratic terrorism") but with a battery of oblique tactics: innuendos and irony and telling particulars. Analyze her methods in "Bureaucrats."

2. Didion often writes extended passages of three or more sentences that culminate in some point of impact. An example is the way ¶ 2 works its way through explanations of Caltrans' special jargon to end with a decoding of "gawk effect," which has been puzzling readers since ¶ 1. Find and study other instances (such as the one in the final three sentences of the essay).

3. Didion's use of direct quotation is especially deft. Reread her essay, asking the following questions each time you find words in quotation marks.
    a. Why does Didion identify or not identify the source of the quotation?
    b. Why does she use as much of the material as she does but no more?
    c. Why does she quote at all instead of paraphrasing?
    d. What is the rhetorical effect of the quotation in context, in connection with the sentence or paragraph containing it?

4. Identify Didion's tone in this essay, paying particular attention to its remarkable consistency.

Intellectual Analysis

1. Why does Didion repeat so many proper nouns and expressions: for example, "120 South Spring," "Operations Center" (and windowless, at that), "the 42-Mile

Loop," "the Xerox Sigma V"? So much heavy-handed repetition would normally be thought a weakness in an essay, yet here it is part of Didion's brilliant style, and certainly central to the point she is making.
   a. The "42-Mile Loop" may be a controlling image because it matches with several other details: "closed circuit," Didion's drive to "120 South Spring" and her return home; "the circle seemed intact" in the last paragraph. All are references to circularity. What are we to make of that metaphor?
   b. Didion also suggests that this circularity in bureaucracy is inevitable and reductive, or diminishing in its returns. Find details that support this view (for example, there are more "Diamond Lanes" forthcoming).
2. From the amalgamation of such repeated details, Didion's analysis of bureaucracy can be derived. Several of her phrases—which are clearly value-judgments—are worth considering as touchstones.
   a. The Operations Center maintains a "kind of tranced distance" (¶ 3). What is the implication of that expression?
   b. In ¶ 4, what does Didion mean by "a foray into bureaucratic terrorism," which ought to link up to ¶s 8 and 9, and the "rearrangement of people's daily planning"?
   c. In ¶ 6, she mentions "a visionary precision" about some statistics that failed to "create confidence." What is her point?
   d. Didion suggests that 120 South Spring may have its own "kind of rapture," and she would call it, "Perpetuating the Department." What does that suggest about bureaucracy?

Suggestions for Writing

1. How does bureaucracy affect the school you are presently attending? Write an essay on the subject. (You could substitute some other large organization with which you have had some direct experience.)
2. "Bureaucrats" conveys, as does much contemporary reportage, most of its criticism by letting facts speak for themselves. Select a target you can investigate first hand, and try this method.
3. Besides bureaucracies, what else do you think puts on a show of good intentions to cover its true motive, which is self-perpetuation?

ON MORALITY

As it happens I am in Death Valley, in a room at the Enterprise Motel and Trailer Park, and it is July, and it is hot. In fact it is 119°. I cannot

1

seem to make the air conditioner work, but there is a small refrigerator, and I can wrap ice cubes in a towel and hold them against the small of my back. With the help of the ice cubes I have been trying to think, because *The American Scholar* asked me to, in some abstract way about "morality," a word I distrust more every day, but my mind veers inflexibly toward the particular.

Here are some particulars. At midnight last night, on the road in from Las Vegas to Death Valley Junction, a car hit a shoulder and turned over. The driver, very young and apparently drunk, was killed instantly. His girl was found alive but bleeding internally, deep in shock. I talked this afternoon to the nurse who had driven the girl to the nearest doctor, 185 miles across the floor of the Valley and three ranges of lethal mountain road. The nurse explained that her husband, a talc miner, had stayed on the highway with the boy's body until the coroner could get over the mountains from Bishop, at dawn today. "You can't just leave a body on the highway," she said. "It's immoral."

It was one instance in which I did not distrust the word, because she meant something quite specific. She meant that if a body is left alone for even a few minutes on the desert, the coyotes close in and eat the flesh. Whether or not a corpse is torn apart by coyotes may seem only a sentimental consideration, but of course it is more: one of the promises we make to one another is that we will try to retrieve our casualties, try not to abandon our dead to the coyotes. If we have been taught to keep our promises—if, in the simplest terms, our upbringing is good enough—we stay with the body, or have bad dreams.

I am talking, of course, about the kind of social code that is sometimes called, usually pejoratively, "wagon-train morality." In fact that is precisely what it is. For better or worse, we are what we learned as children: my own childhood was illuminated by graphic litanies of the grief awaiting those who failed in their loyalties to each other. The Donner-Reed Party, starving in the Sierra snows, all the ephemera of civilization gone save that one vestigial taboo, the provision that no one should eat his own blood kin. The Jayhawkers, who quarreled and separated not far from where I am tonight. Some of them died in the Funerals and some of them died down near Badwater and most of the rest of them died in the Panamints. A woman who got through gave the Valley its name. Some might say that the Jayhawkers were killed by the desert summer, and the Donner Party by the mountain winter, by circumstances beyond control; we were taught instead that they had somewhere abdicated their responsibilities, somehow breached their primary loyalties, or they would not have found themselves helpless in the mountain winter or the desert summer, would not have given way to acrimony, would not have deserted one another, would not have *failed*. In brief, we heard such stories as cautionary tales, and they still suggest the only kind of "morality" that seems to me to have any but the most potentially mendacious meaning.

You are quite possibly impatient with me by now; I am talking, you want to say, about a "morality" so primitive that it scarcely deserves the name, a code that has as its point only survival, not the attainment of the ideal good. Exactly. Particularly out here tonight, in this country so ominous and terrible that to live in it is to live with antimatter, it is difficult to believe that "the good" is a knowable quantity. Let me tell you what it is like out here tonight. Stories travel at night on the desert. Someone gets in his pickup and drives a couple of hundred miles for a beer, and he carries news of what is happening, back wherever he came from. Then he drives another hundred miles for another beer, and passes along stories from the last place as well as from the one before; it is a network kept alive by people whose instincts tell them that if they do not keep moving at night on the desert they will lose all reason. Here is a story that is going around the desert tonight: over across the Nevada line, sheriff's deputies are diving in some underground pools, trying to retrieve a couple of bodies known to be in the hole. The widow of one of the drowned boys is over there; she is eighteen, and pregnant, and is said not to leave the hole. The divers go down and come up, and she just stands there and stares into the water. They have been diving for ten days but have found no bottom to the caves, no bodies and no trace of them, only the black 90° water going down and down and down, and a single translucent fish, not classified. The story tonight is that one of the divers has been hauled up incoherent, out of his head, shouting—until they got him out of there so that the widow could not hear—about water that got hotter instead of cooler as he went down, about light flickering through the water, about magma, about underground nuclear testing.

That is the tone stories take out here, and there are quite a few of them tonight. And it is more than the stories alone. Across the road at the Faith Community Church a couple of dozen old people, come here to live in trailers and die in the sun, are holding a prayer sing. I cannot hear them and do not want to. What I can hear are occasional coyotes and a constant chorus of "Baby the Rain Must Fall" from the jukebox in the Snake Room next door, and if I were also to hear those dying

5

6

voices, those Midwestern voices drawn to this lunar country for some unimaginable atavistic rites, *rock of ages cleft for me*, I think I would lose my own reason. Every now and then I imagine I hear a rattlesnake, but my husband says that it is a faucet, a paper rustling, the wind. Then he stands by a window, and plays a flashlight over the dry wash outside.

What does it mean? It means nothing manageable. There is some sinister hysteria in the air out here tonight, some hint of the monstrous perversion to which any human idea can come. "I followed my own conscience." "I did what I thought was right." How many madmen have said it and meant it? How many murderers? Klaus Fuchs said it, and the men who committed the Mountain Meadows Massacre said it, and Alfred Rosenberg said it. And, as we are rotely and rather presumptuously reminded by those who would say it now, Jesus said it. Maybe we have all said it, and maybe we have been wrong. Except on that most primitive level—our loyalties to those we love—what could be more arrogant than to claim the primacy of personal conscience? ("Tell me," a rabbi asked Daniel Bell when he said, as a child, that he did not believe in God. "Do you think God cares?") At least some of the time, the world appears to me as a painting by Hieronymous Bosch; were I to follow my conscience then, it would lead me out onto the desert with Marion Faye, out to where he stood in *The Deer Park* looking east to Los Alamos and praying, as if for rain, that it would happen: ". . . *let it come and clear the rot and the stench and the stink, let it come for all of everywhere, just so it comes and the world stands clear in the white dead dawn.*"

Of course you will say that I do not have the right, even if I had the power, to inflict that unreasonable conscience upon you; nor do I want you to inflict your conscience, however reasonable, however enlightened, upon me. ("We must be aware of the dangers which lie in our most generous wishes," Lionel Trilling once wrote. "Some paradox of our nature leads us, when once we have made our fellow men the objects of our enlightened interest, to go on to make them the objects of our pity, then of our wisdom, ultimately of our coercion.") That the ethic of conscience is intrinsically insidious seems scarcely a revelatory point, but it is one raised with increasing infrequency; even those who do raise it tend to *segue* with troubling readiness into the quite contradictory position that the ethic of conscience is dangerous when it is "wrong," and admirable when it is "right."

You see I want to be quite obstinate about insisting that we have 9
no way of knowing—beyond that fundamental loyalty to the social
code—what is "right" and what is "wrong," what is "good" and what
"evil." I dwell so upon this because the most disturbing aspect of
"morality" seems to me to be the frequency with which the word now
appears; in the press, on television, in the most perfunctory kinds of
conversation. Questions of straightforward power (or survival) politics, questions of quite indifferent public policy, questions of almost
anything: they are all assigned these factitious moral burdens. There is
something facile going on, some self-indulgence at work. Of course we
would all like to "believe" in something, like to assuage our private
guilts in public causes, like to lose our tiresome selves; like, perhaps, to
transform the white flag of defeat at home into the brave white banner
of battle away from home. And of course it is all right to do that; that is
how, immemorially, things have gotten done. But I think it is all right
only so long as we do not delude ourselves about what we are doing,
and why. It is all right only so long as we remember that all the *ad hoc*
committees, all the picket lines, all the brave signatures in *The New
York Times*, all the tools of agitprop straight across the spectrum, do
not confer upon anyone any *ipso facto* virtue. It is all right only so long
as we recognize that the end may or may not be expedient, may or may
not be a good idea, but in any case has nothing to do with "morality."
Because when we start deceiving ourselves into thinking not that we
want something or need something, not that it is a pragmatic necessity
for us to have it, but that it is a *moral imperative* that we have it, then is
when we join the fashionable madmen, and then is when the thin
whine of hysteria is heard in the land, and then is when we are in bad
trouble. And I suspect we are already there.

Rhetorical Analysis

1. From the first paragraph on, this essay insists on "particulars."
    a. A question ought to occur immediately: What effect does such particularity have on style? What is gained from the details of the first paragraph? What of "Death Valley," and "Enterprise Motel and Trailer Park"?
    b. Consider the broader question of the effect of setting: how does Didion use the scene as a rhetorical base for the essay? She returns to different details of the scene again and again: where and how and to what rhetorical effect?

c. Consider, too, the writer's own involvement in the setting, the interchange that takes place between herself and the surrounding landscape. How does this affect the tone, mood, etc., of the essay?
2. Didion's prose is well known for its compactness.
   a. Look at ¶ 9. Note the frequency, and variety, of punctuation. How does the punctuation indicate the number of issues and ideas, often with their attendant emotional responses, that she is trying to gather together in this paragraph? Look at two or three sentences and explain, punctuation mark by punctuation mark, the particular function of each.
   b. Despite the many-layered density of this ninth paragraph, Didion gives it focus in an image—one that is almost a cliche: "we would all like," she says, "to transform the white flag of defeat at home into the brave white banner of battle away from home." How does this sentence give focus not only to the paragraph but to the essay?
   c. In considering the essay as a whole, the impression one gets is not of heaviness, or slowness, but of lightness and rapidity. This is partly the result of the simplicity and grace in Didion's transitions. Identify these transitions and explain how they contribute to the briskness of Didion's prose.

Intellectual Analysis

1. Since "particulars" are so stressed here, particularity is also of central intellectual importance. Didion says at the outset that her mind "veers inflexibly toward the particular": what does this indicate about her intellectual procedure and her argument? What about the role of abstractions? What does this comment say about what we know and how we come to know it?
2. When Didion speaks of the dissemination of news on the desert, she says, "it is a network kept alive by people whose instincts tell them that if they do not keep moving at night on the desert they will lose all reason." What does she imply about any meaning in life, or about morality, or our relationship to the natural world?
3. Didion worries that the "ethic of conscience is intrinsically insidious" (¶ 8): what is implied by that claim and how do its implications relate to the idea of particularity?
4. Didion's description of the deputies diving into warm pools to recover two bodies might be seen as an image of the whole essay, and of our moral dilemma. How?

Suggestions for Writing

1. Examine the morality of some campus situation or question with which you are intimately familiar, such as cheating on tests, stealing books, racism, sexism, or some other kind of discrimination. Develop an essay, taking that question or

situation as your topic, and stick to the particulars of the subject. Didion confines herself to the night, the desert, to immediate events; try to do likewise so as to avoid abstractions.

2. Didion begins with a rather ironic reference to her immediate reason for writing this essay, and the difficulties of carrying it out. Try using that stratagem to open an essay of your own (whether on morality or something else); you might also try imitating the ironic-but-earnest tone of Didion.

3. Critique Didion's essay, "On Morality," in the light of criteria set down in Barbara Tuchman's essay, "The Historian as Artist."

Bertrand Russell

In 1948, Bertrand Russell swam to safety after an airliner, carrying him to Sweden for a lecture series, crashed in a Norwegian harbor. He was 76. Having survived this episode, which almost certainly should have killed him, he lived on to accept, two years later, the Nobel Prize for literature. And at 80, Russell mused that, "it is reasonable to suppose that the bulk of one's work is done." Reasonable for most people, perhaps. But Russell's work was simply entering a new phase. At this very time, he married Edith Finch—who became his fourth wife—and with her entered a period of energetic political activity, mostly involving anti-nuclear and anti-war demonstrations, which lasted almost until his death in 1970. The last of the three volumes of his magnificent autobiography had appeared just before, in 1969.

When Russell entered Cambridge University, at the age of 18, he came as a brilliant descendant of a distinguished family (his grandfather, Lord John Russell, had introduced into Parliament the famous Reform Bill of 1832, and had earlier visited Napoleon, exiled on Elba). At Cambridge, Russell studied mathematics and philosophy with Alfred North Whitehead. These two became friends, and later collaborated in writing the Principia Mathematica (1910, 1911, and 1913), one of the most important philosophical works of the century.

Russell's seemingly assured career as an academic philosopher was interrupted by World War I (1914–1918). Russell, who all his life thought this particular war one of the greatest mistakes of a mistake-prone humanity, argued against it throughout its duration. In 1918 he was imprisoned for six months for the "libel" of an ally. From that time onward, Russell was constantly the center of public controversies, which were often fueled (if not provoked) by his unorthodox educational and religious views.

Although Russell had opposed the conflicts of 1914–1918, he supported World War II (1939–1945) as a necessary war. Later, Russell outraged many with his liberal views on sex and marriage. He rankled others when he insisted that children should be brought up with a judicious mixture of freedom and discipline. And in religion, he preached a fundamental agnosticism. That none of these positions seems outrageous today is partly due to Russell's vigorous advocacy of them.

Besides his great intellect, Russell brought to the liberal side immense wit and charm—and the passionate zeal of an evangelistic Victorian reformer. Whatever the issue, Russell always insisted that the human condition could be improved. "Neither misery nor folly seems to me any part of the inevitable lot of man. And I am convinced that intelligence, patience and eloquence can, sooner or later, lead the human race out of its self-imposed tortures provided it does not exterminate itself meanwhile."

NIGHTMARES

(1) THE FISHERMAN'S NIGHTMARE OR 'MAGNA EST VERITAS'

Sir Peter Simon had been from early youth passionately fond of fishing and, although he became a very busy and successful professional man, he always devoted the summer holidays to his favourite sport. After testing various regions, he finally came to prefer the Highlands of Scotland. He was, however, deeply distressed by what he considered the vulgar notoriety conferred by the Loch Ness Monster. Although he had often fished in that Loch, he had never come upon any sign of this curious animal, and his nature was such that he thought everything not visible to himself must be mythical.

One evening, after reading in Izaak Walton about respectable fishes such as the chavender or chubb, he fell asleep, and his waking thoughts took shape in the form of a strange nightmare. He dreamt that the Loch Ness Monster had inspired some ingenious people who lived on a loch in a nearby glen. These people—so he dreamt—were actuated by a motive, that of ambitious competition, which he could but applaud. The influx of tourists from the degenerate South following upon the discovery of the Loch Ness Monster had been noted by the hardy Highlanders of the neighbouring glen, and they had observed with envy that the development of tourism had brought whole swarms of chars-à-bancs that made the month of August hideous but, for the dwellers on Loch Ness, extremely lucrative. Sir Peter's sleeping imagination presented these people as having manufactured a monster to inhabit their own lake who was made in part like a car tyre, but with the addition of a long tail that waved in the current like seaweed. This horrid creature was provided with a cleverly contrived device by which, when the air was let out, he uttered loud and dismal howls, at the same time 'Swinging the scaley horror of his folded tail'. On dark nights, especially when there was a thunder storm, this device succeeded in inspiring terror among the more timorous fishermen—a terror far greater than the Loch Ness Monster had ever created.

But, alas, the land-owners of the neighbourhood, who had invented the monster, though they soon succeeded in out-doing the Loch Ness Monster, had underestimated the scientific curiosity of our impertinent age. A rather young FRS, Mr Jonas MacPherson, who had been born and bred in the neighbourhood and who was a fanatic votary of fishing, discovered the hoax by circumambulating the lake on stormy nights and observing the presence of a rowing boat in the neighbourhood of the dreadful howls. In the works of that eminent Lord Chancellor Francis Bacon, he had come across the statement that knowledge is power, and it occurred to him that his knowledge about the Monster gave him power of a very useful kind. Being by no means well-off, he had, hitherto, had great difficulty in paying for his Highland holidays. But now he went to the local hotel-keeper telling of his discovery and promising to keep silence if he was allowed fishing rights and free board and lodging at the hotel. The hotel-keeper, who was one of the ring-leaders in the plot, summoned the committee of conspirators; and Mr MacPherson's terms were reluctantly accepted.

For a time, all went well, but the fame of the new monster continued to grow, and, at last, the pressure of the sensational press combined with the desire of Sir Theophilus Thwackum to add the beast to his private zoo, compelled the Royal Society to send a deputation to investigate the phenomena. The deputation consisted of ten eminent men of science who, it was confidently believed, would not easily be taken in by any hocus-pocus if, indeed, something of the sort were involved. Mr MacPherson, who was not without gratitude to the conspirators and also wished to preserve his free holidays, felt that he should earn his keep. He therefore proceeded to supply the creature with howls and yells far more horrible than before; and he inserted in its inside tape-recordings which loudly wailed, 'Repent, Ye Unbelievers!' All the ten Fellows heard the dreadful message on a dark night of thunder and lightning. Alas, each one of them was deeply conscious that there was that in his past which called for repentance. All ten feared that if they repeated the experiment the awe-inspiring monster would no longer be content with generalities, but would specify the items in which these hitherto respected citizens had sinned. All returned to London with hair completely white. Their cronies would endeavour on social evenings to elicit at least some hint of what had occurred on those northern waters, but not one of these great men could be induced to make even the smallest revelation. All of them, when compelled to speak of their experiences, remarked in grave and awe-stricken tones: 'There are some things which it is not for mortals to investigate.'

And there the matter might have rested if good taste and proper reticence had had due sway. Unfortunately, the results of the investigation seemed unsatisfying to a certain rash young scientist, Mr Adam Monkhouse. Mr Monkhouse was even younger than Mr MacPherson, and, although on the road to scientific success, had not yet become a Fellow of the Royal Society. He had a personal grudge against Mr MacPherson who had adversely criticized a hypothesis of his which he was very loath to abandon. He spent a month at the hotel with which Mr MacPherson had his agreement, and devoted himself to the cultivation of friendly relations with the hotel-keeper. Late one evening, by the expenditure of considerable sums on the very best Highland whisky, he succeeded in producing in the hotel-keeper a mellow mood in which, for the moment, nothing seemed worth concealing. The hotel-keeper told all; and Mr Monkhouse returned jubilant from the gloomy glens and fastnesses which his cheerful soul abominated. He published the results of his researches, with unkind remarks about the investigating committee. The result, however, was not what he had hoped. The Royal Society was indignant at the slur upon ten of its foremost members, and it became clear that he no longer had any hope of himself becoming one of that August Body. All the ten members of the investigating committee sued him for libel. All ten were supported by the whole body of organized science. All ten were awarded heavy damages, which at first he saw no means of paying. But, being a resourceful person, he found a way out: he saw the error of his ways, and joined the Society for Psychical Research.

Sir Peter Simon awoke. The sweat was cold upon him. But with awakening came warmth and understanding. 'Ah', he cried, 'how useful is faith when properly directed! How more than useful is even curiosity—is investigation—when properly curbed by faith!'

Note: After writing the above, I learnt, from the following article in the *Guardian*, that my fantasy was nearer to the truth than I had supposed.

IN HOSPITAL AFTER LOCH NESS DIVE

Search for 'monster'

John Newbold, aged 31, of Stafford, known as Beppo, the clown, was detained in hospital yesterday after diving into Loch Ness in a frogman's outfit to try to get evidence about the 'monster'.

He made a dive lasting ten minutes and surfaced in a semiconscious state. He was taken aboard a yacht belonging to Mr Bernard Mills, the circus proprietor, and recovered partly after artificial respiration had been applied.

Mr Newbold, who was unable to say what had happened while he was underwater, is an experienced high diver and swimmer. He had made several practice dives to a depth of more than 30 feet before yesterday's attempt. The water is several hundred feet deep at this part of the loch.

The late Mr Bertram Mills offered £10,000 before the war for the capture of the 'monster' and nine years ago his sons, Bernard and Cyril, increased the offer to £20,000.

(2) THE THEOLOGIAN'S NIGHTMARE

The eminent theologian, Dr Thaddeus, dreamed that he died and pursued his course toward heaven. His studies had prepared him and he had no difficulty in finding the way. He knocked at the door of heaven, and was met with a closer scrutiny than he expected. 'I ask admission', he said, 'because I was a good man and devoted my life to the glory of God.' 'Man?' said the janitor, 'What is that? And how could such a funny creature as you are do anything to promote the glory of God?' Dr Thaddeus was astonished. 'You surely cannot be ignorant of man. You must be aware that man is the supreme work of the Creator.' 'As to that,' said the janitor, 'I am sorry to hurt your feelings, but what you're saying is news to me. I doubt if anybody up here has ever heard of this thing you call "man". However, since you seem distressed, you shall have a chance of consulting our librarian.'

The librarian, a globular being with a thousand eyes and one mouth, bent some of his eyes upon Dr Thaddeus. 'What is this?' he asked of the janitor. 'This', replied the janitor, 'says that it is a member of a species called "man", which lives in a place called "Earth". It has some odd notion that the Creator takes special interest in this place and this species. I thought perhaps you could enlighten it.' 'Well,' said the librarian kindly to the theologian, 'perhaps you can tell me where this place is that you call "Earth".' 'Oh,' said the theologian, 'it's part of the Solar System.' 'And what is the Solar System?' asked the librarian. 'Oh,' said the theologian, somewhat disconcerted, 'my province was Sacred Knowledge, but the question that you are asking belongs to profane knowledge. However, I have learnt enough from my astronomical friends to be able to tell you that the Solar System is part of the Milky Way.' 'And what is the Milky Way?' asked the librarian. 'Oh, the Milky Way is one of the Galaxies, of which, I am told, there are some hundred million.' 'Well, well,' said the librarian, 'you could hardly expect me to remember one out of so many. But I do remember to have heard the word "galaxy" before. In fact, I believe that one of our sub-librarians specializes in galaxies. Let us send for him and see whether he can help.'

After no very long time, the galactic sub-librarian made his appearance. In shape, he was a dodecahedron. It was clear that at one time his surface had been bright, but the dust of the shelves had rendered him dim and opaque. The librarian explained to him that Dr Thaddeus, in endeavouring to account for his origin, had mentioned galaxies, and it was hoped that information could be obtained from the galactic section of the library. 'Well,' said the sub-librarian, 'I suppose it might become possible in time, but as there are a hundred million galaxies, and each has a volume to itself, it takes some time to find any particular volume. Which is it that this odd molecule desires?' 'It is the one called "the Milky Way" ', Dr Thaddeus falteringly replied. 'All right,' said the sub-librarian, 'I will find it if I can.'

Some three weeks later, he returned, explaining that the extraordinarily efficient card-index in the galactic section of the library had enabled them to locate the galaxy as number XQ 321,762. 'We have employed', he said, 'all the five thousand clerks in the galactic section on this search. Perhaps you would like to see the clerk who is specially concerned with the galaxy in question?' The clerk was sent for and turned out to be an octohedron with an eye in each face and a mouth in one of them. He was surprised and dazed to find himself in such a glittering region, away from the shadowy limbo of his shelves. Pulling himself together, he asked, rather shyly, 'What is it you wish to know about my galaxy?' Dr Thaddeus spoke up: 'What I want is to know about the Solar System, a collection of heavenly bodies revolving about one of the stars in your galaxy. The star about which they revolve is called "the Sun".' 'Humph,' said the librarian of the Milky Way, 'it was hard enough to hit upon the right galaxy, but to hit upon the right star in the galaxy is far more difficult. I know that there are about three hundred billion stars in the galaxy, but I have no knowledge, myself, that would distinguish one of them from another. I believe, however, that at one time a list of the whole three hundred billion was demanded by the Administration and that it is still stored in the basement. If you think it worth while, I will engage special labour from the Other Place to search for this particular star.'

It was agreed that, since the question had arisen and since Dr Thaddeus was evidently suffering some distress, this might be the wisest course.

Several years later, a very weary and dispirited tetrahedron presented himself before the galactic sub-librarian. 'I have', he said, 'at last discovered the particular star concerning which inquiries have been made, but I am quite at a loss to imagine why it has aroused any special interest. It closely resembles a great many other stars in the same galaxy. It is of average size and temperature, and is surrounded by very much smaller bodies called "planets". After minute investigation, I discovered that some, at least, of these planets have parasites, and I think that this thing which has been making inquiries must be one of them.'

At this point, Dr Thaddeus burst out in a passionate and indignant lament: 'Why, oh why, did the Creator conceal from us poor inhabitants of Earth that it was not we who prompted Him to create the Heavens? Throughout my long life, I have served Him diligently, believing that He would notice my service and reward me with Eternal Bliss. And now, it seems that He was not even aware that I existed. You tell me that I am an infinitesimal animalcule on a tiny body revolving round an insignificant member of a collection of three hundred billion stars, which is only one of many millions of such collections. I cannot bear it, and can no longer adore my Creator.' 'Very well,' said the janitor, 'then you can go to the Other Place.' 14

Here the theologian awoke. 'The power of Satan over our sleeping imagination is terrifying', he muttered. 15

Rhetorical Analysis

1. In an ironic essay the writer says one thing but intends another. Therefore, the reader must be clued as to the reversal of meaning. In Russell's first nightmare, what ironic clues does he give? Consider the following:
    a. The name "Sir Peter Simon" (¶ 1).
    b. "he thought everything not visible to himself must be mythical" (¶ 1).
    c. "the degenerate South" (¶ 2).
    d. "that eminent Lord Chancellor Francis Bacon" (¶ 3; see also ¶ 1 of " 'Useless' Knowledge").
    e. The name "Sir Theophilus Thwackum" (¶ 4).
    f. "but being a resourceful person" (¶ 5).
   There are many other ironic touches. How does Russell bring them to bear on the central target of his satire?

2. It is difficult for humans to read anything without conjuring up the personality behind the words. Thus, just as writing presents ideas, inevitably it also presents a certain persona (a "face" or "mask") through which the ideas are projected. Sometimes this feature of writing is called "voice."
    a. It might appear, in the second nightmare, that Russell is not projecting a voice because he is simply recounting someone else's dream. But he is. What kind of person would retell this kind of dream, in the particular way it is retold?
    b. We know it is not a real dream, but one invented by Russell. What does that knowledge add to our interpretation of voice?

c. We also know that Russell has satiric motives in inventing this dream. What more does that knowledge add to the voice?

Intellectual Analysis

1. "Nightmares" is not an essay in the usual sense. But neither may it be classed as a story. Why not? Look at such elements as characterization, scene, and plot. Might it be said that it is the intention of the writer that removes these two "Nightmares" from the realm of fiction? Their main intent seems to be to raise certain intellectual questions. What are these questions?
    a. In "The Fisherman's Nightmare," the first irony is in the title: "Great is truth." Here the truth means very little, does harm to Mr. Monkhouse, and seems to be of no concern to scientists.
        (1) Is the point of the satire that scientists are easily duped? Play out that possibility.
        (2) Is it that science should be limited always by faith, as Sir Peter Simon says on waking?
        (3) Is the attack also on the "FRS," the Fellows of the Royal Society (the most distinguished scientific organization in England)?
    b. In "The Theologian's Nightmare," the prevailing irony seems to be that Dr. Thaddeus's life and study are misguided, limited, and feeble. Your analysis should follow from that irony.
        (1) Is the point of this attack Dr. Thaddeus, or the metaphysics which he represents?
        (2) What is the importance of the cosmology, with its great size and complexity, this essay sets forward?
        (3) Why all the playfulness with the persons of Heaven, the researchers there, and the immensity of the library?
        (4) What does the literal meaning of the name Thaddeus ("praise," "wise," or "gift of God") have to do with Russell's point?
2. Question 1 above begins by observing that "Nightmares" is not characteristic of essays generally. Many essayists in the nineteenth century, including Lamb, Hazlitt and DeQuincy, practiced a kind of subgenre of the essay known as the "reverie." In our own century the Argentine writer, Jorge Luis Borges, often wrote essays that are mistaken for stories and vice-versa. Barry Lopez's piece, "Buffalo," extends that tradition. What sorts of problems do such genres pose to the reader? Does the reader have the right to feel cheated if he finds halfway through a piece that what he thought were an author's factual statements are simply fantasy? Or is it mere fantasy? Why would Russell, a notoriously outspoken truthseeker, dissemble so? Or were these, in fact, real nightmares? (See question 2b of Rhetorical Analysis.) Would it make a difference to your understanding and enjoyment if they were?

Suggestions for Writing

1. Write a satiric reverie or nightmare—about, say, a college dean, a lawyer, a doctor, or even a parent. Make certain that your satiric intent is clear.
2. Write an essay comparing Russell's "voice" techniques in this essay with Barbara Tuchman's "point of view" technique in "Perdicaris Alive or Raisuli Dead." Which of the two is more realistic? Entertaining? Inspiring? Defend your view with specific details from both essays.
3. Both of the short "dreams" deal with the subject of objectivity, its great value to us, and human nature's rejection of it. Write an essay analyzing that theme and evaluating Russell's implied position.

How I Write

I cannot pretend to know how writing ought to be done, or what a wise critic would advise me to do with a view to improving my own writing. The most that I can do is to relate some things about my own attempts.

Until I was twenty-one, I wished to write more or less in the style of John Stuart Mill. I liked the structure of his sentences and his manner of developing a subject. I had, however, already a different ideal, derived, I suppose, from mathematics. I wished to say everything in the smallest number of words in which it could be said clearly. Perhaps, I thought, one should imitate Baedeker rather than any more literary model. I would spend hours trying to find the shortest way of saying something without ambiguity, and to this aim I was willing to sacrifice all attempts at aesthetic excellence.

At the age of twenty-one, however, I came under a new influence, that of my future brother-in-law, Logan Pearsall Smith. He was at that time exclusively interested in style as opposed to matter. His gods were Flaubert and Walter Pater, and I was quite ready to believe that the way to learn how to write was to copy their technique. He gave me various simple rules, of which I remember only two: "Put a comma every four words," and "never use 'and' except at the beginning of a sentence." His most emphatic advice was that one must always rewrite. I conscientiously tried this, but found that my first draft was almost always better than my second. This discovery has saved me an immense amount of time. I do not, of course, apply it to the substance, but only to the form. When I discover an error of an important kind, I rewrite the whole. What I do not find is that I can improve a sentence when I am satisfied with what it means.

Very gradually I have discovered ways of writing with a minimum of worry and anxiety. When I was young each fresh piece of serious work used to seem to me for a time—perhaps a long time—to be beyond my powers. I would fret myself into a nervous state from fear that it was never going to come right. I would make one unsatisfying attempt after another, and in the end have to discard them all. At last I found that such fumbling attempts were a waste of time. It appeared that after first contemplating a book on some subject, and after giving serious preliminary attention to it, I needed a period of subconscious incubation which could not be hurried and was if anything impeded by deliberate thinking. Sometimes I would find, after a time, that I had made a mistake, and that I could not write the book I had had in mind. But often I was more fortunate. Having, by a time of very intense concentration, planted the problem in my subconsciousness, it would germinate underground until, suddenly, the solution emerged with blinding clarity, so that it only remained to write down what had appeared as if in a revelation.

The most curious example of this process, and the one which led me subsequently to rely upon it, occurred at the beginning of 1914. I had undertaken to give the Lowell Lectures at Boston, and had chosen as my subject "Our Knowledge of the External World." Throughout 1913 I thought about this topic. In term time in my rooms at Cambridge, in vacations in a quiet inn on the upper reaches of the Thames, I concentrated with such intensity that I sometimes forgot to breathe and emerged panting as from a trance. But all to no avail. To every theory that I could think of I could perceive fatal objections. At last, in despair, I went off to Rome for Christmas, hoping that a holiday would revive my flagging energy. I got back to Cambridge on the last day of 1913, and although my difficulties were still completely unresolved I arranged, because the remaining time was short, to dictate as best as I could to a stenographer. Next morning, as she came in at the door, I suddenly saw exactly what I had to say, and proceeded to dictate the whole book without a moment's hesitation.

I do not want to convey an exaggerated impression. The book was very imperfect, and I now think that it contains serious errors. But it was the best that I could have done at that time, and a more leisurely method (within the time at my disposal) would almost certainly have produced something worse. Whatever may be true of other people, this is the right method for me. Flaubert and Pater, I have found, are best forgotten so far as I am concerned.

Although what I now think about how to write is not so very different from what I thought at the age of eighteen, my development has not been by any means rectilinear. There was a time, in the first years of this century, when I had more florid and rhetorical ambitions. This was the time when I wrote *A Free Man's Worship*, a work of which I do not now think well. At that time I was steeped in Milton's prose, and his rolling periods reverberated through the caverns of my mind. I cannot say that I no longer admire them, but for me to imitate them involves a certain insincerity. In fact, all imitation is dangerous. Nothing could be better in style than the Prayer Book and the Authorized Version of the Bible, but they express a way of thinking and feeling which is different from that of our time. A style is not good unless it is an intimate and almost involuntary expression of the personality of the writer, and then only if the writer's personality is worth expressing. But although direct imitation is always to be deprecated, there is much to be gained by familiarity with good prose, especially in cultivating a sense for prose rhythm.

There are some simple maxims—not perhaps quite so simple as those which my brother-in-law Logan Pearsall Smith offered me—which I think might be commended to writers of expository prose. First: never use a long word if a short word will do. Second: if you want to make a statement with a great many qualifications, put some of the qualifications in separate sentences. Third: do not let the beginning of your sentence lead the reader to an expectation which is contradicted by the end. Take, say, such a sentence as the following, which might occur in a work on sociology: "Human beings are completely exempt from undesirable behavior patterns only when certain prerequisites, not satisfied except in a small percentage of actual cases, have, through some fortuitous concourse of favorable circumstances, whether congenital or environmental, chanced to combine in producing an individual in whom many factors deviate from the norm in a socially advantageous manner." Let us see if we can translate this sentence into English. I suggest the following: "All men are scoundrels, or at any rate almost all. The men who are not must have had unusual luck, both in their birth and in their upbringing." This is shorter and more intelligible, and says just the same thing. But I am afraid any professor who used the second sentence instead of the first would get the sack.

This suggests a word of advice to such of my readers as may happen to be professors. I am allowed to use plain English because everybody knows that I could use mathematical logic if I chose. Take the statement: "Some people marry their deceased wives' sisters." I can express this in language which only becomes intelligible after years of study, and this gives me freedom. I suggest to young professors that their first work should be written in a jargon only to be understood by the erudite few. With that behind them, they can ever after say what they have to say in a language "understanded of the people." In these days, when our very lives are at the mercy of the professors, I cannot but think that they would deserve our gratitude if they adopted my advice. 9

Rhetorical Analysis

1. "We are born on earth only once," says the Nobel-prize-winning writer, Czeslaw Milosz, "and we indulge in much mimicking and posing, dimly aware of the truth." But Milosz immediately adds that "with pen in hand it is difficult to escape that awareness: then, at least, one wants to keep one's self-respect."
   a. How does Russell, through his title and comments in the essay, persuade the reader that "How I Write" is an effort to be fully truthful, to avoid any kind of posing?
   b. Consider the second sentence in ¶ 4. What devices of language are used by Russell to express accurately and honestly, the situation he is describing? Read other sentences with this question in mind: what kinds of language are needed to express the truth? (Compare Orwell's analysis in "Politics and the English Language" of the ways language distorts the truth!)
   c. If Milosz is correct, then writers gain self-respect to the degree they avoid posing. But what if the subject is a writer's own life and that life has disrespectful episodes in it? Study how Russell writes of his embarrassing moments. Does he gain or lose the *reader's* respect by his candor?
2. Russell alludes to six examples of writing style: the King James version of the Bible, John Stuart Mill, Gustave Flaubert, Walter Pater, the academician Logan Pearsall Smith, and the publications of the famous travel firm of Baedecker. Select one of these and study a few passages. Stylistically, how are they different from Russell's writing? What does he achieve distinctly of his own?

Intellectual Analysis

1. Russell says some striking things about his methods, most of which seem to contradict what is now often taught concerning the writing process. On closer reading, however, we see that his position may not be as radical as it first appears.
    a. Contrary to what we are told about the value of revision, Russell says that his first draft is "almost always better than my second." Yet notice that he rewrites "the whole" if he discovers any important error (¶ 3), and that, before writing anything at all, he "plants" the idea in his subconscious for a period of "intense concentration" (¶ 4). What do these procedures reveal about the kind or amount of revision in Russell's technique (note especially the image of planting)?
    b. In another statement that seems to discount revision, Russell insists that he cannot improve a sentence "when I am satisfied with what it means" (¶ 3). What does this actually say about revision, style, and sense?
    c. With respect to the 1914 Lowell lectures, Russell says they were the best he could do "at that time." What does this add to what we know about Russell's notion of composition?
    d. Finally, in a comment that reverses a time-honored method of learning to write, Russell says that "imitation is always to be deprecated" (¶ 7). But how much does he qualify that statement?
        (1) How does that statement square with the history of his own writing development?
        (2) How does Russell's comment tally with the importance he places on reading "good prose" and on his insistence that a good style must be "an intimate and almost involuntary expression of personality"?
2. Russell offers some advice to all writers, and especially to professors.
    a. In ¶ 8 his three suggestions seem rather plain. Are they more comprehensive than they appear? (Compare them with Orwell's in "Politics and the English Language.")
    b. In ¶ 9 Russell's advice to professors seems, on first reading anyway, rather cynical and tangential to the rest of the essay. By "mathematical logic" Russell refers to his early book with Whitehead, which represented his hope that, compared to ordinary language, a new language of mathematical signs might lead to "certain knowledge." This last paragraph addresses three concerns that, it turns out, underlie the whole essay: language, truth, and style. What does this last paragraph say, then, to summarize Russell's view of these three?

Suggestions for Writing

1. Write your own autobiographical essay, using Russell's title and his insistence on telling the truth.

2. Select another complex skill, besides writing, that you have learned or are in the process of learning. Describe honestly and fully the way you actually learned it, comparing that process with the ideal or conventional notions about how it should be learned, as given forth by parents, "how-to books," or teachers.
3. Russell's comments about writing are so simple they make other discussions about writing, as in textbooks, seem pale and artificial. Write an essay critiquing the academic approach to learning the art of writing.

"Useless" Knowledge

Francis Bacon, a man who rose to eminence by betraying his friends, asserted, no doubt as one of the ripe lessons of experience, that "knowledge is power." But this is not true of *all* knowledge. Sir Thomas Browne wished to know what song the sirens sang, but if he had ascertained this it would not have enabled him to rise from being a magistrate to being High Sheriff of his county. The sort of knowledge that Bacon had in mind was that which we call scientific. In emphasizing the importance of science, he was belatedly carrying on the tradition of the Arabs and the early Middle Ages, according to which knowledge consisted mainly of astrology, alchemy, and pharmacology, all of which were branches of science. A learned man was one who, having mastered these studies, had acquired magical powers. In the early eleventh century, Pope Silvester II, for no reason except that he read books, was universally believed to be a magician in league with the devil. Prospero, who in Shakespeare's time was a mere phantasy, represented what had been for centuries the generally received conception of a learned man, so far at least as his powers of sorcery were concerned. Bacon believed—rightly, as we now know—that science could provide a more powerful magician's wand than any that had been dreamed of by the necromancers of former ages.

The Renaissance, which was at its height in England at the time of Bacon, involved a revolt against the utilitarian conception of knowledge. The Greeks had acquired a familiarity with Homer, as we do with music-hall songs, because they enjoyed him, and without feeling that they were engaged in the pursuit of learning. But the men of the sixteenth century could not begin to understand him without first absorbing a very considerable amount of linguistic erudition. They admired the Greeks, and did not wish to be shut out from their pleasures; they therefore copied them, both in reading the classics and in other less avowable ways. Learning, in the Renaissance, was part of the *joie de vivre*, just as much as drinking or love-making. And this was true not only of literature, but also of sterner studies. Every one knows the story of Hobbes's first contact with Euclid: opening the book, by chance, at the theorem of Pythagoras, he exclaimed, "By God, this is impossible," and proceeded to read the proofs backwards until, reaching the axioms, he became convinced. No one can doubt that this was for him a voluptuous moment, unsullied by the thought of the utility of geometry in measuring fields.

It is true that the Renaissance found a practical use for the ancient languages in connection with theology. One of the earliest results of the new feeling for classical Latin was the discrediting of the forged decretals and the donation of Constantine. The inaccuracies which were discovered in the Vulgate and the Septuagint made Greek and Hebrew a necessary part of the controversial equipment of Protestant divines. The republican maxims of Greece and Rome were invoked to justify the resistance of Puritans to the Stuarts and of Jesuits to monarchs who had thrown off allegiance to the Pope. But all this was an effect, rather than a cause, of the revival of classical learning, which had been in full swing in Italy for nearly a century before Luther. The main motive of the Renaissance was mental delight, the restoration of a certain richness and freedom in art and speculation which had been lost while ignorance and superstition kept the mind's eye in blinkers.

The Greeks, it was found, had devoted a part of their attention to matters not purely literary or artistic, such as philosophy, geometry, and astronomy. These studies, therefore, were respectable, but other sciences were more open to question. Medicine, it was true, was dignified by the names of Hippocrates and Galen; but in the intervening period it had become almost confined to Arabs and Jews, and inextricably intertwined with magic. Hence the dubious reputation of such men as Paracelsus. Chemistry was in even worse odor, and hardly became respectable until the eighteenth century.

In this way it was brought about that knowledge of Greek and Latin, with a smattering of geometry and perhaps astronomy, came to be considered the intellectual equipment of a gentleman. The Greeks disdained the practical applications of geometry, and it was only in their decadence that they found a use for astronomy in the guise of astrology. The sixteenth and seventeenth centuries, in the main, studied mathematics with Hellenic disinterestedness, and tended to ignore the sciences which had been degraded by their connection with sorcery. A gradual change towards a wider and more practical conception of knowledge, which was going on throughout the eighteenth century, was suddenly accelerated at the end of that period by the French Revolution and the growth of machinery, of which the former gave a blow to gentlemanly culture while the latter offered new and astonishing scope for the exercise of ungentlemanly skill. Throughout the last hundred and fifty years, men have questioned more and more vigorously the value of "useless" knowledge, and have come increasingly to believe that the only knowledge worth having is that which is applicable to some part of the economic life of the community.

In countries such as France and England, which have a traditional educational system, the utilitarian view of knowledge has only partially prevailed. There are still, for example, professors of Chinese in the universities who read the Chinese classics but are unacquainted with the works of Sun Yat-sen, which created modern China. There are still men who know ancient history in so far as it was related by authors whose style was pure, that is to say, up to Alexander in Greece and Nero in Rome, but refuse to know the much more important later history because of the literary inferiority of the historians who related it. Even in France and England, however, the old tradition is dying, and in more up-to-date countries, such as Russia and the United States, it is utterly extinct. In America, for example, educational commissions point out that fifteen hundred words are all that most people employ in business correspondence, and therefore suggest that all others should be avoided in the school curriculum. Basic English, a British invention, goes still further, and reduces the necessary vocabulary to eight hundred words. The conception of speech as something capable of aesthetic value is dying out, and it is coming to be thought that the sole purpose of words is to convey practical information. In Russia the pursuit of practical aims is even more whole-hearted than in America: all that is taught in educational institutions is intended to serve some obvious purpose in education or government. The only escape is afforded by theology: the sacred Scriptures must be studied by some in the original German, and a few professors must learn philosophy in order to defend dialectical materialism against the criticisms of bourgeois metaphysicians. But as orthodoxy becomes more firmly established, even this tiny loophole will be closed.

Knowledge, everywhere, is coming to be regarded not as a good in itself, or as a means of creating a broad and humane outlook on life in general, but as merely an ingredient in technical skill. This is part of the greater integration of society which has been brought about by scientific technique and military necessity. There is more economic and political interdependence than there was in former times, and therefore there is more social pressure to compel a man to live in a way that his neighbors think useful. Educational establishments, except those for the very rich, or (in England) such as have become invulnerable through antiquity, are not allowed to spend their money as they like, but must satisfy the State that they are serving a useful purpose by imparting skill and instilling loyalty. This is part and parcel of the same movement which has led to compulsory military service, boy scouts, the organization of political parties, and the dissemination of political passion by the Press. We are all more aware of our fellow-citizens than we used to be, more anxious, if we are virtuous, to do them good, and in any case to make them do us good. We do not like to think of any one lazily enjoying life, however refined may be the quality of his enjoyment. We feel that everybody ought to be doing something to help on the great cause (whatever it may be), the more so as so many bad men are working against it and ought to be stopped. We have not leisure of mind, therefore, to acquire any knowledge except such as will help us in the fight for whatever it may happen to be that we think important.

There is much to be said for the narrowly utilitarian view of education. There is not time to learn everything before beginning to make a living, and undoubtedly "useful" knowledge is *very* useful. It has made the modern world. Without it, we should not have machines or motor cars or railways or aeroplanes; it should be added that we should not have modern advertising or modern propaganda. Modern knowledge has brought about an immense improvement in average health, and at the same time has discovered how to exterminate large cities by poison gas. Whatever is distinctive of our world, as compared with former times, has its source in "useful" knowledge. No community as yet has enough of it, and undoubtedly education must continue to promote it.

It must also be admitted that a great deal of the traditional cultural education was foolish. Boys spent many years acquiring Latin and Greek grammar, without being, at the end, either capable or desirous (except in a small percentage of cases) of reading a Greek or

Latin author. Modern languages and history are preferable, from every point of view, to Latin and Greek. They are not only more useful, but they give much more culture in much less time. For an Italian of the fifteenth century, since practically everything worth reading, if not in his own language, was in Greek or Latin, these languages were the indispensable keys to culture. But since that time great literatures have grown up in various modern languages, and the development of civilization has been so rapid that knowledge of antiquity has become much less useful in understanding our problems than knowledge of modern nations and their comparatively recent history. The traditional schoolmaster's point of view, which was admirable at the time of the Revival of Learning, became gradually unduly narrow, since it ignored what the world has done since the fifteenth century. And not only history and modern languages, but science also, when properly taught, contributes to culture. It is therefore possible to maintain that education should have other aims than direct utility, without defending the traditional curriculum. Utility and culture, when both are conceived broadly, are found to be less incompatible than they appear to the fanatical advocates of either.

10 Apart, however, from the cases in which culture and direct utility can be combined, there is indirect utility, of various different kinds, in the possession of knowledge which does not contribute to technical efficiency. I think some of the worst features of the modern world could be improved by a greater encouragement of such knowledge and a less ruthless pursuit of mere professional competence.

11 When conscious activity is wholly concentrated on some one definite purpose, the ultimate result, for most people, is lack of balance accompanied by some form of nervous disorder. The men who directed German policy during the War made mistakes, for example, as regards the submarine campaign which brought America on to the side of the Allies, which any person coming fresh to the subject could have seen to be unwise, but which they could not judge sanely owing to mental concentration and lack of holidays. The same sort of thing may be seen wherever bodies of men attempt tasks which put a prolonged strain upon spontaneous impulses. Japanese Imperialists, Russian Communists, and German Nazis all have a kind of tense fanaticism which comes of living too exclusively in the mental world of certain tasks to be accomplished. When the tasks are as important and as feasible as the fanatics suppose, the result may be magnificent; but in most cases narrowness of outlook has caused oblivion of some power-

ful counteracting force, or has made all such forces seem the work of the devil, to be met by punishment and terror. Men as well as children have need of play, that is to say, of periods of activity having no purpose beyond present enjoyment. But if play is to serve its purpose, it must be possible to find pleasure and interest in matters not connected with work.

12   The amusements of modern urban populations tend more and more to be passive and collective, and to consist of inactive observation of the skilled activities of others. Undoubtedly such amusements are much better than none, but they are not as good as would be those of a population which had, through education, a wider range of intelligent interests not connected with work. Better economic organization, allowing mankind to benefit by the productivity of machines, should lead to a very great increase of leisure, and much leisure is apt to be tedious except to those who have considerable intelligent activities and interests. If a leisured population is to be happy, it must be an educated population, and must be educated with a view to mental enjoyment as well as to the direct usefulness of technical knowledge.

13   The cultural element in the acquisition of knowledge, when it is successfully assimilated, forms the character of a man's thoughts and desires, making them concern themselves, in part at least, with large impersonal objects, not only with matters of immediate importance to himself. It has been too readily assumed that, when a man has acquired certain capacities by means of knowledge, he will use them in ways that are socially beneficial. The narrowly utilitarian conception of education ignores the necessity of training a man's purposes as well as his skill. There is in untrained human nature a very considerable element of cruelty, which shows itself in many ways, great and small. Boys at school tend to be unkind to a new boy, or to one whose clothes are not quite conventional. Many women (and not a few men) inflict as much pain as they can by means of malicious gossip. The Spaniards enjoy bullfights; the British enjoy hunting and shooting. The same cruel impulses take more serious forms in the hunting of Jews in Germany and kulaks in Russia. All imperialism affords scope for them, and in war they become sanctified as the highest form of public duty.

14   Now while it must be admitted that highly educated people are sometimes cruel, I think there can be no doubt that they are less often so than people whose minds have lain fallow. The bully in a school is seldom a boy whose proficiency in learning is up to the average. When a lynching takes place, the ringleaders are almost invariably very

ignorant men. This is not because mental cultivation produces positive humanitarian feelings, though it may do so; it is rather because it gives other interests than the ill-treatment of neighbors, and other sources of self-respect than the assertion of domination. The two things most universally desired are power and admiration. Ignorant men can, as a rule, only achieve either by brutal means, involving the acquisition of physical mastery. Culture gives a man less harmful forms of power and more deserving ways of making himself admired. Galileo did more than any monarch has done to change the world, and his power immeasurably exceeded that of his persecutors. He had therefore no need to aim at becoming a persecutor in his turn.

Perhaps the most important advantage of "useless" knowledge is that it promotes a contemplative habit of mind. There is in the world much too much readiness, not only for action without adequate previous reflection, but also for some sort of action on occasions on which wisdom would counsel inaction. People show their bias on this matter in various curious ways. Mephistopheles tells the young student that theory is gray but the tree of life is green, and every one quotes this as if it were Goethe's opinion, instead of what he supposes the devil would be likely to say to an undergraduate. Hamlet is held up as an awful warning against thought without action, but no one holds up Othello as a warning against action without thought. Professors such as Bergson, from a kind of snobbery towards the practical man, decry philosophy, and say that life at its best should resemble a cavalry charge. For my part, I think action is best when it emerges from a profound apprehension of the universe and human destiny, not from some wildly passionate impulse of romantic but disproportioned self-assertion. A habit of finding pleasure in thought rather than in action is a safeguard against unwisdom and excessive love of power, a means of preserving serenity in misfortune and peace of mind among worries. A life confined to what is personal is likely, sooner or later, to become unbearably painful; it is only by windows into a larger and less fretful cosmos that the more tragic parts of life become endurable.

A contemplative habit of mind has advantages ranging from the most trivial to the most profound. To begin with minor vexations, such as fleas, missing trains, or cantankerous business associates. Such troubles seem hardly worthy to be met by reflections on the excellence of heroism or the transitoriness of all human ills, and yet the irritation to which they give rise destroys many people's good temper and enjoyment of life. On such occasions, there is much consolation to be found in out-of-the-way bits of knowledge which have some real or fancied connection with the trouble of the moment; or even if they have none, they serve to obliterate the present from one's thoughts. When assailed by people who are white with fury, it is pleasant to remember the chapter in Descartes' *Treatise on the Passions* entitled "Why those who grow pale with rage are more to be feared than those who grow red." When one feels impatient over the difficulty of securing international coöperation, one's impatience is diminished if one happens to think of the sainted King Louis IX, before embarking on his crusade, allying himself with the Old Man of the Mountain, who appears in the Arabian Nights as the dark source of half the wickedness in the world. When the rapacity of capitalists grows oppressive, one may be suddenly consoled by the recollection that Brutus, that exemplar of republican virtue, lent money to a city at 40 per cent, and hired a private army to besiege it when it failed to pay the interest.

Curious learning not only makes unpleasant things less unpleasant, but also makes pleasant things more pleasant. I have enjoyed peaches and apricots more since I have known that they were first cultivated in China in the early days of the Han dynasty; that Chinese hostages held by the great King Kaniska introduced them into India, whence they spread to Persia, reaching the Roman Empire in the first century of our era; that the word "apricot" is derived from the same Latin source as the word "precocious," because the apricot ripens early; and that the A at the beginning was added by mistake, owing to a false etymology. All this makes the fruit taste much sweeter.

About a hundred years ago, a number of well-meaning philanthropists started societies "for the diffusion of useful knowledge," with the result that people have ceased to appreciate the delicious savor of "useless" knowledge. Opening Burton's *Anatomy of Melancholy* at haphazard on a day when I was threatened by that mood, I learnt that there is a "melancholy matter," but that, while some think it may be engendered of all four humors, "Galen holds that it may be engendered of three alone, excluding phlegm or pituita, whose true assertion Valerius and Menardus stiffly maintain, and so doth Fuscius, Montaltus, Montanus. How (say they) can white become black?" In spite of this unanswerable argument, Hercules de Saxonia and Cardan, Guianerius and Laurentius, are (so Burton tells us) of the opposite opinion. Soothed by these historical reflections, my melancholy, whether due to three humors or to four, was dissipated. As a cure for too much zeal, I can imagine few measures more effective than a course of such ancient controversies.

19   But while the trivial pleasures of culture have their place as a relief from the trivial worries of practical life, the more important merits of contemplation are in relation to the greater evils of life, death and pain and cruelty, and the blind march of nations into unnecessary disaster. For those to whom dogmatic religion can no longer bring comfort, there is need of some substitute, if life is not to become dusty and harsh and filled with trivial self-assertion. The world at present is full of angry self-centered groups, each incapable of viewing human life as a whole, each willing to destroy civilization rather than yield an inch. To this narrowness no amount of technical instruction will provide an antidote. The antidote, in so far as it is matter of individual psychology, is to be found in history, biology, astronomy, and all those studies which, without destroying self-respect, enable the individual to see himself in his proper perspective. What is needed is not this or that specific piece of information, but such knowledge as inspires a conception of the ends of human life as a whole: art and history, acquaintance with the lives of heroic individuals, and some understanding of the strangely accidental and ephemeral position of man in the cosmos—all this touched with an emotion of pride in what is distinctly human, the power to see and to know, to feel magnanimously and to think with understanding. It is from large perceptions combined with impersonal emotion that wisdom most readily springs.

20   Life, at all times full of pain, is more painful in our time than in the two centuries that preceded it. The attempt to escape from pain drives men to triviality, to self-deception, to the invention of vast collective myths. But these momentary alleviations do but increase the sources of suffering in the long run. Both private and public misfortune can only be mastered by a process in which will and intelligence interact: the part of will is to refuse to shirk the evil or accept an unreal solution, while the part of intelligence is to understand it, to find a cure if it is curable, and, if not, to make it bearable by seeing it in its relations, accepting it as unavoidable, and remembering what lies outside it in other regions, other ages, and the abysses of interstellar space.

Rhetorical Analysis

1. The mode of this essay is primarily argumentative. Russell has a controversial point to argue, and he hopes to bring enough evidence to bear upon it to convince his readers. Why then does he delay the point he wants to prove until the tenth

paragraph? What use are the nine preceding paragraphs? Would you have found the essay easier to understand if he had stated his thesis at the beginning of the essay?

2. Generally speaking, Russell's paragraphs form logical units. The shape that each paragraph takes—its length, its internal movement—is determined by its contribution to the argument. It is worthwhile to outline several of Russell's paragraphs, to witness the subtle skills of a master logician and writer. Look in particular for such choices as where he states the main point, which points he substantiates, how much proof he includes, where he puts in or leaves out logical connectives, where he qualifies or restates or admits reservations, and so on.

3. Russell's sense of shape (he might like to call it nonutilitarian) also shows itself at the level of the sentence. Frequently he constructs sentence patterns elegant and classical in their complex, balanced rhythms. The style of the essay may seem excessively formal, but it can be adapted successfully to informal patterns. Perhaps the quickest way to appreciate Russell's sentence craft is to write some of your own. Recreate some of his more complex sentences by transferring his syntax to your own content. Replace adjective with adjective, noun with noun, verb with verb—but retain prepositions, pronouns, and connectives. Where Russell repeats a word in his sentence, be sure to repeat the word you have substituted. Thus, the second sentence of ¶ 15 might be rewritten, "There is in the government much too much desire, not only for taxation without clear public support, but also for some sort of taxation in programs for which people would demand non-taxation."

Intellectual Analysis

1. " 'Useless' Knowledge" was first published in 1935, so you should first ask whether Russell's argument is still valid. If it is, one reason might be the author's intellectual detachment. Throughout this essay one glimpses the tone and stance of an intellect trying to examine a complicated problem in an unbiased way. Russell is not out to defend old against new, or humanism against science, without reason or justification. To get at this point directly, look for spots (such as ¶ 9) where Russell's scrutiny seems especially even-handed. Look for places where you think he may have exaggerated or overstated the truth. On balance, what is your assessment of Russell's relative fairness?

2. How does Russell move from a seemingly frivolous topic, such as useless knowledge, to national and international politics? You might begin by carefully examining ¶ 11. Consider his remarks on fanaticism: presumably fanaticism can be for utility or its opposite. What, then, is he advocating?

3. Consider Russell's theory of leisure—how he thinks it ought to be spent, and how, increasingly, it is spent: "The amusements of modern urban populations tend more and more to be passive and collective. . . ." What else is implied here? Less individuality and greater conformity? Does this implication match his earlier

comments on what we demand of education in terms of utility? (See ¶ 7 for a start.) Are there passages connected by the idea of conformity in people?

4. Ponder Russell's argument that a "contemplative habit of mind" is the "most important advantage of 'useless' knowledge" (¶ 15). How does the one feed the other? Why contemplation over action? (The whole of this paragraph is, in fact, rich with implication.)

5. Consider the possible extensions of meaning in Russell's statement: "It is only by windows into a larger and less fretful cosmos that the more tragic parts of life become endurable." Russell uses two metaphors here—"windows" and "cosmos"—the implications of which ought to lead to some discussion of the mind of man, and what constitutes a properly human pursuit.

Suggestions for Writing

1. Argue, in an essay of your own, for or against one of the many controversial assertions in Russell's essay, perhaps one of those referred to above. Here are two possibilities: "As a cure for too much zeal, I can imagine few measures more effective than a course of such ancient controversies" (¶ 18); and, "The world at present is full of angry self-centered groups, each incapable of viewing human life as a whole, each willing to destroy civilization rather than yield an inch" (¶ 19).

2. Russell contends (¶ 14) that highly educated people are less likely to be cruel. Does this contradict what he has been arguing? Write an essay in which you discuss his assertion.

3. Write an essay in which you treat the subject of leisure time. Take Russell's comments (see ¶ 12) as a point of departure.

BARBARA TUCHMAN

The historian Barbara Tuchman comes from a family that has itself made part of the history of the twentieth century. Her grandfather, Henry Morgenthau, Sr., was President Woodrow Wilson's ambassador to Turkey. Her uncle, Henry Morgenthau, Jr., was Franklin Roosevelt's secretary of the treasury and later the chairman of the United Jewish Appeal, when it was collecting donations for the survival of the state of Israel (1947–1950). But Tuchman has performed a different kind of public service. She has written history not merely for politicians and other historians, but for "general readers" who are sometimes given lip service but usually ignored. Her own interest in history was spurred, she says, not by discovery in the classroom, but by her reading of Dumas' historical novels and Conan Doyle's The White Company—"fourteenth-century mercenaries fighting for popes and princes." Sometime later she accompanied her parents to Europe and, in France, she says, "went to the Loire, and to Blois, and I suddenly recognized rooms in which Dumas characters had actually lived, or been murdered. The rooms themselves, the room of the Duc de Guise!" The energy released by that early recognition still crackles in her most recent books.

Tuchman attained her eminence as a historian by means characteristic of the nineteenth century but unusual in our own. That is, she apprenticed as a journalist, not as an academic. After Radcliffe (B.A., 1933), she worked as a research assistant in the Tokyo offices of the Institute of Public Relations. She returned to America in 1935 via Moscow, by way of the Trans-Siberian railway, and Paris—and then traveled to Spain in 1936 to cover the civil war there for the liberal magazine, the Nation. (Her father had recently bought the magazine to keep it from bankruptcy.) Then came marriage, the raising of three daughters, and in 1956 her first major historical work, The Bible and the Sword, on British relations in Palestine from the time of the Crusades to the present. A series of increasingly popular works followed: in 1958 The Zimmermann Telegram (on World War I); in 1962 The Guns of August (on August, 1914, and the outbreak of World War I); in 1966 The Proud Tower (on the prelude to the war); in 1978 A Distant Mirror (on fourteenth-century Europe); and in 1984 The March of Folly.

Tuchman's early journalistic experience is clearly evident in her writing. She has been criticized for making history seem too much like a cracking good yarn. But while her narratives captivate the imagination, they also record solid and credible history. "Perdicaris Alive or Raisuli Dead" presents Tuchman at her best. Her recreation makes these events seem as fresh as today's news, without the disadvantage of undigested fact or ephemeral event. What she combines is not only the artistry of the poet and the historian's knowledge of before and after, but also the ironist's clear eye for the gaps between intention and action that make up so much of history. While history, of course, includes all of us, Tuchman's effort to make it popular in the retelling confirms Oscar Wilde's wry assertion in "The Critic as Artist": "Anyone can make history, but only a great person can write it." Great or not, she has written best-sellers, won two Pulitzer prizes, and gained the esteem of fellow historians and politicians as well.

ON OUR BIRTHDAY—AMERICA AS IDEA

The United States is a nation consciously conceived, not one that evolved slowly out of an ancient past. It was a planned idea of democracy, of liberty of conscience and pursuit of happiness. It was the promise of equality of opportunity and individual freedom within a just social order, as opposed to the restrictions and repressions of the Old World. In contrast to the militarism of Europe, it would renounce

1

standing armies and "sheathe the desolating sword of war." It was an experiment in Utopia to test the thesis that, given freedom, independence, and local self-government, people, in Kossuth's words, "will in due time ripen into all the excellence and all the dignity of humanity." It was a new life for the oppressed, it was enlightenment, it was optimism.

Regardless of hypocrisy and corruption, of greed, chicanery, brutality, and all the other bad habits man carries with him whether in the New World or Old, the founding idea of the United States remained, on the whole, dominant through the first hundred years. With reservations, it was believed in by Americans, by visitors who came to aid our Revolution or later to observe our progress, by immigrants who came by the hundreds of thousands to escape an intolerable situation in their native lands.

The idea shaped our politics, our institutions, and to some extent our national character, but it was never the only influence at work. Material circumstances exerted an opposing force. The open frontier, the hardships of homesteading from scratch, the wealth of natural resources, the whole vast challenge of a continent waiting to be exploited, combined to produce a prevailing materialism and an American drive bent as much, if not more, on money, property, and power than was true of the Old World from which we had fled. The human resources we drew upon were significant: Every wave of immigration brought here those people who had the extra energy, gumption, or restlessness to uproot themselves and cross an unknown ocean to seek a better life. Two other factors entered the shaping process—the shadow of slavery and the destruction of the native Indian.

At its Centennial the United States was a material success. Through its second century the idea and the success have struggled in continuing conflict. The Statue of Liberty, erected in 1886, still symbolized the promise to those "yearning to breathe free." Hope, to them, as seen by a foreign visitor, was "domiciled in America as the Pope is in Rome." But slowly in the struggle the idea lost ground, and at a turning point around 1900, with American acceptance of a rather half-hearted imperialism, it lost dominance. Increasingly invaded since then by self-doubt and disillusion, it survives in the disenchantment of today, battered and crippled but not vanquished.

What has happened to the United States in the twentieth century is not a peculiarly American phenomenon but a part of the experience of the West. In the Middle Ages plague, wars, and social violence were seen as God's punishment upon man for his sins. If the concept of God can be taken as man's conscience, the same explanation may be applicable today. Our sins in the twentieth century—greed, violence, inhumanity—have been profound, with the result that the pride and self-confidence of the nineteenth century have turned to dismay and self-disgust.

In the United States we have a society pervaded from top to bottom by contempt for the law. Government—including the agencies of law enforcement—business, labor, students, the military, the poor no less than the rich, outdo each other in breaking the rules and violating the ethics that society has established for its protection. The average citizen, trying to hold a footing in standards of morality and conduct he once believed in, is daily knocked over by incoming waves of venality, vulgarity, irresponsibility, ignorance, ugliness, and trash in all senses of the word. Our government collaborates abroad with the worst enemies of humanity and liberty. It wastes our substance on useless proliferation of military hardware that can never buy security no matter how high the pile. It learns no lessons, employs no wisdom, and corrupts all who succumb to Potomac fever.

Yet the idea does not die. Americans are not passive under their faults. We expose them and combat them. Somewhere every day some group is fighting a public abuse—openly and, on the whole, notwithstanding the FBI, with confidence in the First Amendment. The U.S. has slid a long way from the original idea. Nevertheless, somewhere between Gulag Archipelago and the featherbed of cradle-to-the-grave welfare, it still offers a greater opportunity for social happiness—that is to say, for well-being combined with individual freedom and initiative—than is likely elsewhere. The ideal society for which mankind has been striving through the ages will remain forever beyond our grasp. But if the great question, whether it is still possible to reconcile democracy with social order and individual liberty, is to find a positive answer, it will be here.

6

7

Rhetorical Analysis

1. "On Our Birthday" appeared in *Newsweek*, July 12, 1976, at the time of our nation's Bicentennial. Its topic clearly fits the occasion, but how Tuchman has used that fit rhetorically is neither simple nor obvious. Study ¶s 1, 4, and 7 closely, and analyze the subtle connections between occasion and topic.

2. Giving shape to this short essay is an appropriately brief but very powerful rhetorical and intellectual scheme. It is a framework that structures much modern discourse: dialectic.
   a. A dialectic moves through three stages, each with *its* own name:
      (1) An initial position or state (the *thesis*).
      (2) A second position or state in opposition or conflict with the first one (the *antithesis*).
      (3) A third position or state, resolving the conflict of the previous two, and blending elements of both to create a new position or state (the *synthesis*).
   Identify the thesis, antithesis, and synthesis of Tuchman's essay.
   b. This kind of logic may operate with opposed attitudes, or emotions. In this piece, Tuchman's unabashed idealism is balanced by her realistic assessment of American culture. Look, for example, at the opening of ¶ 2, or at the opening of ¶ 5 (where the argument broadens). Find other such elements of balance, and determine how they are synthesized.
   c. How else does Tuchman clue the reader to dialectical structures and strategies? How else does she reason dialectically to solve problems?
3. Tuchman's essay was probably commissioned by *Newsweek* a few months *before* its Bicentennial issue. Here is what one might expect if the topic were forced on the average citizen:
   a. Unsupported generalities.
   b. Syrupy patriotism.
   c. Hackneyed ideas.
   But, rhetorically, how has Tuchman avoided these dangers?

Intellectual Analysis

1. Though this essay is short, it deals in history, social philosophy, and psychology all at once.
   a. Where do these subjects, and others, occur in Tuchman's piece?
   b. Do you think that addressing such huge concerns in a short piece forces Tuchman to be simplistic? If not, how does she avoid it?
2. As noted above, the basic logic and structure and strategy of this essay is dialectical. The fundamental clash of opposites is between "the idea" of the country, and the "opposing force" of "material circumstances" (¶ 3).
   a. What, precisely, are these "circumstances" which oppose the "idea of America," and what have been their effects?
   b. How does Tuchman extend this basic dialectical opposition through the rest of the essay? For example, note that material circumstances translates into "contempt for the law" in ¶ 5.
   c. These fundamental opposites reached, in Tuchman's opinion, a "turning point" about 1900. What does she have in mind? What clues does she give?
   d. Does "On Our Birthday" really describe a synthesis which has actually

occurred, or is that synthesis merely stated as a proposal or dream for the future? Notice the phrase "continuing conflict" in ¶ 4.
3. "Yet the idea does not die" (¶ 7). Can Tuchman make that assertion? A great many other questions ought to surface in answering that question. For example, do we "expose our faults and face them"? Do we have "confidence" in the First Amendment? What about the "great question" with which she ends?

Suggestions for Writing

1. The newspaper or magazine editorial is a familiar genre of the short essay. Most people probably attempt to write one at some time or other. Choose a subject of current popular interest and write an editorial or "Letter to the Editor," but think of it as facing possible publication. Remember that editorials are short, often of a specified length. Study some published models before you begin.
2. Write a short essay under the title, "This University (or College) as Idea," and present your argument dialectically, as in Tuchman's essay.

THE HISTORIAN AS ARTIST

I would like to share some good news with you. I recently came back from skiing at Aspen, where on one occasion I shared the double-chair ski-lift with an advertising man from Chicago. He told me he was in charge of all copy for his firm in all media: TV, radio, *and* the printed word. On the strength of this he assured me—and I quote—that "Writing is coming back. *Books* are coming back." I cannot tell you how pleased I was, and I knew you would be too.

Now that we know that the future is safe for writing, I want to talk about a particular kind of writer—the Historian—not just as historian but as artist; that is, as a creative writer on the same level as the poet or novelist. What follows will sound less immodest if you will take the word "artist" in the way I think of it, not as a form of praise but as a category, like clerk or laborer or actor.

Why is it generally assumed that in writing, the creative process is the exclusive property of poets and novelists? I would like to suggest that the thought applied by the historian to his subject matter can be no less creative than the imagination applied by the novelist to his. And when it comes to writing as an art, is Gibbon necessarily less of an artist in words than, let us say, Dickens? Or Winston Churchill less so than William Faulkner or Sinclair Lewis?

George Macaulay Trevelyan, the late professor of modern history at Cambridge and the great champion of literary as opposed to scientific history, said in a famous essay on his muse that ideally history should be the exposition of facts about the past, "in their full emotional and intellectual value to a wide public by the difficult art of literature." Notice "wide public." Trevelyan always stressed writing for the general reader as opposed to writing just for fellow scholars because he knew that when you write for the public you have to be *clear* and you have to be *interesting* and these are the two criteria which make for good writing. He had no patience with the idea that only imaginative writing is literature. Novels, he pointed out, if they are bad enough, are *not* literature, while even pamphlets, if they are good enough, and he cites those of Milton, Swift, and Burke, are.

The "difficult art of literature" is well said. Trevelyan was a dirt farmer in that field and he knew. I may as well admit now that I have always *felt* like an artist when I work on a book but I did not think I ought to say so until someone else said it first (it's like waiting to be proposed to). Now that an occasional reviewer here and there has made the observation, I feel I can talk about it. I see no reason why the word should always be confined to writers of fiction and poetry while the rest of us are lumped together under that despicable term "Nonfiction"—as if we were some sort of remainder. I do not feel like a Non-something; I feel quite specific. I wish I could think of a name in place of "Nonfiction." In the hope of finding an antonym I looked up "Fiction" in Webster and found it defined as opposed to "Fact, Truth and Reality." I thought for a while of adopting FTR, standing for Fact, Truth, and Reality, as my new term, but it is awkward to use. "Writers of Reality" is the nearest I can come to what I want, but I cannot very well call us "Realtors" because that has been pre-empted—although as a matter of fact I would like to. "Real Estate," when you come to think of it, is a very fine phrase and it is exactly the sphere that writers of nonfiction deal in: the real estate of man, of human conduct. I wish we could get it back from the dealers in land. Then the categories could be poets, novelists, and realtors.

I should add that I do not entirely go along with Webster's statement that fiction is what is distinct from fact, truth, and reality because good fiction (as opposed to junk), even if it has nothing to do with fact, is usually *founded* on reality and *perceives* truth—often more truly than some historians. It is exactly this quality of perceiving truth, extracting it from irrelevant surroundings and conveying it to the reader or the viewer of a picture, which distinguishes the artist. What the artist has is an *extra* vision and an *inner* vision plus the ability to express it. He supplies a view or an understanding that the viewer or reader would not have gained without the aid of the artist's creative vision. This is what Monet does in one of those shimmering rivers reflecting poplars, or El Greco in the stormy sky over Toledo, or Jane Austen compressing a whole society into Mr. and Mrs. Bennet, Lady Catherine, and Mr. Darcy. We realtors, at least those of us who aspire to write literature, do the same thing. Lytton Strachey perceived a truth about Queen Victoria and the Eminent Victorians, and the style and form which he created to portray what he saw have changed the whole approach to biography since his time. Rachel Carson perceived truth about the seashore or the silent spring, Thoreau about Walden Pond, De Tocqueville and James Bryce about America, Gibbon about Rome, Karl Marx about Capital, Carlyle about the French Revolution. Their work is based on study, observation, and accumulation of fact, but does anyone suppose that these realtors did not make use of their imagination? Certainly they did; that is what gave them their extra vision.

Trevelyan wrote that the best historian was he who combined knowledge of the evidence with "the largest intellect, the warmest human sympathy and the highest imaginative powers." The last two qualities are no different than those necessary to a great novelist. They are a necessary part of the historian's equipment because they are what enable him to *understand* the evidence he has accumulated. Imagination stretches the available facts—extrapolates from them, so to speak, thus often supplying an otherwise missing answer to the "Why" of what happened. Sympathy is essential to the understanding of motive. Without sympathy and imagination the historian can copy figures from a tax roll forever—or count them by computer as they do nowadays—but he will never know or be able to portray the people who paid the taxes.

When I say that I felt like an artist, I mean that I constantly found myself perceiving a historical truth (at least, what *I* believe to be truth) by seizing upon a suggestion; then, after careful gathering of the evidence, conveying it in turn to the reader, not by piling up a list of all the facts I have collected, which is the way of the Ph.D., but by exercising the artist's privilege of selection.

Actually the idea for *The Proud Tower* evolved in that way from a number of such perceptions. The initial impulse was a line I quoted in *The Guns of August* from Belgian Socialist poet Emile Verhaeren. After a lifetime as a pacifist dedicated to the social and humanitarian ideas which were then believed to erase national lines, he found himself filled with hatred of the German invader and disillusioned in all he had formerly believed in. And yet, as he wrote, "Since it seems to me that in this state of hatred my conscience becomes diminished, I dedicate these pages, with emotion, to the man I used to be."

I was deeply moved by this. His confession seemed to me so poignant, so evocative of a time and mood, that it decided me to try to retrieve that vanished era. It led to the last chapter in *The Proud Tower* on the Socialists, to Jaurès the authentic Socialist, to his prophetic lines, "I summon the living, I mourn the dead," and to his assassination as the perfect and dramatically right ending for the book, both chronologically and symbolically.

Then there was Lord Ribblesdale. I owe this to *American Heritage*, which back in October 1961 published a piece on Sargent and Whistler with a handsome reproduction of the Ribblesdale portrait. In Sargent's painting Ribblesdale stared out upon the world, as I later wrote in *The Proud Tower*, "in an attitude of such natural arrogance, elegance and self-confidence as no man of a later day would ever achieve." Here too was a vanished era which came together in my mind with Verhaeren's line, "the man I used to be"—like two globules of mercury making a single mass. From that came the idea for the book. Ribblesdale, of course, was the suggestion that ultimately became the opening chapter on the Patricians. This is the reward of the artist's eye: It always leads you to the right thing.

As I see it, there are three parts to the creative process: first, the extra vision with which the artist perceives a truth and conveys it by suggestion. Second, medium of expression: language for writers, paint for painters, clay or stone for sculptors, sound expressed in musical notes for composers. Third, design or structure.

When it comes to language, nothing is more satisfying than to write a good sentence. It is no fun to write lumpishly, dully, in prose the reader must plod through like wet sand. But it is a pleasure to achieve, if one can, a clear running prose that is simple yet full of surprises. This does not just happen. It requires skill, hard work, a good ear, and continued practice, as much as it takes Heifetz to play the violin. The goals, as I have said, are clarity, interest, and aesthetic pleasure. On the first of these I would like to quote Macaulay, a great historian and great writer, who once wrote to a friend, "How little the all important art of making meaning pellucid is studied now! Hardly any popular writer except myself thinks of it."

As to structure, my own form is narrative, which is not every historian's, I may say—indeed, it is rather looked down on now by the advanced academics, but I don't mind because no one could possibly persuade me that telling a story is not the most desirable thing a writer can do. Narrative history is neither as simple nor as straightforward as it might seem. It requires arrangement, composition, planning just like a painting—Rembrandt's "Night Watch," for example. He did not fit in all those figures with certain ones in the foreground and others in back and the light falling on them just so, without much trial and error and innumerable preliminary sketches. It is the same with writing history. Although the finished result may look to the reader natural and inevitable, as if the author had only to follow the sequence of events, it is not that easy. Sometimes, to catch attention, the crucial event and the causative circumstance have to be reversed in order—the event first and the cause afterwards, as in *The Zimmermann Telegram*. One must juggle with time.

In *The Proud Tower*, for instance, the two English chapters were originally conceived as one. I divided them and placed them well apart in order to give a feeling of progression, of forward chronological movement to the book. The story of the Anarchists with their ideas and deeds set in counterpoint to each other was a problem in arrangement. The middle section of the Hague chapter on the Paris Exposition of 1900 was originally planned as a separate short centerpiece, marking the turn of the century, until I saw it as a bridge linking the two Hague Conferences, where it now seems to belong.

Structure is chiefly a problem of selection, an agonizing business because there is always more material than one can use or fit into a story. The problem is how and what to select out of all that happened without, by the very process of selection, giving an over- or under-emphasis which violates truth. One cannot put in everything: The result would be a shapeless mass. The job is to achieve a narrative line without straying from the essential facts or leaving out any essential facts and without twisting the material to suit one's convenience. To do so is a temptation, but if you do it with history you invariably get tripped up by later events. I have been tempted once or twice and I know.

The most difficult task of selection I had was in the Dreyfus chapter. To try to skip over the facts about the *bordereau* and the handwriting and the forgeries—all the elements of the Case as distinct from the Affair—in order to focus instead on what happened to France and yet at the same time give the reader enough background information to enable him to understand what was going on, nearly drove me to despair. My writing slowed down to a trickle until one dreadful day when I went to my study at nine and stayed there all day in a blank coma until five, when I emerged without having written a single word. Anyone who is a writer will know how frightening that was. You feel you have come to the end of your powers; you will not finish the book; you may never write again.

There are other problems of structure peculiar to writing history: how to explain background and yet keep the story moving; how to create suspense and sustain interest in a narrative of which the outcome (like who won the war) is, to put it mildly, known. If anyone thinks this does not take creative writing, I can only say, try it.

Mr. Capote's *In Cold Blood*, for example, which deals with real life as does mine, is notable for conscious design. One can see him planning, arranging, composing his material until he achieves his perfectly balanced structure. That is art, although the hand is too obtrusive and the design too contrived to qualify as history. His method of investigation, moreover, is hardly so new as he thinks. He is merely applying to contemporary material what historians have been doing for years. Herodotus started it more than two thousand years ago, walking all over Asia Minor asking questions. Francis Parkman went to live among the Indians: hunted, traveled, and ate with them so that his pages would be steeped in understanding; E. A. Freeman, before he wrote *The Norman Conquest*, visited every spot the Conqueror had set foot on. New to these techniques, Mr. Capote is perhaps naïvely impressed by them. He uses them in a deliberate effort to raise what might be called "creative" journalism to the level of literature. A great company from Herodotus to Trevelyan have been doing the same with history for quite some time.

Rhetorical Analysis

1. Tuchman says that the practice of writing includes "aesthetic pleasure" involving language (¶ 13), structuring (¶ 14), selection (¶s 16–17), and interest (¶ 18).

    a. How useful are these terms? (Be sure you understand what she means by them). Are they equally applicable to all "good writing"?
    b. Tuchman implies that she is willing to "play" or "tinker" with her material abundantly. What evidence is there in the essay that she indeed adopts a playful attitude in her work?
        (1) Consider ¶ 12, which serves primarily to help organize the entire essay. Why does Tuchman place that paragraph right here? Many writers would, for their own reasons, place it earlier in the essay.
        (2) Consider Tuchman's satisfaction in writing "good" sentences (¶ 13). What does she mean by "good"? Locate a number of sentences in this essay that you think must have given her pleasure as she wrote them; by inference, amplify her definition of good sentences.
2. Since Tuchman's subject (historiography) is so abstract, she must continually depend on concrete details to carry the load: specific paintings by El Greco and Rembrandt, specific books such as Jane Austen's *Pride and Prejudice* and Carson's *Silent Spring*, specific words and acts of historians such as Trevelyan and Parkman.
    a. Is Tuchman's purpose merely to illustrate ideas, or do the specifics accomplish more than just that?
    b. Make a special study of the way Tuchman integrates detail into her text—smoothly and with economy. She rarely uses phrases such as "for example" or explains more than she has to. Study of ¶ 6 is especially rewarding.
    c. Do you think Tuchman's allusions are too academic? Would they be appropriate for the *New York Times Book Review*, (or the *New York Herald Tribune Book Week*, where in fact the essay first appeared)?

Intellectual Analysis

1. For our purposes the most interesting aspect of this essay is Tuchman's excellent commentary on what constitutes "good writing" (¶ 4).
    a. It involves, she says "imagination." Track this word, through the essay and through its use in context formulate a definition. (Note that the poet Coleridge called imagination the "shaping power" of the mind.)
    b. It involves perception, both "an *extra* vision and an *inner* vision" (¶ 6). Pursue these terms, and evaluate their meaning or usefulness.
    c. It requires "*understanding*" (¶ 7). Does understanding involve the perception of facts and imagination? If so, how?
2. Tuchman's essay has something to say about *fact* and *truth*; they are key words in her professional vocabulary.
    a. The historian must study and observe the facts (¶ 6) and not distort them; but what else is required? Are the facts ever absolute in themselves? Are they ever enough? Does retelling key facts adequately summarize the principal role of the historian?

b. As to "truth," one of Tuchman's major statements is in ¶ 8. Whatever "truth" is, it is certainly dependent on perception, and a perceiver. Evaluate this dependence carefully.
   c. Tuchman also uses the word, "evidence." Based on a reading of the whole essay, what do you suppose constitutes "evidence" for Tuchman?
3. Tuchman's argument raises many problems, some of which are beyond the scope of this book. But here are two for discussion:
   a. If the historian can be an artist, can the artist be historian? Would Tuchman's argument allow for this? Does she maintain separate provinces for art and history, or is one subsumed under the other?
   b. In ¶ 11, Tuchman claims, "This is the reward of the artist's eye: It always leads you to the right thing." That is a very bold statement: do you see any difficulties with it?

Suggestions for Writing

1. Write an essay in which you compare Tuchman's stand with the stance toward history which Barry Lopez seems to hold in "Buffalo."
2. Our introduction to Tuchman mentions Oscar Wilde's often reprinted essay, "The Critic as Artist." In writing "The Historian as Artist," Tuchman could well have had Wilde's essay in mind. Find the essay by Wilde, and study the way in which it extends our general notion of "artist." Compare Wilde's perspective with that of Tuchman's.
3. Write your own essay entitled "The _____ as Artist." Fill in the blank with something original: student? engineering major? linebacker? dutiful child?

"Perdicaris Alive or Raisuli Dead"

On a scented Mediterranean May evening in 1904 Mr. Ion Perdicaris, an elderly, wealthy American, was dining with his family on the vine-covered terrace of the Place of Nightingales, his summer villa in the hills above Tangier. Besides a tame demoiselle crane and two monkeys who ate orange blossoms, the family included Mrs. Perdicaris; her son by a former marriage, Cromwell Oliver Varley, who (though wearing a great name backward) was a British subject; and Mrs. Varley. Suddenly a cacophony of shrieks, commands, and barking of dogs burst from the servants' quarters at the rear. Assuming the uproar to be a further episode in the chronic feud between their

1

German housekeeper and their French-Zouave chef, the family headed for the servants' hall to frustrate mayhem. They ran into the butler flying madly past them, pursued by a number of armed Moors whom at first they took to be their own household guards. Astonishingly, these persons fell upon the two gentlemen, bound them, clubbed two of the servants with their gunstocks, knocked Mrs. Varley to the floor, drew a knife against Varley's throat when he struggled toward his wife, dragged off the housekeeper, who was screaming into the telephone, "Robbers! Help!," cut the wire, and shoved their captives out of the house with guns pressed in their backs.

Waiting at the villa's gate was a handsome, black-bearded Moor with blazing eyes and a Greek profile, who, raising his arm in a theatrical gesture, announced in the tones of Henry Irving playing King Lear, "I am the Raisuli!" Awed, Perdicaris and Varley knew they stood face to face with the renowned Berber chief, lord of the Rif and last of the Barbary pirates, whose personal struggle for power against his nominal overlord, the Sultan of Morocco, periodically erupted over Tangier in raids, rapine, and interesting varieties of pillage. He now ordered his prisoners hoisted onto their horses and, thoughtfully stealing Perdicaris' best mount, a black stallion, for himself, fired the signal for departure. The bandit cavalcade, in a mad confusion of shouts, shots, rearing horses, and trampled bodies, scrambled off down the rocky hillside, avoiding the road, and disappeared into the night in the general direction of the Atlas Mountains.

A moment later Samuel R. Gummere, United States Consul General, was interrupted at dinner by the telephone operator, who passed on the alarm from the villa. After a hasty visit to the scene of the outrage, where he ascertained the facts, assuaged the hysterical ladies, and posted guards, Gummere returned to confer with his colleague Sir Arthur Nicolson, the British Minister. Both envoys saw alarming prospects of danger to all foreigners in Morocco as the result of Raisuli's latest pounce.

Morocco's already anarchic affairs had just been thrown into even greater turmoil by the month-old Anglo-French entente. Under this arrangement England, in exchange for a free hand in Egypt, had given France a free hand in Morocco, much to the annoyance of all Moroccans. The Sultan, Abdul-Aziz, was a well-meaning but helpless young man uneasily balanced on the shaky throne of the last independent Moslem country west of Constantinople. He was a puppet of a corrupt clique headed by Ben Sliman, the able and wicked old Grand

Vizier. To keep his young master harmlessly occupied while he kept the reins, not to mention the funds, of government in his own hands, Ben Sliman taught the Sultan a taste for, and indulged him in all manner of, extravagant luxuries of foreign manufacture. But Abdul-Aziz's tastes got out of bounds. Not content with innumerable bicycles, six hundred cameras, twenty-five grand pianos, and a gold automobile (though there were no roads), he wanted Western reforms to go with them. These, requiring foreign loans, willingly supplied by the French, opened the age-old avenue of foreign penetration. The Sultan's Western tastes and Western debts roused resentment among his fanatic tribes. Rebellions and risings had kept the country in strife for some years past, and European rivalries complicated the chaos. France, already deep in Algeria, was pressing against Morocco's borders. Spain had special interests along the Mediterranean coast. Germany was eyeing Morocco for commercial opportunities and as a convenient site for naval coaling bases. England, eyeing Germany, determined to patch up old feuds with France and had just signed the entente in April. The Moroccan government, embittered by what it considered England's betrayal, hating France, harassed by rebellion, tottering on the brink of bankruptcy, had yet one more scourge to suffer. This was the Sherif Mulai Ahmed ibn-Muhammed er Raisuli, who now seized his moment. To show up the Sultan's weakness, proportionately increase his own prestige, and extract political concessions as ransom, he kidnapped the prominent American resident Mr. Perdicaris.

"Situation serious," telegraphed Gummere to the State Department on May 19. "Request man-of-war to enforce demands." No request could have been more relished by President Theodore Roosevelt. Not yet forty-six, bursting with vigor, he delighted to make the Navy the vehicle of his exuberant view of national policy. At the moment of Perdicaris' kidnapping he faced, within the next month, a nominating convention that could give him what he most coveted: a chance to be elected President "in my own right." Although there was no possibility of the convention's nominating anyone else, Roosevelt knew it would be dominated by professional politicians and standpatters who were unanimous in their distaste for "that damned cowboy," as their late revered leader, Mark Hanna, had called him. The prospect did not intimidate Roosevelt. "The President," said his great friend Ambassador Jean Jules Jusserand of France, "is in his best mood. He is always in his best mood." The President promptly ordered to Morocco not one warship but four, the entire South Atlantic Squadron—due shortly to coal at Tenerife in the Canaries, where it could receive its orders to proceed at once to Tangier. Roosevelt knew it to be under the command of a man exactly suited to the circumstances, Admiral French Ensor Chadwick, a decorated veteran of the Battle of Santiago and, like Roosevelt, an ardent disciple of Admiral Alfred Thayer Mahan's strenuous theories of naval instrumentality.

Roosevelt's second in foreign policy was that melancholy and cultivated gentleman and wit, John Hay, who had been Lincoln's private secretary, wanted only to be a poet, and was, often to his own disgust, Secretary of State. On the day of the kidnapping he was absent, delivering a speech at the St. Louis Fair. His subordinates, however, recognized Gummere, who was senior diplomatic officer in Tangier in the absence of any American minister and had six years' experience at that post, as a man to be listened to. The victim, Perdicaris, was also a man of some repute, whose name was known in the State Department through a public crusade he had waged back in 1886-7 against certain diplomatic abuses practiced in Tangier. His associate in that battle had been Gummere himself, then a junior member of the foreign service and Perdicaris' friend and fellow townsman from Trenton, New Jersey. 6

"Warships will be sent to Tangier as soon as possible," the Department wired Gummere. "May be three or four days before one arrives." "Ships" in the plural was gratifying, but the promised delay was not. Gummere feared the chances of rescuing Perdicaris and Varley were slim. Nicolson gloomily concurred. They agreed that the only hope was to insist upon the Sultan's government giving in to whatever demands Raisuli might make as his price for release of his prisoners. Most inconveniently, the government was split, its Foreign Minister, Mohammed Torres, being resident at Tangier, where the foreign legations were located, while the Sultan, Grand Vizier, and court were at Fez, which was three days' journey by camel or mule into the interior. Gummere and Nicolson told Mohammed Torres they expected immediate acquiescence to Raisuli's demands, whatever these might prove to be, and dispatched their vice-consuls to Fez to impress the same view urgently upon the Sultan. 7

The French Minister, St. René Taillandier, did likewise, but since the Anglo-French entente was still too new to have erased old jealousies, he acted throughout the affair more or less independently. France had her own reasons for wishing to see Perdicaris and Varley safely restored as quickly as possible. Their abduction had put the 8 foreign colony in an uproar that would soon become panic if they were not rescued. The approach of the American fleet would seem to require equal action by France as the paramount power in the area, but France was anxious to avoid a display of force. She was "very nervous," Admiral Chadwick wrote later, at the prospect of taking over "the most fanatic and troublesome eight or ten millions in the world"; she had hoped to begin her penetration as unobtrusively as possible without stirring up Moroccan feelings any further against her. Hurriedly St. René Taillandier sent off two noble mediators to Raisuli; they were the young brother sherifs of the Wazan family, who occupied a sort of religious primacy among sherifs and whom France found it worthwhile to subsidize as her protégés.

While awaiting word from the mediators, Gummere and Nicolson anxiously conferred with an old Moroccan hand, Walter B. Harris, correspondent of the London *Times*, who had himself been kidnapped by Raisuli the year before. Raisuli had used that occasion to force the Bashaw, or local governor, of Tangier to call off a punitive expedition sent against him. This Bashaw, who played Sheriff of Nottingham to Raisuli's Robin Hood, was Raisuli's foster brother and chief hate; the two had carried on a feud ever since the Bashaw had tricked Raisuli into prison eight years before. The Bashaw sent troops to harass and tax Raisuli's tribes and burn his villages; at intervals he dispatched emissaries instructed to lure his enemy to parley. Raisuli ambushed and slaughtered the troops and returned the emissaries—or parts of them. The head of one was delivered in a basket of melons. Another came back in one piece, soaked in oil and set on fire. The eyes of another had been burned out with hot copper coins.

Despite such grisly tactics, Harris reported to Gummere and Nicolson, his late captor was a stimulating conversationalist who discoursed on philosophy in the accents of the Moorish aristocracy and denied interest in ransom for its own sake. "Men think I care about money," he had told Harris, "but, I tell you, it is only useful in politics." He had freed Harris in return for the release of his own partisans from government prisons, but since then more of these had been captured. This time Raisuli's demands would be larger and the Sultan less inclined to concede them. Sir Arthur recalled that on the last occasion Mohammed Torres had "behaved like an old brute" and shrugged off Harris' fate as being in the hands of the Lord, when in fact, as Nicolson had pointed out to him, Harris was "in the hands of a devil." Sir Arthur had suffered acutely. "I *boil*," he confessed, "to have to humiliate myself and negotiate with these miserable brigands within three hours of Gibraltar." Gummere thought sadly of his poor friend Perdicaris. "I cannot conceal from myself and the Department," he wrote that night, "that only by extremely delicate negotiations can we hope to escape from the most terrible consequences."

Back in America, the Perdicaris case provided a welcome sensation to compete in the headlines with the faraway fortunes of the Russo-Japanese War. A rich old gentleman held for ransom by a cruel but romantic brigand, the American Navy steaming to the rescue—here was personal drama more immediate than the complicated rattle of unpronounceable generals battling over unintelligible terrain. The President's instant and energetic action on behalf of a single citizen fallen among thieves in a foreign land made Perdicaris a symbol of America's new role on the world stage.

The man himself was oddly cast for the part. Digging up all available information, the press discovered that he was the son of Gregory Perdicaris, a native of Greece who had become a naturalized American, taught Greek at Harvard, married a lady of property from South Carolina, made a fortune in illuminating gas, settled in Trenton, New Jersey, and served for a time as United States Consul in his native land. The son entered Harvard with the class of 1860, but left in his sophomore year to study abroad. For a young man who was twenty-one at the opening of the Civil War, his history during the next few years was strangely obscure, a fact which the press ascribed to a conflict between his father, a Union sympathizer, and his mother, an ardent Confederate. Subsequently the son lived peripatetically in England, Morocco, and Trenton as a dilettante of literature and the arts, producing magazine articles, a verse play, and a painting called "Tent Life." He had built the now famous Villa Aidonia (otherwise Place of Nightingales) in 1877 and settled permanently in Tangier in 1884. There he lavishly entertained English and American friends among Oriental rugs, damasks, rare porcelains, and Moorish attendants in scarlet knee-pants and gold-embroidered jackets. He was known as a benefactor of the Moors and as a supporter of a private philanthropy that endowed Tangier with a modern sanitation system. He rode a splendid Arab steed—followed by his wife on a white mule—produced an occasional literary exercise or allegorical painting, and enjoyed an Edwardian gentleman's life amid elegant bric-a-brac.

A new telegram from the State Department desired Gummere to urge "energetic" efforts by the authorities to rescue Perdicaris and punish his captor—"if practicable," it added, with a bow to realities. Gummere replied that this was the difficulty: Raisuli, among his native crags, was immune from reprisal. The Sultan, who had a tatterdemalion army of some two thousand, had been trying vainly to capture him for years. Gummere became quite agitated. United action by the powers was necessary to prevent further abductions of Christians; Morocco was "fast drifting into a state of complete anarchy," the Sultan and his advisers were weak or worse, governors were corrupt, and very soon "neither life nor property will be safe."

On May 22 the younger Wazan returned with Raisuli's terms. They demanded everything: prompt withdrawal of government troops from the Rif; dismissal of the Bashaw of Tangier; arrest and imprisonment of certain officials who had harmed Raisuli in the past; release of Raisuli's partisans from prison; payment of an indemnity of $70,000 to be imposed personally upon the Bashaw, whose property must be sold to raise the amount; appointment of Raisuli as governor of two districts around Tangier that should be relieved of taxes and ceded to him absolutely; and, finally, safe-conduct for all Raisuli's tribesmen to come and go freely in the towns and markets.

Gummere was horrified; Mohammed Torres declared his government would never consent. Meanwhile European residents, increasingly agitated, were flocking in from outlying estates, voicing indignant protests, petitioning for a police force, guards, and gunboats. The local Moors, stimulated by Raisuli's audacity, were showing an aggressive mood. Gummere, scanning the horizon for Admiral Chadwick's smokestacks, hourly expected an outbreak. Situation "not reassuring," he wired; progress of talks "most unsatisfactory"; warship "anxiously awaited. Can it be hastened?"

The American public awaited Chadwick's arrival as eagerly as Gummere. Excitement rose when the press reported that Admiral Theodore F. Jewell, in command of the European Squadron, three days' sail behind Chadwick, would be ordered to reinforce him if the emergency continued.

Tangier received further word from the sherifs of Wazan that Raisuli had not only absolutely declined to abate his demands but had added an even more impossible condition: a British and American guarantee of fulfillment of the terms by the Moroccan government.

Knowing his government could not make itself responsible for the performance or non-performance of promises by another government, Gummere despairingly cabled the terms to Washington. As soon as he saw them, Roosevelt sent "in a hurry" for Secretary Hay (who had meanwhile returned to the capital). "I told him," wrote Hay that night in his diary, "I considered the demands of the outlaw Raisuli preposterous and the proposed guarantee of them by us and by England impossible of fulfillment." Roosevelt agreed. Two measures were decided upon and carried out within the hour: Admiral Jewell's squadron was ordered to reinforce Chadwick at Tangier, and France was officially requested to lend her good offices. (By recognizing France's special status in Morocco, this step, consciously taken, was of international significance in the train of crises that was to lead through Algeciras and Agadir to 1914.) Roosevelt and Hay felt they had done their utmost. "I hope they may not murder Mr. Perdicaris," recorded Hay none too hopefully, "but a nation cannot degrade itself to prevent ill-treatment of a citizen."

An uninhibited press told the public that in response to Raisuli's "insulting" ultimatum, "all available naval forces" in European waters were being ordered to the spot. Inspired by memory of U.S. troops chasing Aguinaldo in the Philippines, the press suggested that "if other means fail," marines could make a forced march into the interior to "bring the outlaw to book for his crimes." Such talk terrified Gummere, who knew that leathernecks would have as much chance against Berbers in the Rif as General Braddock's redcoats against Indians in the Alleghenies; and besides, the first marine ashore would simply provoke Raisuli to kill his prisoners.

On May 29 the elder Wazan brought word that Raisuli threatened to do just that if all his demands were not met in two days. Two days! This was the twentieth century, but as far as communications with Fez were concerned it might as well have been the time of the Crusades. Nevertheless Gummere and Nicolson sent couriers to meet their vice-consuls at Fez (or intercept them if they had already left) with orders to demand a new audience with the Sultan and obtain his acceptance of Raisuli's terms.

At five-thirty next morning a gray shape slid into the harbor. Gummere, awakened from a troubled sleep, heard the welcome news that Admiral Chadwick had arrived at last aboard his flagship, the *Brooklyn*. Relieved, yet worried that the military mind might display more valor than discretion, he hurried down to confer with the Admiral. In him he found a crisp and incisive officer whose quick intelligence grasped the situation at once. Chadwick agreed that the point at which to apply pressure was Mohammed Torres. Although up in the hills the brigand's patience might be wearing thin, the niceties of diplomatic protocol, plus the extra flourishes required by Moslem practice, called for an exchange of courtesy calls before business could be done. Admiral and Consul proceeded at once to wait upon the Foreign Minister, who returned the call upon the flagship that afternoon. It was a sight to see, Chadwick wrote to Hay, his royal progress through the streets, "a mass of beautiful white wool draperies, his old calves bare and his feet naked but for his yellow slippers," while "these wild fellows stoop and kiss his shoulder as he goes by."

Mohammed Torres was greeted by a salute from the flagship's guns and a review of the squadron's other three ships, which had just arrived. Unimpressed by these attentions, he continued to reject Raisuli's terms. "Situation critical," reported Chadwick. [22]

The situation was even more critical in Washington. On June 1 an extraordinary letter reached the State Department. Its writer, one A. H. Slocumb, a cotton broker of Fayetteville, North Carolina, said he had read with interest about the Perdicaris case and then, without warning, asked a startling question, "But is Perdicaris an American?" In the winter of 1863, Mr. Slocumb went on to say, he had been in Athens, and Perdicaris had come there "for the express purpose, as he stated, to become naturalized as a Greek citizen." His object, he had said, was to prevent confiscation by the Confederacy of some valuable property in South Carolina inherited from his mother. Mr. Slocumb could not be sure whether Perdicaris had since resumed American citizenship, but he was "positive" that Perdicaris had become a Greek subject forty years before, and he suggested that the Athens records would bear out his statement. [23]

What blushes reddened official faces we can only imagine. Hay's diary for June 1 records that the President sent for him and Secretary of the Navy Moody "for a few words about Perdicaris," but, maddeningly discreet, Hay wrote no more. A pregnant silence of three days ensues between the Slocumb letter and the next document in the case. On June 4 the State Department queried our Minister in Athens, John B. Jackson, asking him to investigate the charge—"important if true," added the Department, facing bravely into the wind. Although Slocumb had mentioned only 1863, the telegram to Jackson asked him to search the records for the two previous years as well; apparently the Department had been making frenzied inquiries of its own during the [24] interval. On June 7 Jackson telegraphed in reply that a person named Ion Perdicaris, described as an artist, unmarried, aged twenty-two, had indeed been naturalized as a Greek on March 19, 1862.

Posterity will never know what Roosevelt or Hay thought or said at this moment, because the archives are empty of evidence. But neither the strenuous President nor the suave Secretary of State was a man easily rattled. The game must be played out. Already Admiral Jewell's squadron of three cruisers had arrived to reinforce Chadwick, making a total of seven American warships at Tangier. America's fleet, flag, and honor were committed. Wheels had been set turning in foreign capitals. Hay had requested the good offices of France. The French Foreign Minister, Théophile Delcassé, was himself bringing pressure. A British warship, the *Prince of Wales*, had also come to Tangier. Spain wanted to know if the United States was wedging into Morocco.

And just at this juncture the Sultan's government, succumbing to French pressure, ordered Mohammed Torres to accede to all Raisuli's demands. Four days later, on June 12, a French loan to the government of Morocco was signed at Fez in the amount of 62.5 million francs, secured by the customs of all Moroccan ports. It seemed hardly a tactful moment to reveal the fraudulent claim of Mr. Perdicaris.

He was not yet out of danger, for Raisuli refused to release him before all the demands were actually met, and the authorities were proving evasive. Washington was trapped. Impossible to reveal Perdicaris' status now; equally impossible to withdraw the fleet and leave him, whom the world still supposed to be an American, at the brigand's mercy.

During the next few days suspense was kept taut by a stream of telegrams from Gummere and Chadwick reporting one impasse after another in the negotiations with Raisuli. When the Sultan balked at meeting all the terms in advance of the release, Raisuli merely raised his ante, demanding that four districts instead of two be ceded to him and returning to the idea of an Anglo-American guarantee. "You see there is no end to the insolence of this blackguard," wrote Hay in a note to the President on June 15; Roosevelt, replying the same day, agreed that we had gone "as far as we possibly can go for Perdicaris" and could now only "demand the death of those that harm him if he is harmed." He dashed off an alarming postscript: "I think it would be well to enter into negotiations with England and France looking to the possibility of an expedition to punish the brigands if Gummere's statement as to the impotence of the Sultan is true."

No further action was taken in pursuit of this proposal because Gummere's telegrams now grew cautiously hopeful; on the nineteenth he wired that all arrangements had been settled for the release to take place on the twenty-first. But on the twentieth all was off. Raisuli suspected the good faith of the government, a sentiment which Gummere and Chadwick evidently shared, for they blamed the delay on "intrigue of authorities here." Finally the exasperated Gummere telegraphed on the twenty-first that the United States position was "becoming humiliating." He asked to be empowered to deliver an ultimatum to the Moroccan government claiming an indemnity for each day's further delay, backed by a threat to land marines and seize the customs as security. Admiral Chadwick concurred in a separate telegram.

June 21 was the day the Republican National Convention met in Chicago. "There is a great deal of sullen grumbling," Roosevelt wrote that day to his son Kermit, "but they don't dare oppose me for the nomination. . . . How the election will turn out no one can tell." If a poll of Republican party leaders had been taken at any time during the past year, one newspaper estimated, it would have shown a majority opposed to Roosevelt's nomination. But the country agreed with Viscount Bryce, who said Roosevelt was the greatest President since Washington (prompting a Roosevelt friend to recall Whistler's remark when told he was the greatest painter since Velázquez: "Why drag in Velázquez?"). The country wanted Teddy and, however distasteful that fact was, the politicians saw the handwriting on the bandwagon. On the death of Mark Hanna four months before, active opposition had collapsed, and the disgruntled leaders were now arriving in Chicago prepared to register the inevitable as ungraciously as possible.

They were the more sullen because Roosevelt and his strategists, preparing against any possible slip-up, had so steamrollered and stage-managed the proceedings ahead of time that there was nothing left for the delegates to do. No scurrying, no back-room bargaining, no fights, no trades, no smoke-filled deals. *Harper's Weekly* reported an Alabama delegate's summation: "There ain't nobody who can do nothin'" and added: "It is not a Republican Convention, it is no kind of a convention; it is a roosevelt."

The resulting listlessness and pervading dullness were unfortunate. Although Elihu Root, Henry Cabot Lodge, and other handpicked

Roosevelt choices filled the key posts, most of the delegates and party professionals did not make even a pretense of enthusiasm. The ostentatious coldness of the delegation from New York, Roosevelt's home state, was such that one reporter predicted they would all go home with pneumonia. There were no bands, no parades, and for the first time in forty years there were hundreds of empty seats.

Roosevelt knew he had the nomination in his pocket, but all his life, like Lincoln, he had a haunting fear of being defeated in elections. He was worried lest the dislike and distrust of him so openly exhibited at Chicago should gather volume and explode at the ballot box. Something was needed to prick the sulks and dispel the gloom of the convention before it made a lasting impression upon the public.

At this moment came Gummere's plea for an ultimatum. Again we have no record of what went on in high councils, but President and Secretary must have agreed upon their historic answer within a matter of hours. The only relevant piece of evidence is a verbal statement made to Hay's biographer, the late Tyler Dennett, by Gaillard Hunt, who was chief of the State Department's Citizenship Bureau during the Perdicaris affair. Hunt said he showed the correspondence about Perdicaris' citizenship to Hay, who told him to show it to the President; on seeing it, the President decided to overlook the difficulty and instructed Hunt to tell Hay to send the telegram anyway, at once. No date is given for this performance, so one is left with the implication that Roosevelt was not informed of the facts until this last moment—a supposition which the present writer finds improbable.

When Roosevelt made up his mind to accomplish an objective, he did not worry too much about legality of method. Before any unusual procedure he would ask an opinion from his Attorney General, Philander Knox, but Knox rather admired Roosevelt's way of overriding his advice. Once, when asked for his opinion, he replied, "Ah, Mr. President, why have such a beautiful action marred by any taint of legality?" Another close adviser, Admiral Mahan, when asked by Roosevelt how to solve the political problem of annexing the Hawaiian Islands, answered, "Do nothing unrighteous but . . . take the islands first and solve afterward." It may be that the problem of Perdicaris seemed susceptible of the same treatment.

The opportunity was irresistible. Every newspaperman who ever knew him testified to Roosevelt's extraordinary sense of news value, to his ability to create news, to dramatize himself to the public.

He had a genius for it. "Consciously or unconsciously," said the journalist Isaac Marcosson, "he was the master press agent of all time." The risk, of course, was great, for it would be acutely embarrassing if the facts leaked out during the coming campaign. It may have been the risk itself that tempted Roosevelt, for he loved a prank and loved danger for its own sake; if he could combine danger with what William Allen White called a "frolicking intrigue," his happiness was complete.

Next day, June 22, the memorable telegram "This Government wants Perdicaris alive or Raisuli dead" flashed across the Atlantic cable over Hay's signature and was simultaneously given to the press at home. It was not an ultimatum, because Hay deliberately deprived it of meaningfulness by adding to Gummere, "Do not land marines or seize customs without Department's specific instructions." But this sentence was not allowed to spoil the effect: It was withheld from the press.

At Chicago, Uncle Joe Cannon, the salty perennial Speaker of the House, who was convention chairman, rapped with his gavel and read the telegram. The convention was electrified. Delegates sprang upon their chairs and hurrahed. Flags and handkerchiefs waved. Despite Hay's signature, everyone saw the Roosevelt teeth, cliché of a hundred cartoons, gleaming whitely behind it. "Magnificent, magnificent!" pronounced Senator Depew. "The people want an administration that will stand by its citizens, even if it takes the fleet to do it," said Representative Dwight of New York, expressing the essence of popular feeling. "Roosevelt and Hay know what they are doing," said a Kansas delegate. "Our people like courage. We'll stand for anything those two men do." "Good hot stuff and echoes my sentiments," said another delegate. The genius of its timing and phrasing, wrote a reporter, "gave the candidate the maximum benefit of the thrill that was needed." Although the public was inclined to credit authorship to Roosevelt, the Baltimore *Sun* pointed out that Mr. Hay too knew how to make the eagle scream when he wanted to. Hay's diary agreed. "My telegram to Gummere," he noted comfortably the day afterward, "had an uncalled for success. It is curious how a concise impropriety hits the public."

After nominating Roosevelt by acclamation, the convention departed in an exhilarated mood. In Morocco a settlement had been reached before receipt of the telegram. Raisuli was ready at last to return his captives. Mounted on a "great, grey charger," he personally escorted Perdicaris and Varley on the ride down from the mountains, pointing out on the way the admirable effect of pink and violet shadows cast by the rising sun on the rocks. They met the ransom party, with thirty pack mules bearing boxes of Spanish silver dollars, halfway down. Payment was made and prisoners exchanged, and Perdicaris took leave, as he afterward wrote, of "one of the most interesting and kindly-hearted native gentlemen" he had ever known, whose "singular gentleness and courtesy . . . quite endeared him to us." At nightfall, as he rode into Tangier and saw the signal lights of the American warships twinkling the news of his release, Perdicaris was overcome with patriotic emotion at "such proof of his country's solicitude for its citizens and for the honor of its flag!" Few indeed are the Americans, he wrote to Gummere in a masterpiece of understatement, "who can have appreciated as keenly as I did then what the presence of our Flag in foreign waters meant at such a moment and in such circumstances."

Only afterward, when it was all over, did the State Department inform Gummere how keen indeed was Perdicaris' cause for appreciation. "Overwhelmed with amazement" and highly indignant, Gummere extracted from Perdicaris a full, written confession of his forty-year-old secret. He admitted that he had never in ensuing years taken steps to resume American citizenship because, as he ingenuously explained, having been born an American, he disliked the idea of having to become naturalized, and so "I continued to consider myself an American citizen." Since Perdicaris perfectly understood that the American government was in no position to take action against him, his letter made no great pretension of remorse.

Perdicaris retired to England for his remaining years. Raisuli duly became governor of the Tangier districts in place of the false-hearted Bashaw. The French, in view of recent disorders, acquired the right to police Morocco (provoking the Kaiser's notorious descent upon Tangier). The Sultan, weakened and humiliated by Raisuli's triumph, was shortly dethroned by a brother. Gummere was officially congratulated and subsequently appointed minister to Morocco and American delegate to the Algeciras Conference. Sir Arthur Nicolson took "a long leave of absence," the Wazan brothers received handsomely decorated Winchester rifles with suitable inscriptions from Mr. Roosevelt, Hay received the Grand Cross of the Legion of Honor, and Roosevelt was elected in November by the largest popular majority ever given to a presidential candidate.

"As to Paregoric or is it Pericarditis," wrote Hay to Assistant Secretary Adee on September 3, "it is a bad business. We must keep it excessively confidential for the present." They succeeded. Officials in the know held their breath during the campaign, but no hint leaked out either then or during the remaining year of Hay's lifetime or during Roosevelt's lifetime. As a result of the episode, Roosevelt's administration proposed a new citizenship law which was introduced in Congress in 1905 and enacted in 1907, but the name of the errant gentleman who inspired it was never mentioned during the debates. The truth about Perdicaris remained unknown to the public until 1933, when Tyler Dennett gave it away—in one paragraph in his biography of John Hay.

42

Rhetorical Analysis

1. Some of Tuchman's paragraphs are arranged, even orchestrated, to rise toward a crescendo, for example, or to shift from theme to theme in counterpoint. Attend to the orchestration of ¶s 9, 21, 22, 37, and especially 40. Are there others you appreciate for the elegant arrangement?
2. Historical narrative might seem no more difficult than keeping a diary, or writing a long letter home. But narrative is no more easily mastered than any other mode of writing. One reason is that history is, as Tuchman says in "The Historian as Artist," "neither as simple nor as straightforward as it might seem."
    a. In the first 9 paragraphs of this simple historical episode, there are 21 individuals for Tuchman to introduce and keep distinct. What rhetorical devices does Tuchman use to keep the reader from getting confused? Note especially her use of the appositive and her care (and cleverness) with antecedent references.
    b. Since raw events make no sense unless humans interpret them, the historian—like the TV news reporter—must frequently cut and splice the record in order to present a meaningful report. Thus, a mere chronological presentation ("Adam begot Cain begot Seth begot Noah begot X") is often quite useless in explaining "why." In the eight sentences of ¶ 18, for example, Tuchman departs from strict chronology four times, once jumping ten years forward to the outbreak of World War I. Study ¶ 18 carefully. How does Tuchman keep such twists in chronology straight in the reader's mind? Why is it important for her to switch so frequently?
3. One does not have to be a historian to relish eccentric and colorful description ("the head of one was delivered in a basket of melons") or quotations ("The President . . . is in his best mood. He is always in his best mood.") Find other

details you like. What do they add to the reader's enjoyment? to the reader's acceptance of the author's qualifications to write history?

Intellectual Analysis

1. Consider Tuchman's success as a storyteller (which is what she claims to be in "The Historian as Artist"). How well does she achieve in practice the ideals she lays down in theory?
    a. Does Tuchman's cleverness or her artfulness ever get in the way of the facts, the evidence, or the story itself?
    b. Consider the author's skillful handling of point of view. When Tuchman is describing Perdicaris, for example, she recreates the perspective of a rich dilettante; when she is dealing with Raisuli, Tuchman recreates his speech and his views. To appreciate her skill further, list characteristics of each point of view in the essay and show how Tuchman mirrors them in her prose.
2. This historical episode is entirely shot through with irony, from the "scented Mediterranean May evening" of the first sentence, to the final sentence where we are informed that we almost did not know of this event at all. Analyze how Tuchman's view of history, as a colorful, ironic pageant or a ship of fools (note that "the game must be played out"), shines through particular details. Here are some details to ponder:
    a. The personality and looks of Raisuli, as compared to the "grisly tactics" he employs.
    b. The French and English involvement, the deal they cut over Morocco and Egypt, and the darker irony of that deal in light of the Conference at Algeciras and the outbreak of war in 1914.
    c. The Sultan, and others involved in the bizarre politics of Morocco.
    d. Theodore Roosevelt: his character generally, and his use of this incident for his own ends.
    e. The American public and the press.
    f. The amazing irony of A. H. Slocumb's letter, and its shrewd placement in this essay (¶s 23–25).
    g. The telegram itself, with its second sentence withheld from the press.
    h. The fact that an agreement had already been worked out with Raisuli when the telegram arrived.

There are many, many more ironic details, large and small, which you may discover upon rereading.

Suggestions for Writing

1. Choose your favorite paragraph from this essay and analyze it. What rhetorical techniques does Tuchman use to establish tone, rhythm, pace, etc. How does the paragraph you have chosen serve to advance the major concerns of the essay?

2. Research the *New York Time*'s coverage of the incident. Better yet, compare the *Times* of London's account with one other paper and see how perspectives differ. Use the dates Tuchman provides in her essay to track down the contemporary newspaper accounts.
3. Write an essay in which you assess what Tuchman's essay implies about our culture.

LOREN EISELEY

Loren Eiseley thought of himself as a "changeling," as he says in his autobiography, All the Strange Hours. He was born, in 1907, to a father who was 40, a mother who was "stone deaf," and a household of "facial distortions" and silence. The young Eiseley felt kinship less with his natural mother and father than with the local salt flats and ponds and with the prehistoric bones held in a brick museum on the campus of the University of Nebraska, near the Eiseley home in Lincoln. During the Great Depression of the 1930s, Eiseley rode the freight cars with other hoboes—seemingly alienated from home and society.

And something of the hobo, the outsider, or the changeling stayed with Eiseley as an adult. In 1937 he began his career as assistant professor of Sociology and Anthropology at the University of Kansas. In twenty-two years he became a provost of the University of Pennsylvania and a well-known anthropologist and writer. Ironically, as a student he had turned from English after his Freshman Composition teacher had accused him of plagiarism. "You didn't compose this," Eiseley was told, "it is too well written." His career, however, transcended English and anthropology and the several other disciplines (archeology, biology, anatomy) in which he was well trained. Eiseley's vast learning is woven into the fabric of books like The Immense Journey, The Unexpected Universe, and The Firmament of

Time; in these, Eiseley discusses such cosmic subjects as time, evolution, the history of science, and the human condition.

Despite this range, however, Eiseley's work is held together by the contemplative quality of his mind and the recognizable tone of his prose. Respect for the past—history in the deeper sense of biology and geology—causes him to be somber, brooding, and elegiac. "I have remarked that I was born in the central plains, compacted out of glacial dust and winter cold.... My eye is round, open, and undomesticated as an owl's in a primeval forest, a world that for me has never truly departed."

From this perspective, almost out of time, Eiseley observes the linked movements of crows, spiders, wasps, chemicals, and humans. The season is frequently autumn, turning toward winter; the landscape is often desolate (or seemingly so); and the creatures he is watching are often struggling to stay alive. Eiseley discerns, in a flock of birds flying overhead, the very molecules that articulate their bones, flesh, and feathers, and he sees, in the dust beneath his feet, the long-extinct creatures (as though alive) mingled with the earth. This steadiness of attention, which saves his vision from being remote, or forbidding, or bitter, is transmuted to a kind of love of all nature. Apparently, this love is so great that it can curve to the time as well as the space of the world.

Eiseley's distance from life finally became his connection to it. The Immense Journey is dedicated to the memory of his father, "who lies in the grass of the prairie frontier but is not forgotten by his son."

How Flowers Changed the World

If it had been possible to observe the Earth from the far side of the solar system over the long course of geological epochs, the watchers might have been able to discern a subtle change in the light emanating from our planet. That world of long ago would, like the red deserts of Mars, have reflected light from vast drifts of stone and gravel, the sands of wandering wastes, the blackness of naked basalt, the yellow dust of endlessly moving storms. Only the ceaseless marching of the clouds and the intermittent flashes from the restless surface of the sea would have told a different story, but still essentially a barren one. Then, as the millennia rolled away and age followed age, a new and greener light would, by degrees, have come to twinkle across those endless miles.

This is the only difference those far watchers, by the use of subtle instruments, might have perceived in the whole history of the planet Earth. Yet that slowly growing green twinkle would have contained the epic march of life from the tidal oozes upward across the raw and unclothed continents. Out of the vast chemical bath of the sea—not from the deeps, but from the element-rich, light-exposed platforms of the continental shelves—wandering fingers of green had crept upward along the meanderings of river systems and fringed the gravels of forgotten lakes.

In those first ages plants clung of necessity to swamps and watercourses. Their reproductive processes demanded direct access to water. Beyond the primitive ferns and mosses that enclosed the borders of swamps and streams the rocks still lay vast and bare, the winds still swirled the dust of a naked planet. The grass cover that holds our world secure in place was still millions of years in the future. The green marchers had gained a soggy foothold upon the land, but that was all. They did not reproduce by seeds but by microscopic swimming sperm that had to wriggle their way through water to fertilize the female cell. Such plants in their higher forms had clever adaptations for the use of rain water in their sexual phases, and survived with increasing success in a wet land environment. They now seem part of man's normal environment. The truth is, however, that there is nothing very "normal" about nature. Once upon a time there were no flowers at all.

A little while ago—about one hundred million years, as the geologist estimates time in the history of our four-billion-year-old planet—flowers were not to be found anywhere on the five continents. Wherever one might have looked, from the poles to the equator, one would have seen only the cold dark monotonous green of a world whose plant life possessed no other color.

Somewhere, just a short time before the close of the Age of Reptiles, there occurred a soundless, violent explosion. It lasted millions of years, but it was an explosion, nevertheless. It marked the emergence of the angiosperms—the flowering plants. Even the great evolutionist, Charles Darwin, called them "an abominable mystery," because they appeared so suddenly and spread so fast.

Flowers changed the face of the planet. Without them, the world we know—even man himself—would never have existed. Francis Thompson, the English poet, once wrote that one could not pluck a flower without troubling a star. Intuitively he had sensed like a naturalist the enormous interlinked complexity of life. Today we know that the appearance of the flowers contained also the equally mystifying emergence of man.

If we were to go back into the Age of Reptiles, its drowned swamps and birdless forests would reveal to us a warmer but, on the whole, a sleepier world than that of today. Here and there, it is true, the serpent heads of bottom-feeding dinosaurs might be upreared in suspicion of their huge flesh-eating compatriots. Tyrannosaurs, enormous bipedal caricatures of men, would stalk mindlessly across the sites of future cities and go their slow way down into the dark of geologic time.

In all that world of living things nothing saw save with the intense concentration of the hunt, nothing moved except with the grave sleepwalking intentness of the instinct-driven brain. Judged by modern standards, it was a world in slow motion, a cold-blooded world whose occupants were most active at noonday but torpid on chill nights, their brains damped by a slower metabolism than any known to even the most primitive of warm-blooded animals today.

A high metabolic rate and the maintenance of a constant body temperature are supreme achievements in the evolution of life. They enable an animal to escape, within broad limits, from the overheating or the chilling of its immediate surroundings, and at the same time to maintain a peak mental efficiency. Creatures without a high metabolic rate are slaves to weather. Insects in the first frosts of autumn all run down like little clocks. Yet if you pick one up and breathe warmly upon it, it will begin to move about once more.

In a sheltered spot such creatures may sleep away the winter, but they are hopelessly immobilized. Though a few warm-blooded mammals, such as the woodchuck of our day, have evolved a way of reducing their metabolic rate in order to undergo winter hibernation, it is a survival mechanism with drawbacks, for it leaves the animal helplessly exposed if enemies discover him during his period of suspended animation. Thus bear or woodchuck, big animal or small, must seek, in this time of descending sleep, a safe refuge in some hidden den or burrow. Hibernation is, therefore, primarily a winter refuge of small, easily concealed animals rather than of large ones.

A high metabolic rate, however, means a heavy intake of energy in order to sustain body warmth and efficiency. It is for this reason that even some of these later warm-blooded mammals existing in our day have learned to descend into a slower, unconscious rate of living during the winter months when food may be difficult to obtain. On a slightly higher plane they are following the procedure of the cold-blooded frog sleeping in the mud at the bottom of a frozen pond.

The agile brain of the warm-blooded birds and mammals demands a high oxygen consumption and food in concentrated forms, or the creatures cannot long sustain themselves. It was the rise of the flowering plants that provided that energy and changed the nature of the living world. Their appearance parallels in a quite surprising manner the rise of the birds and mammals.

Slowly, toward the dawn of the Age of Reptiles, something over two hundred and fifty million years ago, the little naked sperm cells wriggling their way through dew and raindrops had given way to a kind of pollen carried by the wind. Our present-day pine forests represent plants of a pollen-disseminating variety. Once fertilization was no longer dependent on exterior water, the march over drier regions could be extended. Instead of spores simple primitive seeds carrying some nourishment for the young plant had developed, but true flowers were still scores of millions of years away. After a long period of hesitant evolutionary groping, they exploded upon the world with truly revolutionary violence.

The event occurred in Cretaceous times in the close of the Age of Reptiles. Before the coming of the flowering plants our own ancestral stock, the warm-blooded mammals, consisted of a few mousy little creatures hidden in trees and underbrush. A few lizard-like birds with carnivorous teeth flapped awkwardly on ill-aimed flights among archaic shrubbery. None of these insignificant creatures gave evidence of any remarkable talents. The mammals in particular had been around for some millions of years, but had remained well lost in the shadow of the mighty reptiles. Truth to tell, man was still, like the genie in the bottle, encased in the body of a creature about the size of a rat.

As for the birds, their reptilian cousins the Pterodactyls, flew farther and better. There was just one thing about the birds that paralleled the physiology of the mammals. They, too, had evolved warm blood and its accompanying temperature control. Nevertheless, if one had been seen stripped of his feathers, he would still have seemed a slightly uncanny and unsightly lizard.

Neither the birds nor the mammals, however, were quite what they seemed. They were waiting for the Age of Flowers. They were waiting for what flowers, and with them the true encased seed, would bring. Fish-eating, gigantic leather-winged reptiles, twenty-eight feet from wing tip to wing tip, hovered over the coasts that one day would be swarming with gulls.

Inland the monotonous green of the pine and spruce forests with their primitive wooden cone flowers stretched everywhere. No grass hindered the fall of the naked seeds to earth. Great sequoias towered to the skies. The world of that time has a certain appeal but it is a giant's world, a world moving slowly like the reptiles who stalked magnificently among the boles of its trees.

The trees themselves are ancient, slow-growing and immense, like the redwood groves that have survived to our day on the California coast. All is stiff, formal, upright and green, monotonously green. There is no grass as yet; there are no wide plains rolling in the sun, no tiny daisies dotting the meadows underfoot. There is little versatility about this scene; it is, in truth, a giant's world.

A few nights ago it was brought home vividly to me that the world has changed since that far epoch. I was awakened out of sleep by an unknown sound in my living room. Not a small sound—not a creaking timber or a mouse's scurry—but a sharp, rending explosion as though an unwary foot had been put down upon a wine glass. I had come instantly out of sleep and lay tense, unbreathing. I listened for another step. There was none.

Unable to stand the suspense any longer, I turned on the light and passed from room to room glancing uneasily behind chairs and into closets. Nothing seemed disturbed, and I stood puzzled in the center of the living room floor. Then a small button-shaped object upon the rug caught my eye. It was hard and polished and glistening. Scattered over the length of the room were several more shining up at me like wary little eyes. A pine cone that had been lying in a dish had been blown the length of the coffee table. The dish itself could hardly have been the source of the explosion. Beside it I found two ribbon-like strips of a velvety-green. I tried to place the two strips together to make a pod. They twisted resolutely away from each other and would no longer fit.

I relaxed in a chair, then, for I had reached a solution of the midnight disturbance. The twisted strips were wistaria pods that I had brought in a day or two previously and placed in the dish. They had chosen midnight to explode and distribute their multiplying fund of life down the length of the room. A plant, a fixed, rooted thing, immobilized in a single spot, had devised a way of propelling its offspring across open space. Immediately there passed before my eyes the million airy troopers of the milkweed pod and the clutching hooks of the sandburs. Seeds on the coyote's tail, seeds on the hunter's coat, thistledown mounting on the winds—all were somehow triumphing over life's limitations. Yet the ability to do this had not been with them at the beginning. It was the product of endless effort and experiment.

The seeds on my carpet were not going to lie stiffly where they had dropped like their antiquated cousins, the naked seeds on the pine-cone scales. They were travelers. Struck by the thought, I went out next day and collected several other varieties. I line them up now in a row on my desk—so many little capsules of life, winged, hooked or spiked. Every one is an angiosperm, a product of the true flowering plants. Contained in these little boxes is the secret of that far-off Cretaceous explosion of a hundred million years ago that changed the face of the planet. And somewhere in here, I think, as I poke seriously at one particularly resistant seedcase of a wild grass, was once man himself.

When the first simple flower bloomed on some raw upland late in the Dinosaur Age, it was wind pollinated, just like its early pine-cone relatives. It was a very inconspicuous flower because it had not yet evolved the idea of using the surer attraction of birds and insects to achieve the transportation of pollen. It sowed its own pollen and received the pollen of other flowers by the simple vagaries of the wind. Many plants in regions where insect life is scant still follow this principle today. Nevertheless, the true flower—and the seed that it produced—was a profound innovation in the world of life.

In a way, this event parallels, in the plant world, what happened among animals. Consider the relative chance for survival of the exteriorly deposited egg of a fish in contrast with the fertilized egg of a mammal, carefully retained for months in the mother's body until the young animal (or human being) is developed to a point where it may survive. The biological wastage is less—and so it is with the flowering plants. The primitive spore, a single cell fertilized in the beginning by a swimming sperm, did not promote rapid distribution, and the young plant, moreover, had to struggle up from nothing. No one had left it any food except what it could get by its own unaided efforts.

By contrast, the true flowering plants (angiosperm itself means "encased seed") grew a seed in the heart of a flower, a seed whose development was initiated by a fertilizing pollen grain independent of outside moisture. But the seed, unlike the developing spore, is already a fully equipped *embryonic plant* packed in a little enclosed box stuffed full of nutritious food. Moreover, by featherdown attachments, as in dandelion or milkweed seed, it can be wafted upward on gusts and ride the wind for miles; or with hooks it can cling to a bear's or a rabbit's hide; or like some of the berries, it can be covered with a juicy, attractive fruit to lure birds, pass undigested through their intestinal tracts and be voided miles away.

26 The ramifications of this biological invention were endless. Plants traveled as they had never traveled before. They got into strange environments heretofore never entered by the old spore plants or stiff pine-cone-seed plants. The well-fed, carefully cherished little embryos raised their heads everywhere. Many of the older plants with more primitive reproductive mechanisms began to fade away under this unequal contest. They contracted their range into secluded environments. Some, like the giant redwoods, lingered on as relics; many vanished entirely.

27 The world of the giants was a dying world. These fantastic little seeds skipping and hopping and flying about the woods and valleys brought with them an amazing adaptability. If our whole lives had not been spent in the midst of it, it would astound us. The old, stiff, sky-reaching wooden world had changed into something that glowed here and there with strange colors, put out queer, unheard-of fruits and little intricately carved seed cases, and, most important of all, produced concentrated foods in a way that the land had never seen before, or dreamed of back in the fish-eating, leaf-crunching days of the dinosaurs.

28 That food came from three sources, all produced by the reproductive system of the flowering plants. There were the tantalizing nectars and pollens intended to draw insects for pollenizing purposes, and which are responsible also for that wonderful jeweled creation, the hummingbird. There were the juicy and enticing fruits to attract larger animals, and in which tough-coated seeds were concealed, as in the tomato, for example. Then, as if this were not enough, there was the food in the actual seed itself, the food intended to nourish the embryo. All over the world, like hot corn in a popper, these incredible elaborations of the flowering plants kept exploding. In a movement that was almost instantaneous, geologically speaking, the angio-

sperms had taken over the world. Grass was beginning to cover the bare earth until, today, there are over six thousand species. All kinds of vines and bushes squirmed and writhed under new trees with flying seeds.

The explosion was having its effect on animal life also. Specialized groups of insects were arising to feed on the new sources of food and, incidentally and unknowingly, to pollinate the plant. The flowers bloomed and bloomed in ever larger and more spectacular varieties. Some were pale unearthly night flowers intended to lure moths in the evening twilight, some among the orchids even took the shape of female spiders in order to attract wandering males, some flamed redly in the light of noon or twinkled modestly in the meadow grasses. Intricate mechanisms splashed pollen on the breasts of hummingbirds, or stamped it on the bellies of black, grumbling bees droning assiduously from blossom to blossom. Honey ran, insects multiplied, and even the descendants of that toothed and ancient lizard-bird had become strangely altered. Equipped with prodding beaks instead of biting teeth they pecked the seeds and gobbled the insects that were really converted nectar.

Across the planet grasslands were now spreading. A slow continental upthrust which had been a part of the early Age of Flowers had cooled the world's climates. The stalking reptiles and the leather-winged black imps of the seashore cliffs had vanished. Only birds roamed the air now, hot-blooded and high-speed metabolic machines.

The mammals, too, had survived and were venturing into new domains, staring about perhaps a bit bewildered at their sudden eminence now that the thunder lizards were gone. Many of them, beginning as small browsers upon leaves in the forest, began to venture out upon this new sunlit world of the grass. Grass has a high silica content and demands a new type of very tough and resistant tooth enamel, but the seeds taken incidentally in the cropping of the grass are highly nutritious. A new world had opened out for the warm-blooded mammals. Great herbivores like the mammoths, horses and bisons appeared. Skulking about them had arisen savage flesh-feeding carnivores like the now extinct dire wolves and the saber-toothed tiger.

Flesh eaters though these creatures were, they were being sustained on nutritious grasses one step removed. Their fierce energy was being maintained on a high, effective level, through hot days and frosty nights, by the concentrated energy of the angiosperms. That energy, thirty per cent or more of the weight of the entire plant among some of the cereal grasses, was being accumulated and concentrated in the rich proteins and fats of the enormous game herds of the grasslands.

On the edge of the forest, a strange, old-fashioned animal still hesitated. His body was the body of a tree dweller, and though tough and knotty by human standards, he was, in terms of that world into which he gazed, a weakling. His teeth, though strong for chewing on the tough fruits of the forest, or for crunching an occasional unwary bird caught with his prehensile hands, were not the tearing sabers of the great cats. He had a passion for lifting himself up to see about, in his restless, roving curiosity. He would run a little stiffly and uncertainly, perhaps, on his hind legs, but only in those rare moments when he ventured out upon the ground. All this was the legacy of his climbing days; he had a hand with flexible fingers and no fine specialized hoofs upon which to gallop like the wind.

If he had any idea of competing in that new world, he had better forget it; teeth or hooves, he was much too late for either. He was a ne'er-do-well, an in-betweener. Nature had not done well by him. It was as if she had hesitated and never quite made up her mind. Perhaps as a consequence he had a malicious gleam in his eye, the gleam of an outcast who has been left nothing and knows he is going to have to take what he gets. One day a little band of these odd apes—for apes they were—shambled out upon the grass; the human story had begun.

Apes were to become men, in the inscrutable wisdom of nature, because flowers had produced seeds and fruits in such tremendous quantities that a new and totally different store of energy had become available in concentrated form. Impressive as the slow-moving, dim-brained dinosaurs had been, it is doubtful if their age had supported anything like the diversity of life that now rioted across the planet or flashed in and out among the trees. Down on the grass by a streamside, one of those apes with inquisitive fingers turned over a stone and hefted it vaguely. The group clucked together in a throaty tongue and moved off through the tall grass foraging for seeds and insects. The one still held, sniffed, and hefted the stone he had found. He liked the feel of it in his fingers. The attack on the animal world was about to begin.

If one could run the story of that first human group like a speeded-up motion picture through a million years of time, one might see the stone in the hand change to the flint ax and the torch. All that swarming grassland world with its giant bison and trumpeting mammoths would go down in ruin to feed the insatiable and growing numbers of a carnivore who, like the great cats before him, was taking his energy indirectly from the grass. Later he found fire and it altered the tough meats and drained their energy even faster into a stomach ill adapted for the ferocious turn man's habits had taken.

His limbs grew longer, he strode more purposefully over the grass. The stolen energy that would take man across the continents would fail him at last. The great Ice Age herds were destined to vanish. When they did so, another hand like the hand that grasped the stone by the river long ago would pluck a handful of grass seed and hold it contemplatively. 37

In that moment, the golden towers of man, his swarming millions, his turning wheels, the vast learning of his packed libraries, would glimmer dimly there in the ancestor of wheat, a few seeds held in a muddy hand. Without the gift of flowers and the infinite diversity of their fruits, man and bird, if they had continued to exist at all, would be today unrecognizable. Archaeopteryx, the lizard-bird, might still be snapping at beetles on a sequoia limb; man might still be a nocturnal insectivore gnawing a roach in the dark. The weight of a petal has changed the face of the world and made it ours. 38

Rhetorical Analysis

1. In essence, the biologist attempts to read the past just as the political scientist attempts to predict the future, by creating connections between known facts and by extrapolating from them. Here are two rhetorical tactics useful to both kinds of scientists in interpretation and analysis:
    a. Causation, as a relationship between cause and effect, is essentially a reasoned connection between two events. But causal relationships can be extremely complex. "How Flowers Changed the World" proposes one long chain of cause and effect, but the links are complicated. Select two or three paragraphs and diagram Eiseley's pattern of causation. Then study how Eiseley clearly communicates that pattern to the reader no matter how complex it is, through vocabulary, syntax, and transitional phrases (for examples, see ¶s 10, 13, 21, 25, 29).
    b. A more imaginative tactic in reading the past requires the writer to visualize hypothetical situations. Eiseley's ability to visualize the past is astonishing,

and without it, "How Flowers Changed the World" would read very differently. When Eiseley talks about the dispersal power of seeds, for example, he sees them "skipping and hopping and flying about the woods and valleys" (¶ 27). Choose any two or three paragraphs and study this distinctive writing tactic.
2. In a sense, "How Flowers Changed the World" is constructed like the last chapter of a detective story. How does Eiseley whet our appetite for the solution to the "crime," yet postpone that solution until nearly the end?

Intellectual Analysis

1. The tone and diction of Eiseley's essay are quite different from the other essays by him in this book. How? Can you describe and exemplify Eiseley's tone and attitude? How do they affect his meaning?
    a. Eiseley's enthusiasm for his subject is striking. Characterize it.
    b. How, in his enthusiasm, does he avoid absurdity, sentimentality, or gushiness? For example, examine ¶ 28 carefully.
    c. How does Eiseley make use of the senses in his language? For example, study ¶s 4, 8, and 18.
2. By way of admiring Eiseley's intellect, tote up the number of disciplines he incorporates in this essay. Eiseley is simultaneously drawing on his studies in several fields. How does he manage them all without strain or confusion?
3. The chain of causes that Eiseley traces might be outlined this way: (1) A planet with no life on it; (2) a world covered with green; (3) a planet with emerging animal life; (4) a world populated with flowers and warm-blooded animals; (5) a world with proto-human life, imaged by stone and then a handful of seeds.
    a. First, mark the key spots in the essay where this progression is made clear, and make note of tactics Eiseley uses to link the parts into a whole.
    b. Secondly, notice that this progression might be further simplified to a preoccupation with two subjects, each of which may be clearly traced throughout the essay: flowers and metabolism. See, for example, ¶s 11, 12, and 16.
    c. Finally, the progression of the whole essay might admit of one further simplification: the word "explosion" and its derivatives. Follow that metaphor from ¶ 5 onward, and notice how many ways the word and the idea are extended or mutated.
4. One of Eiseley's major concerns in this essay is time, the immensity of it, played against a geological or biological event. In what sense can Eiseley speak of epochs, "some millions of years" (¶ 14), and yet say "In that moment" in ¶ 38? What other such opposites—matchings of large and small, for example—does Eiseley use just as freely? And what overall impression do we gain from that pattern?

Suggestions for Writing

1. "How Flowers Changed the World" aims to make technical generalizations (such as "angiosperms arose in Cretaceous times") vivid and meaningful. Choose an area in which you have some technical knowledge and do the same for a lay reader, perhaps for either your instructor or another student. As a second model for your essay, you might observe how Thomas pursues the same aim in "Seven Wonders of the Modern World."
2. Write an essay in which you evaluate Eiseley's essay from the point of view expressed in Stephen Jay Gould's "The Nonscience of Human Nature."
3. How is this essay similar to the other two by Eiseley in this book, and how is it different? Or, compare this essay structurally and stylistically to a comparable chapter in a biology textbook. What differences do you find? Write an essay discussing the reasons for the differences.

THE JUDGMENT OF THE BIRDS

*I*t is a commonplace of all religious thought, even the most primitive, that the man seeking visions and insight must go apart from his fellows and live for a time in the wilderness. If he is of the proper sort, he will return with a message. It may not be a message from the god he set out to seek, but even if he has failed in that particular, he will have had a vision or seen a marvel, and these are always worth listening to and thinking about.

The world, I have come to believe, is a very queer place, but we have been part of this queerness for so long that we tend to take it for granted. We rush to and fro like Mad Hatters upon our peculiar errands, all the time imagining our surroundings to be dull and ourselves quite ordinary creatures. Actually, there is nothing in the world to encourage this idea, but such is the mind of man, and this is why he finds it necessary from time to time to send emissaries into the wilderness in the hope of learning of great events, or plans in store for him, that will resuscitate his waning taste for life. His great news services, his world-wide radio network, he knows with a last remnant of healthy distrust will be of no use to him in this matter. No miracle can withstand a radio broadcast, and it is certain that it would be no miracle if it could. One must seek, then, what only the solitary approach can give—a natural revelation.

Let it be understood that I am not the sort of man to whom is entrusted direct knowledge of great events or prophecies. A naturalist, however, spends much of his life alone, and my life is no exception. Even in New York City there are patches of wilderness, and a man by himself is bound to undergo certain experiences falling into the class of which I speak. I set mine down, therefore: a matter of pigeons, a flight of chemicals, and a judgment of birds, in the hope that they will come to the eye of those who have retained a true taste for the marvelous, and who are capable of discerning in the flow of ordinary events the point at which the mundane world gives way to quite another dimension.

New York is not, on the whole, the best place to enjoy the downright miraculous nature of the planet. There are, I do not doubt, many remarkable stories to be heard there and many strange sights to be seen, but to grasp a marvel fully it must be savored from all aspects. This cannot be done while one is being jostled and hustled along a crowded street. Nevertheless, in any city there are true wildernesses where a man can be alone. It can happen in a hotel room, or on the high roofs at dawn.

One night on the twentieth floor of a midtown hotel I awoke in the dark and grew restless. On an impulse I climbed upon the broad old-fashioned window sill, opened the curtains and peered out. It was the hour just before dawn, the hour when men sigh in their sleep, or, if awake, strive to focus their wavering eyesight upon a world emerging from the shadows. I leaned out sleepily through the open window. I had expected depths, but not the sight I saw.

I found I was looking down from that great height into a series of curious cupolas or lofts that I could just barely make out in the darkness. As I looked, the outlines of these lofts became more distinct because the light was being reflected from the wings of pigeons who, in utter silence, were beginning to float outward upon the city. In and out through the open slits in the cupolas passed the white-winged birds on their mysterious errands. At this hour the city was theirs, and quietly, without the brush of a single wing tip against stone in that high, eerie place, they were taking over the spires of Manhattan. They were pouring upward in a light that was not yet perceptible to human eyes, while far down in the black darkness of the alleys it was still midnight.

As I crouched half asleep across the sill, I had a moment's

illusion that the world had changed in the night, as in some immense snowfall, and that if I were to leave, it would have to be as these other inhabitants were doing, by the window. I should have to launch out into that great bottomless void with the simple confidence of young birds reared high up there among the familiar chimney pots and interposed horrors of the abyss.

I leaned farther out. To and fro went the white wings, to and fro. There were no sounds from any of them. They knew man was asleep and this light for a little while was theirs. Or perhaps I had only dreamed about man in this city of wings—which he could surely never have built. Perhaps I, myself, was one of these birds dreaming unpleasantly a moment of old dangers far below as I teetered on a window ledge.

Around and around went the wings. It needed only a little courage, only a little shove from the window ledge to enter that city of light. The muscles of my hands were already making little premonitory lunges. I wanted to enter that city and go away over the roofs in the first dawn. I wanted to enter it so badly that I drew back carefully into the room and opened the hall door. I found my coat on the chair, and it slowly became clear to me that there was a way down through the floors, that I was, after all, only a man.

I dressed then and went back to my own kind, and I have been rather more than usually careful ever since not to look into the city of light. I had seen, just once, man's greatest creation from a strange inverted angle, and it was not really his at all. I will never forget how those wings went round and round, and how, by the merest pressure of the fingers and a feeling for air, one might go away over the roofs. It is a knowledge, however, that is better kept to oneself. I think of it sometimes in such a way that the wings, beginning far down in the black depths of the mind, begin to rise and whirl till all the mind is lit by their spinning, and there is a sense of things passing away, but lightly, as a wing might veer over an obstacle.

To see from an inverted angle, however, is not a gift allotted merely to the human imagination. I have come to suspect that within their degree it is sensed by animals, though perhaps as rarely as among men. The time has to be right; one has to be, by chance or intention, upon the border of two worlds. And sometimes these two borders may shift or interpenetrate and one sees the miraculous.

I once saw this happen to a crow.

This crow lives near my house, and though I have never injured him, he takes good care to stay up in the very highest trees and, in general, to avoid humanity. His world begins at about the limit of my eyesight.

On the particular morning when this episode occurred, the whole countryside was buried in one of the thickest fogs in years. The ceiling was absolutely zero. All planes were grounded, and even a pedestrian could hardly see his outstretched hand before him.

I was groping across a field in the general direction of the railroad station, following a dimly outlined path. Suddenly out of the fog, at about the level of my eyes, and so closely that I flinched, there flashed a pair of immense black wings and a huge beak. The whole bird rushed over my head with a frantic cawing outcry of such hideous terror as I have never heard in a crow's voice before, and never expect to hear again.

He was lost and startled, I thought, as I recovered my poise. He ought not to have flown out in this fog. He'd knock his silly brains out.

All afternoon that great awkward cry rang in my head. Merely being lost in a fog seemed scarcely to account for it—especially in a tough, intelligent old bandit such as I knew that particular crow to be. I even looked once in the mirror to see what it might be about me that had so revolted him that he had cried out in protest to the very stones.

Finally, as I worked my way homeward along the path, the solution came to me. It should have been clear before. The borders of our worlds had shifted. It was the fog that had done it. That crow, and I knew him well, never under normal circumstances flew low near men. He had been lost all right, but it was more than that. He had thought he was high up, and when he encountered me looming gigantically through the fog, he had perceived a ghastly and, to the crow mind, unnatural sight. He had seen a man walking on air, desecrating the very heart of the crow kingdom, a harbinger of the most profound evil a crow mind could conceive of—air-walking men. The encounter, he must have thought, had taken place a hundred feet over the roofs.

He caws now when he sees me leaving for the station in the morning, and I fancy that in that note I catch the uncertainty of a mind that has come to know things are not always what they seem. He has seen a marvel in his heights of air and is no longer as other crows. He has experienced the human world from an unlikely perspective. He and I share a viewpoint in common: our worlds have interpenetrated, and we both have faith in the miraculous.

It is a faith that in my own case has been augmented by two

remarkable sights. As I have hinted previously, I once saw some very odd chemicals fly across a waste so dead it might have been upon the moon, and once, by an even more fantastic piece of luck, I was present when a group of birds passed a judgment upon life.

On the maps of the old voyageurs it is called *Mauvaises Terres*, the evil lands, and, slurred a little with the passage through many minds, it has come down to us anglicized as the Badlands. The soft shuffle of moccasins has passed through its canyons on the grim business of war and flight, but the last of those slight disturbances of immemorial silences died out almost a century ago. The land, if one can call it a land, is a waste as lifeless as that valley in which lie the kings of Egypt. Like the Valley of the Kings, it is a mausoleum, a place of dry bones in what once was a place of life. Now it has silences as deep as those in the moon's airless chasms.

Nothing grows among its pinnacles; there is no shade except under great toadstools of sandstone whose bases have been eaten to the shape of wine glasses by the wind. Everything is flaking, cracking, disintegrating, wearing away in the long, imperceptible weather of time. The ash of ancient volcanic outbursts still sterilizes its soil, and its colors in that waste are the colors that flame in the lonely sunsets on dead planets. Men come there but rarely, and for one purpose only, the collection of bones.

It was a late hour on a cold, wind-bitten autumn day when I climbed a great hill spined like a dinosaur's back and tried to take my bearings. The tumbled waste fell away in waves in all directions. Blue air was darkening into purple along the bases of the hills. I shifted my knapsack, heavy with the petrified bones of long-vanished creatures, and studied my compass. I wanted to be out of there by nightfall, and already the sun was going sullenly down in the west.

It was then that I saw the flight coming on. It was moving like a little close-knit body of black specks that danced and darted and closed again. It was pouring from the north and heading toward me with the undeviating relentlessness of a compass needle. It streamed through the shadows rising out of monstrous gorges. It rushed over towering pinnacles in the red light of the sun, or momentarily sank from sight within their shade. Across that desert of eroding clay and wind-worn stone they came with a faint wild twittering that filled all the air about me as those tiny living bullets hurtled past into the night.

It may not strike you as a marvel. It would not, perhaps, unless you stood in the middle of a dead world at sunset, but that was where I stood. Fifty million years lay under my feet, fifty million years of bellowing monsters moving in a green world now gone so utterly that its very light was travelling on the farther edge of space. The chemicals of all that vanished age lay about me in the ground. Around me still lay the shearing molars of dead titanotheres, the delicate sabers of soft-stepping cats, the hollow sockets that had held the eyes of many a strange, outmoded beast. Those eyes had looked out upon a world as real as ours; dark, savage brains had roamed and roared their challenges into the steaming night.

Now they were still here, or, put it as you will, the chemicals that made them were here about me in the ground. The carbon that had driven them ran blackly in the eroding stone. The stain of iron was in the clays. The iron did not remember the blood it had once moved within, the phosphorus had forgot the savage brain. The little individual moment had ebbed from all those strange combinations of chemicals as it would ebb from our living bodies into the sinks and runnels of oncoming time.

I had lifted up a fistful of that ground. I held it while that wild flight of south-bound warblers hurtled over me into the oncoming dark. There went phosphorus, there went iron, there went carbon, there beat the calcium in those hurrying wings. Alone on a dead planet I watched that incredible miracle speeding past. It ran by some true compass over field and waste land. It cried its individual ecstasies into the air until the gullies rang. It swerved like a single body, it knew itself and, lonely, it bunched close in the racing darkness, its individual entities feeling about them the rising night. And so, crying to each other their identity, they passed away out of my view.

I dropped my fistful of earth. I heard it roll inanimate back into the gully at the base of the hill: iron, carbon, the chemicals of life. Like men from those wild tribes who had haunted these hills before me seeking visions, I made my sign to the great darkness. It was not a mocking sign, and I was not mocked. As I walked into my camp late that night, one man, rousing from his blankets beside the fire, asked sleepily, "What did you see?"

"I think, a miracle," I said softly, but I said it to myself. Behind me that vast waste began to glow under the rising moon.

I have said that I saw a judgment upon life, and that it was not passed by men. Those who stare at birds in cages or who test minds by their closeness to our own may not care for it. It comes from far away out of my past, in a place of pouring waters and green leaves. I shall never see an episode like it again if I live to be a hundred, nor do I think that one man in a million has ever seen it, because man is an intruder into such silences. The light must be right, and the observer must remain unseen. No man sets up such an experiment. What he sees, he sees by chance.

You may put it that I had come over a mountain, that I had slogged through fern and pine needles for half a long day, and that on the edge of a little glade with one long, crooked branch extending across it, I had sat down to rest with my back against a stump. Through accident I was concealed from the glade, although I could see into it perfectly.

The sun was warm there, and the murmurs of forest life blurred softly away into my sleep. When I awoke, dimly aware of some commotion and outcry in the clearing, the light was slanting down through the pines in such a way that the glade was lit like some vast cathedral. I could see the dust motes of wood pollen in the long shaft of light, and there on the extended branch sat an enormous raven with a red and squirming nestling in his beak.

The sound that awoke me was the outraged cries of the nestling's parents, who flew helplessly in circles about the clearing. The sleek black monster was indifferent to them. He gulped, whetted his beak on the dead branch a moment and sat still. Up to that point the little tragedy had followed the usual pattern. But suddenly, out of all that area of woodland, a soft sound of complaint began to rise. Into the glade fluttered small birds of half a dozen varieties drawn by the anguished outcries of the tiny parents.

No one dared to attack the raven. But they cried there in some instinctive common misery, the bereaved and the unbereaved. The glade filled with their soft rustling and their cries. They fluttered as though to point their wings at the murderer. There was a dim intangible ethic he had violated, that they knew. He was a bird of death.

And he, the murderer, the black bird at the heart of life, sat on there, glistening in the common light, formidable, unmoving, unperturbed, untouchable.

The sighing died. It was then I saw the judgment. It was the judgment of life against death. I will never see it again so forcefully presented. I will never hear it again in notes so tragically prolonged. For in the midst of protest, they forgot the violence. There, in that clearing, the crystal note of a song sparrow lifted hesitantly in the hush. And finally, after painful fluttering, another took the song, and then another, the song passing from one bird to another, doubtfully at first, as though some evil thing were being slowly forgotten. Till suddenly they took heart and sang from many throats joyously together as birds are known to sing. They sang because life is sweet and sunlight beautiful. They sang under the brooding shadow of the raven. In simple truth they had forgotten the raven, for they were the singers of life, and not of death.

I was not of that airy company. My limbs were the heavy limbs of an earthbound creature who could climb mountains, even the mountains of the mind, only by a great effort of will. I knew I had seen a marvel and observed a judgment, but the mind which was my human endowment was sure to question it and to be at me day by day with its heresies until I grew to doubt the meaning of what I had seen. Eventually darkness and subtleties would ring me round once more.

And so it proved until, on the top of a stepladder, I made one more observation upon life. It was cold that autumn evening, and, standing under a suburban street light in a spate of leaves and beginning snow, I was suddenly conscious of some huge and hairy shadows dancing over the pavement. They seemed attached to an odd, globular shape that was magnified above me. There was no mistaking it. I was standing under the shadow of an orb-weaving spider. Gigantically projected against the street, she was about her spinning when everything was going underground. Even her cables were magnified upon the sidewalk and already I was half-entangled in their shadows.

"Good Lord," I thought, "she has found herself a kind of minor sun and is going to upset the course of nature."

I procured a ladder from my yard and climbed up to inspect the situation. There she was, the universe running down around her, warmly arranged among her guy ropes attached to the lamp supports—a great black and yellow embodiment of the life force, not giving up to either frost or stepladders. She ignored me and went on tightening and improving her web.

I stood over her on the ladder, a faint snow touching my cheeks, and surveyed her universe. There were a couple of iridescent green beetle cases turning slowly on a loose strand of web, a fragment of luminescent eye from a moth's wing and a large indeterminable object, perhaps a cicada, that had struggled and been wrapped in silk. There were also little bits and slivers, little red and blue flashes from the scales of anonymous wings that had crashed there.

Some days, I thought, they will be dull and gray and the shine will be out of them; then the dew will polish them again and drops hang on the silk until everything is gleaming and turning in the light. It is like a mind, really, where everything changes but remains, and in the end you have these eaten-out bits of experience like beetle wings.

I stood over her a moment longer, comprehending somewhat reluctantly that her adventure against the great blind forces of winter, her seizure of this warming globe of light, would come to nothing and was hopeless. Nevertheless it brought the birds back into my mind, and that faraway song which had traveled with growing strength around a forest clearing years ago—a kind of heroism, a world where even a spider refuses to lie down and die if a rope can still be spun on to a star. Maybe man himself will fight like this in the end, I thought, slowly realizing that the web and its threatening yellow occupant had been added to some luminous store of experience, shining for a moment in the fogbound reaches of my brain. 43

The mind, it came to me as I slowly descended the ladder, is a very remarkable thing; it has gotten itself a kind of courage by looking at a spider in a street lamp. Here was something that ought to be passed on to those who will fight our final freezing battle with the void. I thought of setting it down carefully as a message to the future: *In the days of the frost seek a minor sun.* 44

But as I hesitated, it became plain that something was wrong. The marvel was escaping—a sense of bigness beyond man's power to grasp, the essence of life in its great dealings with the universe. It was better, I decided, for the emissaries returning from the wilderness, even if they were merely descending from a stepladder, to record their marvel, not to define its meaning. In that way it would go echoing on through the minds of men, each grasping at that beyond out of which the miracles emerge, and which, once defined, ceases to satisfy the human need for symbols. 45

In the end I merely made a mental note: One specimen of Epeira observed building a web in a street light. Late autumn and cold for spiders. Cold for men, too. I shivered and left the lamp glowing there in my mind. The last I saw of Epeira she was hauling steadily on a cable. I stepped carefully over her shadow as I walked away. 46

Rhetorical Analysis

1. The introduction (¶s 1–3) is adroit. It is divided into three parts for more than just logical construction. Analyze its structure. It also introduces verbal strands which help tie the essay together—for instance, "vision," "wilderness," "message," "the

marvelous," "natural revelation," and "another dimension." Trace some of these strands through the essay.

2. The body of the essay consists of five episodes. Their sequence is meaningful. For instance, the essay moves from the city (the pigeons) to the green country (the crow) to the barren Badlands (the warblers) back to the green country (the songbirds and the raven) and then finally back to the city (the spider). This sequence repeats the Biblical search for vision alluded to in the first paragraph: the retreat into a desert wilderness and a return with a prophetic message. In what other ways is the ordering of the five episodes meaningful?

3. Eiseley's extreme care in writing this essay can be illustrated by noting the verbal parallels binding Eiseley to the animals which provide him with "natural revelations." In the first episode he "leaned out sleepily through the open window" while the pigeons "were beginning to float outward upon the city." In the second episode he "was groping across the field" and "flinches" upon encountering the crow, while the crow is also "lost and startled." On the Badlands he "studied [his] compass" and the warblers migrate with the "undeviating relentlessness of a compass needle." There are other such verbal connections. What is Eiseley's purpose in using them?

Intellectual Analysis

1. As noted above, Eiseley begins and ends the essay with a reference to prophets and their retreats to the wilderness.
    a. What does Eiseley gain by framing his essay in this idea? Consider such a question as this: Why does one retreat—for a better vision of nature, or a vision inside the mind? In answering, identify internal evidence from the essay to prove your point.
    b. What are the characteristics of each retreat? (For example, why is solitude necessary? What does being alone have to do with perception?) In answering this question, consider Eiseley's definition of the miraculous (in ¶ 11 see "the border of two worlds").

2. You are encouraged above to notice the rhetorical effect of the essay's five-part structure; now consider the same structure from the aspect of intellectual content.
    a. What does Eiseley learn from each of the incidents? Are the revelations always about the relationship between man and nature?
    b. How do the incidents differ? For example, with the pigeons, Eiseley sees the world as they do; with the crow in the fog, the bird sees our world as we do; hence the perspective of up and down, of human toward animal, has changed. What, then, do we make of the "flight of chemicals"? The last two episodes are both akin to the first three, yet set apart. How is the raven incident different from the preceding three, and how does the spider episode draw the entire series of episodes together?

Suggestions for Writing

1. Eiseley's final sentence is, "I stepped carefully over her shadow as I walked away." Write an essay defining "shadow" and discussing the author's meaning here. What has this concluding sentence to do with the essay as a whole? What would happen to the meaning of the essay if this final sentence were omitted?
2. Eiseley sees some deeper lesson for man in the spider's web—and hence in each incident—and he describes it at one point as, "Here was something that ought to be passed on to those who will fight our final freezing battle with the void." Consider the meaning of this sentence, and interpret it more generally in terms of contemporary politics and culture.
3. Consider the raven episode in ¶s 30–37. In the preceding episodes, our relationship to birds, and birds' to us, have been considered, and in "the flight of chemicals," both birds and humans are related to time. Here, Eiseley seems to see imaged, in the kingdom of birds, humanity's own situation. Develop, by means of close interpretation of this section, an essay on the view this episode takes of our world.
4. Compare Eiseley's attitude toward birds with Lopez's attitude toward wolves in "Wolfing for Sport" or toward buffalo in "Buffalo."

ONE NIGHT'S DYING

There is always a soft radiance beyond the bedroom door from a night-light behind my chair. I have lived this way for many years now. I sleep or I do not sleep, and the light makes no difference except if I wake. Then, as I awaken, the dim forms of objects sustain my grip on reality. The familiar chair, the walls of the book-lined study reassert my own existence.

I do not lie and toss with doubt any longer, as I did in earlier years. I get up and write, as I am writing now, or I read in the old chair that is as worn as I am. I read philosophy, metaphysics, difficult works that sometime, soon or late, draw a veil over my eyes so that I drowse in my chair.

It is not that I fail to learn from these midnight examinations of the world. It is merely that I choose that examination to remain as remote and abstruse as possible. Even so, I cannot always prophesy the result. An obscure line may whirl me into a wide-awake, ferocious concentration in which ideas like animals leap at me out of the dark, in which sudden odd trains of thought drive me inexorably to my desk and paper. I am, in short, a victim of insomnia—sporadic, wearing, violent, and melancholic. In the words of Shakespeare, for me the world "does murder sleep." It has been so since my twentieth year.

In that year my father died—a man well loved, the mainstay of our small afflicted family. He died slowly in severe bodily torture. My mother was stone-deaf. I, his son, saw and heard him die. We lived in a place and time not free with the pain-alleviating drugs of later decades. When the episode of many weeks' duration was over, a curious thing happened: I could no longer bear the ticking of the alarm clock in my own bedroom.

At first I smothered it with an extra blanket in a box beside my cot, but the ticking persisted as though it came from my own head. I used to lie for hours staring into the dark of the sleeping house, feeling the loneliness that only the sleepless know when the queer feeling comes that it is the sleeping who are alive and those awake are disembodied ghosts. Finally, in desperation, I gave up the attempt to sleep and turned to reading, though it was difficult to concentrate.

It was then that human help appeared. My grandmother saw the light burning through the curtains of my door and came to sit with me. A few years later, when I touched her hair in farewell at the beginning of a journey from which I would not return to see her alive, I knew she had saved my sanity. Into that lonely room at midnight she had come, abandoning her own sleep, in order to sit with one in trouble. We had not talked much, but we had sat together by the lamp, reasserting our common humanity before the great empty dark that is the universe.

Grandmother knew nothing of psychiatry. She had not reestablished my sleep patterns, but she had done something more important. She had brought me out of a dark room and retied my thread of life to the living world. Henceforward, by night or day, though I have been subject to the moods of depression or gaiety which are a part of the lives of all of us, I have been able not merely to endure but to make the best of what many regard as an unbearable affliction.

It is true that as an educational administrator I can occasionally be caught nodding in lengthy committee meetings, but so, I have observed, can men who come from sound nights on their pillows. Strangely, I, who frequently grow round-eyed and alert as an owl at the stroke of midnight, find it pleasant to nap in daylight among friends. I can roll up on a couch and sleep peacefully while my wife and chatting friends who know my peculiarities keep the daytime universe safely under control. Or so it seems. For, deep-seated in my subconscious, is perhaps the idea that the black bedroom door is the gateway to the tomb.

I try in that bedroom to sleep high on two pillows, to have ears and eyes alert. Something shadowy has to be held in place and controlled. At night one has to sustain reality without help. One has to hear lest hearing be lost, see lest sight not return to follow moonbeams across the floor, touch lest the sense of objects vanish. Oh, sleeping, soundlessly sleeping ones, do you ever think who knits your universe together safely from one day's memory to the next? It is the insomniac, not the night policeman on his beat.

Many will challenge this point of view. They will say that electric power does the trick, that many a roisterer stumbles down the long street at dawn, after having served his purpose of holding the links of the mad world together. There are parts of the nighttime world, men say to me, that it is just as well I do not know. Go home and sleep, man. Others will keep your giddy world together. Let the thief pass quickly in the shadow, he is awake. Let the juvenile gangs which sidle like bands of evil crabs up from the dark waters of poverty into prosperous streets pass without finding you at midnight.

The advice is good, but in the city or the country small things important to our lives have no reporter except as he who does not sleep may observe them. And that man must be disencumbered of reality. He must have no commitments to the dark, as do the murderer and thief. Only he must see, though what he sees may come from the night side of the planet that no man knows well. For even in the early dawn, while men lie unstirring in their sleep or stumble sleepy-eyed to work, some single episode may turn the whole world for a moment into the place of marvel that it is, but that we grow too day-worn to accept.

For example, I call the place where I am writing now the bay of broken things. In the February storms, spume wraiths climb the hundred-foot cliff to fight and fall like bitter rain in the moonlight upon the cabin roof. The earth shakes from the drum roll of the surf. I lie awake and watch through the window beyond my bed. This is no ticking in my brain; this is the elemental night of chaos. This is the sea chewing its million-year way into the heart of the continent.

The caves beneath the cliff resound with thunder. Again those warring wraiths shoot high over the house. Impelled as though I were a part of all those leaping ghosts, I dress in the dark and come forth.

With my back against the door, like an ancient necromancer, I hurl my mind into the white spray and try to summon back, among those leaping forms, the faces and features of the dead I know. The shapes rise endlessly, but they pass inland before the wind, indifferent to my mortal voice.

I walk a half mile to a pathway that descends upon a little beach. Below me is a stretch of white sand. No shell is ever found unbroken, even on quiet days, upon that shore. Everything comes over the rocks to seaward. Wood is riven into splinters; the bones of seamen and of sea lions are pounded equally into white and shining sand. Throughout the night the long black rollers, like lines of frothing cavalry, form ranks, drum towering forward, and fall, fall till the mind is dizzy with the spume that fills it. I wait in the shelter of a rock for daybreak. At last the sea eases a trifle. The tide is going out.

I stroll shivering along the shore, and there, exposed in inescapable nakedness, I see the elemental cruelty of the natural world. A broken-winged gull, hurled by the wind against the cliff, runs before me wearily along the beach. It will starve or, mercifully, the dogs will find it. I try not to hurry it, and walk on. A little later in a quieter bend of the shore, I see ahead of me a bleeding, bedraggled blot on the edge of the white surf. As I approach, it starts warily to its feet. We look at each other. It is a wild duck, also with a shattered wing. It does not run ahead of me like the longer-limbed gull. Before I can cut off its retreat it waddles painfully from its brief refuge into the water.

The sea continues to fall heavily. The duck dives awkwardly, but with long knowledge and instinctive skill, under the fall of the first two inshore waves. I see its head working seaward. A long green roller, far taller than my head, rises and crashes forward. The black head of the waterlogged duck disappears. This is the way wild things die, without question, without knowledge of mercy in the universe, knowing only themselves and their own pathway to the end. I wonder, walking farther up the beach, if the man who shot that bird will die as well.

This is the chaos before man came, before sages imbued with pity walked the earth. Indeed it is true, and in my faraway study my hands have often touched with affection the backs of the volumes which line my shelves. Nevertheless, I have endured the nights and mornings of the city. I have seen old homeless men who have slept for hours sitting upright on ledges along the outer hallway of one of the great Eastern stations straighten stiffly in the dawn and limp away with feigned businesslike aloofness before the approach of the policeman on his rounds. I know that on these cold winter mornings sometimes a man, like the pigeons I have seen roosting as closely as possible over warm hotel air vents, will fall stiffly and not awaken. It is true that there are shelters for the homeless, but some men, like their ice-age forebears, prefer their independence to the end.

The loneliness of the city was brought home to me one early sleepless morning, not by men like me tossing in lonely rooms, not by poverty and degradation, not by old men trying with desperate futility to be out among others in the great roaring hive, but by a single one of those same pigeons which I had seen from my hotel window, looking down at midnight upon the smoking air vents and chimneys.

The pigeon, *Columba livia*, is the city bird *par excellence*. He is a descendant of the rock pigeon that in the Old World lived among the cliffs and crevices above the caves that early man inhabited. He has been with us since our beginning and has adapted as readily as ourselves to the artificial cliffs of man's first cities. He has known the Roman palaces and the cities of Byzantium. His little flat feet, suited to high and precarious walking, have sauntered in the temples of vanished gods as readily as in New York's old Pennsylvania Station. In my dim morning strolls, waiting for the restaurants to open, I have seen him march quickly into the back end of a delivery truck while the driver was inside a store engaged in his orders with the proprietor. Yet for all its apparent tolerance of these highly adapted and often comic birds, New York also has a beach of broken things more merciless than the reefs and rollers of the ocean shore.

One morning, strolling sleepless as usual toward early breakfast time in Manhattan, I saw a sick pigeon huddled at an uncomfortable slant against a building wall on a street corner. I felt sorry for the bird, but I had no box, no instrument of help, and had learned long ago that pursuing wounded birds on city streets is a hopeless, dangerous activity. Pigeons, like men, die in scores every day in New York. As I hesitantly walked on, however, I wondered why the doomed bird was assuming such a desperately contorted position under the cornice that projected slightly over it.

At this moment I grew aware of something I had heard more loudly in European streets as the factory whistles blew, but never in such intensity as here, even though American shoes are built of softer materials. All around me the march of people was intensifying. It was New York on the way to work. Space was shrinking before my eyes. The tread of innumerable feet passed from an echo to the steady murmuring of a stream, then to a drumming. A dreadful robot rhythm began to rack my head, a sound like the boots of Nazis in their heyday of power. I was carried along in an irresistible surge of bodies.

A block away, jamming myself between a waste-disposal basket and a lightpost, I managed to look back. No one hesitated at that corner. The human tide pressed on, jostling and pushing. My bird had vanished under that crunching, multi-footed current as remorselessly as the wounded duck under the indifferent combers of the sea. I watched this human ocean, of which I was an unwilling droplet, rolling past, its individual faces like whitecaps passing on a night of storm, fixed, merciless, indifferent; man in the mass marching like the machinery of which he is already a replaceable part, toward desks, computers, missiles, and machines, marching like the waves toward his own death with a conscious ruthlessness no watery shore could ever duplicate. I have never returned to search in that particular street for the face of humanity. I prefer the endlessly rolling pebbles of the tide, the moonstones polished by the pulling moon.

And yet, plunged as I am in dire memories and midnight reading, I have said that it is the sufferer from insomnia who knits the torn edges of men's dreams together in the hour before dawn. It is he who from his hidden, winter vantage point sees the desperate high-hearted bird fly through the doorway of the grand hotel while the sleepy doorman nods, a deed equivalent in human terms to that of some starving wretch evading Peter at heaven's gate, and an act, I think, very likely to be forgiven.

It is a night more mystical, however, that haunts my memory. Around me I see again the parchment of old books and remember how, on one rare evening, I sat in the shadows while a firefly flew from volume to volume lighting its small flame, as if in literate curiosity. Choosing the last title it had illuminated, I came immediately upon these words from St. Paul: "Beareth all things, believeth all things, hopeth all things, endureth all things." In this final episode I shall ask you to bear with me and also to believe.

I sat, once more in the late hours of darkness, in the airport of a foreign city. I was tired as only both the sufferer from insomnia and the traveler can be tired. I had missed a plane and had almost a whole night's wait before me. I could not sleep. The long corridor was deserted. Even the cleaning woman had passed by.

In that white efficient glare I grew ever more depressed and weary. I was tired of the endless comings and goings of my profession;

I was tired of customs officers and police. I was lonely for home. My eyes hurt. I was, unconsciously perhaps, looking for that warm stone, that hawthorn leaf, where, in the words of the poet, man trades in at last his wife and friend. I had an ocean to cross; the effort seemed unbearable. I rested my aching head upon my hand.

Later, beginning at the far end of that desolate corridor, I saw a man moving slowly toward me. In a small corner of my eye I merely noted him. He limped, painfully and grotesquely, upon a heavy cane. He was far away, and it was no matter to me. I shifted the unpleasant mote out of my eye.

But, after a time, I could still feel him approaching, and in one of those white moments of penetration which are so dreadful, my eyes were drawn back to him as he came on. With an anatomist's eye I saw this amazing conglomeration of sticks and broken, misshapen pulleys which make up the body of man. Here was an apt subject, and I flew to a raging mental dissection. How could anyone, I contended, trapped in this mechanical thing of joints and sliding wires expect the acts it performed to go other than awry?

The man limped on, relentlessly.

How, oh God, I entreated, did we become trapped within this substance out of which we stare so hopelessly upon our own eventual dissolution? How for a single minute could we dream or imagine that thought would save us, children deliver us, from the body of this death? Not in time, my mind rang with my despair; not in mortal time, not in this place, not anywhere in the world would blood be staunched, or the dark wrong be forever righted, or the parted be rejoined. Not in this time, not mortal time. The substance was too gross, our utopias bought with too much pain.

The man was almost upon me, breathing heavily, lunging and shuffling upon his cane. Though an odor emanated from him, I did not draw back. I had lived with death too many years. And then this strange thing happened, which I do not mean physically and cannot explain. The man entered me. From that moment I saw him no more. For a moment I was contorted within his shape, and then out of his body—our bodies, rather—there arose some inexplicable sweetness of union, some understanding between spirit and body which I had never before experienced. Was it I, the joints and pulleys only, who desired this peace so much?

I limped with growing age as I gathered up my luggage. Something of that terrible passer lingered in my bones, yet I was released, the very room had dilated. As I went toward my plane the words the firefly had found for me came automatically to my lips. "Beareth all things," believe, believe. It is thus that one day and the next are welded together, that one night's dying becomes tomorrow's birth. I, who do not sleep, can tell you this.

Rhetorical Analysis

1. Perhaps more than any other essay in this anthology, "One Night's Dying" is shaped by emotion, intuition, and imagination.
    a. The reader senses a division of the essay into these main parts: ¶s 1–3, 4–7, 8–11, 12–16, 17–23, and 24–32. Yet the seams between sections are not as distinct as they might be in a more analytical essay. One section simply flows into the next. How, in particular, does Eiseley's writing style communicate both the continuous flow and the sense of design—of periodic closure and of segmentation among the parts?
    b. A second organizational method not often found in more analytical essays is the particular way Eiseley connects the final climactic episode (¶s 25–32) to the rest of the essay. Eiseley says that the event "haunts my memory" (¶ 24), and indeed it is eerily present throughout the rest of the piece. Reread, noting the foreshadowing. How effective is this technique for you?
    c. Emotionally, the essay rises from matter-of-fact placidity to a rather oracular intensity. Study the ways Eiseley modulates his tone, paying attention especially to distinctive choice of words ("day-worn" in ¶ 11), unusual sentence structure ("Into that lonely room at midnight she had come," ¶ 6), repetition ("Not in time, not mortal time," ¶ 30), apostrophe ("Oh, sleeping, soundlessly sleeping ones," ¶ 9), and metaphoric language ("holding the links of the mad world together," ¶ 10).
2. Should we interpret the "terrible passer" (¶s 24–32) as vision, dream, omen, hallucination, or fictional character? Reread these paragraphs to judge the rhetorical clues that help us to choose among these options. Or are they clues that are intended to prevent us from choosing?

Intellectual Analysis

1. "One Night's Dying" is ostensibly about insomnia, and what one does in the watches of the night. Eiseley assures us at the outset (¶ 2) that he does not toss "with doubt any longer." He then proceeds to recount events that do not necessarily fit together. But they do. How does the author link these events?
    a. Eiseley gives us a clue in ¶ 11: "some single episode may turn the whole world for a moment into the place of marvel that it is. . . ." What does he

mean by "marvel," and how does it have to do with each of the episodes?
   b. Each episode also has to do with waking reality, or one's grip on it, from ¶ 1 onward. Explore this relationship and decide how it resounds through the whole essay. For example, see ¶ 9.
   c. From ¶ 4 on, death, as well as the night, figures in each episode. Study that connection and decide what it has to do with the "marvel" mentioned above.
   d. Finally, all of these episodes have to do with the "elemental cruelty of the natural world" (¶ 15). Ponder this theme, along with the others mentioned above.
2. Another way to divide the essay (see "Rhetorical Analysis") is to look at the major episodes: ¶ 4, his father's death; ¶ 12, the scene at the beach; ¶ 18, the pigeon in the city; ¶ 24, the encounter at the airport. But:
   a. Notice the rich material by means of which Eiseley links these episodes together. These passages cannot be called "filler," because of the new and interesting ideas they add.
   b. Notice ¶s 16–17; what do they accomplish? Certainly they too are transitional, but they accomplish much more than that.
   c. For another fine example, notice the minute details of language and metaphor in ¶ 22, and how Eiseley's whole intellectual design is simultaneously held together and moved forward.

Suggestions for Writing

1. "Some single episode may turn the whole world into the place of marvel that it is" (¶ 11). Write an account of an event in your life that has had such an effect.
2. Paragraphs 18–22 could stand as a self-contained essay, a recounting of a moment that produced insight into the nature of humanity ("man in the mass marching like the machinery of which he is already a replaceable part") and a judgment on that insight ("I prefer the endlessly rolling pebbles of the tide"). Write your own essay that provides both an insight *and* a commentary on the insight.
3. Recount a particularly vivid dream that you've had in the past few weeks—its content, its meaning, its effects.

PAUL TILLICH

His life spanned from the German Empire of Otto van Bismarck to the divided Germany of the Berlin blockade—and from a settled past to an uncertain future. Born in Prussia (northeastern Germany) in 1886, Paul Tillich died in Chicago in 1965. He is considered to be one of the most important theologians of the twentieth century.

Tillich grew to manhood in Central Europe in the late nineteenth century—during what many contemporaries later called a Golden Age, a time of peace, relative stability, and—for the middle classes, at least—progress. But in 1914, World War I marked the end of that age, golden or not. Though Tillich served as chaplain with the German forces, he was deeply opposed both to the "Great War" and to the German militarism that helped bring it about. After the Armistice, he returned to Berlin to teach religion and philosophy—in a nation that soon began consuming itself in the mendacities, barbarism, and horrors that culminated in the Third Reich. A variety of posts eventually found him at Frankfurt.

When Hitler was named chancellor of the Reich in 1933, Tillich lost his professorship and fled; "I had the great honor and luck," Tillich said, "to be about the first non-Jewish professor dismissed from a German university." He arrived in New York that same year, and began almost immediately to teach at the Union Theological Seminary in New York. He became a naturalized citizen in 1940. In 1954 he was appointed to the faculty of the Harvard Divinity school; in later years he taught at the University of Chicago.

Tillich saw his turbulent life as an engagement with history. This engagement he traced to the circumstances of his birth: "I have never doubted," he wrote in his autobiographical On the Boundary, "that the union of a father from Brandenburg and a mother from the Rhineland implanted in me the tension between eastern and western Germany. In eastern Germany, an inclination to meditation tinged with melancholy, a heightened consciousness of duty and personal sin, and a strong regard for authority and feudal traditions are still alive. Western Germany is characterized by a zest for life, love of the concrete, mobility, rationality and democracy." That those conflicting qualities parallel the struggle between East and West on the historical scale was not lost on Tillich. At the core of his theology is a "theory of dynamic truth, which holds that truth is found in the midst of struggle and destiny, and not, as Plato thought, in an unchanging 'beyond'." Tillich's theology reached a wide audience—in the last year of his life, 7,000 people came to hear him lecture at the University of California at Berkeley—a sign that the paradoxes of his temperament and his exile from his native land made him particularly suited to interpret the contradictions at the heart of our very troubled century.

FAITH AND UNCERTAINTY

*I*n his book, On the Bondage of the Will, Martin Luther writes, "What is more miserable than uncertainty!" He challenges the half-sceptical attitude of his great opponent, Erasmus of Rotterdam, who had declared that he would rather go over at once to the camp of the sceptics, if the authority of Scripture and the Church would permit him to do so. Luther demands *certainty* in the matter of our ultimate concern. He demands *assertions* and not sceptical possibilities or academic probabilities. "Take away assertions," he says, "and you take away Christianity." It is not the character of the Christian mind to avoid assertions, he declares. Every word of the prophets and the writers of the New Testament confirms his attitude and disproves that of Erasmus. Nei-

1

ther Jesus nor Paul nor John speaks in terms of probability or of accumulation of experiences. They make assertions with a certainty and an unshaken confidence about the truth of their message, which is often hard to stand and harder to understand for the modern mind. Paul writes to the Galatians, ". . . Even if we, or an angel from heaven, should preach to you a gospel contrary to that which we preached to you, let him be accursed." We feel a kind of resistance and even resentment against this unbroken certainty, the immediate consequence of which is the "Anathema" against heretics. Have we all become Erasmians, consciously or unconsciously? Do we approach Christianity as just another possibility among so many others? As, perhaps, a probability, but by no means a certainty? Was it not embarrassing for all of us when Karl Barth, following the attitude of the Reformers, said his uncompromising "No!" to all attempts to approach God in terms of progressive assurance? Did we not hear in his words the voices of ancient and modern dictators? Is the fight between Paul and the Jewish perfectionists, between Augustine and the Pelagian rationalists, between Luther and the Erasmian humanists decided by a compromise in which, in reality, Paul, Augustine and Luther are defeated? I do not speak here of a theological defeat. I speak of a defeat in our hearts, in our lives, in the depths of our souls. Or can we still realize what Luther means when he exclaims, "What is more miserable than uncertainty!"

But let us look more exactly at the nature of that certainty which Paul and Luther defend. The words of Paul show clearly that it is not *self*-certainty: ". . . Even if *we* . . . should preach to you a gospel contrary to that which we preached to you. . . ." The truth of the gospel Paul has preached is not dependent on Paul. The certainty he has is not dependent on the changes in his personal experience. He can imagine that some day he might preach a distorted gospel; he can even imagine that an angel from heaven might bring another message than that which the Church has already received. He is not sure of himself and he is not even sure of angelic visions. But he is sure of the gospel, so sure that he places himself and the highest spiritual powers under the threat of a divine curse if he or they should distort the gospel. For, he continues, the gospel I preach is not a human affair; no man put it into my head. I, yet not I; my gospel and yet not my gospel; my certainty and yet not my certainty. This is a description of our situation before God which runs through the whole Bible and the confessions of all the great Christian witnesses. It *is* our certainty, but it is lost the moment we begin to regard it as our certainty. We are certain only as long as we look at the content of our certainty and not at the rational or irrational experiences in which we have received it. Looking at ourselves and our certainty as *ours*, we discover its weakness, its vulnerability to every critical thought; we discover the small amount of probability which our reasoning can give to the idea of God and to the reality of the Christ. We discover the contradictions in the emotional side of our religious life, its oscillation between ecstatic confidence and despairing doubt. But looking at God, we realize that all the shortcomings of our experience are of no importance. Looking at God, we see that we do not have Him as an object of our knowledge, but that He has us as the subject of our existence. Looking at God we feel that we cannot escape Him even by making Him an object of sceptical arguments or of irresistible emotions. We realize that in our uncertainty there is one fixed point of certainty, however we may name it and describe it and explain it. *We* may not comprehend, but we *are* comprehended. We may not grasp anything in the depth of our uncertainty, but that we are grasped by something ultimate, which keeps us in its grasp and from which we may strive in vain to escape, remains absolutely certain.

In this sense Luther speaks of Christian certainty. "By assertion," he writes, "I mean a constant adhering, affirming, defending and invincibly persevering." This certainty was not something he possessed as his own. Nobody has experienced the profundity of doubt more than he. The refuge in authority finally taken by both Augustine and Erasmus was made impossible by Luther. So were all possible arguments for religious truth and all confidence in his vocation as a reformer, in his religious strength and his accumulated experience. All these do not count in the ultimate uncertainty. But sometimes, when, in this worst of all Hells, the First Commandment, "I am the Lord, *thy* God," came to his mind, he knew that one certainty had not left him, and this was the only one which is ultimately needed.

Can we maintain this certainty in spite of the fundamental uncertainties which are the character of our period in religion as well as in all other realms of life? Can we maintain it in spite of our personal doubts and despairs and of our sceptical heritage? The answer to these questions does not depend on us. We can attain the certainty of the Reformers and Apostles whenever it is given to us to touch the Ground of our existence and to look beyond ourselves. When we have left behind all objective probabilities about God and the Christ, and all subjective approximations to God and the Christ, when all preliminary certainties have disappeared, the ultimate certainty may appear to us. And in the power of this certainty, though never secure and never without temptation, we may walk from certainty to certainty.

Rhetorical Analysis

This essay is short, and one may more easily see its progression of ideas than with longer pieces.
1. The first paragraph sets forth an old theological debate over predestination and free will. On the one side are St. Paul, St. Augustine, Martin Luther, and Karl Barth—all of whom argue that humans have absolute need of divine grace for salvation. On the other are the Jewish perfectionists, the followers of Pelagius, Erasmus, and certain modern existential theologians, all of whom argue that, for salvation, humans have perfect freedom of will and no absolute need of God's grace. Why, rhetorically, does Tillich launch his essay in this way—that is, by reviewing an ancient controversy?
2. The long second paragraph ends by stating firmly the side Tillich takes in this debate. In this paragraph, how does Tillich lead up to that affirmation?
3. Tillich's third paragraph returns to Luther. Why? Does Tillich advance his own position in any way by reverting to the views of another?
4. The fourth paragraph does not function as summary (which would hardly be necessary in such a short essay). What does that paragraph do?

Intellectual Analysis

1. This brief essay, from its very title on, is built on paradox: that is, the putting together of things which are contradictory and incongruous. In this essay, such paradoxes are seen as being at the very center of faith.
    a. Luther demands, for example, certainty regarding that which by definition is never secure, and he wants to make "assertions" about that which is ineffable (God).
    b. When Tillich comes to explain what we might call "uncertain certitude," he uses paradoxically opposed terms: for example, "We realize that in our uncertainty there is one fixed point of certainty . . ." (¶ 2).
    Find other such logically contradictory statements, concepts, or feelings.
2. Some central theological issues lie behind these paradoxes, and they are worth further study:
    a. By mentioning Augustine and Erasmus and the "refuge" they take in "authority" (¶ 3), Tillich is pointing to some fundamental differences between Protestantism and Catholicism.

      (1) He implies an opposition between Catholic "substance" (dogma) and Protestant skepticism.
      (2) He affirms Protestantism's demand for the synthesis of paradoxical opposites.
  b. Tillich also places the responsibility of faith and the burden of synthesis squarely on the individual, not on the church. Examine ¶ 4 and the "Ground of our existence" carefully.
  c. The Protestant emphasis on salvation being won out daily (instead of once-and-for-all, at baptism) is also implicit here. How is that implication introduced and how does Tillich develop it?

Suggestions for Writing

1. Write an essay about college life in which you express your thesis as a paradox. For example: "Only what is forgotten has been best learned," or "Students truly pass a course only when they enroll in it for life."

2. Write an essay, the title of which expresses polar opposites (such as "Success and Failure," or "Leisure and Work"), but whose thesis reconciles or merges or recombines them. Other possible titles include "Comedy and Tragedy," "Conscious and Unconscious," "Realism and Idealism," "Classic and Romantic," and so on. You may use the *Dictionary of the History of Ideas* in your library as a springboard to other topics or to gather information on one of the above.

THE DECLINE AND THE VALIDITY OF THE IDEA OF PROGRESS

My subject is the idea of progress, which I will examine from the point of view that it is valid, that it has declined very much in its importance, and that in a new form it might be revived. Therefore, my title is "The Decline and the Validity of the Idea of Progress."

    Let us, first, examine some basic considerations about the concepts involved. This is where my semantic critics are right. Every discussion today in philosophy and theology demands a semantic clearing up of the concepts which are used, because we are living in Babylon after the tower has been destroyed and the languages of man have been disturbed and dispersed all over the world. This is the situation one faces today in reading theological and philosophical books. Therefore, I must guide you through some burdensome logical, semantic, and historical journeys.

Now, first, there is a difference between the concept of progress and the idea of progress. The concept of progress is an abstraction, based on the description of a group of facts, of objects of observation which may well be verified or falsified; but the idea of progress is an interpretation of existence as a whole, which means first of all our own existence. Thus, it is a matter of decision. It is an answer everybody has to give about the meaning of his life. Progress as an idea is a symbol for an attitude toward our existence. As so often in history, a concept open to logical and empirical description and analysis has become a symbol, and in the case of progress this is particularly true—the concept has become a symbol. What is extracted from a special realm of facts has become an expression of a general attitude toward life. Therefore, we must look at progress both as concept and as symbol. Since observation always precedes interpretation, I will give most attention to progress as a concept, because most of the confusions about progress as a symbol come from a limited and wrong analysis of progress as a concept.

Obviously progress is a universal experience which everybody has. The word is derived from *gressus* which means step, progress means stepping ahead from a less satisfactory situation to a more satisfactory situation. Imagine a lecture like this about progress, yet denying the idea of progress; someone might attempt this. But even such a person in denying the idea of progress works for progress; that is, he wants the less informed of his listeners to be better informed at the end of his lecture. In this sense, even if he speaks against the idea of progress, he accepts the concept of progress. He is implicitly progressivistic. I call this kind of thinking about progress "progressivism," which is implied in every action. Everybody who acts, acts in order to change a state of things in the direction of a better state of things. He wants to make progress. This is the most simple, the most fundamental, and actually the least contradictory way of understanding progress—the progressivism implied in every action. Nobody can get away from this. Yet this simple sense of progress is far from progress as the universal way of life, and as the law of human history. Therefore, we ask how could the idea have arisen that human history and, even preceding it, the history of all life, the history of the universe, has a progressivistic character—is progress from something lower to something higher. How could this idea develop? What are the motives behind it?

Now I must first guide you on the thorny path—especially so for Americans—of historical reminder. I hope it is a reminder because I presume that all of you know what I am referring to, but if not, be patient with me because the historical question gives the basis for the understanding of what today seems natural to us. The idea of this country is that it represents a new beginning in the history of mankind. This is true in many respects. But the new beginning is never fully new. It is always a result of preceding events, and if I may comment on my experience on two continents, I would say that Europe is endangered by its past and by all the curses coming from that past. America, on the other hand, is endangered by going ahead without looking back at the creative forces which have determined the whole of Western culture. So I wish to direct your thoughts in the first part of this paper to the past. You will discover how relevant this is to our present understanding of such an idea as that of progress.

Let us first consider the religious background of the idea of progress. The fundamental factor in this respect is prophetic religion as expressed in the Old Testament and in many forms ever since in the Christian church as well as in Judaism and Islam. It involves the idea that God has elected a nation and, later on in Christianity, people from all over the world, that he has promised something related to the future, and that in spite of all resistance on the part of the people, he will fulfill his promise. There is the vision of progress toward the future in this idea. The belief of the prophets that Yahweh, the God of Israel, will establish his heavenly rule or his kingdom over all the world is the primary basis of an interpretation of history as the place where the divine reveals itself in progress toward an end. Now this idea has always been important in the development of Christianity. There was, for example, a man whose name should be remembered, Joachim De Fiore, an abbot in Southern Italy in the twelfth century, who expressed this idea of progress in the doctrine that there were three stages in history, the stage of the Father in the Old Testament, the stage of the Son (the last thousand years of church history), and the coming or third stage of the Divine Spirit in which there will be no more church since everyone will be taught directly by the spirit. In this last stage, too, there will be equality and there will be no more marriage: history will come to an end.

Now this half-fantastic, half-realistic idea had many consequences for the whole subsequent church history, and also for this country. The idea of the third stage was taken on by the radical evangelicals in the time of the Reformation, which underlies most of this country's religion, and is seen in the idea of a revolutionary or progressivistic realization of the kingdom of God in Calvinism. It became the religious basis deep-rooted in every Western man. If you don't believe it, go to Asia—to India or Japan. I had the privilege of being in Japan for ten weeks talking everyday with Buddhist priests and scholars. There is nothing like this. "The religions of the East are of the past," I was told, "not of the future." For the religious people of the East, one wants to return to the Eternal from which one came directly, not caring for history, going out of history at some time of one's life into the desert, if possible. If you contrast this with the Western religious feeling of progressive activity, then you see what the difference is.

However, this was only the religious basis for the idea of progress. Now we come to the secular motives, and the secular elaboration of the idea of progress, which, of course, starts with the Renaissance. The man of the Renaissance is something new, not only as compared with the Middle Ages but also as compared with the late ancient world. The most important impact of the ancient world on Renaissance man was made by Stoic philosophy, but it was a transformed Stoicism. It was not the Stoicism of resignation, as it was under the Roman empire in the later Greek world, but it was the Stoicism of action. The Romans—some of the Roman emperors even—were partly mediators in this direction. However, the man of the Renaissance does not feel he is dependent on fate as the Stoics did. Rather, he feels—as expressed in painting—that when the destiny of man is compared with a sailboat, driven by the winds of contingency, man stands at the rudder and directs it. Of course, he knows that destiny gives the winds, but nevertheless, man directs destiny. This conception is unheard of in all Greek culture and is a presupposition of the idea of progress in the modern world. Out of this arose the great Renaissance Utopian writings, that is, the anticipation of a reality—*outopos*—which "has no place" in history, but which is nevertheless being expected. Such Utopias have been written ever since, into the twentieth century. It was the idea of the third stage of history, the stage of reason in bourgeois society, the stage of the classless society in the working-class movements. It was a secularized idea of the third stage, the religious foundations of which we saw. But it was not only ideas which produced this passion for purpose, it was also the social reality, the activities of bourgeois society at this time, such as the colonial extension of Europe in all directions; space extension, which has remained an element in the idea of progress up to the space exploration we are doing today; and technical extension—continuous progress in controlling nature and putting it into the service of man. All this has been based on the boundary lines of science which we have trespassed year by year since the beginning of the Renaissance up until today.

But there was another element of great importance in the idea of progress, namely the vision of nature as a progressive process from the atom to the molecule, to the cell, to the developed organism, and finally to man. This is evolution, progress in largeness of elements united in one being, with centeredness and, therefore, power being in the individual. And this line, then, was drawn beyond nature through humanity, from primitive to civilized man, to us as the representatives of the age of reason in which the potentialities of creation have come to their fulfillment.

When I tell you this, you yourself can feel how overwhelmingly impressive it is, and how virtually impossible it was to escape this idea as a symbol of faith. Progress became in the nineteenth century not only a conscious doctrine but also an unconscious dogma. When I came to this country in 1933 and spoke with students of theology, and criticized certain ideas of God, of Christ, of the Spirit, of the Church, or of sin or salvation, it didn't touch them very much but when I criticized the idea of progress, they said to me, "In what then can we believe? What do you do with our real faith?" And these were students of theology. It means that all the Christian dogmas had been transformed in the unconscious of these people (which my questions brought out) into a faith in progress. But then something happened! This dogma was shaken in the twentieth century, as foreseen by some prophetic minds in the nineteenth, first in Europe, then in America.

In Europe one of the greatest expressions of the shaking of this faith was Nietzsche's prophecy of—what unfortunately today has become a fashionable phrase—the death of God. This doesn't mean primitive, materialistic atheism; Nietzsche was far from this. But it meant the undercutting of the value-systems, Christian as well as secular, and the view of the human predicament as something in conflict, in destruction, in estrangement from true humanity.

Nietzsche was one of the predecessors of what today is called "existentialist" literature. The trend was further supported by the historical pessimism of men like Spengler, who wrote two important volumes on *The Decline of the West* in which much historical imagination was connected with much true prophecy. In the year 1916 he prophesied the coming of the period of the dictators, and in the early thirties the Communist and the Fascist dictators were a reality. The first World War and then the rise of what he prophesied of the totalitarian powers—this was the end of the belief in progress as an idea in Europe. In America it started somehow with the great economic crisis in the thirties. In Germany it started with the beginning of the Hitler period and the experience that history can fall back and that a rebarbarization can happen in any moment even in the highest culture. Then came the second World War, the cold war, and the atomic crisis. And with all this there came in this country the end of the crusading utopianism of the first third of the century. Instead, opposite Utopias appeared in literature—negative Utopias—like Huxley's *Brave New World*, or Orwell's *1984*. In many other novels and treatises the future is painted in terms of negative utopianism, in terms not of fulfillment but of dehumanization. The same can be seen in the existentialist style in the arts—whether you call it expressionist, cubist, or abstract—wherein the expression of the demonic in the underground of the individual or the group moves away from the figures and faces of human beings toward the abstract elements in the underground of reality. In philosophy there is a withdrawal into a merely formal analysis of the possibility of thinking without going into a reality itself with one's thinking. This was the end of a phase in the idea of progress, but the active motive of all our behavior cannot die, nor can the lure of future possibilities.

Today we need a new inquiry into the validity and the limits of the idea of progress. There are symptoms of reconsideration: for instance, in philosophy now there is an attempt finally to use the sharpened instruments of logical analysis to go into the real problems of human existence; and in the arts at least an attempt to use the elementary forms discovered in the last fifty years to express in a new way reality as manifestly encountered. There are other elements too: the extension of national independence; the real fight about the racial problem; and the increasing awareness, even among conservative theologians, that our attitude toward the non-Christian religions has to be one of dialogue—even the present Pope used that term. But, of course, these are symptoms and not yet fulfillments, and the threat of a relapse into the predominant pessimism (if you use that word which shouldn't be used by a philosopher) is always a danger.

We must now contribute to this reappraisal by going through a serious and perhaps painstaking analysis of the concept of progress as it appears in the different realms of life. After this somewhat dramatic historical section, I ask you to follow me through an analytic section, through an analysis of all the things one does oneself, especially in academic surroundings.

II

The tremendous force of the progressivistic idea was rooted, firstly, in observations about particular instances of progress in technical and scientific matters. But this observation was inadequate, and what is needed now is to show the non-progressive elements in reality and culture, and to demonstrate in some way how they are related to the progressive elements. There is a general principle for all this which one can follow through more fully when one thinks about these ideas. The general principle is: where there is freedom to contradict fulfillment, there the rule of progress is broken. Freedom to contradict one's fulfillment breaks the rule of the law of progress. This freedom is nothing else but another word for the moral act, which we perform every day innumerable times. There is no progress with respect to the moral act because there is no morality without free decisions, without the awareness of the power to turn with one's centered self in the one or the other direction. It means that every individual starts anew and has to make decisions for himself, whether he be on the lowest or highest level of culture or education. The German rebarbarization was looked at with great astonishment by a world which was adhering to the faith in progress. But there it was. In one of the most highly civilized nations, decisions were made by individuals and followed by many which contradicted anything we consider to be human nature and human fulfillment. This was a tremendous shock. And here is the first answer to the whole problem of progress. Every newborn infant has, when it comes to a certain point of self-awareness, the possibility of stopping progress by contradicting fulfillment in man's essential nature.

There is something else in what we usually call progress in the ethical realm, namely, coming to maturity—maturation. The child matures, and in this respect, there is progress. There is as in nature a progression from the seed to the fruit of the tree, or to the fully grown tree, but this element of maturity belongs to the individual first, and he may at any moment break out of it. We know how much this happens even in people whom we consider to be mature, and we know many who never become mature. There is something like maturing also in social groups. It means deeper understanding of man's essential nature in individual and social relations. This is not moral progress but it is cultural progress in the moral realm. It is cultural because it sees better what human nature is, but it doesn't make people better. If we had attained the full idea now of the social interrelation between the races in this country, we would be on a higher, on a more mature level; we would have deeper insight into human nature and into the content of the moral demand, but we would not have better human beings, because the goodness or not-goodness of a human being appears on all levels of culture and insight. So we can say—and this is very important for our whole consideration of this idea and for our whole culture today with respect to the free moral decisions of individuals—there are always new beginnings in the individual and sometimes in the group, but the contents can mature and can grow from one generation to another. This is the difference between civilized ethics and primitive ethics, but do not believe that on the level of primitive ethics people were worse than we are. In the smallest decisions you make in your classes, or in your homes, or wherever it may be, there is the same problem of ethical decision which is found in the crudeness of the cavemen; you are not better than they. You may be better than one of them, but one of them may be better than you. The distinction between moral decision and progress in moral content is fundamental for our judging the whole of past history.

When we look at education, we arrive at the same result. Education leads to higher cultural levels, to progress and maturity, to a production of habits of good behavior. As a consequence, education can be a kind of second nature in each of you, useful for society but, when it comes to moral freedom, you are still able to become rebarbarized, even if not openly as it was in Germany, in your personal relation to another person, to your children, your husband, your wife, or your friends. You can again start on a level which is that of freedom to contradict what you ought to be. When we add to the ordinary educational process, as we have it in a college or university, when we add to it education in psychotherapy, psychoanalysis, counselling, and all these things which are so important, what can they do? They can heal you from disturbances, they can help you to become free, but when you have been set free, let us say by successful analysis, you still have to decide. This is not moral progress; it is progress in healing, but the moral decision remains free, and now has become really free by medical or psychoanalytical help.

Besides moral freedom, the freedom of contradicting every possible instance of progress, there is a second element where there is no progress, namely, the freedom of spiritual creativity—creation in culture.

Let us look at the different cultural functions. There are the arts. Is there progress in the arts? There is progress in the technical use of materials, in the better mixing of colors, and in things like that, but is there progress in the arts? Has Homer ever been surpassed by anyone? Has Shakespeare ever been surpassed by anyone? Is an early Greek frieze worse than a classical sculpture, or is a classical worse than a modern expressionist? No. There is maturity of styles; there are good and bad representatives of style, but you cannot compare artistic styles in terms of progress. A style starts, often very modestly and preliminarily. It grows, it becomes mature, it produces its greatest expressions, then it decays. But there is no progress from one style to another. There is no progress from the Gothic to the Classical style. (And this needs to be said against our Gothic church buildings—we shouldn't pretend that we can go back to the Gothic style, after our modern stylistic feelings and developmental possibilities have become so different.) So, creativity in the arts admits of maturity, admits of "great moments"—*kairoi*—right times, decisive times, turning points, all this, but it does not admit progress from one style to another.

The same is true in the realm of knowledge. If you look at philosophy, you see an analytic element in our great philosophers as well as a visionary element. Take Aristotle, for example, who unites both of them so clearly. In every kind of knowledge a philosophical element is present. You can also speak of a logical and empirical element in knowledge which is detached and necessary, and an existentialist and inspirational element which is involved. Both are there, and the very fact that in all great philosophers there was this visionary, involved, inspirational element makes it impossible to speak about progress in the history of philosophy except in those elements which are connected with a sharpened logical analysis or a tremendous increase in empirical knowledge. I have never found a philosopher who I could say progressed over Parmenides the Eleatic of the sixth century B.C. Of course, there is much more empirical knowledge, there is much more refined analysis, but the vision of this man, and of Heraclitus, his polar friend and opposite, cannot be surpassed. There is no qualitative progress from Heraclitus to Whitehead.

And there is no progress in humanity, that is, in the formation of the individual person. I was struck by this once when I saw a photograph of an old Sumerian sculpture, perhaps of a priestess, and looking at it said to myself, "Look at the sculptures and paintings of great representatives of humanity in the following history of three or four thousand years." I found no progress at all. I found differences, but I didn't find progress. This means that even justice as well as humanity are not matters of progress except in technical elements. If I think, for instance, of democracy there is progress in largeness of the number of people involved, and progress in maturity in some respects, but there was justice in the state of Athens, justice in old Israel, in Rome, in the Middle Ages, and there is justice in modern democracy. The progress is quantitative, but the quality of the ideas of humanity and justice has not progressed.

Now I come to the most difficult problem—progress in religion. Of course, it is simple if you follow the conservative or fundamentalist idea that there is one true religion and many false ones. Then, needless to say, there is no progress. But even if you hold this view, you have a difficulty, namely, the Old Testament—what about that? Isn't there something then like progress—progressive revelation? So the problem appears even in Christianity. There is development, there is progress. Even in church history there is supposed to be progress according to the Gospel of John where Jesus is reported to have said that the Spirit will introduce you into all truth. This is progress. Furthermore, there are Christian theologies which expect new revelations even beyond Jesus the Christ. This, of course, would be post-Christian religion. Now if we look at this, we encounter great difficulties. On the one hand, Christianity claims that there is no possible progress beyond what is given in Jesus the Christ; on the other hand, there is great progress in world history in many respects—in knowledge as well as in other areas. How shall we deal with this problem?

Here is where religion might provide the standpoint from which we might understand the whole problem better. I would say that we must replace the idea of progress by two other concepts: the concept of maturing, and the concept of "the decisive moment." What we need is an understanding of history in which there are two things, rather than a single, continuous line of progress. (I hope that what I have said about all the other realms—the ethical, the cultural, the artistic, the scientific, the philosophical, the religious—showed this clearly.) "Great moments" or, if you want to accept the term I like very much, taken from the New Testament or from classical Greek, the term *kairos*, the right time, fulfilled time, time in which something decisive happens, is not the same as *chronos*, chronological time, which is watch time, but it means the qualitative time in which "something happens." I would say, therefore, that in history we have two processes, not progress as a universal event, but the maturing of potentialities, the maturing of a style, for instance, or the maturing in the education of a human being. It is not progress beyond this human being. He or she may give something to their children, but children must decide again on their own. There is no progress; they must start anew. Two things then we can see in history. One is the process of maturing in terms of potentialities; the other is the great moments, the *kairoi*, in history in which something new happens. However, that new thing which happens is not in a progressivistic line with the other new things before and after it. This is only true in the technical and scientific realm so far as the logical elements are implied, but it is not so in the realm of spiritual creativity and of the moral act.

My description and analysis of progress has been been more careful than is usual, but I believe that the service an academic lecturer can give is to show his listeners where the problems lie, and to steer them away from the popular talk about such weighty problems. This I have tried to do, and now perhaps we will have some of the fruits of this. When progress is elevated into a symbol or an idea, as I said in the beginning, then it can take on two forms. The one is the idea of endless progress, without a limit, in which one moves further and further along, and things get better and better. The other is the Utopian form, which is historically much more important; namely, that at some point in time man's essential nature will be fulfilled. What is possible for man will then exist. Now, what happens with these two? In the first type, progress runs ahead without aim, unless progress itself is taken to be the aim, but there is no goal at the end of the progression. Thus, it is simply a matter of going ahead, and of course, if my analysis before was right, this is possible to a certain extent in the technical and scientific realms. But it is not possible in the realms where vision and inspiration play a role. The other type, the Utopian, has produced all the tremendous passions in history for it is the principle of revolution. However, after the revolution is successful, the great disappointment follows, and this disappointment produces cynicism and sometimes complete withdrawal from history. We have it in some forms of Christianity—we have it strongly in Lutheranism and in the Greek Orthodox Church; we have it less in Calvinism and Evangelical radicalism, which underlies this country; and we have it in an anti-Christian way as a result of the terrible experiences of suffering in Asiatic religions, especially in Buddhism with its withdrawal from history.

Now the question is, is there a way of avoiding the Utopianism which sees the fulfillment of history around the corner; which says, only one step more and we will be in the classless society; only one step more and we will be an educated nation; only one step more and all our youngsters will reach full humanity, or all our social groups will stand for true justice. If only all men of good will—that means we—stand together, everything will be all right. All this is Utopianism. In contrast, I want to save you, by my criticism of the idea of progress, from the cynical consequences of disappointed Utopianism. In my long life I have experienced the breakdown of the Utopianism of the Western intelligentsia both in Europe and America and the tremendous cynicism and despair which followed it and, finally, the emptiness of not being ultimately concerned about anything. Therefore, I think that we must put something else in place of these two types of progressivism. Endless progress may be symbolized by running ahead indefinitely into an empty space. We will do that, but it is not the meaning of life; nor are better and better gadgets the meaning of life. What is the meaning of life then? Perhaps it is something else. Perhaps there are great moments in history. There is in these great moments not total fulfillment but there is the victory over a particular power of destruction, a victory over a demonic power which was creative and now has become destructive. This is a possibility, but don't expect that it *must* happen. It might not happen; that is a continuous threat hanging over development in history. But there *may* be a *kairos*.

After the first World War in Germany, we believed, just because of the defeat of Germany, that there was a *kairos*, a great moment, in which something new could be created. In this sense we were progressive, but we did not believe that it was necessary that this would happen. Inevitable progress should not be sought by us, for there is no such thing. Of course, what we hoped for then was completely destroyed by the Hitler movement. Out of these experiences we came to see that there is a possibility of victory over a particular demonic power—a particular force of destruction—or to put it simply, there is a possibility of solving a particular problem, as for instance, the race problem in our time. But even if this does happen, it doesn't mean inevitable progress. We must fight for it, and we may be defeated, but even if not, new demonic powers will arise.

There is a wonderful symbolism in the last book of the Bible, in the idea of the thousand years' rule of Christ in history. In these thousand years, which is a symbolic number, of course, the demonic forces will be banned—put into chains in the underworld. This is all symbolism. But they are not annihilated and they may come to the surface again, as they will in the final struggle. When we thought about our problems after the first World War, we used this symbol—not in its literal sense, of course—as expressing the awareness that you can ban a particular demonic force. Hitler was banned, but the powers behind Hitler, the demonic forces in mankind and in every individual are not definitely annihilated; they are banned for a moment and they may return again. So instead of a progressivistic, Utopian, or empty vision of history, let us think of the great moments for which we must keep ourselves open, and in which the struggle of the divine and the demonic in history may be decided for one moment for the divine against the demonic, though there is no guarantee that this will happen. On the contrary, in the view of the Bible, especially the book of Revelation, the growth of the divine powers in history are contradicted by a growth of the demonic powers.

So in every moment the fight is going on and the only thing we can say is this: If there is a new beginning, let us mature in it; if there is a new beginning in world history as we have it now in this country and beyond this country, let us follow it and develop it to its maturity. But let us not look at history in the sense of progress which will be going on and finally come to an end which is wonderful and fulfilling. There is no such thing in history, because man is free, free to contradict his own essential nature and his own fulfillment. As a Christian theologian I would say that fulfillment is going on in every moment here and now beyond history, not some time in the future, but here and now above ourselves. When I have to apply this to a meeting like this, then I would say it might well be that in such a meeting in the inner movements of some of us, something might happen which is elevated out of time into eternity. This then is a non-Utopian and a true fulfillment of the meaning of history and of our own individual life.

Rhetorical Analysis

1. Verbal definition, which is simply a statement of the meaning of a word or phrase, has one purpose: to reduce confusion, to keep the reader from confounding the word or phrase with any other. When used in essays, definition usually has a tacit but no less important purpose: to help prepare the reader for the argument which follows. Study and discuss the reasons Tillich takes the care to define "progress" (¶s 3 and 4), "Utopia" (¶ 8), "the death of God" (¶ 11), "moral act" (¶ 15), and "kairos" (¶ 23).
2. Essential to definition is another logical maneuver—distinction, the act of drawing boundaries between two or more concepts. Again, one purpose may be to prevent confusion, but secondary purposes usually are served as well. Study the distinctions Tillich draws between "idea" and "concept" (¶ 3), "Europe" and "America" (¶ 5), "moral decision" and "progress in moral content" (¶ 16), and "kairos" and "chronos" (¶ 23). What secondary purposes might these distinctions serve? What quality of mind do these and other distinctions convey to the reader?
3. Look at the beginnings of each paragraph. What have they to do with the fact that the essay was first presented as a university lecture (at Ohio State University in 1964)?

Intellectual Analysis

Tillich opens his essay by distinguishing between the concept and the idea of progress. Generally, the first half of the essay traces the concept and the second the idea of progress; these terms, however, do not remain separated since either concept or idea can become a symbol, and Tillich ultimately rejects both.

1. Tillich defines the "concept of progress" as an abstraction "based on the description of a group of facts, of objects of observation which may well be verified or falsified" (¶ 3). The history of the concept of progress is thereafter traced in the balance of Part I.
    a. Tillich places great weight on Joachim De Fiore's theory of the three stages of history (¶ 6): What are those three stages?
        (1) What influence did Joachim's theory have on the concept of progress in religious matters subsequently?
        (2) What impact did the theory have on secular history?
    b. By the nineteenth century, Tillich claims, the concept of progress had

become both "conscious doctrine" and "unconscious dogma" (¶ 10). What other intellectual and social developments contributed to this faith in progress?
  c. Tillich next analyzes the decline of this faith in progress in western culture.
    (1) Nietzsche is a key factor in the "undercutting of the value-systems" (¶ 11) of the concept of progress. What did Nietzsche stand for, and how was his thinking corrosive to the idea of progress?
    (2) Tillich also underscores the significance of World War I in the decline of the idea of progress. In what ways?
  d. He ends this first section by claiming a present reappraisal of the idea of progress, after the near total bankruptcy of the concept. Carefully study the argument and details of ¶s 12 and 13.
2. The idea of progress Tillich defines as "an interpretation of existence as a whole, which means first of all our own existence" (¶ 3). We can infer from that sentence that the first part of the essay deals with nature and society, the second, with the individual. In general this is true.
  a. Tillich's first step is to point out those facts which are irreconcilable with the idea of progress. These are of two kinds, and both need to be evaluated.
    (1) Matters of "spiritual creativity" do not progress.
    (2) Human maturation and morality do not progress. Here, a key word, "rebarbarization" (first used in ¶ 12 of Part I), comes into play. Follow its usage through the rest of the essay.
  b. The idea of progress, elevated to a symbol, can take two turns: utopianism and endless linear progress. Both forms are riddled with problems: examine ¶s 24–25 with care.
3. Finally, Tillich argues for a new, third concept of progress, and he struggles to define it through the rest of the essay. The following are three avenues for analysis:
  a. Tillich offers a pair of opposed terms, quantities and qualities, which become essential to his own idea of progress. Trace these terms.
  b. Tillich insists on two concepts of time, *chronos* and *kairos*.
  c. Tillich suggests that both utopianism and endless linear progress should be replaced by two different concepts: first that of "great moments" to which we must all be open; and the idea of the struggle between the divine and the demonic in any moral event. Discuss Tillich's point and intentions here. What hope does he finally have for progress?

Suggestions for Writing

1. Tillich notes the importance of defining his terms clearly, and attempts to do so with the words "concept" and "idea." Choose two personally significant, yet abstract, terms that seem closely related ("freedom" and "democracy," for exam-

ple) and, in a brief essay, clarify their relationships, noting both differences and similarities, resisting the natural temptation to oversimplify.
2. Tillich says in his essay that he was able to criticize his students' religion, but when he brought his criticism to bear on the idea of progress, those same students reacted very strongly against it. State your position on this issue, and either defend or attack Tillich's notions about progress and its function in human life (both social and individual).
3. Tillich's life span (1886—1965) stretched over a long and violent period in German history and in the history of civilization generally. He witnessed the end of the German empire in World War I, the fall of the Third Reich in World War II, and the early years of the Cold War after 1945. During his life, the West declined from a group of imperial powers to its present position as leading (but no longer dominant) powers. How does Tillich's essay mirror this "decline"?

THE RIDDLE OF INEQUALITY

> *For to him who has will more be given; and from him who has not, even what he has will be taken away.*
>
> MARK 4:25

One day a learned colleague called me up and cried angrily, "There is a saying in the New Testament which I consider to be one of the most immoral and unjust statements ever made!" And he began to quote our text—"To him who has will more be given," his anger increasing as he continued, "and from him who has not, *even what he has will be taken away.*" I believe that most of us cannot but feel equally offended. And we cannot easily excuse the passage by suggesting what this colleague suggested—that the words may be due to a misunderstanding on the part of the disciples. No, they appear at least four times in the gospels with great emphasis. And furthermore, it is clear that the writers of the gospels feel exactly as we do. For them, the statement is a stumbling block, and they tried to interpret it in different ways. Probably none of the explanations satisfied them fully, for this particular saying of Jesus confronts us immediately with the greatest and perhaps most painful riddle of life—the inequality of all beings. We certainly cannot hope to

1

solve it. Neither the Bible nor any of the great religions and philosophies was able to do so. But this we can do: we can explore the breadth and depth of the riddle of inequality; and we can try to find a way to live with it, unsolved as it may remain.

I

When we consider the words, "to him who has will more be given," we ask ourselves—what *do* we have? And we may discover that much has been given us in terms of external goods, of friends, of intellectual gifts, and even of a comparatively high morality on which to base our action. So we can expect that even more will accrue to us, while, at the same time, those who are lacking in all these attributes will lose the little they already have. Even further, according to Jesus' parable, the one poor talent they possess shall be handed over to those who have five or ten talents. We shall be richer because they will be poorer. And cry out as we may against such an injustice, we cannot deny that life abounds in it. We cannot deny it, but we might well ask—do we really *have* what we believe we have, so that it cannot be taken from us? It is a question full of anxiety, intensified by Luke's version of our text: "From him who has not, even what he *thinks* that he has will be taken away." Perhaps our having of those many things is not the kind of having that can be increased. Perhaps the having of a few things on the part of the poor is the kind of having that makes them grow. Jesus confirms this thought in the parable of the talents. The talents that are used, at the risk of their being lost, are the talents that we really have. Those that we try to preserve, without risking their use for growth, are those that we do not really have, and that will therefore be taken from us. They begin to disappear, until suddenly we feel that we have lost them, perhaps forever.

Let us apply the principle to our own life, be it long or short. In the memory of all of us, there are many things that we seemed to have, but that we really did *not* have, and that were therefore taken away from us. Some of them were lost because of the tragic limitations of life. They had to be sacrificed so that other things might grow. We were all given childish innocence, but innocence cannot be used and increased. The growth of our lives is made possible only by the sacrifice of the original gift of innocence. Sometimes, nevertheless, a melancholy longing arises in us for a purity that has been taken from us. We were all given youthful enthusiasm for many things and goals. But all this enthusiasm also cannot be used and increased. Most of the objects of our early enthusiasm must be sacrificed for a few, and those few approached soberly. No maturity is possible without this sacrifice. Yet often a deep yearning for the lost possibilities and that enthusiasm takes hold of us. Innocence and youthful enthusiasm: we had them, and we did not have them. Life itself demanded that they be taken from us.

But there are other things that we had and that were taken from us because we were guilty of taking them too much for granted. Some of us were deeply sensitive to the wonder of life as it is revealed in nature. Slowly, under the pressure of work and social life and the lure of cheap pleasures, we lost the wonder of our earlier years—the intense joy and sense of the mystery of life in the freshness of the young day or the glory of the dying afternoon, the splendor of the mountains and the infinity of the sea, or in the perfection of the movements of a young animal or of a flower breaking through the soil. We try perhaps to evoke such feelings again, but we find ourselves empty and do not succeed. We had that sensitivity and we did not have it, and it was taken from us.

Others of us have had the same experience with respect to music, poetry, great literature and the drama. We desired to devour all of these; we lived in them, and through them created for ourselves a life beyond our daily life. We had this experience and we did not have it. We did not allow it to grow. Our love for it was not strong enough, and so it was taken from us.

Many people remember a time when the desire to solve the riddles of the universe and to find *truth* was the driving force in their lives. They entered college and the university not in order to gain access to the upper middle classes or the preconditions for social and economic success, but because they felt driven by their thirst for knowledge. They had something to which, seemingly, more could be added. But their desire was not strong enough. They failed to nurture it, and so it was taken from them. Expediency and indifference towards truth took the place of genuine academic interest. Because their love for the truth was let go, they sometimes feel sick at heart; they realize that what they have lost may never be returned to them.

We all know that any deep relationship to another human being requires watchfulness and nourishment; otherwise, it is taken from us. And we cannot recapture it. This is a form of having and not having that is the root of innumerable human tragedies. We are all familiar with them.

And there is the most fundamental kind of having and not having—our having and losing God. Perhaps in our childhood, and even beyond it, our experience of God was rich. We may remember the moments in which we felt His presence intensely. We may remember our praying with an overflowing heart, our encounter with the holy in words and music and holy places. We communicated with God; but this communication was taken from us, because we had it and did not have it. We failed to let it grow, and therefore, it slowly disappeared, leaving only an empty space. We became unconcerned, cynical and indifferent, not because we doubted our religious traditions—such doubt belongs to a life rich in God—but because we turned away from what once concerned us infinitely.

Such thoughts mark the first step in approaching the riddle of inequality. Those who have, receive more if they *really* have what they have, if they use it and cause it to grow. And those who have not, lose what they seem to have, because they really do *not* have.

II

But the question of inequality has not yet been answered. For now we must ask—why do some of us receive more than others in the very beginning, before using or wasting our talents is even possible? Why does the one servant receive five talents, and the second, two, and the third, one? Why is one person born to desperate poverty, and another to affluence? To reply that much will be demanded of those to whom much is given, and little of those to whom little is given, is not adequate. For it is just this original inequality, internal and external, that gives rise to the question. Why is the power to gain so much more out of his being human given to one human being rather than to another? Why is so much given to one that much *can* be asked of him, while little can be asked of another, because little was given him? If we consider this problem in relation not only to individual men, but also to classes, races and nations, the question of political inequality also arises, and with it the many ways in which men have tried to abolish inequality. In every revolution and war, the will to solve the riddle of inequality is a driving force. But neither war nor revolution can answer it. And even though we may imagine that most social inequalities will be conquered in the future, there remain three realities: the inequality of talents in body and mind, the inequality created by freedom and destiny, and the inequality of justice deriving from the fact that all generations before the time of such equality would by nature be excluded from its blessings. This last would be the greatest inequality possible! No! In the face of one of the deepest and most tormenting problems of life, we cannot permit ourselves to be so shallow or foolish as to try to escape into a social dreamland. We have to live now. We have to live *this* life. We must face the riddle of inequality today.

Let us not confuse the riddle of inequality with the fact that each of us is a unique and incomparable self. Our being individual certainly belongs to our dignity as men. This being was given to us, and must be made use of and intensified, not drowned in the gray waters of conformity that threaten us so much today. One should defend every individuality and the uniqueness of every human self. But one should not be deluded into believing that this is a solution to the riddle of inequality. Unfortunately, there are social and political reactionaries who exploit this confusion in order to justify social injustice. They are at least as foolish as those who dream of the future abolition of inequality. He who has witnessed hospitals for the ill and insane, prisons, sweat shops, battlefields, people starving, family tragedies, or moral aberrations should be cured of any confusion of the gift of individuality with the riddle of inequality. He should be cured of any sense of easy consolation.

III

And now we must take the third step in our attempt to penetrate the riddle of inequality by asking—why do some of us use and increase what was given to us, while others do not and thus lose what was given them? Why does God say to the prophet in the Old Testament that the ears and eyes of a nation are made insensitive to the divine message? Is it sufficient to answer—because some use their freedom responsibly and do what they ought to do, while others fail through their own guilt? This answer, which seems so obvious, *is* sufficient only when we apply it to ourselves. Each one of us must consider the increase or loss of what was given as a matter for his own responsibility. Our conscience tells us that we cannot blame anybody or anything other than ourselves for our losses.

But when we consider the plight of others, this answer is *not* sufficient. We cannot tell somebody who comes to us in great distress about himself—"Make use of what was given you," for he may have come to us precisely because he is unable to do so! And we cannot tell those in despair because of what they are—"Be something else," for the inability to get rid of oneself is the exact meaning of despair. We cannot tell those who failed to conquer the destructive influences of their surroundings and thence were driven into crime and misery— "You should have been stronger," for it was just this strength of which they were deprived by heritage or environment. Certainly they are all men, and freedom is given to them all. But they are also all subject to destiny. It is not for us to condemn others because they *were* free, as it is also not for us to excuse them because of the burden of their destiny. We cannot judge them. And when we judge ourselves, we must keep in mind that even this judgment has no finality, because we, like them, stand under an ultimate judgment. In it the riddle of inequality is eternally answered. But the answer is not ours. It is our predicament that we must ask the question, and we ask with an uneasy conscience—why are they in such misery? Why not we? Thinking of those near to us, we ask—are we partly responsible? But even though we are, the riddle of inequality is not solved. The uneasy conscience asks also about those most distant from us—why they, why not we?

Why did my child, or any one of millions of children, die before he had the chance to grow out of infancy? Why was my child, or any child, born crippled in mind or body? Why has my friend or relative, or anyone's friend or relative, disintegrated in his mind, and thus lost both his freedom and his destiny? Why has my son or daughter, gifted as they were with many talents, wasted them and been deprived of them? Why do such things happen to any parent at all? And why have the creative powers of this boy or that girl been broken by a tyrannical father or a possessive mother?

None of these questions concern our own misery. At present, we are not asking—why did this happen to me? It is not Job's question that God answered by humiliating him and then elevating him into communion with Him. It is not the old and urgent question—where is divine justice, where is divine love, for me? It is almost an opposite question—why did this *not* happen to me, while it did happen to another, to innumerable other ones, to whom not even Job's power to accept the divine answer was given? Why, Jesus asks also, are many called but few elected? He does not answer the question, but states simply that this is the human predicament. Shall we therefore cease to ask, and humbly accept a divine judgment that would hurl most human beings out of community with the divine and condemn them to despair and self-destruction? Can we accept the eternal victory of judgment over love? We can *not*, nor can any human being, though he may preach and threaten in such terms. As long as he is unable to visualize himself with absolute certainty as eternally rejected, his preaching and threats are self-deceptive. For who can see himself eternally rejected?

But if this is not the solution of the riddle of inequality at its deepest level, may we go outside the boundaries of Christian tradition to listen to those who would tell us that this life does not determine our eternal destiny? There will be other lives, they would say, predicated, like our present life, on previous ones and what we wasted or achieved in them. This is a serious doctrine and not completely strange to Christianity. But since we don't know and never shall know what each of us was in a previous existence, or will be in a future one, it is not really *our* destiny developing from life to life, but in each life, the destiny of someone *else*. Therefore, this doctrine also fails to solve the riddle of inequality.

Actually, there is no answer at all to our question concerning the temporal and eternal destiny of a single being separated from the destiny of the whole. Only in the unity of all beings in time and eternity can there be a humanly possible answer to the riddle of inequality. "Humanly possible" does not mean an answer that removes the riddle of inequality, but one with which we can live.

There is an ultimate unity of all beings, rooted in the divine life from which they emerge and to which they return. All beings, non-human as well as human, participate in it. And therefore they all participate in each other. And we participate in each other's having and in each other's not having. When we become aware of this unity of all beings, something happens to us. The fact that others do *not* have changes the character of our having: it undercuts our security and drives us beyond ourselves, to understand, to give, to share, to help. The fact that others fall into sin, crime and misery alters the character of the grace that is given us: it makes us recognize our own hidden guilt; it shows us that those who suffer for their sin and crime suffer also for us, for we are guilty of their guilt and ought to suffer as they suffer. Our becoming aware of the fact that others who *could* have developed into full human beings did not, changes our state of full humanity. Their early death, their early or late disintegration, brings to our own personal life and health a continuous risk, a dying that is not yet death, a disintegration that is not yet destruction. In every death we encounter, something of us dies, and in every disease, something of us tends towards disintegration.

Can we live with this answer? We can to the degree to which we are liberated from seclusion in ourselves. But no one can be liberated from himself unless he is grasped by that power which is present in everyone and everything—the eternal, from which we come and to which we go, and which gives us *to* ourselves and liberates us *from* ourselves. It is the greatness and heart of the Christian message that God, as manifest in the Christ on the Cross, totally participates in the dying of a child, in the condemnation of the criminal, in the disintegration of a mind, in starvation and famine, and even in the human rejection of Himself. There is no human condition into which the divine presence does not penetrate. This is what the Cross, the most extreme of all human conditions, tells us. The riddle of inequality cannot be solved on the level of our separation from each other. It is eternally solved through the divine participation in the life of all of us and every being. The certainty of divine participation gives us the courage to endure the riddle of inequality, although our finite minds cannot solve it. 19

Rhetorical Analysis

1. In practice good writers often follow a general guideline: the more complex and difficult the ideas, the simpler the organization. Illustrate this observation using paragraphs from Tillich's essay. Point to specifics, passages which seem to be rendered simply yet without violence to the facts.

2. This essay, in the form of a sermon, is written on a rather abstract level. Tillich uses no proper names (except God, Mark, Job, and Christ), even where he is referring to specific people. For instance, at the end of Part II he speaks only of "social and political reactionaries who use this confusion in order to justify social injustice." Try to imagine how Orwell would have rewritten or edited this sentence using principles enunciated in ¶ 18 of "Politics and the English Language"; on the other hand, how might you defend Tillich? Does the level of abstraction accord with his stated purposes in the essay?

3. It is axiomatic in rhetoric that items arranged in a series imply a similar order in reality, and that the order of reality is one of increasing importance. Thus, for

example, in the second sentence of Part I, Tillich arranges four items in climactic order: "And then we may find that much is given to us in terms of external goods, of friends, of intellectual gifts and even of a comparatively high moral level of action." Notice how the sequence allows Tillich to indicate his own ranking of these four gifts (material wealth lowest, morality highest) without taking time and space to make that ranking explicit. Find and study other sequences in sentences of this essay. Is the order always a hierarchical one of increasing emphasis, or does Tillich use some alternative principles of ordering? Does Tillich ever use a random sequence? Does he ever invert a sequence, causing it to dwindle from the most important object to the least?

4. Some extended sequences bear careful analysis—for example, the three-fold sequence in the next-to-last paragraph of the essay, or the long series of gifts taken away from us in the middle five paragraphs of Part I. Finally, do the three parts of this essay also form a sequence?

Intellectual Analysis

1. Tillich calls inequality "the greatest and perhaps most painful riddle of life" and provides no solution to it; instead, he attempts to explore the contours of the riddle, and to propose a way to live with it. Nevertheless, what is the effect of the opening statement on the rest of the essay?

2. With his overall structure clear, Tillich proceeds to speculate on what we have, and why some people seem to have a headstart (or a handicap) at the beginning of life.
   a. As to the first speculation, there seems to be *nothing* that we possess or have for certain. Consider the effect of this realization on most people. What does it drive them to do as a result?
      (1) Tillich identifies, however, a true and lasting possession, although its essence is paradoxical: "Those talents which are used, even with a risk of losing them, are those we really have. . . ." How do you resolve the paradox? Does this resolution affect the way you look at talents and material goods?
      (2) Do we lose all of what we possess regardless of category? There would seem to be a difference between losing one's innocence and losing one's love of music, or nature, or study.
   b. As to the second point, Tillich claims, in the strongest terms of his essay, "*No!* . . . it is unpermittably shallow and foolish to escape into a social dreamland. We have to live now. . . ." Here, Tillich speaks passionately for the "unique and incomparable self," for human dignity, and individuality. Try relating Tillich's anguish over "conformity" to the similar points in Russell, Dinesen, Gould, Orwell, and Baldwin.

3. Tillich's third question, signaled with equal clarity, is, Why do some use what they

have and prosper, while others seem unable to use what they are given and therefore fail?
   a. The question finally resolves itself, in Tillich's argument, to "Why has this not happened to me?" What does the negative imply in that question?
   b. Tillich's answer to the third question seems to be that "There is an ultimate unity of all being. . . ." But notice that this answer contains a leap of faith which Tillich does not here attempt to prove. Is Tillich's "leap" philosophically defensible? It will not be enough simply to say, reductively, that Tillich is a believer, a theologian; he is also a fine logician and philosopher, and his argument must be met (defended or attacked) on its own terms.
4. In his final paragraph, Tillich seems poised, even "high centered," on his own question: "Can we live with this answer? We can to the degree to which we are liberated from seclusion in ourselves." To be liberated from self is a broad topic. Is it a suitable conclusion to end the essay? May it even be seen as a kind of victory?

Suggestions for Writing

1. The basic form of this essay is that of a sermon: selection of a scriptural text and explication of it. Write your own explication of Mark 4:25. Do not feel constrained to present the Christian interpretation of the text as Tillich does.
2. You may not agree with some opinions expressed by Tillich. Perhaps you question some of his basic premises. Write an essay outlining your own theory of equality or inequality, and support your position with specific evidence.
3. Write an essay in which you either defend or attack Tillich's basic theology. Can you take God out of this argument and still make sense of it?

COPYRIGHTS AND ACKNOWLEDGMENTS

GEORGE ALLEN & UNWIN LTD   For "Nightmares," from *Fact and Fiction* by Bertrand Russell. © George Allen & Unwin Ltd, 1961. For "How I Write," from *Portraits from Memory and Other Essays* by Bertrand Russell. Copyright © 1951, 1952, 1956 by Bertrand Russell. And for "'Useless' Knowledge," from *In Praise of Idleness and Other Essays* by Bertrand Russell. Copyright, 1935, by Bertrand Russell. Reprinted by permission of George Allen & Unwin, Ltd.

ANDREWS, MCMEEL & PARKER   For "The Log Jam" from *River Notes: The Dance of Herons* by Barry Holstun Lopez. Copyright 1979 Barry Holstun Lopez. Reprinted with permission of Andrews, McMeel & Parker. All rights reserved.

JAMES BALDWIN   For "An Open Letter to My Sister, Miss Angela Davis," by James Baldwin. For "Notes of a Native Son" and "If Black English Isn't a Language, Then Tell Me, What Is?" from *The Price of the Ticket: Collected Nonfiction 1948–1985*, by James Baldwin. Reprinted by permission of James Baldwin.

FARRAR, STRAUS & GIROUX, INC.   For "On Keeping a Notebook" and "On Morality," from *Slouching Towards Bethlehem* by Joan Didion. Copyright © 1965, 1966, 1968 by Joan Didion. Reprinted by permission of Farrar, Straus & Giroux, Inc.

FLORENCE FEILER   For "On Mottoes of My Life" from *Daguerreotypes and Other Essays* by Isak Dinesen. The University of Chicago Press, USA. William Heinemann Ltd., London. Copyright 1979 by the Rungstedlund Foundation.

HARCOURT BRACE JOVANOVICH, INC.   For "Tolerance" from *Two Cheers for Democracy*, copyright 1951 by E. M. Forster; renewed 1979 by Donald Parry. For "My Wood" from *Abinger Harvest*, copyright 1936, 1964 by Edward Morgan Forster. For "Old Mrs. Grey" and "Professions for Women" from *The Death of the Moth* by Virginia Woolf, copyright 1942 by Harcourt Brace Jovanovich, Inc.; renewed 1970 by Marjorie T. Parsons, Executrix. Reprinted by permission of the publisher. For "Gas" from *The Captain's Death Bed and Other Essays* by Virginia Woolf, copyright 1950, 1978 by Harcourt Brace Jovanovich, Inc. Reprinted by permission of the publisher. For "Beauty: When the Other Dancer Is the Self," copyright © 1983 by Alice Walker; for "Nuclear Madness: What You Can Do," copyright © 1982 by Alice Walker; and for "In Search of Our Mothers' Gardens," copyright © 1974 by Alice Walker. Reprinted from her volume *In Search of Our Mothers' Gardens*. For "As I Please" from *The Collected Essays, Journalism and Letters of George Orwell*, Vol. III, copyright © 1968 by Sonia Brownell Orwell. For "Politics and the English Language," copyright 1946, 1974 by Sonia Orwell, and for "A Hanging," copyright 1950 by Sonia Brownell Orwell, renewed 1978 by Sonia Pitt-Rivers; both from *Shooting an Elephant and Other Essays* by George Orwell. All reprinted by permission of Harcourt Brace Jovanovich, Inc.

HAROLD OBER ASSOCIATES INCORPORATED   For "Theme for English B" from *Montage of a Dream Deferred* by Langston Hughes. Copyright 1951 by Langston Hughes. Copyright renewed 1979 by George Houston Bass. And for "Brown America in Jail: Kilby" by Langston Hughes, from *Good Morning Revolution*. Copyright © 1973 by Faith Berry. Reprinted by permission of Harold Ober Associates Incorporated. Copyright © 1951, 1973, and 1979.

HARPER & ROW, PUBLISHERS, INC.   For "The Gastropods" and "Calculating Machine," from *Poems and Sketches of E. B. White*. Copyright 1925–1954, © 1955–1981 by E. B. White. For "Death of a Pig" from *Essays of E. B. White*. Copyright © 1934–1977 by E. B. White. All rights reserved. And for "The Decline and the Validity of the Idea of Progress" by Paul Tillich, from *The Future of Religion: Paul Tillich*, ed. Jerald C. Brauer. Copyright © 1966 by Hannah Tillich. Reprinted by permission of Harper & Row, Publishers, Inc.

HARVARD UNIVERSITY PRESS   For "My Grandmother's House" by Eudora Welty. Reprinted by permission of the publishers from *One Writer's Beginnings* by Eudora Welty, Cambridge, Mass., Harvard University Press. Copyright © 1983, 1984 by Eudora Welty.

HILL & WANG   For "Salvation" from *The Big Sea* by Langston Hughes. Copyright 1940 by Langston Hughes. Copyright renewed © 1968 by Arna Bontemps and George Houston Bass. Reprinted by permission of Hill & Wang, a division of Farrar, Straus & Giroux, Inc.

THE HOGARTH PRESS   For "Anonymity: An Enquiry" in *Two Cheers for Democracy* by E. M. Forster (London: Edwin Arnold, 1972). © 1951, 1972 The Trustees of the Late E. M. Forster. Reprinted by permission of the author's estate and the Hogarth Press.

ALFRED A. KNOPF, INC.   For "A Dream Deferred" by Langston Hughes. Copyright 1951 by Langston Hughes. Reprinted from *The Panther and the Lash*, by Langston Hughes. For "On Our Birthday—America as Idea." Copyright © 1976 by Alma Tuchman, Lucy T. Eisenberg and Jessica Tuchman Matthews. For "The Historian as Artist." Copyright © 1966 by Alma Tuchman, Lucy T. Eisenberg and Jessica Tuchman Matthews. And for "'Perdicaris Alive or Raisuli Dead.'" Copyright © 1959 by Alma Tuchman, Lucy T. Eisenberg and Jessica Tuchman Matthews. Reprinted from *Practicing History* by Barbara Tuchman. All selections reprinted by permission of Alfred A. Knopf, Inc.

W. W. NORTON & COMPANY, INC.   "The Nonscience of Human Nature" is reprinted from *Ever Since Darwin: Reflections in Natural History*, by Stephen Jay Gould. Copyright © 1977 by Stephen Jay Gould. Copyright © 1973, 1974, 1975, 1976, 1977 by The American Museum of Natural History. And for "Crazy Old Randolph Kirkpatrick" and "A Biological Homage to Mickey Mouse," reprinted from *The Panda's Thumb: More Reflections in Natural History*, by Stephen Jay Gould. Copyright © 1980 by Stephen Jay Gould. All selections reprinted with the permission of W. W. Norton & Company, Inc.

RANDOM HOUSE, INC. For "A Sweet Devouring," copyright © 1957 by Eudora Welty, and "The Little Store," copyright © 1975 by Eudora Welty. Reprinted from *The Eye of the Story: Selected Essays and Reviews* by Eudora Welty. And for "The Iguana" and "Pooran Singh," from *Out of Africa* by Isak Dinesen. Copyright 1937 by Random House, Inc. and renewed 1965 by Rungstedlundfonden. For "The Habit," copyright © 1963 by William Styron; "The Oldest America," copyright © 1968 by William Styron; and "This Quiet Dust," copyright © 1965 by William Styron. Reprinted from *This Quiet Dust and Other Writings*, by William Styron. And for "How Flowers Changed the World," copyright © 1957 by Loren Eiseley, and "The Judgment of the Birds," copyright © 1956 by Loren Eiseley. Reprinted from *the Immense Journey*, by Loren Eiseley. All selections reprinted by permission of Random House, Inc.

CHARLES SCRIBNER'S SONS Barry Lopez, "Wolfing for Sport," from *Of Wolves and Men*. Copyright © 1978 Barry Holstun Lopez. Barry Lopez, "Buffalo," from *Winter Count*. Copyright © 1981 Barry Holstun Lopez. (Originally appeared in *Chouteau Review* as "Intentions in North America: The Buffalo.") Loren Eiseley, "One Night's Dying" from *The Night Country*. Copyright © 1971 Loren Eiseley. Paul Tillich, "Faith and Uncertainty" from *The New Being*. Copyright © 1955 Paul Tillich; copyright renewed © 1983 Hannah Tillich. Paul Tillich, "The Riddle of Inequality" from *The Eternal Now*. Copyright © 1963 Paul Tillich. All selections reprinted with the permission of Charles Scribner's Sons.

SIMON & SCHUSTER, INC. For "Bureaucrats," from *The White Album* by Joan Didion. Copyright © 1979 by Joan Didion. Reprinted by permission of Simon & Schuster, Inc.

VIKING PENGUIN, INC. For "How to Fix the Premedical Curriculum," from *The Medusa and the Snail* by Lewis Thomas. Copyright © 1978 by Lewis Thomas. Originally published in the *New England Journal of Medicine*. And for "Late Night Thoughts on Listening to Mahler's Ninth Symphony" and "Seven Wonders," from *Late Night Thoughts on Listening to Mahler's Ninth Symphony* by Lewis Thomas. Copyright © 1982, 1983 by Lewis Thomas. Reprinted by permission of Viking Penguin, Inc.

Glossary of Useful Terms

Abstraction A concept presented as divorced from any object or thing, as with "honor" or "compactness." In writing, there will be degrees in the expression of abstraction. The statement "Government-sponsored transportation is in difficulty" is more abstract, less concrete, than the statement "Ventures like Amtrak are periodically threatened with cuts in Congress."

Allusion Mention of persons, places, or events in an informal way because the writer assumes they are familiar to the reader: "Radio station XYZ is another *Tower of Babel*." Allusions may also be the direct quotation of, or oblique reference to, some other writer or discourse. These can be rare or frequent, identified or not, familiar or arcane, depending on the writer and on the audience which the writer assumes.

Antecedent Grammatically, the previous item to which pronouns (and other words like *such* and *thus*) refer. In the following two sentences, *Congress* is the antecedent of the pronoun *It*. "Congress adjourned early for the holidays. It will reconvene on the 15th." It is a courtesy of writers to make antecedents clear to the reader.

Antithesis Generally, in rhetoric, a phrase, sentence, figure of speech, or idea which is opposite in meaning, though usually similar in structure, to a previously stated sentence or phrase, as in Charles Dickens's famous opening to *A Tale of Two Cities:* "It was the best of times, it was the worst of times. . . ." In "On Morality," Didion sets up her concept of concrete experience as an antithesis to the notion of abstract moralizing. In logic, antithesis leads to synthesis (see **dialectic**). Didion's resulting synthesis is what she calls "wagon train morality," embodied in the concern of the nurse who waits by the young man's body in the desert until help can be brought.

Appeal Any tactic of persuasive writing in which an argument is supported by virtue of a connection made to implicit opinions or emotions. The argument that "the States should assert their prerogatives" contains at least one appeal, to the assumption that it is good to be independent. Such an appeal may be either more subtle or more open. Tuchman's "On Our Birthday—America as Idea" overtly appeals to our common heritage as Americans, as does Styron's "The Oldest America"; but in "'Useless' Knowledge" Russell's appeal is more subtle—to our Puritan background and our blind dependency on expediency. In any case, it is the writers' responsibility to know what appeals they are making or implying.

Apposition A noun or noun phrase standing next to another with no grammatical link. Apposition is a syntactic form of real economy: "Francis Hopkinson, *signer of the Declaration,* said he designed the American flag."

Argument A reason given to support or refute an opinion or assertion. In this sense, an argument is an element in **argumentation.** Sometimes argument is used in the broader sense of **thesis,** the basic contention of the author. For example, the argument of Gould's "Crazy Old Randolph Kirkpatrick" is that "foolish" obsessions can result in legitimate advances in scientific knowledge.

Argumentation Generally, the method by which discourse is ordered and its logic advanced. More specifically, argumentation is the mode of writing whose aim is to present and defend an opinion. Opinion may be argued by **definition,** by evidence, by **example,** through **cause and effect,** from circumstance, by means of **narration,** by **comparison and contrast,** etc. Most methods of argumentation imply a particular logic and structure: e.g., to argue by definition implies deductive logic (see **deduction**), and hence implies a structure beginning with a general definition, which is then applied to particular cases. But in most essays, the mode of argumentation is not pure.

Assertion Any verbal statement that can be responded to as true or false. "How long will it take?" is not an assertion, but "It will take a long time" is. Assertions need to be carefully examined by the writer, or false ones will result. Advertising sometimes deliberately deals in "loaded" assertions, which appear true but cannot be verified ("a better buy").

Audience Literally, those who hear, or listen. In rhetoric, the audience is those to whom one addresses a particular speech or piece of writing. Determining one's audience is one of the first steps toward effective communication, involving anticipation of age of the typical audience member, as well as economic and social position, cultural and educational background, sex, biases, and even eccentricities. In writing, where the readers often must be hypothesized, insufficient anticipation of audience is one of the most common reasons for the failure to communicate.

Authority The sense, projected by a piece of writing, of its trustworthiness. This sense is mainly conveyed through the reader's perception of the author as knowledgeable, reliable, faithful to sources and experiences, forthright, and fair. Authority may automatically accompany a piece of writing (as where Virginia Woolf can speak with authority about a woman writing novels) or generated by the way the piece is written.

Body That part of a composition exclusive of **introduction** and **conclusion.** It provides the main development and support of the **thesis** (see also **unity** and **coherence**).

Cause and effect Both a mode of **argumentation** and a method of organization, which analyzes the sources of a situation and the results of it, and which orders discourse in that essential, two-fold way. Cause and effect relation-

Cause and effect (cont.)
    ships, of course, may be complicated, with multiple causes for one effect, or multiple effects from one cause, or the effect of one cause becoming the cause for new effects, etc. Argument by cause and effect may begin with the observation of results, and then induce, or search out, the causes; or it may analyze present difficulties and deduce the likely consequences. Baldwin's "Notes of a Native Son" is, in part, argued by cause and effect.

Classification   A more systematic form of **division,** in which a class of things or ideas is sorted into several categories. In a working classification, there is a logically consistent relationship between the categories of a class, and between the categories themselves and the class as a whole. Consider a classification which sorts college students into three categories: those living in Greek houses, those living in dormitories, and those living elsewhere. The classification is *exhaustive* (no student fails to fall into one of the categories), *consistent* (the categories are divided by the same principle, of place of residence), and *mutually exclusive* (no student falls into more than one category). Classification can provide a useful organization to writing, as may be seen in ¶s 12–19 of Tuchman's "The Historian as Artist."

Cliché   An expression, often a metaphor, which has lost its impact, even meaning, through overuse: e.g., "drunk as a skunk," "crystal clear," "smooth as velvet," all three phrases which have lost their original freshness. More recent coinages that have quickly become clichés are "ballpark figure," "bottom line," and "the whole nine yards." As a test, ask yourself what is the literal meaning of a phrase like "ballpark figure." If you are not sure, then you probably have a cliché. George Orwell provides an insightful discussion of the cliché in "Politics and the English Language" (he calls it "dying metaphor").

Coherence   The quality in a piece of writing that readers sense when each sentence easily follows the preceding sentence. In other words, coherence generates that sense of ever-present continuity needed for a reader to perceive a piece of writing as a whole. The devices a writer uses to maintain coherence are varied and numerous. They can be pronouns (see **antecedent**), repeated words, **transitions,** an assumed intellectual or cultural framework, etc. Ideally, writers will provide enough coherence to keep readers from losing track and having to scan back over the writing previously read.

Comparison and contrast   One of the traditional methods of **argumentation,** observing likeness and differences between two objects, positions, ideas, etc. Although it serves a number of rhetorical purposes, comparison and contrast functions most commonly as a way to put a subject in perspective and thereby to make it understandable, as in Orwell's "Politics and the English Language," where good practices of writing are defined by contrasting them with bad.

Concession   An admission of facts or opinions that argue against one's position. Typically, writers indulge only in partial concessions: "*Of course, fans quickly forget a game,* but during it they are nothing but serious."

Conclusion That leave-taking part of an essay that steps away from the main argument to review or reconsider it. Most pieces of writing, and all essays, include an **introduction, body,** and conclusion. A conclusion can summarize and round off an essay neatly, or it can leave the reader puzzlng over a vital question (as in Lopez's "Buffalo"), but it should never leave the reader simply hanging. See Forster's "My Wood" for a classic example of an essay conclusion.

Deduction Reasoning from generalizations to particulars; e.g., "More and more people are feeling the need to exercise [generalization]; this town ought to build a bike and jogging path through the park [particulars]." Deduction is one of the two classic methods of logical reasoning (the other is **induction**). Along with **dialectics,** deduction and induction form the basic modes of **argumentation.** Gould often starts his essays in a deductive mode of argumentation.

Definition The literal meaning of definition, from the Latin *definire,* is to limit, to fix the boundaries of a thing or term. There are four basic types of definition commonly used in discourse: informal (definition in a word or brief phrase), formal, extended, and stipulative. The phrase in parentheses in the previous sentence is an *informal definition.* A *formal definition* is at least a full sentence, containing the term to be defined, the species to which the term belongs, and the differentia to distinguish between members of the species; e.g., a campanini [term] is a canary bird [species] that teaches other canaries to sing [differentia]. An *extended definition* usually runs from a few sentences to several paragraphs, but can carry on even for several hundred pages. A *stipulative definition* is one in which the definer uses a term in a special way for the purposes of a particular argument and for a clearly determined period of time.

Detail The specifics or particulars of a subject in writing, as opposed to the general argument. Good detail may add to an argument by providing support for **generalizations,** but detail provides other important functions. It can make a subject believable, graspable, graphic, and interesting, as can be seen by the detail that places the reader physically in the scene at the beginning of Didion's "On Morality," or the detail that helps readers visualize the hunting incident described in ¶ 23 of Lopez's "Wolfing for Sport."

Description Sometimes classified as one of the four basic modes of discourse, along with **narration, exposition,** and **argumentation.** To describe something is to create a verbal picture of it. The descriptive essay is a kind of subgenre in which description predominates (although the essay may, and usually does, develop through other modes as well), but description is also useful as a technique or strategy to present or clarify a narration, exposition, or argument. See Eiseley, "How Flowers Changed the World," ¶ 20, for a passage which begins with a narrative sentence but subsequently moves to description.

Dialectic As defined by Aristotle, dialectic is the art of logical **argumentation** as distinguished from rhetoric, which is the art of **persuasion**. In the formulation of the German philosopher Hegel, dialectic is a particular form of logical reasoning, where one considers opposites to arrive at a third position, thus the terms *thesis, antithesis, synthesis;* e.g., "This university needs to increase its enrollment [thesis], yet it is unethical to enroll unqualified students who will not make it on their own [antithesis]; the school ought to establish special programs for the poorly qualified [synthesis]."

Diction A writer's choice of words as distinct from choice of subject matter. Writing "police officer" instead of "cop" is a question of diction. Diction can be distinguished from **style** (though obviously diction affects style) by thinking of style as the manner in which words are put together, diction as simply the choice of individual words. Diction can be formal, informal, colloquial, slang, or anywhere in between. The proper use of diction depends upon the meaning the speaker or writer intends, and the **audience** to whom the words are addressed. "Cop" would not be used in a formal piece of writing (say, in a lawyer's brief) or face to face with a police officer, but it might be perfectly appropriate in an informal essay.

Didactic Referring to discourse that intends mainly to instruct (from the Greek, *didaskein,* to teach). The Roman poet, Horace, distinguished three purposes of art (and later rhetoricians applied his formula to discourse): to "instruct, or please, or both." Most essays, though they may lean toward either instructing or pleasing, both instruct and please. Tillich's sermon, "Faith and Uncertainty," is almost purely didactic, though those who are convinced by its argument may well be pleased by the grace with which it convinces.

Division A common process of reasoning, in which a subject matter is broken down into some of its component parts. Also called *partition* or *analysis,* division can provide useful schemes of organization in writing, for sentences all the way up to entire essays. Witness how the fifth sentence of the first paragraph of Tuchman's "On Our Birthday—America as Idea" divides the gifts allowed the American colonists in their experiment with democracy into three: "freedom, independence, and local self-government." Yet the entire paragraph divides the idea of the new nation into many more parts.

Emphasis The placing of words or ideas in a sentence, paragraph, or composition to have greater or lesser impact. Placing words or ideas at the beginning or end gives them the most emphasis, placing them in between the least. Emphasis is also achieved by repeating, by giving greater space for development, by arranging into a cumulative series, by contrasting, and by using punctuation, italics, headings, or other mechanical means. In the second of the following two sentences, the italicized word receives more emphasis: "In grade school, Brahms, *Stravinsky,* and Strauss were his favorite composers"; "In grade school, his favorite composers were not only Brahms and Strauss but even *Stravinsky.*"

Evaluation A primary aim of writing, distinguished by an effort of the writer to establish the value or worth of the subject. If **definition** explains what the writer takes to be the subject at hand, and **exposition** conveys how the writer envisions the subject, evaluation continues by showing how the writer judges the subject as good or bad. A book review, for example, not only defines what book is under consideration and describes its contents, but also evaluates the book's worth (see also **exhortation**).

Example In writing, presentation of instances that are encompassed by a **generalization**. Examples of "innovative contemporary technology" are compact disks, car telephones, laser printers, etc. Note that examples may be generalizations themselves that can be broken down into even more specific examples, as compact disks may be exemplified by different models. The two main writing purposes of example are to argue the validity of a generalization (see **induction**) and to make a generalization concrete and understandable.

Exhortation A particular aim of writing, where the writer intends to persuade the audience to take some specific action concerning the subject. In this, exhortation may be distinguished from **evaluation**, which judges the subject as good or bad but does not necessarily recommend any action to be taken about it. Exhortation may be the avowed intention of a piece of writing right from the start of it (as in Thomas's "How to Fix the Premedical Curriculum") or only a part, usually toward the end (as in Dinesen's "The Iguana").

Explicit Referring to a point or fact clearly and overtly stated (cf. **implicit**).

Exposition A general mode of writing in which the subject is presented or explained in a way that does not criticize it or argue for a position concerning it. Pure exposition will be found in telephone directories, assembly directions, repair manuals, news items on the front page of most newspapers, etc. None of the essays in this anthology is purely expository since each has a definite argument. Tuchman's "'Perdicaris Alive or Raisuli Dead'" and Lopez's "Wolfing for Sport" come closest. But even the most **argumentative** essays will have patches of exposition, for example ¶ 6 of Gould's "Crazy Old Randolph Kirkpatrick" or the first six sentences of ¶ 2 in Styron's "The Habit."

Fantasy Generally, a common mental activity taking the form of reverie, daydream, dream, or even hallucination, characterized by the formation of mental images that contradict our everyday waking sense of reality. As a writing genre, fantasy is closely related to science fiction, usually having a fairy-tale or myth-like plot, as in *Alice in Wonderland*, *The War of the Worlds*, or *Lord of the Rings*. But elements of fantasy may add interest and meaning to any kind of writing (as in Lopez's "Buffalo").

Fiction That mode of writing which is story-like, where the material has the status not of fact (as in **nonfiction**) but of a feigned or made-up reality. Fiction has also been defined as discourse in figurative (as opposed to discursive) language, the object of which is not to convey information, but to symbolize, to image, or to tell a story (see **metaphoric language** and **synecdoche**).

Figures of Speech   Words used in other than their literal sense. Without figures of speech, much writing would lack color and spirit. Examples of figurative language—once studied as a major component of **rhetoric**—include hyperbole, **irony, metaphoric language, paradox,** simile, **synecdoche,** and understatement.

Free modification   Information in a sentence that is not essential to the meaning of the sentence. The italicized clause in the following sentence is free (or nonrestricted) modification: "Children, *who are careless*, should be monitored." But in the following sentence it is bound (or restricted) modification: "Children *who are careless* should be monitored." Notice the change in meaning. The first sentence asserts that all children should be monitored. The second sentence asserts that only certain children should be monitored, namely those who are careless.

Generalizations and specifics   A generalization is a statement which asserts a broad truth, one that embraces a number of specifics. Generalization has to do with statement and the realm of reality to which the writer is referring; specifics indicate the support the writer offers. Generalizations may be reasonable and useful, especially if they are upheld by clear specific evidence or **example.** Several varieties of *false generalizations*, however, plague much bad writing: those that cannot be proved, those based on bias, those which are unexamined, etc.

Imagery   One of the traditional figures of speech in which a thing or idea is pictured by the way it is physically sensed. In "A Sweet Devouring," Eudora Welty images, by her title and subsequent references to appetite, her youthful attitude toward reading. In this instance, the image of "devouring" books gets extended into a pattern of imagery through the whole essay. Imagery may, of course, become symbolic, as do the buffalo of Lopez's essay and the "third class carriage" in Woolf's "Gas." Nearly all good writers employ images, whether for descriptive vividness or for more symbolic purposes.

Imagination   The creative mental faculty (as distinguished from reason) which gives shape to data or information. It is the constructive faculty of mind which is able to build or perceive connections among disparate elements or facts: in science, the ability to hypothesize beyond presently observed facts; in literature, the ability to image or metaphorize; in history, the ability to make discovered facts into narrative, etc. (see **fiction** and **intuition**).

Implicit   Referring to a point or fact which is not stated but which can be clearly inferred by the reader. In the sentence "She has never been sued for malpractice," it is implicit that the woman is a medical doctor. A writer may convey information implicitly not only to save words, but also to give readers the feeling that they share with the author a common body of knowledge and of cultural attitude. Implicit information in the first paragraph of Didion's "On Morality," for example, shows readers that Didion has confidence in their knowledge about the geography and climate of Death Valley and about

Implicit (cont.)
  Didion's status as a professional writer who could well have been commissioned by a national magazine, *The American Scholar,* to write an article.

Induction   Reasoning from particulars to generalization; e.g., "My experience in foreign countries [particulars] leads me to believe that high-school education in the United States should be speeded up [generalization]. (One of the three traditional methods of logic; cf. **deduction** and **dialectic**).

Introduction   That part of an essay, as distinguished from the **body** and the **conclusion,** that, like an usher, helps place the reader in a position to begin understanding the main argument. Introductions may be short or long, depending upon how much information the reader will need. Functions of introductions include defining terms, narrowing the topic, emphasizing the importance of the topic, suggesting the central **thesis,** indicating the organization that the essay will follow, establishing the **authority** of the writer, describing the setting, setting the tone, and engaging the interest of the reader.

Intuition   A function of the mind characterized by direct perception of a thing or idea, independent of logic or of reasoning about it. To intuit something is to understand it whole, usually without benefit of complete empirical proof or evidence.

Irony   When what is explicitly declared is not what is meant (often the opposite): "Meanwhile, nations continue to stockpile chemical weapons—*another gesture of international good will.*" Irony can exist at the verbal level (a single word or sentence), as when Styron in the last paragraph of "The Habit" calls a crude and self-serving statement from the tobacco industry "a prodigious thought." Or it can operate as a central aspect of a whole work (e.g., Russell's "Nightmares"). It can be a characteristic tone or **voice** of a piece (e.g., Didion's "Bureaucrats"). It can be signalled and made obvious, or simply embedded and implied.

Metaphoric language   Figures of speech in which one thing is identified by analogy with another. If a *simile* draws an **explicit** analogy ("this is like that"), then a *metaphor* states an **implicit** identification ("this is that"). By using metaphoric language, a writer calls one thing by a different name (usually a surprising and vivid one). Such a figure of speech, as a tactic, is one of the most powerful weapons in language, for it both compares and contrasts at the same time. When Thomas calls Greek the "foundation" on which all else in education should be built, he speaks metaphorically ("How to Fix the Premedical Curriculum").

Mode   Any one of various ways in which writing can be ordered and presented. The various modes therefore indicate structure in discourse, as well as an approach to persuasion.

Motif   A significant or dominant feature, theme, or idea, often repeated throughout a piece of discourse (or work of literature, music, art). Sometimes a motif

Motif (cont.) is an indirect allusion, by means of an image or a group of related images or ideas, that supports the main subject. The subject, for example, of Thomas's "Late Night Thoughts on Listening to Mahler's Ninth Symphony" is death—the contrast between natural death and human suicide by thermonuclear bombs. Recurrent motifs are age, loss, and sound—Thomas listening to Mahler, the young having to listen to politicians speculate about the number of deaths in a nuclear war.

Myth A story or **fiction** that embodies or expresses certain elemental human ideas or emotions. The myth of Sisyphus expresses the central human anxiety about the ends or purposes of life. The myth of Oedipus, who killed his father and married his mother, was placed by Sigmund Freud at the center of his psychology as expressing, in his eyes, a complex of elemental male emotions, consisting of the son's fear of the father and desire for the mother. Freud took the myth of Electra as the expression of a corresponding complex of emotion in the daughter. A myth can be a type of story or tale, usually anonymous and occurring early in the development of a culture, but there are often mythic elements in modern fiction, as well as in other forms of discourse, including essays. Dinesen's "Pooran Singh," with depiction of the primitive figure of the blacksmith, is mythic both in intent and structure.

Nonfiction The language with which authors speak most directly to readers, written to convey information or argumentation based on facts or observations. Nearly all discursive writing is nonfictional. Occasionally the difference between **fiction** and nonfiction breaks down, as with Orwell's "A Hanging," where both modes of writing are in operation at once.

Paradox A seemingly absurd or self-contradictory statement which actually expresses a possible truth. "If the fool would persist in his folly, he would become wise" (William Blake). Gould approaches paradox in his essay "Crazy Old Randolph Kirkpatrick" when he asserts that the obsessive, wrong-headed scientist can sometimes bring about more fruitful results than many orthodox scientists, by virtue of that very wrong-headed obsessiveness. Paradox is often useful when one is attempting to express either a truth that is very complex or one not fully understood. For that reason, though, it can also be misleading, for its wit may well hide untruth or confusion.

Parallelism Coordination of similar syntactic forms, either within or between sentences. "The war ended; the economy collapsed" is parallel, but "When the war ended, there was a collapse in the economy" is not. On a small scale, individual words can be parallel ("The grief and pain of illness"). On a large scale, whole paragraphs can have coordinated and therefore parallel forms (e.g., the series of questions in ¶ 42 of Styron's "This Quiet Dust"). Whatever forms are made parallel will have equal weight, both in grammar and meaning.

Persuasion The main goal of **rhetoric**. The object of nearly all discursive language—essays, letters, reports, articles—is to persuade an audience of something. Traditionally, different styles were developed, suitable to different subject matter and different audiences, to carry persuasion. Aristotle, the first to analyze rhetoric, claimed there were three "grounds" for persuasion: the **appeal** to emotions, to logic, and to morality. Others have extended or adapted his terms endlessly, but in any case we can reiterate that persuasion implies an awareness of an **audience** for the discourse.

Point of view The intellectual or emotional stand writers adopt, or embody, from which they view reality, their material, or the point they are trying to make. Point of view may shift or change with the particular occasion, or it may stem from a central belief or philosophy which remains steady.

Process A logical organization of writing that describes a subject as a sequence of steps leading to a planned goal. The narration of steps to take in making a recipe in a cookbook is organized by process, as is Welty's account in "The Little Store" of the procedure she followed to bring home her mother's grocery order. As such, process is distinguished from chronology, which is a narrative of events arranged by sequence in time but not necessarily directed toward a pre-set goal.

Qualification Any verbal reservation or restriction or limitation. To change "It will cause trouble" to "It will probably cause trouble" qualifies the first statement.

Refutation The attempt to prove that an argument—usually someone else's—is wholly or partly wrong. This may be accomplished by showing that the facts are erroneous, the reasoning is unsound, or that the conclusions do not apply. See ¶s 13–19 of Gould's "The Nonscience of Human Nature" for an extended refutation.

Reminiscence A narrative that is the product of the narrator's remembering the past, as Eudora Welty's "The Little Store."

Rhetoric The art, and the technique of that art, of presenting facts and ideas in clear, well-ordered, and hence convincing language. Aristotle distinguishes rhetoric, the art of public, persuasive speaking, from **dialectic,** the art of logical reasoning. More modern usage of the term tends to include both persuasion and reasoning. Though the word "rhetoric" has in our own time negative connotations ("the congressman's speech last night was mere rhetoric"), the basic rhetorical principles and techniques (**argumentation, exhortation, exposition,** the use of **figures of speech,** etc.) are used consciously or unconsciously in any speaking or writing that aims at an audience with good effect.

Rhetorical question A question for which the speaker or writer of the question obviously already has an answer: "Can we tolerate such blackmail?" The rhetorical question is useful as a means to raise an issue, and sometimes can

Rhetorical question (cont.) have a dramatic effect, especially when it is put to an audience the speaker knows with some immediacy, and is usually found in persuasive or oratorical speaking or writing. But overuse of the rhetorical question can make one's argument seem leading, formulaic, or even silly.

Self-expression A major aim in much writing, in which the ideas, feelings, emotions, and imagination of the writer are expressed. Some writing situations encourage the suppression of self-expressive content, such as scientific papers, office memoranda, news items, legal briefs, government reports, etc. At the other pole from this effort at objectivity are strongly self-expressive writings like personal letters and diary entries. The proportion of self-expressive content to objective content is an important matter to consider in composing any public piece of writing.

Setting What the author describes of that environment in which any action takes place: surrounding landscape, time of year, weather, political situation, etc.

Speaker The controlling sensibility that produces a piece of discourse; in essays, the speaker is usually assumed to be the author (see **voice** and **tone**).

Style In discourse, the distinctive manner of a piece of writing, as distinguished from its content (although any too-rigid distinction would be artificial). For instance, Didion's style generally is more concrete than Loren Eiseley's. The elements that together make up a particular style are numerous, ranging from punctuation to overall organization.

Synecdoche A figure of speech which images the whole of something by one part: e.g., referring to Mark Twain's writing skill as "his pen." Many metaphors and images operate in this manner, and thus become tools for economy and concision in discourse. The danger of synecdoche is oversimplification.

Syntax The way words are arranged to form sentences. "The first objection" and "the objection which is first" express more or less the same meaning with two different syntactic constructions. Syntax must be seen as the relationship of any one word to the group of which it is a part. Thus the term is distinguished from a simple grammar which merely classifies individual words as nouns, adverbs, etc.

Synthesis See **dialectic, thesis, antithesis.**

Tactic A conscious manipulation of language by the composing writer to produce intended effects on readers. Tactics, then, are maneuvers which together form the basic strategies of a piece of writing, such as telling the truth or moving the reader emotionally. Writing tactics are infinite, ranging from spelling words conventionally, to producing a surprise final twist for a paragraph, to adding entire sections in order to strengthen an argument.

Thesis An author's central and controlling idea about a subject. The thesis is central because other ideas in the piece lead up to it or follow from it. It is controlling because all elements of an essay—from tone to detail—should

Thesis (cont.)
   ultimately serve to advance it. (Hence the virtue of a thesis in providing a sense of unity.) Note the essential difference between subject and thesis. The subject is the arena of reality that the author wishes to discuss. The thesis is the basic contention the author wishes to make about that arena. The subject of Thomas's "How to Fix the Premedical Curriculum" is the premedical curriculum. His thesis is that the curriculum ought to be changed in a certain way.

Thesis statement   The sentence (or few sentences) that best express an essay's **thesis,** stating the main point the writer wishes to develop, to which the essay's ideas and their supporting details are directly or indirectly related. With an **explicit** thesis statement, the writer usually intends for the reader to recognize it as such. But it is possible for a perfectly good essay not to condense the thesis into one or two sentences—in which case, the thesis remains **implicit.**

Tone   The emotion and attitude of mind conveyed by diction (cf. **voice**). Thus tone may point to the relationship between the writer and his material; it may also refer to **point of view** in discourse. Tone can also be associated with a writer's characteristic or habitual **style.** In discussions of writing, the use of this term is based on an analogy with music and with public speaking (tone of voice).

Transition   An explicit verbal linkage between sentences, or between paragraphs, or among larger units of discourse: e.g., "however," "on the other hand," "a more important consideration is. . . ."

Unity   From the Latin, *unitas,* meaning oneness. The unity of a written composition refers to the way in which seemingly unconnected images, ideas, themes, or details work to develop and support the main **argument** or **thesis.** There are several techniques and devices which may contribute to the unity of an essay, including the cogent and logical organization of ideas and supporting detail, the effective use of transitional phrases between sentences and paragraphs and main sections, the proper use of emphasis, the clear statement of thesis, the use of topic sentences, and the construction of a helpful conclusion.

Voice   An essay's point of view, or tone, or attitude, revealing the relationship between writer and material. Sometimes voice is the recognizable tone or attitude of a given writer (cf. **style**).

Index of Rhetorical Modes

Though individual essays are difficult to classify, certain kinds of discourse—whether one calls them modes or aims or forms or genres—have acquired traditional names. The categories below overlap also because rarely is an essay purely of one kind. Basically, these groupings are intended merely to suggest linkages among the essays for purposes of comparison and extended study. Essays under any one heading may help illuminate each other.

Mode	Author	Short Title	Page
Argumentation (Issues/Answers)	Thomas	"Thoughts"	112
	Orwell	"As I Please"	133
	Forster	"Tolerance"	218
	Forster	"Anonymity"	224
	Gould	"Homage"	254
	Gould	"Nonscience"	265
	Baldwin	"Black English"	312
	Russell	"'Useless'"	357
	Tuchman	"Historian"	374
	Tillich	"Faith"	432
	Tillich	"Progress"	436
Causation	Dinesen	"On Mottoes"	94
	Orwell	"Politics"	136
	Styron	"The Habit"	178
	Forster	"My Wood"	214
	Gould	"Homage"	254
	Didion	"Notebook"	320
	Tuchman	"'Perdicaris'"	381
	Eiseley	"Flowers"	400
Classification	Forster	"My Wood"	214
	Forster	"Anonymity"	224
	Tuchman	"Historian"	374
	Tillich	"Progress"	436
Definition	White	"Gastropods"	68
	Walker	"Beauty"	156

Index of Rhetorical Modes 477

Mode	Author	Short Title	Page
Definition (cont.)	Forster	"Tolerance"	218
	Forster	"Anonymity"	224
	Baldwin	"Black English"	312
	Didion	"Bureaucrats"	329
	Didion	"On Morality"	334
	Tuchman	"Historian"	374
Description	Welty	"House"	8
	Welty	"Store"	14
	White	"Gastropods"	68
	Dinesen	"The Iguana"	88
	Dinesen	"Pooran Singh"	90
	Styron	"Oldest"	183
	Woolf	"Mrs. Grey"	238
	Eiseley	"Judgment"	411
Dialectic	Styron	"Dust"	188
	Didion	"On Morality"	334
	Tuchman	"Birthday"	370
	Tillich	"Progress"	436
Exhortation (Persuasion)	Hughes	"Kilby"	32
	White	"Machine"	72
	Dinesen	"The Iguana"	88
	Thomas	"How to Fix"	108
	Orwell	"Politics"	136
	Walker	"Madness"	152
	Styron	"The Habit"	178
	Baldwin	"Letter"	305
	Tillich	"Riddle"	451
Experience (Insight/ Illumination)	Hughes	"Salvation"	26
	Hughes	"Theme"	30
	Lopez	"Buffalo"	60
	White	"Pig"	76
	Dinesen	"The Iguana"	88
	Orwell	"A Hanging"	126
	Walker	"Beauty"	156
	Styron	"Dust"	188
	Woolf	"Gas"	248
	Didion	"Bureaucrats"	329
	Eiseley	"Judgment"	411
	Eiseley	"Dying"	421

Index of Rhetorical Modes

Mode	Author	Short Title	Page
Exposition	Welty	"House"	8
	Lopez	"Wolfing"	47
	Walker	"Search"	165
	Forster	"Anonymity"	224
	Woolf	"Professions"	241
	Russell	"How I Write"	352
	Tillich	"Progress"	436
Fantasy	Lopez	"Buffalo"	60
	Woolf	"Gas"	248
	Russell	"Nightmares"	344
Illustration	Welty	"Devouring"	2
	Lopez	"The Log Jam"	38
	Lopez	"Wolfing"	47
	Dinesen	"The Iguana"	88
	Orwell	"Politics"	136
	Gould	"Kirkpatrick"	272
	Didion	"Notebook"	320
	Tuchman	"Historian"	374
	Eiseley	"Judgment"	411
Narration	Hughes	"Salvation"	26
	Lopez	"The Log Jam"	38
	White	"Pig"	76
	Orwell	"A Hanging"	126
	Woolf	"Gas"	248
	Baldwin	"Notes"	284
	Russell	"Nightmares"	344
	Eiseley	"Judgment"	411
Partition (Division)	Dinesen	"On Mottoes"	94
	Thomas	"How to Fix"	108
	Thomas	"Wonders"	117
	Orwell	"Politics"	136
	Russell	"How I Write"	352
	Eiseley	"Judgment"	411
Process (and Historical Account)	Welty	"Store"	14
	Thomas	"How to Fix"	108
	Orwell	"Politics"	136
	Walker	"Madness"	152

Mode	Author	Short Title	Page
Process	Woolf	"Professions"	241
(and Historical	Gould	"Homage"	258
Account)	Russell	"'Useless'"	357
(cont.)	Tuchman	"'Perdicaris'"	381

Index of Subject Matter

This clustering by topic, highly suggestive, is for teachers who may want to assign related essays, and for students who may want to pursue a particular subject.

Subject	Author	Short Title	Page
Ancestors	Welty	"House"	8
	Walker	"Search"	165
	Baldwin	"Notes"	284
Animals	Lopez	"Wolfing"	47
	Lopez	"Buffalo"	60
	White	"Gastropods"	68
	White	"Pig"	76
	Dinesen	"The Iguana"	88
	Eiseley	"Flowers"	400
	Eiseley	"Judgment"	411
The Arts	White	"Machine"	72
	Thomas	"Thoughts"	112
	Walker	"Search"	165
	Forster	"Anonymity"	224
Characters	Welty	"House"	8
	White	"Pig"	76
	Dinesen	"Pooran Singh"	90
	Walker	"Search"	165
	Styron	"Dust"	188
	Woolf	"Mrs. Grey"	238
	Gould	"Kirkpatrick"	272
Childhood/Adolescence	Welty	"Devouring"	2
	Welty	"Store"	14
	Hughes	"Salvation"	26
	Lopez	"The Log Jam"	38
	Thomas	"Wonders"	117
	Walker	"Beauty"	156
	Gould	"Homage"	254
	Baldwin	"Notes"	284

Subject	Author	Short Title	Page
Culture	Lopez	"Buffalo"	60
	Thomas	"How to Fix"	108
	Thomas	"Thoughts"	112
	Orwell	"Politics"	136
	Styron	"Oldest"	183
	Forster	"Tolerance"	218
	Gould	"Homage"	254
	Baldwin	"Notes"	284
	Didion	"On Morality"	334
	Tuchman	"Birthday"	370
	Tillich	"Progress"	436
Death	Hughes	"Kilby"	32
	Lopez	"The Log Jam"	38
	White	"Pig"	76
	Orwell	"A Hanging"	126
	Styron	"Dust"	188
	Woolf	"Mrs. Grey"	238
	Baldwin	"Notes"	284
	Eiseley	"Judgment"	411
	Eiseley	"Dying"	421
Education	Hughes	"Salvation"	26
	Hughes	"Theme"	30
	Dinesen	"On Mottoes"	94
	Thomas	"How to Fix"	108
	Walker	"Beauty"	156
	Forster	"Anonymity"	224
	Russell	"How I Write"	352
	Russell	"'Useless'"	357
Evil	Welty	"Store"	14
	Hughes	"Kilby"	32
	Orwell	"A Hanging"	126
	Forster	"Tolerance"	218
	Baldwin	"Notes"	284
	Baldwin	"Letter"	305
Evolution	White	"Gastropods"	68
	Thomas	"Wonders"	117
	Gould	"Homage"	254
	Gould	"Nonscience"	265
	Eiseley	"Flowers"	400

Subject	Author	Short Title	Page
Fact and Fiction	Lopez	"Buffalo"	60
	Orwell	"A Hanging"	126
	Styron	"Dust"	188
	Forster	"Anonymity"	224
	Woolf	"Gas"	248
	Didion	"Notebook"	320
	Russell	"Nightmares"	344
	Tuchman	"Historian"	374
	Eiseley	"Judgment"	411
	Tillich	"Faith"	432
Feminism	Dinesen	"On Mottoes"	94
	Walker	"Search"	165
	Woolf	"Mrs. Grey"	238
	Woolf	"Professions"	241
The Future	Thomas	"Thoughts"	112
	Walker	"Madness"	152
	Styron	"Oldest"	183
	Forster	"Tolerance"	218
	Woolf	"Professions"	241
	Tillich	"Progress"	436
History	Welty	"House"	8
	Lopez	"Wolfing"	47
	Lopez	"Buffalo"	60
	Orwell	"As I Please"	133
	Walker	"Search"	165
	Styron	"The Habit"	178
	Styron	"Oldest"	183
	Styron	"Dust"	188
	Woolf	"Professions"	241
	Baldwin	"Black English"	312
	Russell	"'Useless'"	357
	Tuchman	"Historian"	374
	Tuchman	"'Perdicaris'"	381
	Tillich	"Progress"	436
Humanities	Thomas	"How to Fix"	108
	Baldwin	"Black English"	312
	Russell	"'Useless'"	357
	Tuchman	"Historian"	374
	Tillich	"Progress"	436

Index of Subject Matter

Subject	Author	Short Title	Page
Human Nature	Lopez	"Wolfing"	47
	White	"Gastropods"	68
	White	"Pig"	76
	Dinesen	"The Iguana"	88
	Orwell	"A Hanging"	126
	Walker	"Beauty"	156
	Styron	"The Habit"	178
	Styron	"Dust"	188
	Forster	"My Wood"	214
	Forster	"Tolerance"	218
	Gould	"Nonscience"	265
	Baldwin	"Notes"	284
	Baldwin	"Letter"	305
	Didion	"On Morality"	334
	Eiseley	"Dying"	421
	Tillich	"Faith"	432
	Tillich	"Riddle"	451
Landscape	Lopez	"The Log Jam"	38
	Dinesen	"The Iguana"	88
	Styron	"Oldest"	183
	Forster	"My Wood"	214
	Didion	"On Morality"	334
	Eiseley	"Judgment"	411
Language/Writing	Hughes	"Theme"	30
	White	"Machine"	72
	Dinesen	"On Mottoes"	94
	Thomas	"How to Fix"	108
	Orwell	"Politics"	136
	Forster	"Anonymity"	224
	Baldwin	"Black English"	312
	Didion	"Notebook"	320
	Russell	"How I Write"	352
	Tuchman	"Historian"	374
Literature	Welty	"Devouring"	2
	Thomas	"How to Fix"	108
	Styron	"Dust"	188
	Forster	"Anonymity"	224
	Woolf	"Professions"	241
	Tuchman	"Historian"	374

Subject	Author	Short Title	Page
Minorities	Hughes	"Theme"	30
	Hughes	"Kilby"	32
	Lopez	"Buffalo"	60
	Walker	"Beauty"	156
	Walker	"Search"	165
	Styron	"Dust"	188
	Gould	"Nonscience"	265
	Baldwin	"Notes"	284
	Baldwin	"Letter"	305
	Baldwin	"Black English"	312
Myth	Lopez	"Wolfing"	47
	Lopez	"Buffalo"	60
	White	"Pig"	76
	Dinesen	"Pooran Singh"	90
	Styron	"Dust"	188
	Woolf	"Gas"	248
	Gould	"Homage"	254
Nuclear Holocaust	Thomas	"Thoughts"	112
	Walker	"Madness"	152
Perception	Welty	"Store"	14
	Hughes	"Kilby"	32
	Dinesen	"The Iguana"	88
	Thomas	"Thoughts"	112
	Woolf	"Gas"	248
	Tuchman	"Historian"	374
	Eiseley	"Judgment"	411
Politics	Orwell	"Politics"	136
	Walker	"Madness"	152
	Gould	"Nonscience"	265
	Baldwin	"Letter"	305
	Baldwin	"Black English"	312
	Didion	"Bureaucrats"	329
	Russell	"Nightmares"	344
	Tuchman	"Birthday"	370
	Tuchman	"'Perdicaris'"	381
Possessions (Material)	Dinesen	"The Iguana"	88
	Forster	"My Wood"	214
	Tillich	"Riddle"	451

Subject	Author	Short Title	Page
Reading	Welty	"Devouring"	2
	White	"Machine"	72
	Dinesen	"On Mottoes"	94
	Thomas	"How to Fix"	108
	Walker	"Madness"	152
	Forster	"Anonymity"	224
	Russell	"How I Write"	352
	Russell	"'Useless'"	357
Recollection	Welty	"House"	8
	Welty	"Store"	14
	Hughes	"Salvation"	26
	Dinesen	"The Iguana"	88
	Dinesen	"Pooran Singh"	90
	Orwell	"A Hanging"	126
	Walker	"Beauty"	156
	Baldwin	"Notes"	284
	Eiseley	"Judgment"	411
	Eiseley	"Dying"	421
Religion	Hughes	"Salvation"	26
	Lopez	"Buffalo"	60
	Woolf	"Gas"	248
	Didion	"On Morality"	334
	Russell	"Nightmares"	344
	Tillich	"Faith"	432
	Tillich	"Progress"	436
	Tillich	"Riddle"	451
Science	Lopez	"Buffalo"	60
	White	"Gastropods"	68
	Thomas	"How to Fix"	108
	Thomas	"Wonders"	117
	Gould	"Homage"	254
	Gould	"Nonscience"	265
	Gould	"Kirkpatrick"	272
	Didion	"Bureaucrats"	329
	Russell	"Nightmares"	344
	Russell	"'Useless'"	357
	Eiseley	"Flowers"	400
	Eiseley	"Judgment"	411

Subject	Author	Short Title	Page
The Self	Welty	"Devouring"	2
	Welty	"House"	8
	Hughes	"Theme"	30
	White	"Pig"	76
	Walker	"Beauty"	156
	Styron	"Dust"	188
	Forster	"My Wood"	214
	Woolf	"Professions"	241
	Baldwin	"Notes"	284
	Didion	"Notebook"	320
	Eiseley	"Dying"	421
	Tillich	"Faith"	432
The Senses	Welty	"Store"	14
	White	"Gastropods"	68
	Walker	"Beauty"	156
	Woolf	"Mrs. Grey"	238
	Woolf	"Gas"	248
	Eiseley	"Judgment"	411
Society	Hughes	"Kilby"	32
	Lopez	"The Log Jam"	38
	Orwell	"As I Please"	133
	Orwell	"Politics"	136
	Walker	"Madness"	152
	Styron	"Oldest"	183
	Woolf	"Gas"	248
	Baldwin	"Letter"	305
	Didion	"Bureaucrats"	329
	Tuchman	"Birthday"	370
The South	Welty	"House"	8
	Welty	"Store"	14
	Hughes	"Kilby"	32
	Walker	"Beauty"	156
	Walker	"Search"	165
	Styron	"Oldest"	183
	Styron	"Dust"	188
War	Lopez	"Buffalo"	60
	Orwell	"As I Please"	133
	Styron	"Dust"	188

Subject	Author	Short Title	Page
War (cont.)	Forster	"Tolerance"	218
	Baldwin	"Notes"	284
	Russell	"'Useless'"	357
	Tuchman	"'Perdicaris'"	381